CLIO'S BATTLES

CLIO'S BATTLES

Historiography in Practice   JEREMY BLACK

INDIANA UNIVERSITY PRESS

Bloomington & Indianapolis

This book is a publication of

INDIANA UNIVERSITY PRESS
Office of Scholarly Publishing
Herman B Wells Library 350
1320 East 10th Street
Bloomington, Indiana 47405 USA

iupress.indiana.edu

The paper used in this publication
meets the minimum requirements of
the American National Standard for
Information Sciences–Permanence of
Paper for Printed Library Materials,
ANSI Z39.48–1992.

*Manufactured in the
United States of America*

Cataloging information is available from
the Library of Congress.

ISBN 978-0-253-01675-1 (hardback)
ISBN 978-0-253-01681-2 (paperback)
ISBN 978-0-253-01687-4 (ebook)

1 2 3 4 5 20 19 18 17 16 15

For

DANIEL JOHNSON

Contents

Preface

THE WEIGHT OF THE PAST IS HEAVY AND INSISTENT, AT TIMES brutally apparent, but frequently more prone to insinuate and influence. This weight is presented as positive – offering continuity and lessons from experience; and yet also as negative, indeed, a curse. As an instance of the latter, empowerment through grievance is especially damaging, in particular, locating both grievance and empowerment in a misleading, as well as destructive, historical context. Linked to this empowerment is the prevalence of "history wars," disputes about how to present the past, which are the heavily historicized equivalent of the American "culture wars." These disputes take the "could" of academic discussions about how the past could be presented, and turn it into a "should" of how the past should, indeed "must," be explained. In this context, the past becomes a validation for the present and, as such, a matter of great significance. History, whose muse is Clio, is thereby made the ammunition of politics, and this ammunition is potent precisely because the past serves as the basis for ideas and practices of identification.

This use of the past is contested and, therefore, there is a variety, even confusion, in this book. This variety reflects not only these "history wars" but also, more broadly, the Janus-faced character of the past, as, at the same time, the solace of continuity and the sore of grievance. Moreover, whether or not they are affected in these cases by politics, memory and history vie as interpreters, each able to take the approach of continuity or that of grievance. In the following study, I focus on some of these aspects of what is, at once, the kaleidoscopic variety of readings offered of the past and yet also, more narrowly, a tension between readings that unite and those that divide. These readings focus on historiography in terms of the content of the past that is offered, and its political implications, and not on the theoretical frameworks of the historical methods employed; although these methods can play a major role in the direction of research, and thus the content, that is offered.

This book takes forward interests I have developed in earlier studies, and is aimed in particular at student courses on historical method and public history. There is, in chapters 2 to 5, a long historical section, an account of history-writing from the ancient world to the here and now, in which I underscore the differences and developments in traditions of history writing. The choice of what to cover in these chapters reflects the need to adopt a multiple perspective on developments in this writing, rather than to envisage simply a central intellectual and political course for historiography. The latter approach, with its assumption that it is obvious what must be covered, is of limited value at the global level, where the range in traditions of history-writing is highly pronounced.

The focus in this book, in chapters 6 to 11, is on recent decades, notably the post–Cold War period; that since 1989. In this focus, there is a deliberate eschewing of "Eurocentrism." There is considerable material on Asia, but without suggesting that it represents one, non-Western view on history. Indeed, the contrasts, in 2014, in content and tone between the claims of re-launching the caliphate and the pursuit of nationalist disputes between China and Japan are striking. I also consider the challenges facing the Western academic concept of history at the present time. In chapter 12, I turn to the possible future use of the then past, which is a way to open up thought about how we do the same today.

Bridging public history and historiography, this book is an ambitious account of the engagement with the past across world history, one focused on "history wars." This book discusses the links between the popular and academic approaches to the events and relevance of the past, and also considers their contrasts. In my discussion of popular history, my emphasis is on the discussion of the past by ministers, other politicians, and opinion leaders – for example the editors of newspapers – and not by academics. That emphasis is not intended to ignore the many practices in which scholarship is engaged in institutions that present history to the public, such as museums, memorials, historical sites, national parks, libraries, schools, historical societies, and films. Indeed, some of this scholarship, and certain aspects of the "heritage industry" connect with this discussion of popular history by ministers, politicians, and commentators, not least with debates about the merits of continuity or change.

There is an instructive problem in the use of the term "public history." In the United States, as in Britain, this term commonly refers to history as it is presented at public sites. In practice, in these countries, "public history" usually represents a consensus view at a given point of time. However, it might also display a highly politicized view of what the public "ought" to think about a particular historical event, as is the case with many American Civil War monuments. Such a politicized view can reflect, as well as lead to, debate and dissension.

The use of the term to refer to the presentation at public sites clashes with another understanding of public history, that of history as it is deployed by news outlets, pundits, and politicians. They aim to create a consensus about how their readers and listeners "ought" to understand their country's past, while frequently decrying other views. There, indeed, is a possible confusion with the official and institutional usage of history referred to above in this very paragraph. It is instructive that the especially helpful publisher suggested "dropping the term 'public history' except when referring to history as it is presented in public contexts and use something along the lines of the employment of a selective interpretation of the past used for partisan purposes – propaganda."[1]

It is unclear, however, as this book will demonstrate, why "public history," in the sense of the history produced by public institutions, should be treated as necessarily less partisan than that deployed by politicians, pundits, and news outlets. That is certainly not the perspective gained from a global approach. Popular history might be seen as an acceptable alternative term to public history to describe the history thus deployed by politicians and others; but it is unclear why the term public should be detached from the people and applied simply to state institutions. As a related point, institutions can be privately owned or managed. A range of issues and practices certainly emerged over the twentieth century to engage and negotiate spaces between academic historians and the public, and there is an important literature linked to this engagement.

One of the central challenges of that literature, of those debates about presentation, is how to deal with the contested perspectives that are a subject of this book. Historians indeed operate through advancing diverse perspectives. However, my focus is not on the academics, but on the politicians and the public, each of whom I see as more significant for historiography.

In a book of this type, there is a tendency for the historian to sink himself or herself into the subject, and to avoid personal comments. That is a worthy tradition, but I feel it necessary in this book on my subject to express my own views. I am a pluralist, aware and respectful of different practices and traditions, but I am also convinced of the value, indeed necessity, of the freedom of thought and expression. In an interaction of past developments and present circumstances, that freedom varies greatly around the world.

I have benefited while writing this work from the opportunity to discuss the subject with fellow scholars, but also with others involved in the presentation and use of history. I am particularly grateful to John Blair, Penelope Corfield, John France, Bill Gibson, Bill Purdue, Kaushik Roy, Nigel Saul, Richard Toye, Peter Wiseman, Neil York, Patrick Zutshi, and two anonymous readers for their comments on all or part of earlier drafts. Conversations with Roger Burt, Duco Hellema, Luigi Loreto, and Maarten Prak proved most instructive. I have also profited, while writing this work, from the opportunity to speak at the Seconda Università di Napoli, Waseda University, the Chalke Valley Historical Festival, Blundell's School, and the Museum of London, and to the D Club. Bob Sloan has again proved a most helpful editor. I am also grateful to Mike Mosbacher for allowing me to use material from the Social Affairs Unit's publication on *Historiography* (2011).

It is a particular pleasure to dedicate this book to Daniel Johnson, as a mark of our friendship, and with respect for his forthright, humane, and interesting writings, which seamlessly link culture and commitment. He is a model of both, and of their significance to intellectual debate. I am proud to enjoy his friendship.

Abbreviations

BL   London, British Library

NA   London, National Archives

Unless otherwise stated, books are published in London.

CLIO'S BATTLES

ONE

Academic, State, and Public Histories

"In the Harry Potter story, the dark wizard Voldemort dies hard because the seven horcruxes, which contain parts of his soul, have been destroyed. If militarism is like the haunting Voldemort of Japan, the Yasukuni Shrine in Tokyo is a kind of horcrux, representing the darkest parts of that nation's soul." Writing in the *Daily Telegraph* on 1 January 2014, Liu Xiaoming, China's ambassador in London, attacked Shinzo Abe, Japan's Prime Minister, for visiting and paying homage at the Yasukuni Shrine in Chiyoda, Tokyo, in December 2013. This shrine memorializes Japanese military personnel who died in war, including fourteen "Class A" World War II criminals who were added in 1978. Liu accused Abe of posing a "serious threat to global peace" by "rekindling" Japan's militaristic spirit and argued that "visits to the shrine by Japanese leaders cannot simply be an internal affair," as they raised "serious questions about attitudes in Japan and its record of militarism, aggression and colonial rule." World War II played a key role not only in Liu's expression of grievance, but also in the proposal for remedy. Liu argued that, as China and Britain were "wartime allies," they "should join together both to uphold the UN Charter and to safeguard regional stability and world peace." Indeed, both China and Britain had fought Japan.[1] This was one of over thirty articles by Chinese ambassadors in newspapers across the world.

When debating the politics of the present, the reference to history is more common than that to imaginative fiction (let alone fantasy literature), although the latter may come to have greater resonance for societies in which visual imagery proves more potent than written arguments. Indeed, the Japanese ambassador in London accused China of playing Voldemort. Nevertheless, the use of both history and imaginative fiction capture the extent to which a wide frame of reference can be employed when addressing present-day issues. Moreover, the references offered are eclectic, reflecting what is judged most helpful at the moment.

The weight of the past in framing senses of identity and in fueling the politics of grievance are themes of this book as part of the broader account of the usage of the past that it offers. This account focuses not on academic approaches to historiography, but on state and popular uses of the past. In these pages, these state and popular uses are seen as more significant than their academic counterparts for the treatment of history – both in form and in content. To discuss this thesis, it is appropriate to consider the development of historiography and also to offer a wide-ranging and up-to-date account of more recent trends. The emphasis will be on the shaping and characteristics of identity and grievance, and on the salience of politics in the usage of history. There will be an attempt to link the analysis to current issues and disputes, in short to show how the past is grasped for the present. Considering this dimension makes the book relevant, which is also a key characteristic of the type of history under discussion, history that may be termed public in the broadest sense, notably as contrasted with academic.

The public use of history has become far more widespread and urgent in recent decades. Since 1945, over 120 new states have been created across the world, each of which has had to define a new public history, even if partly under the guise of reviving older ones. Moreover, earlier independent states have been transformed, in large part due to the pressures of political history, in the shape of developments that made previous arrangements redundant.[2] This shift can be seen with new constitutional and political systems, as, for example, in Germany, Japan, Italy, France, Egypt, Iran, Russia, and South Africa between 1945 and 1994.

At the same time, public histories in both old and new states have been, and are, contested. Far from there being any "Death of the Past" (J. H. Plumb, 1969) or "End of History" (Francis Fukuyama, 1989), this process continues to be active and important, albeit at very different levels. In 1779, the Spanish painter Francisco Goya painted *Truth, Time, and*

History – a benign and harmonious, as well as allusive, account of their relationship – which hangs in the National Museum in Sweden. The reality of this relationship has been very different; and this is not simply a matter of key episodes or major countries. Instead, the corollary of the use of the past to offer identity in continuity, and continuity in identity, is that both also provide a basis for contestation.

Overlapping with that contestation can come academic work, but the pattern of change can differ. Moreover, in many countries, the state approach takes precedence. For example, in China, growing academic stress on the iniquities and harshness of the rule and regime of Mao Zedong, the Communist dictator from 1949 to 1976, clashes with the state orthodoxy, which has been willing to admit to his mistakes but not to there having been a very bloody, cruel, and inefficient tyranny under Mao. As a result, the "Great Leap Forward" of 1958–1962, a murderous and unsuccessful attempt to force-modernize Chinese agriculture, is not discussed in public with the freedom with which it is treated by scholars, notably outside China.

Changes in the public use of history, both by government and by the public as a whole, are crucial to the general understanding of the past, and these developments stem largely from current political shifts and pressures. Thus, for example, the collapse of Communism across much of Eurasia in 1989–1991 was followed by a recovery of non- and anti-Communist themes, topics, and approaches – the theme of chapter 8. For example, in newly independent Estonia, it became possible, indeed appropriate, to emphasize the destructiveness of Soviet conquest in 1940 and, again, 1944 and occupation, and to discuss both the many victims of this occupation, and those who resisted. It will be instructive to see how far the same process occurs in Cuba once the Castro system ends, as is likely to be the case.

At the same time, the collapse of European Communism threw up bitter political contentions that also had strong historical resonances. This was readily apparent in 2013 when the government of Ukraine rejected an agreement for its association with the EU (European Union). Russian pressure was, in part, responsible for this decision by Viktor Yanukovich, the Ukrainian president, and this pressure owed much to history as well as geopolitics. Linkage with Ukraine provided Russians a sense of historical identity, in that Kiev, the capital of Ukraine, was the center of the first Russian state (founded in the late ninth century) and the site that supplied Russia's connection to the Eastern Roman Empire (Byzantium) and Orthodox Christianity. The collapse of the Soviet Union and of Communism made this linkage more important in Russia, not least as Slavic identity and Orthodox Christianity became more significant there, while also requiring definition and inviting expansion. Opposing EU expansion is pertinent to this process of identification as historical foes of Russia, namely Poland, Lithuania, and Germany, are particularly associated with this current expansion as far as Ukraine is concerned. Thus, the seventeenth-century struggle between Russia and Poland-Lithuania over control of Ukraine appears relevant in Russia.

In turn, Ukrainian popular anger with the president's action helped to provoke his overthrow in February 2014. This is discussed at greater length in chapter 8. This overthrow threw to the fore in Russia a different historical reference: the willingness of some Ukrainians to cooperate with the German invasion in 1941. Russian commentators repeatedly, and misleadingly, asserted continuity between this case and that of Ukrainian nationalists in 2014.

The role of history in politics is significant, and it is scarcely surprising that politics accordingly has affected the character of the history that is offered. Issues of national identity and political legitimation are central. The context is often a long-term one. When, for example, members of the Polish Parliament from two populist parties occupied the chamber in 2002, they were criticized for reviving what were presented as the anarchic traditions of the old Polish Commonwealth. This was a very charged comparison. Although other factors, such as a lack of defensible frontiers, were significant, anarchic impulses were seen as a significant factor in the weakness of this Commonwealth that led to the partitions of Poland by Austria, Prussia, and Russia in 1772–1795. These partitions removed Poland from the political map of Europe until these empires collapsed at the close of World War I. Thus, critics discerned a self-destructive politics that was quasi-treasonable in 2002.

More commonly, the frame of historical reference is less distant. The World Wars (1914–1918, 1939–1945) dominate attention, especially the second. World War I attracted attention in 2014 with discussion in terms of what commemoration of the centenary was appropriate. However, it proved easier to deploy memories about World War II and to derive "lessons" from the war, and its background, and thus to make them apparently relevant. For example, the unwillingness of Britain to help the Spanish Republic against the German-backed nationalist uprising during the Spanish Civil War (1936–1939) bolstered the cause of the Communist Soviet Union, which did provide assistance for the Republic. This example was cited as a reason the Western powers were wrong to opt for inaction over Syria in 2010–2014,[3] as, more generally, were the apparent lessons of the "Appeasement" of Hitler's Germany in 1938. On the other hand, the complexities of choice and action were indicated by these examples. Had Franco, the Nationalist leader, not won in Spain, the Cold War with the Communist bloc from 1945 to 1989 would have been more difficult for the West as it would have faced a Communist Spain. The choice in Syria, moreover, looked less attractive if presented in terms of Assad or jihadists as opposed to Assad and liberals; and this contrast is instructive as far as the future historical treatment of the civil war in Syria is concerned.

TIME AND DIVINE PURPOSE

There are broader contexts for political controversies in which history is deployed. History as understood by the public is, in large part, a product of patterns of social experience, such as shifts in collective memory, and of social change, for example the rise of literacy. These patterns of social experience create powerful narratives and analyses. Religious explanations are a prime instance. Different societies have interpreted time in varied ways,[4] not least as a consequence of the diverse nature of creation and revival myths, as well as of ecclesiological accounts of time and of divine intervention in causation.[5]

The varied interpretations of the meaning of time are not simply linked to history, as in an account of causation, but also to history, as in the dating of events. The latter was particularly significant in order to understand the nature and purpose of time and, more particularly, to know when religious ceremonies should be observed – as doing so correctly was a means to propitiate the deities and secure their support, so it helped to ensure that history was a process of benign causation. This knowledge was linked to astrology, a means in many societies to understand the present in the light of supra-human forces in order to help shape the future. Astrology, in many cultures, was a matter not only of personal horoscopes, but also of interpretations related to kings or countries as a whole.[6] These beliefs explained the need to note divine purpose through measuring time, which proved an important drive in the presentation of mathematical knowledge.[7] Time was presented as the sphere in which human agents acted and were acted upon by supra-human forces.[8] Providentialism and storytelling were ways to understand this interaction, helping to ensure that myth was not a separate category to other accounts of causation and change. This situation has lasted to the present.

A crucial element was provided by religion. Indeed, direct divine intervention in the life of humans offered a narrative and analysis that was common both to the ancient world and more recently. Religious agents and themes played a major role in both providentialism and storytelling. Moreover, in retelling history in this fashion, the potency of religious agencies, such as oracles, holy men, relics and saints, and the threat from their opponents, notably demons, became readily apparent.[9] Prophecy played a significant role, but it could draw not only on good agencies but also on those that were more ambiguous, or, at least, secretive, such as astrology and alchemy.[10] The extent to which, for most of the past, histories were written by those with clerical education, interests, and careers greatly affected their approach, content, and tone.[11]

Yet, although religious themes were very important, time was not necessarily understood in a simple fashion, or only in terms of the issues of liturgical time or an apocalyptic future.[12] The influential English monastic scholar Bede (c. 673–735 CE), one of the leading clerical historians, as well as many of his Irish monastic contemporaries, divided time into three kinds: natural, human/customary, and divine. The first of these was rigid and linear, and the third was mysterious; but the second was open-ended, defined only by artificial means, and otherwise amendable to the influence of human actions. As a more general indication that religious interpretations did not entail the absence of choice – a choice that, in turn, had to be explained – eighth- and ninth-century Western

European historians were generally attached to the creativity of the human present and to an undefined future. Believing in Judgment Day at the time of Christ's Second Coming was not the same as believing that everything was already mapped out. Generally, the rhetoric surrounding the Last Judgment and the Apocalypse was that, because their timing was unknown and they could come at any moment, it was necessary to think carefully about how choices in the present would play out in the future.[13] This perception contributed to a situation in which the present was distinguished from the past, creating new opportunities, as well as closing off what became anachronistic because it was less relevant.

Religious accounts of causation remain of great cultural weight. In societies that look to the past for example and validation, societies that are reverential of and referential to history, this weight is of major significance.[14] History as a record of providential action is a theme and approach that is widely seen. It provides a meaning that apparently links past, present, and future,[15] and that seems to give purpose to events, change, and time. Providential interpretations ensure that episodes such as the Holocaust can be apparently explained, both at the time and subsequently, not only with reference to secular interpretations, but also, or instead, with regard to theological counterparts. The latter include arguments that God left Humanity with a degree of free will that made the Holocaust possible, and also that God was present in the Holocaust, both suffering and as Jews testified to their faith. Some Christian theologians have argued that the Holocaust can be understood alongside the suffering of Christ.[16]

Academic works of history and on historiography, however, are generally written in a secular tone, with religious themes treated as an aspect of the past, and historical scholarship, conversely, as a secularizing project. This approach is particularly adopted for the post-medieval age, the last half-millennium, to employ a Western method of organizing time. This account, however, is too limited for this post-medieval age, and may also be inappropriate for the future. Indeed, demographic trends, the rise of religious fundamentalism, and what has been presented as a crisis in secular approaches and an exhaustion of their dreams, have led to the suggestion that the future will be more religious, not least due to the tendency of the devout to have more children and to engage in politics.[17]

Such a future would probably have consequences for the nature of popular history and for the discussion of historiographical trends considered in chapter 12. For example, in India, Hindu activists press hard against accounts of Hinduism they dislike, while there are comparable demands from the Hindu diaspora.

At the same time, religious fundamentalism in part arises today, as in the past, from an urgency in facing challenges from secularism and globalization; in part, moreover, evidence of resurgent fundamentalism has as much to do with the impact of more social, political, and cultural populism. In addition, fundamentalisms are fractured tendencies, rather than coherent movements. There are also the consequences of serious rivalry between religions and sects, both in encouraging fundamentalism and in weakening its impact. This rivalry is an aspect of globalization. Indeed, across time, the diffusion of religions has been one of the most significant, and often lasting, aspects of globalization. The rivalry between religions makes it difficult to offer a unified and clear account of the past based on religious considerations, notably providentialism, whether or not the account is fundamentalist in character.

There are also significant geographical contrasts in the character and impact of religious life, with attendant consequences for the role of religion in establishing and affecting the approach to the past. In some countries, religion is not at the fore in setting this approach. The current situation in China does not suggest that fundamentalism will be the key theme there. However, on the global scale, religion (more particularly religions), which had been regarded by many politicians and commentators – notably modernizers in the twentieth century – as anachronisms, made redundant by scientific progress and marginal by secularism, has, instead, displayed far greater popular vitality than political movements that seemed or declared themselves on the cusp of the future. This situation has consequences for the understanding of history by those societies that are particularly affected.

POPULAR AND ACADEMIC APPROACHES

Leaving aside the issue of divine intervention and religious purpose, there is a tension between popular and academic approaches over the role of contingency and human agency. Popular narratives rely upon the drama of human agency: people make history, or, indeed, in the case of the most popular form of the subject, genealogy and family history constitute history. Television history finds this approach most conducive. Drawing frequently on the social sciences, many academic historians, in contrast, often emphasize the structural aspects of situations. However, the resulting focus on probability, even necessity, can be purchased at the expense of choice and contingency.[18] Such tensions between popular and academic approaches can be seen in the differing responses to shifts in academic historiography. For example, the French *Annales* approach to history, with its emphasis on social structures and economic pressures, was highly influential in the Western academy (the university world) in the twentieth century, specifically from the 1930s to the 1960s.[19] However, this approach had very little impact on popular views. Similarly, the public has shown limited appetite for the more fractured, complex discussions of the past produced by Western scholars during the "cultural turn" of recent decades.

Another major divide between public interest and academic fashion relates to objectivity. Popular history assumes the possibility of objectivity or, at the minimum, detachment. This is something many academic historians, who used to share these ideas, but are now influenced by the "linguistic turn" in historiography, consider epistemologically naive.[20] The contrasting use of oral history sources exemplify this divide, with popular history proving less critical of the sources than its academic counterpart as each seeks to provide a "bottom-up" history focused on individual experience, or on collective practice understood in these terms.[21]

The academic approach to the past is anyway becoming less prominent with the rise of media in which it plays little role. This is certainly the case with the internet. Whereas academic publishing and presentation were an established section of the worlds of book and television history, and, in part, helped to validate them, this is less true, despite major efforts, of the internet. The contrast is also apparent with archives, with official archival systems now supplemented (and thus, in part, challenged) by online archives, such as the Nations' Memorybank, which went public in Britain in 2007. The online activity "from below" was joined in many countries by an increased habit, "from above," of consulting the public in ranking national events and icons. For example, in 2006, the Department for Culture, Media, and Sport asked the public, in the project "Icons – a Portrait of England," to choose and vote on its favorite symbols of English culture. There was similar activity in other states, not least as television companies found the theme of most famous compatriots a suitable basis for programs. Such activity linked ideological and governmental themes, of democratization and accountability, with commercial interest in the public as consumers. An historical world of state-sanctioned democratic capitalism was a consequence, although its character and manifestations varied in particular countries. So, too, did the impact of technology.

The engagement of academics with the popular presentation of history is patchy.[22] Academic history in the West is varied in its approach, but heavily influenced by an idealist approach, one that regards issues of historical theory and method, for example the recovery of truth or the creation of "truths," as more significant and valuable than the expression of popular memory.[23] As a related issue, there is the more general question of the reputation of academic historians outside the profession. In the twentieth century, and notably after World War II, the idea of the intellectual, the notion of professionalism, the practice of free speech, and the institutional autonomy of universities, combined to give academic historians a welcome measure of independence and a degree of respect. But this situation is under challenge in the West. Political and governmental pressures are of particular note. The conflation of political correctness and institutional funding, oversight and direction of research, affect the character, content, and presentation of academic research. The role of governmental and institutional control makes this situation particularly noticeable in Europe, whereas, in the United States, both institutional independence and individual tenure lead to more independence. There are also consequences for academic history that stem directly from the democratization of culture and from popular interests. This was readily apparent in the case of religious history when academic discussion of key aspects of Christian history was swamped in the mid-2000s by the outpourings stemming from Dan Brown's novel *The Da Vinci Code.*

THE GLOBAL DIMENSION

Irrespective of this, and in contrast to the self-image of the modern Western academic, the role of the academic as the servant of the state is more important across much of the world. It is likely that this role will become more significant in the future, not least if economic and political power increasingly focus, both in absolute and relative terms, in East and South Asia. There, although to differing degrees, academics depend on public funding and often operate under the threat of censorship within a context in which the goal and content of most historical research and teaching are very sensitive. History is a crucial aspect of nationalism, and the significance of nationalist perspectives for the discussion of history is a key aspect of the weight of the past. Witness the controversies in China and Japan in the 2000s and 2010s, as well as the impact of Hindu nationalism in India. In the Indian election of 2014, Hindu nationalist groups, notably the *Rashtriya Swayamsevak Sangh,* opposed to the governing Congress Party, argued that, in the rise of the BJP (Bharatiya Janata Party), which won the election, the nation was being restored, correcting losses over the previous millennium.

The situation in East Asia and South Asia, different as they are, raises the question of whether the relationships among academic, state, and popular history in the West are typical for the rest of the world – indeed whether there can be global criteria for historiography, or, an agreed-upon basis for world history.[24] This issue can be clearly seen in debates over the relationship between nationalism and objectivity. Scholars in the West divide over the possibility of recovering the past, as does the literature on method. They generally subscribe to a desire to avoid nationalistic partisanship, not least as a result of their recent emphasis on transnationalism. That approach, however, means little in many states across the world, where partisanship and national identity are intertwined, a key theme of this book.

At the same time, it would be woefully mistaken to imagine that these are only issues in the developing world. In the United States, the controversy over the National History Standards in the early 1990s, and the unease that lay behind the establishment of the Historical Society in 1998 as a conservative alternative to the American Historical Association, reflected the contentiousness of historical content and methods in *both* popular and academic circles. In Europe, there is considerable contention over the historical nature of its identity and culture, both for individual states and for the continent as a whole, a theme considered in chapter 9.[25] In European settlement societies, particularly Australia, Canada, and New Zealand and, to a lesser extent, the Andean states and the United States, there is the question, as part of this debate over identity, of how "first peoples" were and are treated, a topic discussed in chapter 7. What is termed "black armband" history with reference to the treatment of the Aborigines has proved very contentious and divisive in Australia, as has its counterpart in New Zealand. The destructiveness of Western conquest is a major theme, but so too is the extent to which "first peoples" were not just passively living in the wilderness but, instead, actively shaped the pre-conquest environment.[26] This argument has then been taken forward to argue that "first peoples" were not simply savages or victims of annihilation, but, instead, active participants in the creation of a syncretic culture or, at least, a "middle ground."[27]

Global demographics will affect official and popular history around the world. Ninety-five percent of the world's population increase is taking place in the developing world. It is there that the pressures to provide a readily comprehensible popular history, both of individual countries and of the world as a whole, will seem most acute, a topic discussed in chapter 12. Governments in developing countries will need to develop unifying national myths, especially as the liberation accounts employed in the immediate post-colonial period, for example in post-apartheid South Africa from 1994, become less potent, on which see chapter 6. A variety of factors makes this situation more urgent: the volatility of societies in the developing world, with the relatively large percentage of their populations under the age of 25; the disruptive impact of urbanization and industrialization; the breakdown of patterns of deference and social control; and pressures on established political, social, religious, and cultural networks, identities, and systems of explanation. There is the challenge posed by particular constructions of ethnicity and religion within many states, and how they interact with historicized notions of national identity and development. We need to devote more attention in historiography to the process of forging new histories in the developing world. It will be both interesting and important to see how dynamic societies with rapidly growing populations come to grips with their recent, and more distant, past. This will probably be the most significant aspect of historiography over the next century. Unfortunately, as this book suggests, the past may well be defined, both there and elsewhere, in terms of hostilities, a practice that helps make sense of "history wars," politicized accounts of the past, within and between countries.

HISTORIOGRAPHIES AND THEIR USES

"History supplies the defects of our own experience. It shows us causes as in fact they were laid, with their immediate effects, and it enables us to guess at future events."[28] Unsurprisingly, as an accomplished (although, by then, unsuccessful) British politician and an active political writer, Henry, Viscount Bolingbroke (1678–1751) was also expert at a third use of history in addition to those given above: its use for present politics and polemic. This was a use shown in the call to history, and the sense of history as destiny, expressed by President Plevneliev of Bulgaria in an interview with the *Observer,* a liberal British newspaper, on 22 December 2013. He was anxious about the debate in Britain about limiting migration there by Bulgarians, a debate linked to opposition in Britain to the terms of British membership in the European Union, or, indeed, to membership itself:

> Isolating Britain and damaging Britain's reputation is not the right history to write . . . Are we in Great Britain today writing a history of a switch to isolation, nationalism and short-term political decisions . . . politicians should be ready to say the inconvenient truth and fight for unpleasant but necessary decisions which, in the short term, will bring our ratings down but, in the long term, preserve our values and keep the history of our proud tolerant nations as they are.

For both Bolingbroke and Plevneliev, as for others, history is in part about positioning a community within its present, rather than its past. This use is readily apparent in the 2010s; although history has always been written to justify and legitimize or to challenge the current situation. In that sense, history, as political means, has its own long history. Thus, there is a curious disjuncture between courses on historiography, defined in the dictionary to which I refer as "writing of history; study of history-writing,"[29] and the use of history in modern politics and society. The courses may focus on Leopold von Ranke (1795–1886), a key figure in the development of professional history, and, by way of contrasting a supposed, modern exemplar, post-modernism, or, to take a shorter time span, the French *Annales* School of the mid-twentieth century and post-modernism.[30] In contrast, the use of history in politics and society is not primarily a matter of intellectual thought and its academic application, although there is the important overlap of school curricula. Instead, this use is more a case of governmental concerns with national identity, political polemic at the international and domestic levels, social genealogy, especially of families, and a popular cultural curriculum[31] that is often at odds with its educational counterpart.

To emphasize these factors may appear both present-minded and anti-intellectual, but the popular sphere is very important, and creates a historiography of its own. Far more people in the United States saw the harsh portrayal of slavery in the television series *Roots* (1977) than read Robert Fogel's more measured, scholarly *Time on the Cross* (1974), which included an account of the conditions of slave life in the United States. Far more people in Britain in 2010 would have seen Ian Hislop's BBC2 television series *Age of the Do-Gooders,* a lively account of Victorian reformers, than will ever read scholars revealing that the pre-reform age in Britain (and elsewhere) was not simply mired in reaction, corruption, and complacency, as Hislop, an articulate journalist and accomplished popular historian, suggested; and, indeed, that reform was a rhetoric as much as a description, a crucial point that is frequently overlooked.

The significance of television, and of particular television programs, both reflect and sustain a situation whereby, in a process in which commercial and political pressures frequently play a role, people get the history they want to have.[32] Alongside the range of explanations available in any one period comes the account that provides the exemplary narrative and the established analysis, which can be rephrased as the attractive narrative and the desired analysis.

Politics is a key aspect of the context, content, and discussion in public and popular history. Moreover, the use of the past for political and social reasons is highly significant for the employment of history and the development of historiography, and this significance can be extended to other fields. Thus, the extensive British use of the neo-Classical style in architecture in the nineteenth and early-twentieth centuries strengthened the claim to imperial sway, at least in its own mind, with Britain appearing as the worthy successor of the Roman Empire. This understanding of historiography complicates the conventional discussion of the subject as a branch of intellectual history, or, more crudely, as historians' way of looking at themselves and shaping their subject, an approach that emphasizes theory as opposed to utility.

A challenge also arises from a different direction, namely in any attempt to redress the standard approach of the customary focus on the Western tradition. There is still an understandable bias in the West to teach the subject of history within a Western framework. Alongside some excellent recent work that does engage with the "non-West" and that reflects the interest in world history, many accounts of historiography as a distinct subject have been reluctant to embrace an agenda of globalization.[33] This point is also abundantly true – often more so – of the teaching of history elsewhere in the world. Aside from Western-centricity, a characteristic fault of historiographical work is its downplaying of the political thought and historical views of political actors in favor of those of political thinkers.[34] This approach is mistaken, but in keeping with the dominant tendency to look at the theory of history rather than its practice, especially its practice by non-historians. Moreover, there is still insufficient effort to incorporate in work on historiography the dynamics of official or popular interest in history, although this theme has become much more significant in recent decades.

In turn, popular interest and knowledge are affected by the character, content, and context of education. In some countries, the fragmented nature of teaching and, notably the frequent lack of narrative explication, creates problems. In particular, without offering the background of a broad narrative, a narrative that is almost completely absent now in most British universities, teaching there generally focuses on narrow specialisms – such as detailed courses in the field of medical history – to a degree that would be unusual in many other subjects, notably the physical sciences. As a result, British students on history courses are frequently disoriented, which affects their ability to engage with historical works. World history has a more prominent and successful role in the United States. Traditionally, this approach was overly dominated by "Western Civilization" and similar courses, but the pattern in recent decades has been more global. "Western Civilization" has been treated as a branch of world history, and has been re-conceptualized accordingly.[35]

Teaching is a key area for the overlap of public history and historiography, and for the interaction of professionalism with wider currents of interest. This is because the historian is no magician able to unlock the past, but a guide who stimulates students, readers, (and, increasingly, viewers) to think and see with their own minds and eyes. Academics and students/readers/viewers therefore constitute historiography and are all historians. Although that inclusive remark is not intended to discount the great value of the scholarly expertise, research, and reflection offered by the academics, the emphasis in this book is on a broad understanding of historiography.

This understanding underlines the extent to which there is more than one way to approach and discuss the subject. It is certainly the case that the writing of history is not now, and never has been, detached from present political, ideological, social, and cultural controversies. Why otherwise would women's history have arisen as a subject in the West from the 1960s, a period when equality of opportunity was a political and social preoccupation there? So, too, with environmental history. Even when Western academic history adopted a scientific culture and exposition in the nineteenth century, it did so, in practice, as an aspect of a set of norms that implied clear moral values, and, frequently, political ones as well.[36]

REFERRING TO THE PAST

At a time when historical experience plays an increasingly appreciable role in national popular cultures[37] challenged by the rise of globalization, and certainly a greater role than in the more self-consciously new 1960s and 1970s, public discussion of historical matters has become more heated. Social fluidity, the ebbing of deference and respect, the rise of individualism, and the impact of electronic media have each played, and continue to play, a significant role, and one that is seen not only in the West but also across much of the world.

Moreover, in accordance with a longstanding pattern, the past becomes a space of the imagination where people explore the discontents of modern civilization.[38] Contention is unsurprising given that historical work, whether by academics, popularizers, governments, or individual memory, asserts the causality and significance of what occurs, and thereby enables individuals and societies to establish themselves in time, and, perhaps most importantly, in their own contemporary time.

Linked to this, events can be given explanation and resonance by looking for parallels. For example, debate over individual conflicts is given additional bite by reference to past episodes.[39] The Appeasement of the dictators in the 1930s, and the Vietnam War, served, respectively, to encourage and discourage subsequent Western, notably American, intervention in international crises.[40] As a result, scholarship on these apparent lodestars became controversial. Thus, arguments that the Vietnam War was winnable, for example Mark Moyar's *Triumph Forsaken: The Vietnam War 1954–1965* (2006), were challenged, as by John Prados's *Vietnam: The History of an Unwinnable War, 1945–1975* (2009). In turn, fresh conflicts became new sources of reference for the debate, notably the invasion of Iraq in 2003. More generally, the process of comparison between past and present can, potentially, be an incubus, as accounts of the past can readily be used to provide reference points that fix, and thus restrict, options, and can also mislead.

Alongside contestation, the process of establishing identity and arguments in, and through, time helps explain the extent to which education, celebration, and reconciliation focus on accounts of the past. The rise of the memory of persecution as an issue and means in contemporary history contributes strongly to this process. "Truth and Reconciliation Commissions" about contentious past issues, as in post-apartheid South Africa, provide an opportunity to arbitrate memories and, in doing so, can serve as agents of politics and nationalism. Archbishop Desmond Tutu, the South African chairman, described the Commission as "an incubation chamber for national healing, reconciliation and forgiveness," but, across the world, the situation has not always proved so positive. Aside from disagreements, the argument of hardship and persecution is also employed by persecutors and would-be persecutors. A prime instance was Hitler's repeated (and misleading) depiction of the Germans after the Peace of Versailles of 1919 as wronged by most others, and, thus, as entitled to demand a new territorial order. Historical accounts, indeed historiography itself, therefore, become an aspect of the competition of memories, a competition, ranging through time, that records both views of the past and hopes for, and fears of, the future.[41] The internet, moreover, allows many more people to establish and assert their competing position on history and memory through their own or other websites.

The culture or ideology of professional history, notably in the West, argues for a separation from politics, and indeed from nationalism, as a key definition and product of this professionalism. This professionalism, however, does not have a close relationship with the broad current of popular interest in history. We never have had, and never will see, a television series on "Historiography," but there are programs on the history of popular topics, such as television, as well as many of "The Hundred Best" types, for example films, television shows, or novels. In these and other questions, most people are not concerned with datasets, debate, re-interpretation, conceptual answers, or methodological difference. On the contrary, they are interested in history as spectacle, entertaining anecdote, evidence of conspiracy, or simply a dramatic thing. Narrative is the preferred means of explication, not analysis.[42] Today, the development of history in the universities can appear a minor side road to the motorway of the television series, and the publishing phenomenon of *Horrible Histories* and other popular works, or the compelling desire of a frequently rootless population to discover their family origins and past, to write the history of their most precious possession, their house, to indulge their dark fantasies through picture books of ancient weaponry or the uniforms of the ss,[43] or to glory in last summer through coffee-table garden histories. Libraries and archives are filled by largely untutored amateurs working for the love of their subject, unaware of any pre-considered methodological approaches, and publishing in myriad specialized journals that rarely mention, or are mentioned by, "serious" academic journals. Airport bookshops sport a range of "academic light" histories in their "intellectual" sections, which cater to an audience with interests a mile wide and quarter of an inch thick, either by providing fashionable broad sweeps of world history, or by offering personalized "docudramas" of great events and battle.

CONCLUSIONS

There is no reason for complacency when considering the context of popular knowledge of the past. In particular, anxiety about national identity and cohesion has been expressed in many countries, including Britain, France, and the United States, in the 2000s and 2010s. There is also the serious cultural challenge brought out in a 2007 American study of the transmission of historical knowledge: "If school history is to play a major role in shaping the consciousness of the today's iPod-ed, YouTubed, Instant Messengerised, MySpaced American youth, it must find new ways to engage the cultural curriculum that engulfs them. Failing to do so only guarantees school history's irrelevance into the next century."[44]

Such an account of modern youth, an account that, as an instance of the pace of technological change, would today be presented in terms of social media, is "declinist" in the sense that there is the assumption that the loss of prose, let alone interest, means the end of history. That account certainly makes sense in terms of many of the conventions and culture of modern academe. However, it is apparent from looking at historical consciousness and sources across the continuum of the past that prose is only one form of historical expression. Other literary genres have been used,[45] as indeed have visual genres, to express interest in the past. Further, just as mapping has been re-thought in recent decades with a transformation in cartographic perception, notably (but not only) to engage with historic non-Western traditions,[46] so the same may become true for history and historiography. Changes in storytelling about the past will reflect developments in technology and society, but the strength of narrative is such that this form will persist whatever the means. Having established the major themes of this book in the introductory chapter, we will consider their chronological development before focusing on the subject in the modern world. Then, in chapter 12, we will assess possible future changes.

His death was a great turning point in human happiness, for the laws and security of all men and particularly for our own nation, which only just escaped total ruin thanks to his sudden end. I therefore intend to give an exact account of the whole story, not least because it offers a weighty proof of the power of God. It also provides reassurance for those in affliction, and a lesson in prudence for those who think that good fortune lasts forever, and do not realize that unaccompanied by righteousness it will bring them to misery.

THE JEWISH HISTORIAN FLAVIUS JOSEPHUS
on the assassination of the Roman Emperor Caligula in CE 41[1]

TWO

A Selective Narrative to 1650

ORIGINS, PROVIDENTIALISM, AND STORYTELLING

Historiography began as foundation myths, the myths of peoples, dynasties, and religions, and this theme is still powerfully present today. Indeed, there is a parallel between the origin-myths of the nations and states of two and three millennia ago, and those propounded for the new or revived states established from 1945 to the present. One major difference, however, is the role of religion, which played a key part in early origin-myths, but has been conspicuously absent – or negligible – in most recent ones (although with important Muslim exceptions, as well as Israel), or has been presented in secular guises. Indeed, to a degree, nationalism is a modern form of religion, one in which the state worships itself and its community, with the nation encouraged to think in terms of a continuous mission. The weakness of some states, for example Iraq and Syria, is linked not only to very bad government, but also to a failure of nationalism to overcome other allegiances, allegiances that in part reflect, and are reflected in, the nature of this government. Religions themselves have origin-myths,[2] and some religions are aspects of the development of nations, notably in the case of Jews and the Japanese.

Modern history is generally understood in the West as an eighteenth-century Enlightenment project that endorsed the secular analysis of cause and effect, and notably did so in a clear programmatic fashion. This was the type of history that provided the basis for the subsequent rise of university history.[3] It was a type that deliberately departs from religious accounts and, indeed, offers a secular analysis of cause and effect for religious factors and developments such as the Protestant Reformation in sixteenth-century Europe. Bolingbroke wrote "since the ages of prophecy, as well as miracles, are past, we must content ourselves to guess at what will be, by what has been."[4]

In practice, the use of the past in the modern world still frequently demonstrates belief in a providential purpose or effect. Significantly, it is difficult to link this usage to conventional historiographical discussion. Conversely, it is possible that secular narratives and analyses can be regarded as having a providential, or at least privileging, purpose or effect; and, in some cases, very much by intent. Indeed, this point can be regarded as helping explain the particular success of such narratives. Both *The Whig Interpretation of History,* a progressive account that was so influential in Britain in the nineteenth century and with equivalents elsewhere, and the Marxist approach, which was a powerful force in the twentieth century, can be discussed in these terms. Similarly, many Americans regarded themselves as an elect or privileged nation. Nevertheless, in America and elsewhere, there is also an anti-version, born of revisionism and fuelled by concepts of metaphysical guilt.

However quasi-prophetic and providential (religious or secular) popular approaches to history may be, there is no reason for the academic discussion of historiography to be progressive or teleological in character – in short, assuming an improvement in quality. The same point is relevant for the shift from the oral historical tradition to the written account. This development is generally treated in terms of improvement, but that approach and its implications must be handled with care. It is certainly the case that the oral tradition had a characteristic element of storytelling that was scarcely open to later techniques of documentary research. As a result, the content, context, and meaning of history changed with the decline of this tradition. However, as a reminder of the need to avoid simplistic accounts of change and improvement, much of this storytelling continued in popular narrations of history, both during periods dominated by literature and, more recently, by visual media.

Thus, for example, *Downton Abbey,* a successful seven-part television story about the English aristocracy in the early 1910s that was broadcast in 2010, with sequels thereafter, is fictional and depicts an imaginary family. Yet, the series also presented what was claimed to be an accurate account of such a family, was filmed in a real stately home, and included mention of real people, such as the then–Chancellor of the Exchequer, David Lloyd George, and episodes, notably the sinking of the ocean liner the *Titanic* in 1912, which began the story, and British entry into World War I, which closed the first series. Moreover, partly because such a program operates on the popular drama boundary between the educated and the entertained, the viewing public considers the series to be an accurate account. Indeed, this belief led to many complaints over inaccuracies in period detail,[5] while giving rise to many conversations about the plausibility of aspects of the plot. Fiction thereby informs history, in the sense of the perception of the past. Such British series can be compared to American programs on the Civil War (1861–1865) or China's series on the life of Mao Zedong's son, who died in the Korean War (1950–1953).

The reminder of parallels, as well as differences, between particular types of history invites consideration of the problem with the idea of clear contrasts between these types. The counterpointing of reason and religion, or human and providential history, provides the obvious instance of apparent contrasts, but the situation is more complex. For example, for many writers of the Classical period, such as the Roman historian Livy (c. 59 BCE–CE 17), the central problem was that of explaining failure. A common way to do so was to argue that omens had been ignored. However, as the Athenian historian Thucydides, c. 460– c. 400 BCE, author of *The History of the Peloponnesian War*, pointed out, "oracle-mongers" chanted "oracles of every import," and the Athenians listened eagerly to the oracles, "each according to his own preference."[6] This remark suggests, on the part of Thucydides, a degree of skepticism about oracles, unlike the view of Herodotus (c. 485–425 BCE), the other renowned Greek historian of the century. If failure could be explained as arising from ignoring the right oracles, success, conversely, could be attributed to following the correct oracles, for example in terms of delaying battle until the right sign was seen. On the one hand, this approach can be described as an expression of religious conviction, but it also represented an attempt to provide a rational account for developments that might otherwise appear arbitrary: rational in so far as respect for oracles was the accepted way of reasoning at the time, with oracles providing the reason for things and events. There was the assumption that timely or accurate adherence to prophecy would produce desired results with regularity, in fact a naturalistic assertion of cause and effect.

Reading omens was an aspect of a wider process of using knowledge, based on an experience of the past and an understanding of the present, to seek truth about the future. Different treatments of the response to omens and providence, both in the Classical world and more recently, underlined the extent to which history was (and is) both an account of what human agents had done and about what happened to them. Emphases varied by writer and market, and continue to do so, as any discussion of counterfactualism amply demonstrates.[7]

The conventional Western approach presents the writing of the fifth-century BCE Greek world as the origin of modern historical writing, with Herodotus as the father of history, and Thucydides as a key figure emphasizing human, not divine, action and motives. Herodotus was the first to define history as what can be reliably discovered, rather than just stories about the past. At the very beginning of his narrative, which set out to trace the origin of the hostility between Greece and Asia, he gave a set of stories that rationalized myths, and then rejected them, in order to concentrate on Croesus of Lydia. At the limit of reliable oral tradition, Croesus was the man he knew to have been the first to attack the Greeks, about 120 years before Herodotus's own time. About 425 BCE, Herodotus (1. pref. 1) wrote: "This is the display of the research of Herodotus of Halicarnassus, made so that human achievements should not fade with time, and so that great and wondrous deeds displayed by Greeks and barbarians should not be without lasting fame: my particular concern is the reason why they went to war with one another."

The Greek word *historiē* means research or enquiry.[8] Herodotus turned to Croesus, as follows: "This, then, is what the Persians and Phoenicians say. But I am not going to say that these things happened this way or otherwise, rather I shall indicate the man whom I myself know to have begun unjust deeds towards the Greeks, and then I shall advance forwards into my account" (1.5.3). Thucydides began: "Thucydides from Athens wrote his account of the war which the Peloponnesians and the Athenians fought against each other, beginning from when the war broke out, because he expected that it would be major and the most worthy of discussion of previous events" (1.1.1). Thucydides's emphasis is on evidence and probable conclusions:

"Anyone who considered from the aforesaid indications that things were more or less what I have described would not go wrong, neither trusting what the poets have eulogized about them, embellishing them for the purpose of exaggeration, nor what the prose writers have put together for the purpose of entitlement to the audience rather than the truth" (1.21.1). "Perhaps the lack of the mythical element in my history will appear rather unpleasing to an audience; but if those who wish to look at clarity – both of the things that have happened and of those which, in accordance with human nature, are going to happen again some time like this and in similar form – should judge it useful, that will be sufficient. It is set down as a possession for always rather than as a competitive display for instant hearing" (2.22.4). This was not the history of Homer, which depended on divine help, a work on an ancient world for which there was no comparable evidence. In contrast, the methods of Thucydides could be applied to this ancient, mythological world, but only by rationalizing myth, which was what the Greek historian Plutarch (c. CE 46–c. CE 120) sought to do for Theseus, and not by interrogating living memory.[9]

The conventional approach to the origin of modern historical writing has been challenged with the argument that there were significant contrasts between Greek and modern historical work, notably in ideas about temporality and historicity. Nevertheless, historical writing in the Classical West, as in most contexts and periods, sought to present a rational account, to provide an exemplary narrative, and to offer appropriate support for the public accounts and rituals that were central to state myths and to social life.[10] The actions of rulers were a key theme, as in the history of the Roman emperors from 180 to 238 CE by Herodian, who was born in Syria and wrote in Greek but lived in Rome.

At the same time, historical discussion was expressed in different modes and forms in the Classical world, as it also is today.[11] In his *Cyropaedia* [*The Education of Cyrus*], the Greek historian Xenophon (c. 444–357 BCE) declared the lesson of history to be that of respecting omens, specifically in avoiding hubris and misgovernment.[12] Ancient Chinese beliefs, most obviously as advanced by Confucius, made similar points.

To Polybius, (c. 200–118 BCE), a Greek writer in the service of Rome, the work of historians could provide useful lessons: "Fortune has guided almost all the affairs of the world in one direction and has forced them to incline toward one and the same end; a historian should likewise bring before his readers under one synoptical view the operations by which she has accomplished her general purpose."[13] Livy commemorated "the deeds of the foremost people of the world," the Romans. He was in no doubt of the utilitarian purpose of doing so: "What chiefly makes the study of history wholesome and profitable is this, that you behold the lessons of every kind of experience set forth as on a conspicuous monument; from these you may choose for yourself and for your own state what to imitate, from these mark for avoidance."[14] Plutarch wished to treat a mythical character (Theseus) in an historical way, to "succeed in purifying Myth, making her submit to reason and take on the semblance of History."[15] This observation comes at the start of the paired parallel lives of Theseus (Greek) and Romulus (Roman). Hitherto, Plutarch had been dealing with periods that allowed reasoning in terms of probability and a narrative of real events, but now he entered the territory of poets and mythmakers, where everything was uncertain and obscure. That is why he made the point about purifying myth to make it look like proper history. Theseus counted as mythic because his exploits belonged to a period before proper history began. Some authors put the beginning of proper (i.e., dateable) history at the first Olympiad (776 BCE), others at the fall of Troy, which was first dated – to 1184 by BCE – by Eratosthenes in the third century BCE. The most famous Theseus story was his rescue of the Athenian children who had been sent as tribute to Minos, king of Crete. As a son of Zeus and the lawgiver of the underworld, Minos was a figure of myth. The Theseus story implies that Minos controlled the Aegean, including Athens; but when Herodotus (at 3.122) talked about "masters of the sea," he made Polycrates of Samos (c. 520 BCE) the first known example, explicitly excluding Minos as not belonging to "what we may call the time of men."

Providentialism and storytelling were key elements in the interlinked accounts of past, present, and future. These interlinked accounts serve as a reminder that history, as a process of change and explanation, was not seen as distinctive in its effects or even causes, to the past. Concern about the ages of the world, and about demonstrating divine purpose, necessarily encompassed past, present, and future. Indeed, predicting and envisaging the end of time was an aspect of the work of a number of historians such as the Anglo-Saxon monk Bede (c. 673–735 CE).[16] Nor was history solely a particular account of the past. Instead, the sense of the past as different was limited. This belief affected the significance of time, the understanding of change, and the possibility of fixing accounts of cause and effect to particular chronological contexts. Indeed, the role of providentialism and storytelling helped ensure that myth was not (and is not) separate from history, notably history as discussed by the public. Myth serves to structure, and thereby rationalize, events and time in a fashion that satisfies the public need for clarity and exposition. Both myth and history, indeed, represent an exercise of imagination. To modern eyes, myth overlaps more with fiction, but the extent to which ready distinctions can be drawn is sometimes unclear: myth and history certainly overlap and feed on each other, both using imagination.[17] Take, for example, the various editions of John Foxe's *Acts and Monuments of Matters Most Special and Memorable Happenings in the Church with an Universal History of the Same,* popularly known as the *Book of Martyrs,* and first published in 1563. Over time, the various editions were elaborated as people came to believe the account of Protestant suffering and fortitude and demanded editions that conformed to it, bolstering the Protestant heroism and demonizing Catholicism.

This point can be taken further by arguing that there is an overlap in what Adrian Jones terms "vivid history," an attempt to evoke a past, rather than to present it in formal arguments about outcomes and processes.[18] In a number of languages, the same word is used for both story and history, and this has also been the case for English. Moreover, as part of their overlap, history contributed to memory, with the differing forms of narrative providing memory-aids that could be complementary, as well as clashing.[19] In India, ancient Vedic literature, later epics, and medieval tales of the past, all used myth-making to capture essential relationships.[20] Historical texts for the pre-Muslim period in India are limited, however, creating problems of lack of corroboration and lacunae that are, of course, also familiar elsewhere. Portions of the Vedic epics appear authentic in terms of their correspondence with other sources.

At the same time, epics were altered in order to note changing circumstances,[21] a practice also seen with chronicle writing, and, indeed, different editions of modern scholarly books.

The issues and practices of memory, myth, fiction, and history played out in the variety of milieux beside the individual, in which stories were (and are) disseminated and news transformed into history.[22] The most important agencies were community ones: families, localities, and confessional and economic groups. These agencies interacted with more authoritative means of historical formulation and transmission, those centered on the lay and religious agencies of central government, as well as formal educational institutions and, in time, the culture of print. The relationship between these two forms and means of historical formulation and transmission was not one of simple competition, as community agencies could serve for the dissemination of historical accounts received from the more authoritative agencies. And yet, there was (and still is) a basic tension. Through their values, local communities, understood to refer to a specific group, geographical, social, ethnic, religious, economic, or other groups, not necessarily limited to geography alone, could influence the impact of the history received from external agencies. Nevertheless, the local communities played a more limited role in doing so than they did in the establishment, dissemination, and discussion of local histories, where their part was far more prominent, although affected by other local histories. In contrast, external agencies, such as religious bodies and royal governments, both imposed the outside world on local communities and mediated between it and the localities. In particular, these agencies created and sustained narratives and understandings that were not those of the locality. History was both the form and content of the narratives and the process of understanding them. In opposition to the accounts produced by these agencies of external power, rumor provided a way to present information and concern, about past, present, and future, in the localities.[23]

Across the range of agencies, historical accounts were of course closely related to political sympathies. This process owed much to the extent to which works were produced in particular milieux and with the belief that it was appropriate to reflect the relevant values. Thus, in eleventh-century (CE) England, the different texts of the *Anglo-Saxon*

Chronicle were composed in ecclesiastical locations that were linked to their sympathies, with text C produced in Mercia by supporters of the Earls of Mercia who were opposed to the views of text E, which was produced by those who backed the rival Earls of Wessex.[24] More generally, an overlap between secular and religious histories, historians and motivations was frequent.

RELIGIOUS AND SECULAR

History, alongside religion, formed the key way of explaining the world. The past was central to the processes of reference and relevance, and in a way that is alien to many modern cultures. History illuminated God's purpose and the interconnectedness of the cosmic and the earthly, the divine and the human.[25] In doing so, history fulfilled the role commonly given to science today. This interconnectedness of the divine and the human was not only general, but also specific, with history serving to present the importance of particular sites, relics, and individuals. It did so by recording origins and provenance, providing an equivalent to dynastic histories. Religious texts were regarded as history, and vice versa.

The idea of progress in human history was, to a degree, compromised by the strength of religious perspectives. This was particularly so with belief in millenarian outcomes ending human life on Earth, and with the confidence that time and change were cyclical in character, at least prior to the eventual end of the world, for example as outlined by the Christian belief in the Last Judgment. Cyclical concepts appeared natural to societies that could observe the passage of the seasons, and that also saw human life in terms of a cycle of experience from birth to death.[26] The Wheel of Fortune was a powerful idea of cyclical success and failure. Such areas attract interest from historians, but generally are the preserve of anthropologists, although the anthropological approach has been incorporated by some, notably oral, historians.

The nature and impact of divine intervention in human history was presented in very different lights. Alongside sacred history for humanity as a whole, came a history that was a particular dispensation arising from the historicized character of central religious events, such as the Exodus of the Jews from Egypt, or the lives of Christ and Muhammad, as well as a history of local religious sites and individuals. For Christendom, the Creation was the fundamental origin-myth, one that was written in the Bible and regularly proclaimed in readings from it and sermons based on it. The life of Jesus presented the distinctive origin-myth for Christianity.

A focus on origins and ancestry affected not only the contents of historical work, but also the writing of history across the world: in China as in the Islamic lands and Christendom. The authority of earlier accounts encouraged an emphasis on new work largely as a continuation of them, while favoring what is somewhat unfairly seen as "scissors-and-paste" treatments of the past. There was also a large-scale fabrication of historical sources, such as papal decretals and the Donation of Constantine (awarding of rights to the Papacy by the Emperor Constantine, the first Roman emperor to promote Christianity), or the eleventh-century claim that St. Martial of Limoges was one of the Apostles,[27] in order to establish and enhance claims. Such fabrication appeared appropriate as producing what was believed ought to exist.

At the same time, a religious worldview and an interest in origins were scarcely incompatible with scholarly values such as independent judgment, impartiality, and critical acumen.[28] Author of the *Ecclesiastical History of the English People* (c. 731), Bede showed remarkable care to cite sources. Moreover, the structure of his work, moving backward and forward between the various kingdoms to heighten the sense of a coherent "English people" finding their way to salvation, was much more sophisticated than any history written in Western Europe since the Roman period. In addition, although Bede did not actually invent AD (CE) dating, he was the first to use it systematically in order to reckon time, and played a large part in popularizing this dating.

Moreover, policing theological orthodoxy did not necessarily mean a comparable attempt to dictate history, although it often did: the situation varied by religion and within individual religious traditions. In Western Christendom, general histories were written as continuations of the Bible, explaining and interpreting current events in the light of the Christian faith. The discussion of the Crusades provide a key example. However, the papacy made little effort to establish an official historiography in the High Middle Ages. There was much polemic, for example over the Investiture Controversy of the eleventh century concerning the choice and endorsement of bishops, and polemical chronicles were part of that controversy. However, the papacy did not get to the point of seriously trying to establish an official view and rooting out alternatives. The popes carefully monitored the way the emperors formulated their documents, but they did not monitor imperial chronicles, which they had no way to control.

In Western Christendom, as in China and the Islamic world, alongside a strongly didactic character to the presentation of the past, mostly in the form of moral treatises, there was no single "pre-modern" state of historical understanding. Instead, there were important developments, notably in China in the late tenth and early eleventh centuries, and in Western Christendom in the twelfth century. Key figures in what has been seen as a twelfth-century Renaissance and historiographical revolution include Anglo-Norman writers, notably William of Jumièges, Orderic Vitalis, William of Malmesbury, Henry of Huntingdon, William of Newburgh, Gerald of Wales, and Geoffrey of Monmouth. This activity was an aspect of a broader pattern of cultural and intellectual change in Western Europe that included the development of schools and universities, the rise of clerical professionalism – notably a self-conscious clerical class – an emphasis on documentation, a greater interest in individuality, and a more sophisticated historiography. Ideas of knowability were linked to the development of scientific empiricism in works by Adelard of Bath, Thierry of Chartres, and William of Conches. Their argument in favor of a method that combined induction with deductive thought were related to a readiness to accept contingent and changing results, notably in place of a clear-cut certainty. Doubt that was to be clarified by information deployed by a God-given human intellect was crucial in the assertion of this new rationalism.[29]

The historiographical dimension was probably most pronounced in England because monasteries and other Anglo-Saxon religious foundations needed and wished to protect themselves in a Norman world. Thus, very local concerns were linked to a broader pattern of development. As a reminder of the variety of causes that interacted, a marked rise in population and economic activity provided a significant underpinning for historiographical activity; prefiguring the situation in the West since the late eighteenth century.

At the local level, seeking to affirm and exalt their position and claims, religious institutions produced foundation histories in which traditions were invented and history was appropriated. In Western Christendom, this process was seen with individual monasteries, bishoprics and other institutions. For example, the Cistercian abbeys in Yorkshire in England produced such foundation histories in the thirteenth century. These works were specific in their purpose, but also part of a larger engagement with the authority of the past. This engagement was seen in the collection and codification of historic documents, notably for current purposes, especially to defend legal rights.[30] Local histories often sought to join the account of the locality, and its particular historical rights, rites, and magic – for example the relics it cared for, with national and universal history. Such conjunctions occurred foremost in retelling and justifying the protection offered by rulers, notably their grants of land and privileges, and, secondly, in relating signs of the central events of Christian revelation.

Real or alleged local events were also given lasting relevance, as well as being checked carefully, in the case of canonization processes; with the lengthy quasi-legal process that preceded canonization an important aspect of the testing and establishment of sainthood. Witnesses to miracles were questioned. Shrines, relics, and annual celebrations, in turn, were confirmed by this process. They also acquired their own history, notably as miracles took place. Hagiography, the lives of saints, was a key aspect of history. The collection of saints' lives compiled in the 1260s by Jacobus de Voragine, a Dominican friar living in northern Italy, proved especially influential, being translated into most of the languages of Western Europe and providing, as was intended, the basis for numerous sermons. The collection survived into the age of print, when it appeared in many editions in the late fifteenth century. Focusing on the martyr saints of the first four centuries CE (AD), this collection, like the paintings of the period, which were easier to interpret in light of the lives, kept them a real presence for over a millennium.[31] This was history as lesson, but also as wondrous story, an overlap similar to that with the world of Harry Potter suggested in the last chapter. In central Brussels, the Shrine of the Sacrament of the Holy Miracle in the Church of St. Michael and St. Gudula (now Brussels Cathedral), enhanced in the sixteenth century with a separate, much adorned, chapel, commemorated the Eucharistic hosts allegedly desecrated by Jews in 1370, hosts that supposedly had bled miraculously when stabbed.

The historical language of locality was also to be seen at the lay level. It was significant for the process of self-identification as groups differentiated themselves, and were categorized by others. This was a long-term process, one related to what is termed ethnogenesis. History was a core component in the language of difference that was employed in asserting identity and also when rejecting rule that could be stigmatized as outside and illegitimate. The evidence for this process varies. Literacy, and records and their survival, are all crucial factors in determining the availability of evidence. History was to become particularly apparent with towns, entities that had their own legal character and privileges, as well as a population, some of whom were able to write works expressing a sense of local identity.

This idiom of identity politics and power was not restricted to what can be seen as "small countries" resisting larger neighbors. These larger neighbors also found the articulation of an historical identity necessary and valuable in opposing the equivalents of modern super or hyper powers, namely medieval claimants to universal empire. These claimants drew on a tradition that was seen in much of Eurasia. In China, a worldview centered on the Celestial Emperor encouraged this approach, while in Islam the authority of the Caliph, the successor to the Prophet, was the key point of reference. In Christendom, universal empire looked back to the authority and power of Imperial Rome, and one that had been strengthened by the pretensions of the papacy to head the one, true Church. This cesaro-papalism fused in the cooperation of Holy Roman Empire and papacy. It was largely in opposition to this that arguments of national independence were advanced. Similarly, these arguments were asserted by lay rulers, including the Holy Roman emperors, against the jurisdictional, ecclesiastical, and political pretensions of the papacy and the international Church. Thus, in England, there was vocal opposition, notably from the thirteenth and, even more, fourteenth centuries to the appointment of foreign clerics and to the transfer of funds to international religious orders. These and other themes were largely contested not in terms of a presentist legitimacy born of consent, but, instead, with reference to ideas of rights and privileges that were located with regard to the authority of the past. This was an authority that brought together both secular and ecclesiastical legitimacy. Thus, to defy the claims of cesaro-papalism, it was necessary to search for alternative historical pathways to contemporary legitimacy. This search involved the creation of antecedents that entailed a large measure of selective argument, if not downright forgery.

History provided not only legitimacy, but also prestige and glory. This was true for lay and ecclesiastical authority, and at all levels. Thus, rulers, clerics, and municipalities commissioned works, including books and paintings, that enhanced and defended their position, acquired and affirmed prestige, and offered what is now termed "soft power." Dynasties, kingdoms, and countries were enhanced by the presentation of an exemplary history. For example, Henry VI of England (r. 1422–1461, 1470–1471) backed the canonization of the ninth-century King Alfred of Wessex, in order to provide validation for a view of the longevity of English kingship. Manuel I of Portugal (r. 1495–1521), under whom Vasco da Gama reached India in 1498, commissioned, from the historian and chronicler Duart Galvào, the *Chronicle of El-Rei D. Afonso Henriques,* the life and deeds of Portugal's first king, Afonso I Henriques (r. 1139–1185). Finished in 1505, this work dealt with the victory at Ourique over the Moors in 1139 as well as the capture of Lisbon from the Moors in 1147. The role of the Crown as the traditional protector of the Christian faith was therefore made clear, with success vindicating this role. This interpretation was significant as a justification for Portugal's overseas expansion at that juncture, and also in the competition for prestige with neighboring Spain – not least prestige as the defender of Christendom at a time when the papacy was arbitrating between Spain and Portugal over transoceanic territorial claims.

If this is a functional account of the relationship between history and nationalism, and one that, by later standards, omits, or underplays, the groundswell of popular national sentiment, that may indeed appear appropriate. This is particularly so for Christendom in the Middle Ages, and can also be seen as an important thesis thereafter. Indeed, a tension between a historicized sense of nationalism that reflected broadly based support, and one that was more clearly a governmental project, has been crucial to the use of history, and remains so. The former can be regarded as organic and in accordance with the principles of political development outlined by the British politician and commentator Edmund Burke in his *Reflections on the Revolution in France* (1790), even though its manifestations can be malign as well as benign. Conversely, nationalism as a governmental project has little to do with democratic values. Instead, the propagation of a historicized sense of nationalism as a government project is, in a harsh light, an aspect of the false consciousness deliberately advanced by elites in order to justify their role and power, and to win popular support.[32]

CHINA

Concern with the past emerged in China on a very different scale and in a different context compared to Western Christendom. Excluding the older, mythologized "histories" of the Chinese golden age, histories were written at least partially under imperial auspices from Sima Qian's *Records of the Grand Historian* produced under the Han dynasty (206 BCE–CE 220). During the Tang dynasty (618–907 CE), which, until disrupted by the serious An Lushan Rebellion (756–763), was a period of cosmopolitan openness,[33] much thought was given to historical writing, and the evolving formal system of producing history reached its mature form. Although not fully practiced during the Tang itself, mostly due to military upheavals,[34] the Tang system of historical compilation was adopted by all subsequent dynasties, and was actually followed to the greater extent.

The codification of legend was important as a basis for legitimacy. Thus, in 941, an official record was compiled of the legends surrounding Ch'i-shou khaghdan, the founder of the Khitan dynasty, which conquered Manchuria and, in 947, established the Liao dynasty in Beijing, a dynasty that lasted until 1126. By the reign of Sheng-tsung (982–1031), there was already a History Office and a director of the national history. In 991, they presented the first Liao records. During the reign, moreover, a daily calendar was compiled as a draft from which an established later record would be written. There was also an attempt to link Chinese and Khitan accounts. Thus, in the 1040s, the historian Hsiao Han-chia-nu compiled national history, translated Chinese historical works into Khitan, and compiled records for earlier reigns with Khitan scholars.[35]

Dynastic histories were greatly concerned with the lessons that history could teach to present generations or could be presented as teaching. These histories served a specific purpose for dynasties that were Chinese as opposed to those that derived from the steppe. The former histories described the territories controlled by China, an emphasis that presented a way to assert ethnocentric cohesion against non-Chinese neighbors and, at times, rulers. Thus, under the Song dynasty (960–1279), which generally coexisted with the Liao Empire to the north, there was a concern with territorial integrity that can be related to pressure from the north. Thinking in historical terms presented a means to legitimate and strengthen the state, including from the challenge posed by the Liao.

Dynastic references in China also provided a way to set the tone for particular reigns, and to give them resonance. Thus, the Kao-tsung emperor (r. 1127–1162) of the Song dynasty initially admired Han Kuang-wu-ti (r. 25–57) of the later Han dynasty, who had restored the Han after it had been overthrown, thus providing a model for a hoped-for-response by the emperor to the Jin who had taken control of northern China from the Liao in 1126. The Kao-tsung emperor contrasted Han Kuang-wu-ti's reign to that of T'ang T'ai-tsung (r. 626–649), the second ruler of the Tang Empire, who had played a major role in unifying China, on the grounds that the latter had sought fame too much. From 1141, however, Kao-tsung started to admire Wen-ti (r. 180–157 BCE) of the Western Han dynasty on the basis that he had sought to attain success through peace and had emphasized the primacy of civil government. This approach reflected Kao-tsung's attempt to maintain the peace with the Jin, but also was a more general response to his reading of Chinese history, notably his praise for the Song Emperor Jen-tsung (r. 1022–1063), who had made peace with the Liao, which Kao-tsung cited as a precedent. The choice by new popes of papal names in order to establish links and affirm goals as part of a particular legacy is a continuing aspect of the same process.

There were also changes in the process by which history was presented in China. Dynastic histories can be referred to as if they were a static form, which is an aspect of the misleading primitivatization of non-Western history by some Western commentators. Instead, there was, in practice, a considerable process of change and development. Thus, under the Song, dynastic histories stopped being called *shu* (documents) and took on the new description of *shih* (histories). Linked to this, contending versions of major dynastic records were compiled.[36] In the late tenth century, T'ai-tsung (r. 976–997) established the History Office and initiated the *Four Great Compendia of the Song Dynasty*, the last of which, the *Ts'e-fu yüan-kuei* (1005–1013), provided an authoritative history of the earlier Tang dynasty and of the Five Dynasties (881–979).[37] Whereas the early Song emperors had instituted a system under which an official from the History Office compiled a record for each reign based on the Court diary, this process was changed in the reign of Hui-tsung (1100–1126). The History Office was left unstaffed, and the editorial secretaries of the Palace Library were entrusted with collecting the record. The History Office was finally abolished in 1140, and, after a period of gaps and uncertainties, the Palace Library formally took over its role.

This institutional uncertainty was linked to an acute level of politicization in the presentation of Chinese history, with, for example, the dynastic history for the reign of Shen-tsung (1067–1085), revised repeatedly, notably in 1135 and 1138, because of the political implications of his policies. Moreover, Ch'un Kuei, the chief minister from 1138, suppressed much of the archival material about his tenure as a councillor in 1131–1132. The sensitivity of historical accounts led, in the mid-twelfth century, to strict censorship of all unofficial writing of histories and political memoirs.[38] The current Chinese practice of controlling the account of the past is a longstanding one, although without any direct linkage between imperial and Communist days.

At the same time, history served as a way to strengthen the dynastic position because the very process of sponsoring history demonstrated appropriate conduct. Political legitimacy required a respect for history. Thus, Khubilai Khan (the grandson of the great Mongol conqueror, Chinggis Khan), who, as Great Khan of the Mongols from 1260 to 1294, completed the Mongol conquest of China, overthrowing the Song, responded favorably to suggestions that a dynastic history in the traditional Chinese style be produced. This response pleased the Confucian intellectuals as showing respect for the Chinese heritage. Confucianism stressed the role of the past and the value of historical models as guides for conduct: the works of Confucius are primarily about past examples of wise and virtuous men. Khubilai approved the founding of a History Office able to assemble records and compose histories, a policy that had been called for by a prominent Confucian scholar. Crucially, the latter wanted to have the historical records of non-Chinese rulers collected and their dynasties commemorated, an approach that made sense of the Mongols and helped incorporate them in Chinese history.[39]

For the historians of the Mongol Yüan dynasty, which ruled China from 1264 to 1368, there was the question not only of responding to the conventional Chinese approach of cultural supremacy, but also of deciding how best to present previous non-Chinese dynasties. The official histories reluctantly accepted the Liao as a legitimate dynasty, but were unwilling to do the same for the Hsia, who had founded the Xixia Empire in the 1030s.[40] Alongside the imperial dynastic tradition, there was, in China, a more general family history tradition, which similarly testified to the significance of forbears, continuity, and legitimacy.

Dynastic histories went on being important in Chinese historiography, not least providing a way to understand what appeared to be recurrent patterns of rise and decline, or dynastic cycles.[41] Moreover, the Chinese emphasis on government-sponsored official histories was influential across East Asia, notably in Korea and Japan. Official history reflected the linkage of ruling dynasties to powerful deities, a linkage that ensured that history was a sacred text that it was not valid to revise. At the same time, a practice of critical inquiry in the private historiography developed. Patterns of rise and decline, generally presented in terms of dynastic cycles, remained of importance and concern, until the late nineteenth century led to a different focus related to reform within China and to relations with the West. This focus affected the understanding of the past and the presentation of history, which, in the late nineteenth century, was increasingly on the Western model.[42]

Across the world, dynasticism served as a measure of legitimacy and continuity, and not only for rulers. Part of the purpose of history focused on the need to exult dynastic lineage, which was an aspect of self-identification or ethnogenesis. Thus, in Central Asia, there was, from the thirteenth century, a need to establish descent from Chinggis Khan (d. 1227)[43] and, in doing so, to assert precedence over those who could not. Mongol lineages, or at least connections, were linked to political concepts, symbols, and practices in establishing legitimacy, for example with the Kara Qoyunlu and the Aq Qoyunlu, Türkmen tribes that ruled Persia from 1375 to 1508, and with the Jalayirs who ruled much of Iraq from 1336 to 1432. Babur, the Mughal conqueror of Delhi in 1526, was very keen to assert a Mongol lineage.

ISLAM

Islamic societies demonstrated an impressive range in historical activity and treatment. The early traditionalists, namely the biographers of the Prophet, and the chroniclers like Tabari and Baladhuri, provided sacred history, but, rather than being providentialist, it was more like a history of religious legal enactment and proof. Subsequently, there was a shift to more dynastic historians, such as those by Juwaini and Ibn Khaldun. There was an additional tradition of genealogical hero-tales, much of them in Arabic poetry. Young members of the elite, such as Saladin in the twelfth century, had to memorize them.

As far as Islamic rulers were concerned, claims to precedence were linked to caliphal status as successor or deputy to Muhammad, and to guardianship over sacred sites. Both roles entailed history as a means of assertion, as it demonstrated the continuity that established both dynastic legitimacy and providential support. Thus, the process by which the power of the Ottoman Sultan was displayed and recharged depended on the resonance of established patterns of legitimacy and behavior.[44] By conquering Constantinople, the center of Orthodox Christianity, in 1453, and by taking over, from the defeated Mameluke rulers of Egypt, the guardianship of the Holy Cities of Mecca and Medina in 1517, the Ottomans drew on powerful historical resonances of authority.

Dynastic histories also provided a means to pursue competing claims to prestige and renown, as with the anonymous *Holy Wars of Sultan Murad, son of Mehmed Khan*, an account of the Ottoman Sultan Murad II (r. 1421–1451). The deeds of rulers were a key theme. Thus, the Mughal rulers, who dominated northern India from the mid-1520s, both supported the compilation of historical works in order to assert their position, and, in some cases, wrote their own memoirs.[45]

Alongside themes of dynastic continuity and legitimacy came the pursuit of religious goals across time. In particular, Sunni orthodoxy was challenged by Shi'ites, notably with the rapid Safavid conquest of what is now Iran and Iraq, in the 1500s. Sacred time was a key element, as Isma'il, the leader of the Safavids who proclaimed himself Shah in 1501, was seen by many as the reincarnation of Imam Ali, Muhammad's adopted son and son-in-law and the founder of Shi'ite Islam, or as the hidden Iman, a millenarian figure. Control over shrines, notably Karbala, Kayir, Najaf, and Samarra, was another aspect of this grasp of sacred time, while, conversely, Sunni shrines were desecrated by the Safavids. Shi'ite historical accounts remain highly significant in modern Iran and Iraq. In 2014, Ayatollah Sayed Ali Khameni, Iran's supreme religious leader, called on the Islamic Revolutionary Guard Corps to show "heroic flexibility" in accepting talks over Iran's nuclear program. This was an allusion to Hassan, the second Shia imam, who made peace with the Sunni Umayyad caliphate, in contrast to Hussein, his younger brother, the third imam, who died fighting overwhelming odds.[46]

Related to Islamic historiography came the idea of pre-modern customs of legal writing as schools of history. Islamic hadith-collections, like the Jewish Talmud and Christian canon-law collections, as well as common law commentaries, were all forms of historiography. They all add a chronological framework, often allowed for change over time, and were instances of studying vice and virtue in the past in order to teach proper conduct. These practices of legal exposition were important in amplifying the use of the past as a form of authority. There was a parallel with the use of the law and of legal judgments in the Christian world in order to confirm continuity and to advance political views, as with the use of Common Law against royal pretensions in England in the early seventeenth century.

THE EARLY-MODERN PERIOD

The Renaissance, printing, transoceanic exploration, the Protestant Reformation, and major changes in a number of states, all created a great sense of flux in (non-Ottoman) Europe from the fifteenth century, and even more in the sixteenth.[47] This sense affected the presentation of history as well. There is need for care in emphasizing change, however, not least at the expense of traditional religious interpretations of time, such as millenarianism, that were still capable of much dynamism.[48] This is an aspect of a longstanding historiographical problem: an excessive emphasis on a secular reading of modernization, notably with the focus on state formation.[49] Aspects of change, moreover, did not always have the same consequences. For example, printing served the interests of authority and repeated familiar accounts, as much as it challenged either.

An important impetus was provided by the revival of knowledge of, and interest in, Classical (Greek and Roman) literature, by Humanist scholars, a revival that played a major role in the Renaissance of the fifteenth century. There was strong interest in Classical historical texts, with an expanded use of philology as a tool to provide and understand accurate texts. The major role of Classical literature also helps explain why Egypt (until the eighteenth century) and, far more, Mesopotamia (part of Iraq) largely dropped from the cultural, intellectual, and political radar of a Western civilization that was to be focused on Greece and Rome. This revival provided not only information on the ancient world that helped foster further interest, but also models for considering and presenting more recent times and for understanding the current situation. Thus, Spanish historiography on the conquest of the New World owed much to the ideas offered by Classical works, which, notably with Roman expansion, provided a suitable pedigree as well as reference point.[50] The religious element in Western expansion did not only focus on spreading God's word. There was also an historical dimension. For example, the Portuguese initially vindicated their arrival in India from 1498 by drawing on the legacy of the Apostle Thomas. His relics were discovered, allegedly, while the presence of local Christians apparently meant that the Portuguese Crown was reaching out to free them from oppression and to gather in all Christians under the papacy. At Cochin in Kerala, there are sites that recall this history.

As an instance of continuity, the Humanistic narration of politics drew on important strands in Western medieval historical writing, notably providing the reader with news, a key reason for the focus on contemporary history; and also writing to entertain.[51] Rather than emphasizing any rejection of late medieval Christianity, it is important to note the debt of Humanist thought and writing to existing practices and ideas. For example, the cult of relics influenced the recovery of Classical objects and texts. The combination of these strands, interests, and frames of reference provided a distinctive character for Renaissance historical consciousness. The didactic value of history was an aspect both of the medieval presentation of history and of its Renaissance successor. The Renaissance, moreover, saw the continuation of the medieval practice of producing false chronicles, fictional accounts that served to substantiate positions and whose authors appear to have regarded themselves as writing what they believed should be in the historical record. For example, the fictional chronicles of Julián Pérez, which came to attention in the 1590s, apparently demonstrated the Christian steadfastness of the Mozarabs (Christians under Muslim rule) of Toledo, and also gave that city a higher profile in Spanish history.[52] The Lead Books discovered in the Granada excavations in 1595 were another forgery that served present purposes, in this case apparently demonstrating the viability of Christian-Muslim coexistence in Philip II's Spain. The need, in sixteenth-century Spain, to confront the emphasis on being "true Christians" may well have encouraged the forgeries that justified the particular positions of the Mozarabs and the Moriscos (Christian Moors).[53]

Alongside continuity, there was change, with established usages of the past called into question, in part because of new political and cultural questions and configurations, but, in part, because the significance of time, the separation between past and present, came to be more strongly asserted and more readily understood. A notion of modernity, and its separation from what was called the Middle Ages, became apparent in Europe,[54] not least with modernity seen as looking back, beyond the Middle Ages, to antiquity. However, aspects of the latter were rejected as well as accepted. Creating the past more clearly as a distinct subject made how it was understood and depicted as different more of an issue, and also focused attention on the issues of patterns and progress in time.

As with the earlier situation, history in the early modern period established rights, whether by monarchs to territory or by the ordinary people to resources and land in the local environment.[55] Legitimacy was seen to rest not on the consent of the people, but on the weight of rights, rights proven in a relationship between past and present. Although occasionally challenged by individuals claiming divine inspiration, these rights were proved by ancestry and descent. Recent events, therefore, had to be interpreted and presented accordingly. Thus, Polydore Vergil (1470–1555), an Italian in papal service who entered that of the English Crown, provided an account of fifteenth-century England in his *Anglica Historia* that supported the Tudor dynasty that had seized power, in the person of Henry VII, in 1485. Although different in structure and content from their Chinese counterparts – in large part because they were less formulaic and lacked the institutional context – such dynastic histories fulfilled similar functions. Moreover, history served as a key aspect of the representation of authority that was so important to the culture and practice of politics.[56] Vergil was to be criticized in 1545 by John Leland, who was made King's Antiquary by Henry VIII in 1533, for not devoting sufficient attention to Britain's glory,[57] but that argument reflected the exaltation of royal authority as England broke with papal authority, and, therefore, the requirement for a more exemplary history.

If there were no equivalent in Europe to the Chinese History Office, which had been incorporated into the Hanlin Academy, European rulers were naturally concerned to preserve and record their heritage, and, from the sixteenth century, there were more signs of such a determination. Thus, alongside monuments, came archives and the organization of records judged historical that they offered. The role of documents reflected a more general commitment to experience as a basis for credibility, an empiricism seen in science, philosophy, judicial practice, theological arguments, and travel accounts. Experience had scarcely been absent earlier, but authority and reliability had been established largely in terms of political and social status, notably the rank, prominence, and reputation of the witness, rather than what had been seen. This development was also significant to the process of questioning interpretations, and thus establishing them in a process of disputation.[58]

There was also a willingness to try novel approaches in writing history. Experiments with new forms and in mixed-genre writing ensured that, alongside the persistence of the chronicle tradition, as with Holinshed's *Chronicles* (1577; 2nd edn, 1587),[59] many kinds of history were written. These works both contributed to the literature of national identity and fragmented it.[60] A separate literature of historical identity was presented in the texts of plays. For England, the key examples were the history plays of William Shakespeare, notably *King John, Richard II, Henry IV, parts 1 and 2, Henry V, Henry VI, parts 1, 2, and 3, Richard III,* and *Henry VIII.* Drawing in part on Holinshed, these works covered English history over much of the previous four centuries, and offered far more specific accounts than those of more mythic times, such as *King Lear.*

THE REFORMATION

In the sixteenth century, in Western Christendom, the Protestant Reformation was both an attack on the past and a call to remove current excrescences. The Protestant challenge to the efficacy of prayers for the dead and to the existence of Purgatory meant creating a new spiritual cosmology that denied the traditional relationship between past, present, and future. So also with the Protestant attacks on shrines, relics, pilgrimages, and miracles. As the identity and contents of Christianity were contested, the relationships, under the early Church, between papacy and bishops and between clergy and laity, became an issue during the Reformation. New religious entities, such as the Church of England, struggled to settle and ratify their governmental systems, as for example with the all-important claim to apostolic succession of the bishops of the Church of England. The use of history was a key element in such discussions. Identification of doctrine and forms of worship with those of the Primitive Church meant carrying Christ's authority and message through history to the present.

This use of history in a contentious context and fashion reflected, and contributed to, the accentuation of ideological disputation during the sixteenth century and early seventeenth century. Political issues were discussed both in terms of the particular histories of given localities and with reference to wide-ranging tensions. The tensions were shaped as ideological issues in part by providing them an historical pedigree. Ideological suppositions, however, could clash with Humanist critical methods, for history was both a continuation of the Gospel and a process open to scrutiny and debate. Aside from doctrinal orthodoxy, is-sues included the holiness and longevity of particular national churches. These issues were of value to both Catholics and Protestants in linking national identities to an assertion of position within the international context. The primacy of Rome was thereby contested by Catholics as well as Protestants. Thus, in Spain, there was a determination to trace Christian belief to evangelization by St. James, a claim to a lengthy and exemplary national pedigree. The emphasis on history was vindicated because it was regarded as the way to see God's will revealed. As such, history was a continuation of the Gospel and, at once, an experience and an understanding.[61]

History was not only of significance in ecclesiastical history. More generally, traumatic crises, such as the Reformation, the French Wars of Religion, and the English Civil War, were in large part fought out by means of historical works, for history established the frame of reference for these and other crises. Moreover, the enmities of the present were given added value and weight by depicting a pedigree. Rulers, ministers, politicians, and commentators drew on historical examples, presenting them as lessons.[62] Historians and theologians ransacked the Bible to find examples, both of how to live under tyrannical kings and of how far it was appropriate to oppose them. Diplomatic manuals stressed the value of historical examples.[63] Both news and history became part of the world of politics, each being employed to articulate topical grievances and to advance remedies.[64] In a narrowly specific, as well as wider, cul-tural sense, books and the printed word were employed as instruments for expounding religious, political, and cultural policies.[65] This was true across religious and political spectrums. Thus, in Christendom, it was seen with saints' lives, but also with John Foxe's *Book of Martyrs* (1563).[66]

CONCLUSIONS

Spurred by both the Reformation and the Catholic or Counter-Ref-ormation, the encouragement, at times imposition, of state programs of history in Christendom was a central factor in historiography there in the sixteenth and seventeenth centuries. As a reminder, however, of the range of historiography, it is also possible to emphasize other types of activity, and the beliefs to which they were related. An important strand was provided by the antiquarians who searched for evidence of the past such as inscriptions, ancient coins, and other records. This strand can be seen in Europe,[67] but also elsewhere, notably in China. It is also necessary to give due weight to the continuing importance of history at the level of popular culture, particularly the vitality, across the world, of oral traditions. Indeed, folk-tales, local customs, and ancestral traditions have been of lasting significance.[68] At the same time, the relationship between history, folklore, and tradition was far from fixed,[69] notably that "between local memory and an emerging national historical culture . . . authorised by the printed page."[70] This situation in the early modern period looks toward that today.

THREE

The Long Eighteenth Century

AS A REMINDER OF THE NON-CONTINUOUS NATURE OF THE historical imagination and historical writings, the ideological theme, while still present, both changed in character and became less significant in Christian Europe from the mid-seventeenth century, and this remained the case until the French Revolution led to a reconceptualization of the role of history. In the intervening period, conventionally from the Peace of Westphalia in 1648 to 1789, there was still, however, a major commitment to both religion and the Church's role in framing history and identity,[1] as well as a strong interest in the past. Such an interest served a range of interests and drives, notably, as before and as also outside the West, dynastic prestige and the protection of local interests. Ruling houses sought status and legitimation from the past. Thus, in 1701 a medal was struck at the request of Electress Sophia of Hanover to mark her being named heiress to the Crown of England. The reverse depicted "Matilda [c. 1156–1189], daughter of Henry II, King of England, wife of Henry the Lion . . . mother of Emperor Otto IV . . . progenitor of the House of Brunswick." The medal grounded the claim on the succession in primogeniture and the history of the House of Guelph, and not on the Act of Settlement passed by the English Parliament in 1701. History thereby served to establish and strengthen an alternative claim.[2]

Such dynastic locating was scarcely new, and it is too easy to forget such conventional uses of history, and such established goals of new works, when focusing on the new developments in this period and others. Interest in history in the eighteenth-century West more generally reflected a continuing sense that the past had shaped the present, as well as a concern with organic development that is not always associated with the thinkers of the eighteenth-century European Enlightenment(s). History also provided the central source of evidence for political and religious polemic, as with English Royalist historians under Charles II (r. 1660–1685) who, in tracing the origins of seditious ideas, linked Presbyterians, sectarians, and Catholics as opponents of the monarchy.[3]

The location of historical work with reference to the Western Enlightenment of the eighteenth century engages most attention today. Although many eighteenth-century Western writers, in the fields of philosophy, politics, or psychology, advanced theoretical ideas from general principles – an approach that is not focused on historical particularities; there was also an engagement with the social context and with the relationship between theory and practice, both of which provided room for historical investigation and evidence. Thinkers, in practice, were as much concerned with discovery, whether through exploration, observation, or historical study, as with speculation. For example, the application of scholarship to issues of political organization involved theoretical discussion, but also, as in Britain and France, debate about the historical basis and credibility of contrasting views on how best to govern particular states. Though the nature and closeness of the relationship with such discovery varied by individual and subject, they were crucial to the development and application of Enlightenment ideas. In particular, a sense of the transforming possibilities of time invited attention not only to the past but also to the prospect of future change.

As an aspect of their radicalism, the French *philosophes* were happiest to reject history. They disparaged much of the past, the Middle Ages for being barbaric, the age of the Reformation for being fanatical, and the reign of Louis XIV (1643–1715), on which Voltaire wrote *Le Siècle de Louis XIV* (1751), for its supposed obsession with *gloire* alongside the brilliance of the civilization. At the same time, Voltaire's study was impressive for his employment of actual events, rather than presenting simply a parade of facts. This was history as argument, not as chronicle. The *philosophes* also found that history as written by the *érudits*, who focused on textual criticism, could not provide the logical principles and ethical suppositions that were required to support the immutable laws the *philosophes* propounded.[4] In Spain, the local equivalents of the *philosophes* presented a critical account of the country's present and past in order to justify their call for reform. Their arguments have overly influenced later historians, leading to a failure to appreciate other perspectives.[5]

Alongside criticism of the past during the Enlightenment, there was much interest in historical work and theory, not least because Enlightenment historians sought to diminish, if not replace, theological, particularly providential, accounts of time. Instead, they took an approach that worked well with their view of an openness to the non-Christian traditions, and with their desire to explain the here-and-now. History thus served as a means to study progress and civilization, to consider philosophy in, and through, action. History as a form of knowledge offered much to both. It provided knowledge that was not dependent on revelation and offered a way to incorporate the non-Western world into accounts of development. In his *Essai sur les moeurs et l'esprit des nations* (1745–1753), Voltaire wrote a world history within a universal context, rather than within a Christian or nationalist framework.[6] Indeed, as with other branches of eighteenth-century Western enquiry, the development of history as a coherent intellectual project, and, even more, as an academic pursuit, left little role for divine intervention. Thus, in France, historians replaced the customary view of Clovis (r. 481–511), the conquering Frank who converted to Christianity in 493, as a miracle-working royal saint, with that of a royal legislator. As such, historical work paralleled the rise of Newtonian science, which, similarly, did not seek to dethrone God, but, nevertheless, limited the divine role, certainly in terms of causing specific events. This intellectual thrust represented a new form of realism, one separate from direct manifestations of divine action. The ending of the Royal Touch in England with the accession of George I in 1714 was instructive, although in exile, the Stuarts continued the practice.

The eighteenth century also saw theological issues discussed by means of considering secular historical evidence. Linked to this, the renewed origins of modern Western academic culture and practice (in so far as they can be seen as a unity) can be seen in this period, notably with the stronger emphasis on the reality and importance of "facts," and an assertion of their primacy over attempts at expository manipulation. The Scientific Revolution of the late seventeenth century and its popularization in the eighteenth were both relevant to the development of history. Alongside a commitment to the idea of an impartial enquiry into the past, there was a stress on sources. In the preface to his *History of the Reign of Charles V* (1764), the much-praised Scottish cleric-historian William Robertson, Principal of Edinburgh University from 1762 to 1793, noted: "I have carefully pointed out the sources from which I have derived information."[7]

Abandoning a focus on religious accounts, the nature of the historical development of human society attracted much attention, for example in Italy from both Ludovico Muratori (1672–1750) and Giambattista Vico. Vico (1688–1744), Professor of Rhetoric at Naples, emphasized the historical evolution of human societies in his *Scienza Nuova* (*New Science*, 1725) and advanced a cyclical theory of history, which provided a sense of continuity with the past. Philosophical history, as discussed by the great Scots philosopher David Hume in his "On the Study of History" (1741), proposed a comprehensive explanation of long-term trends in social development – rather than an account simply of events focused, in particular, on recovering the Classical world through antiquarian scholarship.

There were also distinctive national circumstances and developments in the West. In Germany, historiographical traditions of Latin humanism and the history of the Holy Roman Empire were very much alive. At the same time, the German university world, pre-eminently the university at Göttingen in the Electorate of Hanover founded by George II in 1737, became the center of an important strand of intellectual activity that included an engagement with history.[8] New universities have generally, although not invariably, been more intellectually fertile than those facing the challenge of ingrained practices; although this fertility has sometimes rushed ahead of practicality and prudence.

The politics of history were also seen in non-Western states. Thus, in China, historians writing on the Five Dynasties (881–979 CE) and Song (960–1279 CE) periods had to be sensitive from the Manchu conquest in the mid-seventeenth century to the ruling dynasty's links with the Khitan rulers of those earlier periods.[9] The official history of the Ming dynasty (1368–1644), printed in 1739, provided a biased account of Ming relations with Manchuria and Mongolia. Moreover, under the Manchu (1644–1912), there was very little study of the Ming period, a situation that changed only with the relaxation of government control in the late nineteenth century.[10] History, not least the compilation of works of history, was important to the image cultivated by the emperors, as they wished to stress a legitimacy that in part rested on continuity with earlier dynasties.[11] There was also a recording of the successes of the ruling dynasty.

THE EXAMPLE OF EIGHTEENTH-CENTURY BRITAIN

The example of eighteenth-century Britain is particularly instructive for a number of reasons. First, there is the extent to which the relative freedom to write and publish made Britain an important instance of both the contemporary European situation, and one that prefigured the modern West. Moreover, the development of history in America was greatly influenced by the situation during the period when America had been part of the British world or, at least, the part of America from which the American state and public culture developed from 1776. Secondly, compared to countries such as Spain, there was a large entrepreneurial world of publishing in Britain, as well as in America. Thirdly, many of the leading British intellectuals of the age, including Henry, Viscount Bolingbroke, Edward Gibbon, David Hume, William Robertson, and Adam Smith, wrote history, or about history, or used history in their writings.[12] Lastly, from the 1960s, much of the theoretical historical literature that has been fashionable and consciously innovative in its conceptualization has deliberately set out to contest the value and relevance of Enlightenment ideas of modernity. It is therefore useful to turn to the eighteenth century to see the world and work of its historians.

Historical work in eighteenth-century Europe was largely grounded in the controversies of the present, notably religious and political struggles. The idea of a separate sphere for scholarship existed, but antiquarianism without relevance excited slight support. In Britain, as elsewhere, there was a habit, instead, of employing the past to warn about present and future, as when people deployed the examples of Mary I of England

(r. 1553–1558) and James II of England and VII of Scotland (r. 1685–1688) as reasons to support the exclusion of Catholic claimants from the throne. Such reasons took precedence over interest in the past itself. For example, the public memorialization and discussion of the traumatic civil wars of the mid-seventeenth century were not concerned with contesting its issues anew, but, rather, those of subsequent political and religious settlements.[13]

Monarchs were particularly interested in history, and not only because of dynastic concerns. George III (r. 1760–1820) had a strong sense of historical consciousness. When his brother Henry, Duke of Cumberland married a commoner in 1771, the outraged and overwrought George was concerned that such a step might threaten civil war, as he claimed that the fifteenth-century Wars of the Roses in England owed much to the intermarriage of crown and nobility.[14] History was a favorite reading of Louis XVI of France (r. 1774–1792), as well as George, and Louis showed a close interest in the fate of Charles I of England (r. 1625–1649): at the time of the French Revolution, the life of the martyr-king played a central role in Louis's sense of impending doom.[15]

Monarchs' interests were widely shared. History played a role in printed and private discussion. The surviving libraries of stately homes contain many handsomely bound historical works from the period. The anonymous pamphlet *Letter from a Gentleman in Worcestershire to a Member of Parliament* (1727) used the ravages of the Vikings to warn about the need to keep Norway and Denmark out of Russian hands, and Edward, Lord Thurlow, the Lord Chancellor, claimed in 1789 that "every page of the Dutch History points" out the problems of supporting a remedy for the political instability in the Austrian Netherlands (Belgium) by organizing its government on the Dutch basis.[16]

Indeed, history offered a vista of possible developments and, if that was a frightening perspective, this was claimed to be part of its educational value. This value, frequently in practice partisan, was often presented directly in the titles of works, as in the 1713 pamphlet of the overweening ambition of great men, *The Life of Edward Seymour, Duke of Somerset ... With Some Parallel Instances to the Case of John Duke of M-h [Marlborough], Late Great Favourite [and] the Sudden Fall of ... John Dudley, Duke of Northumberland*, a linkage of the reigns of Edward VI

(1547–1553) and Queen Anne (1702–1714), with the former called in to provide warnings about the latter.

The historiography of the period is generally discussed, in a top-down fashion, in terms of Bolingbroke, Gibbon, Robertson, and Hume, but it is necessary to note the extent to which this work, which linked erudition and exposition to establish scholarly norms,[17] was grounded in a widespread public interest. This is of relevance for considering the discussion of history today. For the public, historical works were as much approached in terms of relevance and partisanship as of a detached scholarship. Thus, historical works frequently appeared in newspapers, indeed more so than today, and their partisan intention was clear. Newspapers stressed the value of history largely so that they might debate current issues, a pattern also seen with newspapers on the Continent. The *True Briton*, a London newspaper, of 9 September 1723, argued: "No study is so useful to mankind as history, where, as in a glass, men may see the virtues and vices of great persons in former ages, and be taught to pursue the one, and avoid the other." History was deployed not only to make short-term points about inconsistency and hypocrisy, but also to develop and employ the concept of national interests. In turn, opponents were criticized for betraying these interests, and this alleged betrayal was employed to demonstrate their unworthiness.

This argument rose to a facetious height when *Old England,* then the leading opposition essay paper, in its issue of 8 February 1752, turned the arguments of the prominent Whig philosopher, theorist, and office-holder John Locke (1632–1704), specifically his *Essay Concerning Human Understanding* (1689), against the Whig government with reference to peacetime subsidy treaties to foreign powers, a policy that the newspaper opposed:

> As the disapprobation of foreign subsidies has, we have seen, founded itself in the sense or understanding of Britain, it will demand our closest attention effectually, to counterveil these operations of nature, or, as Mr Locke would (for this purpose more conveniently) say, these prejudices of education. The structure we are here to raise for the public good will therefore find its basis in that great man's system of no innate ideas ... the present purpose, which is to make us approve foreign politics, demands no more than that all the books which have been wrote, regarding the particular interests of this kingdom, should be burnt. Polity, History, and Geography, are all the offensive studies ... You observe

all maxims of policy, all knowledge of men, of the trading interests, and of the
advantage of our situation, are utterly lost and dead: For by the wholesome
prohibition of speaking, writing, or printing . . . all dangerous communication
between father and son, will be effectually prevented.

This account reflected the opposition sense of foreign policy as un-
real because it was based on a denial of the national interest. Such a
denial was allegedly possible because corrupt self-interest was linked
to an active attempt to mislead the public. The rejection of history was
presented as central to this malign project. History was seen in this
account both as a public project and as the relationship of continuity
within society; and the two as the protection against the authoritarianism of government and intellectual remodeling. Thus, this Tory paper
prefigured the arguments of the writer Edmund Burke at the time of the
French Revolution.

For opposition newspapers, history provided a safe perspective from
which to attack ministers, as well as to offer the suggestion that the
cause of opposition was both timeless and necessary, and that evil governments would eventually collapse. Similar practices had long been
employed in China: using a figure from history and criticizing him as
an indirect way of attacking some government figure in the present.
On 11 May 1728, in an attack on Sir Robert Walpole, the leading Whig
minister from 1720 to 1742, the *Craftsman,* then the most significant
opposition newspaper, and one in which Bolingbroke played a prominent role, claimed: "History gives us frequent examples where the best
princes have by such ministers lost the affections of the best people; who
are naturally disposed to overlook the personal failings or accidental
miscarriages of their sovereign, and are never so much irritated as when
he endeavors to support a tyrannical over-grown favorite against their
general demand for justice."

Pro-government papers were well able to reply. The *London Journal* of 10 October 1730 complained that, in Bolingbroke's essays in the
Craftsman, "The History of England is racked and tortured," in other
words, misrepresented. Moreover, in 1734, the *Daily Courant* carried a
life of Cola di Rienzi as a warning against popular disorder and pseudo-
patriotism, both of which the ministry linked with the opposition. In
1347, Rienzi (1313–1354) successfully persuaded the citizens of Rome to

rebel against aristocratic rule, but, after being driven out, he tried again in 1354, only to be killed as a result of a hostile rising. Wagner was to write an opera about Rienzi (1842), an individual now largely forgotten in the English-speaking world, whose reputation there rests essentially on this opera that, as it were, "creates" him for the modern audience.

The treatment of history in the press overlapped with the discussion in longer works. The latter frequently appeared, in parts or summary, in the newspapers while the partisan intention or applicability of these works encouraged criticism. Thus, sections of Gilbert Burnet's *History of My Own Time* (2 vols., 1723–1734), a prominent Whig work written by a bishop, were published in *Read's Weekly Journal*, a pro-government London newspaper, but the *History* was attacked in 1723–1724 by *Mist's Weekly Journal*, the leading Tory paper, and also criticized in *Historical and Critical Remarks on Bishop Burnet's History of His Own Time* (1725) by the Jacobite Bevil Higgons (1670–1736). This criticism was countered in the Whig *London Journal* on 30 January and 6 February 1725, which led Higgons to a second edition in 1727 that rebutted the paper's defense of Burnet. Higgons also published *A Short View of the English History; with reflections on the reigns of the kings, their characters and manners, their succession to the throne; and all other remarkable incidents, to the Revolution, 1688* (1723), which refuted Burnet's claims of the Pretender's illegitimacy. As a reminder of the range of media across which history was asserted, Higgons was the author of *The Generous Conqueror* (1702), a play defending the Jacobite claim to the throne.

History was a term deployed to suggest truth and in no way was restricted to factual accounts. Thus, Henry Fielding (1707–1754) insisted that his novels were "true histories" in that they revealed the truth of behavior, an approach particularly suited to the ironic voice he adopted as narrator. In the last chapter of his novel *Joseph Andrews* (1742), "This true history is brought to a happy conclusion." History frequently appeared in the titles of novels, as in James Ridley's *The History of James Lovegrove* (1761). Fielding, moreover, used the term history in his journalism, as in "The Present History of Europe," to suggest that he was offering particularly authentic information.[18]

While novels sought to be true histories, conversely, historical writing was supposed to capture character. Perhaps because biography had not fully emerged as a genre, "lives" were a division of history in a pattern that went back to the Classical world, as with Plutarch's *Lives*. For example, the anonymous *Reflections on Ancient and Modern History* (1746) praised Classical writers because of "that nice discernment of the several lines and features of human nature, which are so strongly expressed in all the characters, throughout their histories."[19] In a somewhat modern style, the established Classical account of history was challenged by Sarah Fielding (1710–1768), the sister of Henry Fielding, in *The Lives of Cleopatra and Octavia* (1757), with her female protagonists returning to tell their tales and to claim the spotlight from a traditionally male-dominated narrative.

History did not only offer character out of interest. There was also the presentation of history as a morally exemplary tale, a presentation that brought history, novels, and the theatre together. Indeed, this presentation, a key element in narratives, has been the main theme in historical writing and, even more, the historical consciousness – albeit one challenged by academic methods and the academic culture. A stress in the eighteenth century on individual free will, or on a providential intervention linked to behavior, led to a world that was best understood in moral terms.

Far from being differentiated, the relationship of history, or politics, with morality was strongly focused in monarchical political systems both because of the obvious importance of a small number of individuals and due to the notion of kingship and governance as moral activities. In time, these assumptions were to be democratized and, in the age of nation states, given an ethno-genesis, but the emphasis on morality remained. The anonymous writer of the *Reflections on Ancient and Modern History* complained in 1746 that "with modern writers everything is either vice or virtue."[20] As the relationship appeared timeless, it seemed pertinent to apply admonitory tales in a modern context, as with the comparisons of Sir Robert Walpole indiscriminately with Charles I's favorite, the Duke of Buckingham, Henry VIII's Cardinal Wolsey, and the Roman emperor Tiberius's Sejanus, and the equivalent use of historical examples on stage. In its issue of 9 October 1762, the *Monitor* published an essay on bad favorites, comparing John, 3rd Earl of Bute, the key advisor of George III, with Roger Mortimer (c. 1287–1330), the lover of Queen Isabella, wife of Edward II, which was a pointed comparison, as Bute was rumored to be the lover of George's mother, Augusta. Mortimer and Isabella were responsible for Edward's overthrow in 1326 and murder in 1327, and were, in turn, to be overthrown in 1330 by Edward II's son, Edward III. Belief that history possessed a cyclical quality contributed to this process, as time was not held to compromise the moral power of Classical and later exemplars.

When history was deployed, Classical references were frequent. For example, in 1722, William, 2nd Earl Cowper, a prominent opposition Whig, formerly a minister, complained about the building of ships in Britain for France, offering a host of reasons, including the danger that the French government, then allied to Britain, would change policy, adding, "Would the Romans have done this for the Carthaginians or vice versa?" and that "it would not be permitted to build forts on a frontier, and sell them to a neighbor – ships are our forts."[21] His reference to the Classical world was typical not only of parliamentary discussion, but also of the printed debates about policy. The Classical narrative threw issues into high and dramatic relief as it tended to encourage a polarization into exemplary and reprobate, thus offering a secular parallel to religious accounts, as well as a parallel that was more readily applicable because it was secular. It was assumed that readers were not only knowledgeable about the Classical world but also interested in it.[22] More particularly, for this throws light on attitudes toward time and history, arguments from the Classical world were believed still to be of direct relevance, so that Cowper could refer to the three Punic Wars between Rome and Carthage, which had occurred in 264–241 BCE, 218–201 BCE, and 149–146 BCE. That Rome only rose on the defeat and destruction of Carthage was a lesson for the relationship between Britain and France. Similarly, commentators on America's condition in the 2000s looked, for parallels, to Classical Rome, as well as to nineteenth-century Britain.

This sense of relevance helped explain the impact of Edward Gibbon's *Decline and Fall of the Roman Empire* (1776–1788). A politician as well as an historian, Gibbon was an MP from 1774 to 1780 and 1781 to 1784, and a member of the Board of Trade from 1779 to 1782. In 1779, at the request of Thomas, 3rd Viscount Weymouth, Secretary of State, he wrote the *Mémoire Justificatif* against the hostile conduct of France and Spain in the War of American Independence. Readers of Gibbon's *Decline and Fall* considered it a possible paradigm for the fate of the British Empire, and thus a timely lesson. Classical references were cited throughout the period, with the renewed struggle with France from 1793 providing new opportunities, leading the writer Richard Bentley to complain in 1798, "We hear of Rome and Carthage every day and in every debate, even to puerility."[23]

The general stress on personal drives, rather than on social, economic, institutional, or geo-political forces, ensured that in history, as in literature, the emphasis was on personality and narrative, the two combining to demonstrate the central role of individuals. A modern parallel is the emphasis on Winston Churchill in popular British accounts of World War II. Moreover, the porosity of history contributed to the same emphasis on individuals, in the case of the power of literary accounts and images in the collective historical understanding. This situation was captured by Elizabeth Montagu in 1762, when she observed to a friend: "Few people know anything of the English history but what they learn from Shakespeare; for our story is rather a tissue of personal adventures and catastrophes than a series of political events."[24] The impact of literary stories on popular views prefigured the modern stress on the impact of visual counterparts.

Both history and novels placed an emphasis on individual free will, not determinism. This emphasis offered a contrast with the Classical world and its faith in oracles, but the response to oracles and portents had itself involved free will. In both cases, a world profoundly affected by the drives and actions of the great was depicted, one that was best understood in moral terms and where there was no sense of fundamentally changing moral standards. The novel offered for many the moral guidance of history, the complexity of which was outlined in the prominent London newspaper the *Test* on 12 February 1757:

> The mechanism of government is too intricate and subtle, in all its various motions, for a common eye to perceive the nice dependencies and the secret springs, that give play to the complex machinery; and, in consequence the generality of people while the great political movements are passing before them, are full of undiscerning astonishment, and only gaze on in expectation of the event. Afterwards indeed when the historian gives his narrative of facts, when

he rejudges the actions of the great, and, from the ends which they had in view, and the means by which they pursued those ends, ascertains the colour of their characters, then the minds of men are opened, and they perceive honour and conquest, or disappointment and disgrace naturally following one another, like necessary effects from their apparent respective causes.

The focus on individuals was seen in the work of historians, whether hack or more prominent, and both Gibbon and Robertson were able to meet this need. So also were the less prominent, such as John Bancks or Banks (1709–1751), who wrote lives of Christ, Oliver Cromwell, Peter the Great of Russia, John, 1st Duke of Marlborough, Marlborough's colleague in arms, the Austrian general Prince Eugene, and William III, as well as a history of the Habsburgs. Bancks also wrote poetry and played a major role in two leading London newspapers, *Old England* and the *Westminster Journal*. His histories were designed to be useful, as well as exemplary and exhortatory. On 8 February 1746, the *Westminster Journal* advertised Bancks's *Compendious History of the House of Austria* [the Habsburgs]*, and the German Empire,* which, it claimed, gave "a more exact and clear idea of the motives and nature of the present war [the War of the Austrian Succession], and what may probably ensue, than is to be met with in any other work."

Similarly, Walter Harte (1709–1774), an Oxford academic who became a country-cleric, wrote a *History of the Life of Gustavus Adolphus,* published in 1759, that was translated into German in 1760. Killed in 1632 at the battle of Lützen, this King of Sweden captured both the sense of an embattled Protestantism and of a heroic, self-sacrificing response. He appeared to prefigure the warrior Protestantism of Frederick II (the Great) of Prussia. These themes fused British ideological concerns and xenophobic responses at the time of the Seven Years' War. The range covered by popular writers can also be seen with John Campbell (1708–1775), who wrote a history of Spanish America, lives of British admirals, part of the *Universal History* (1736–1765), and political pamphlets, as well as editing travel literature.[25]

If much British historical writing lacked intellectual subtlety and philosophical profundity, the vigor of the writing and the clarity of the prejudices expressed meant that these works may have been well-attuned to popular attitudes, and possibly more so than some of the more self-consciously enlightened writers of the period. At the same time, to suggest a crude contrast between "enlightened," "rational" history for an elite readership, and xenophobic, hack-written history for a mass readership, would be misleading. The works of Gibbon, Hume, and Robertson were all extremely popular, and Gibbon, for one, was very concerned about his sales. The principal difference lay in the tendency of "enlightened" history toward skeptical and critical judgment in the use of sources. Emphasis on such judgment was widespread. In 1728, in the preface to his *Complete History of Algiers,* John Morgan complained: "What a monstrous load of gross lies and insufferable absurdities ... does not one fall in with immediately upon laying hands on any tract, treatise, history, memoir, dictionary geographical, historical, or critical, relating to Africa and its affairs! Yet how many wise-acres tell one, scornfully, we have histories enough of that country? Why, truly, so we have. But the question is, have we one that is not rather romance than history?"[26]

A prominent writer of hack history, Richard Rolt (1724–1770) adopted a polemical style and a didactic method, as in *The Lives of the Principal Reformers, Both Englishmen and Foreigners, Comprehending the General History of the Reformation: From its Beginning in 1360, by Dr John Wickliffe, to its Establishment in 1600 under Queen Elizabeth. With an Introduction; Wherein the Reformation is Amply Vindicated and its Necessity Fully Shown From the Degeneracy of the Clergy, and the Tyranny of the Popes* (1759). In this, as in other books, Rolt, an opposition Whig journalist in the early 1750s, presented religious freedom and liberty as inseparable. Oppressed by a corrupt present and by threats of future hazard, Rolt, like other writers, looked back to a glorious past, especially to the reign of Queen Elizabeth I (r. 1558–1603). In 1756, when he jointly edited *The Universal Visiter and Memoralist,* he published a poem in it beginning "Illustrious [Sir Walter] Raleigh! Britain's noblest friend." Raleigh had played a major role in maritime opposition to Spain. Elizabeth was greatly praised in Rolt's work for her defense of Protestantism, her vigorous foreign policy, and the challenge to Spain's position in the Americas. Elizabeth was, unlike the Hanoverian dynasty, English, a key molder of the Church of England, and had apparently ensured that foreign policy served national goals. Elizabeth was also sufficiently historical to prove both uncontroversial and malleable, without being so ancient as to offer only tenuous parallels to the present, as was the case with pre-Reformation monarchs such as Edward III (r. 1327–1777), a hammer of the French. At a time of national humiliation in the early stages of the Seven Years' War, the *Monitor,* a leading London newspaper, in its issue of 26 November 1757, asked, "Who can forget the days when Elizabeth out of her cabinet gave laws to all Europe: set the captives free and of a distressed state made them high and mighty?" Critical of the commitment of British troops to Germany, the issue of 11 March 1758 had to confront the fact that Elizabeth had sent an English army to the Low Countries in 1585, but this commitment was presented as a form of forward-defense for England. Indeed, in its issue of 16 October 1762, the *Monitor* was to criticize George III's abandonment of his alliance with Frederick II of Prussia by making reference to Edward III and Henry V (r. 1413–1422), who had allied with the Dukes of Burgundy against France during the Hundred Years' War.

A belief that the national position, its constitution, liberty, international security and religion, were all under threat, accounted for Rolt's views on the didactic purposes of history. He argued that history revealed the threats challenging the nation, and the fate that would befall the island if vigilance was lost. Thus, Rolt ended his life of Archbishop Cranmer, burnt as a Protestant under Queen Mary in 1556, by stating that her reign "ought to be transmitted down to posterity, in characters of blood, as her persecution was the most terrible that raged since the time of Diocletian [r. 284–305],"[27] a Classical reference that called forward the persecution of early Christians under the Roman Empire. Rolt was quite clear that history should be didactic: "It was not the true intent of history so much to load the memory of the reader with a copious collection of public records, as it is to elevate his thoughts and enrich his understanding."[28] Rolt's works included history for children, notably *A New History of France; by Question and Answer* (1755) and a *New History of England* (1757).

Rolt was far from alone in thinking that religious history was a key element of the understanding of past and present, and thus a vital guide to how the future had to be fought out in the present. Samuel Chandler (1693–1766), a prominent nonconformist London cleric, wrote a preface to a 1732 translation of Limborch's *History of the Inquisition:*

There being, as I apprehend, no way so proper to expose the doctrine and
practice of persecution, as by a fair representation of the unspeakable mischiefs
that have been occasioned by it; nor any other method so likely to render it the
universal abhorrence of mankind, as to let them see, by past examples, what mis-
eries they must expect, if God should ever, for our sins, subject us again to the
yoke of ecclesiastical power; which, wherever it is not kept under strict restraint,
will usurp upon the authority and dignity of princes, and trample under foot all
the civil and religious liberties of mankind.[29]

Chandler's preface led to controversy. An Anglican cleric, William
Berriman, published a criticism in 1733, which led to three replies by
Chandler in 1733–1734, replies collected as a *History of Persecution* (1736).
For Chandler, who was very friendly with the Archbishop of Canter-
bury and other bishops and saw the Church and Dissent as allies rather
than competitors, the battle against Catholicism was central to national
identity, culture, and interest, and linked human and sacred history, as
the Catholic Church, in his view, imposed its own authority over that
of scriptures. Ten editions of his *Great Britain's Memorial against the
Pretender and Popery* (1745) appeared during the Jacobite rising of 1745–
1746, a fundamental crisis for the Hanoverian regime. Chandler also
published a life of King David (1766).

A clear sense of history made present by the Catholic threat, of historical writings firmly located in contemporary ideological suppositions
by their anti-Catholicism, did not cease with the collapse of Jacobit-
ism. In 1769, Edward Lewis, an Oxfordshire rector (1701–1784) who had
written against the Jacobites in 1744–1745, published *The Patriot King:
Displayed in the Life of Henry VIII, King of England, from the Time of his
Quarrel with the Pope till his Death*, a violently anti-Catholic work.

The theme of continuing danger was not adopted uncritically. Thus,
Richard Brinsley Sheridan's brilliant play *The Critic* (1779) ridiculed the
patriotic depiction of the danger of Bourbon (French and Spanish)
invasion in the shape of Puff's absurd play-within-a-play, *The Spanish
Armada*. However, the theatre saw many heroic plays on historical subjects, such as Richard Cumberland's *The Battle of Hastings* (1778), George
Colman the Younger's *The Battle of Hexham* (1789) and *The Surrender
of Calais* (1791), and Edward Jerningham's *The Siege of Berwick* (1793).
The Surrender of Calais, depicting Edward III's capture of the French
fortress in 1346, closed with:

> Rear, rear our English banner high
> In token proud of victory!
> Where'er our god battle strides,
> Land sound the trump of fame!
> Where'er the English warrior rides,
> May laurelled conquest grace his name.

The Hundred Years' War was also celebrated in paintings such as *Edward III Crossing the Somme* (1788) and *The Burghers of Calais* (1789) by Benjamin West, which showed that successful monarchs could be portrayed in a dramatic (and colorful) fashion that reflected glory on their current successor.[30] West also produced Classical history paintings, such as *Agrippina Landing at Brundisium with the Ashes of Germanicus* (1768), as well as religious paintings, such as *Christ Healing the Sick* (1811).

BURKE AND THE FRENCH REVOLUTION

Rolt's themes were to be revived in response to the French Revolution, which began in 1789, and during Britain's wars with Revolutionary, and then Napoleonic, France which continued from 1793 to 1815 with only two brief intervals. The use of history in this period is most readily discussed not with reference to the French but with regard to their opponents. History was a past to be discarded for the French Revolutionaries, who got rid of monarchy in 1792 and followed by destroying the *ancien régime*. They started the calendar anew, with Christianity deliberately repudiated. The new year was to begin on 21 September, the date of the autumnal equinox and of the Declaration of the French Republic in 1792. Society was to be regenerated as well as systematized, in part by using time to replicate natural order as well as the traditions of Classical republicanism. In newly ordering time, a new collective memory was to be created, and thus a new history.[31]

The break with the past was a central part of a wider political stance. Thus, feudal rights and monarchy were abolished, as opposed simply to replacing the monarch, while secularization entailed a rupture with the role of the Church in education. For these reasons, history was not a prime concern of the Revolutionaries, other than in the shape of memorializing their own achievements. For these purposes, there was a stress on instant history in the shape of commemorative ceremonies. The dramatic "texts" produced were paintings, notably the works of Jacques-Louis David, especially *The Death of Marat* (1793), rather than scholarly books. More generally, the emphasis was not on the past, but on a spirit of progress and on uniform modern systems. This emphasis was shown in the *Institut National des Sciences et des Arts* established in 1795. Moreover, history literally became a museum, notably with the *Musée des Monuments Française* founded in 1795. The treasures of the despoiled cathedrals and monasteries were placed there.

The impact of the Revolution in contemporary historical work was strongest in the case of the hostile reaction to it. In Britain, Edmund Burke (1729–1797) argued, in his celebrated and provocative *Reflections on the Revolution in France* (1790), that developments in France were harmful because they were unrelated to any sense of continuity, any historical consciousness. In contrast, at the Restoration of the Stuart dynasty in 1660 and with the Glorious Revolution overthrowing the authoritarian James II in 1688–1689, the English, according to Burke: "regenerated the deficient part of the old constitution through the parts which were not impaired. They kept these old parts exactly as they were, that the part recovered might be suited to them. They acted ... not by the organic *moleculae* of a disbanded people," the latter a reference to contemporary France and to the idea of starting history anew. Burke's view of relatively recent history was related to a more general interpretation of English history. Citing William Blackstone's 1759 edition of Magna Carta, the English constitutional foundation document of 1215, and quoting from the texts of the Petition of Right (1628) and the Declaration of Rights (1689), Burke claimed: "It has been the uniform policy of our Constitution to claim and assert our liberties, as an entailed inheritance delivered to us from our forefathers, and to be transmitted to our posterity. . . . This policy appears to me to be the happy effect of following nature, which is wisdom without reflection ... People will not look forward to posterity who never look backward to their ancestors."[32]

Burke continued, in his *Appeal from the New to the Old Whigs* (1791), to argue that it was his views that were consistent with the Glorious Revolution of 1688–1689, rather than those of Whig radicals such as Richard Price and Joseph Priestley. Burke claimed that the French Revolution was compatible not with the Glorious Revolution, as the Whig radicals argued, but with the regicide of 1649, the execution of Charles I. Thus, history was not only asserted as a principle by Burke, but also contested as a practice. Burke quoted from the prosecution case against the Tory cleric Henry Sacheverell in order to clarify what Whig principles had been in the reign of Queen Anne (1702–1714), and how 1688–1689 had been interpreted then. Burke felt that the events of 1688–1689 could only be appreciated in light of the assumptions they had given rise to, and he did this to deny contemporary radical attempts to interpret the legacy. He cited as his "authorities" for the Revolution Settlement "the acts and declarations of Parliament given in their proper words," and also cited sources for his account of the Peasants' Revolt of 1381 as an instance when the majority had no right to act. In his *Letter to a Member of the National Assembly* (1791), Burke argued that "the last revolution of doctrine and theory" previous to the Revolution was the Reformation, which had produced "principles of internal as well as external division" across Europe.

The details of Burke's use of historical example can be challenged, especially given his failure to accept that the events of 1688–1689 marked a major discontinuity in English history and were only enforced in Ireland and Scotland after considerable violence. However, the polemical purpose of Burke's philosophical discussion of historical development made such an interpretation necessary. To insist upon Burke's historical errors is to miss the point of his understanding of history and his belief in the need to understand history;[33] whereas, to criticize him for thinking of the past as a divinely intended teleological order is to entail a dismissal of most eighteenth-century history, and of the attitudes that illuminated it and gave it both meaning and impact. Burke struck an echo not only thanks to his ability to write powerfully, but also because his understanding and use of history were far from marginal. History was shaped for Burke, as for his contemporaries, including his opponents, by purpose, and was far from being an arbitrary assemblage of events.

The outbreak of war with Britain in 1793, and the move of the French Revolution that year into the Reign of Terror, helped ensure that Burke's arguments also had a powerful public resonance in Britain. Thus, Edward Nares (1763–1841), an Anglican cleric and, from 1813, Regius Professor of Modern History at Oxford,[34] took forward themes advanced by Burke, while underlining their religious implications. Nares made a powerful case for the value of history in a sermon preached in 1797 on a day of public thanksgivings for a series of naval victories. He presented history as of value because it displayed the providential plan, and contrasted the historical perspective with the destructive secular philosophy of present-mindedness, coming to the reassuring conclusion that British victories proved divine support:

> From the first invention of letters, by means of which the history of past ages has been transmitted to us, and the actions of our forefathers preserved, it has ever been the wisdom of man, under all circumstances of public and general concern, to refer to these valuable records, as the faithful depositaries of past experience, and to deduce from thence by comparison of situations, whatever might conduce to his instruction, consolidation, or hope. Thither the statesman of the present day frequently recurs for the conduct and support of the commonwealth . . . Thither . . . the religious man . . . bent upon tracing the finger of God in all concerns of importance to the good and welfare of man, is pleased to discover, in the course of human events, a direction marvellously conducive to the final purposes of Heaven, the constant and eternal will of God: and continually illustrative of his irresistible supremacy, his over-ruling providence, his might, majesty, and power!

To Nares, there was a clear struggle between the historical and the opposition to history:

> the enemy begin their operations on the pretended principle of giving perfect freedom to the mind of man . . . the first step to be taken in vindication of such a principle, is to discard all ancient opinions as prejudices . . . The great point is to discover the heavenly purposes and these can only be fitly studied in the consequences.[35]

The hostile treatment of the French Revolution continued into the nineteenth century, with English novelists joining historians in presenting the Revolution as violent, terrifying, and un-English.[36] The Revolution was also played out by historians in terms of British political divisions.[37] Comparisons between revolutions in Britain and France were important not only to the polemic of current politics, but also to the development of comparative history. The two were linked, as with the career of François Guizot (1787–1874), professor of modern history at Paris from 1812, Minister of Public Instruction from 1832, and subsequently the chief adviser to King Louis-Philippe (r. 1830–1848). Guizot sought in 1830 to make the French revolution of that year, which brought

Louis-Philippe to power, look to the British example, rather than to the French one of 1789.[38]

The impact of politics on the presentation of history was earlier seen under Napoleon, with the frame of reference for historical work changing in France. While not looking back to the *ancien régime* French monarchy, Napoleon was mindful of the past to a degree different to that of the revolutionaries he displaced in 1799. Much of his interest focused on the ancient world, or, at least, on accounts of this world. Egypt, which he successfully invaded in 1798, a focus of esoteric Enlightenment interests,[39] proved an inspiration while also fulfilling the revolutionary agenda in reaching back to the pre-Christian past. The scholars who accompanied him greatly advanced knowledge of ancient Egypt, fusing the widening engagement with antiquity with the Western interest in the East. However, in an important instance of the degree to which such a focus on the past could be used to influence attitudes toward an entire civilization, this was an interest in Egypt past. The massive *Description de l'Egypte* (1809–1822) that resulted from the expedition, presented Egypt as having declined since antiquity, the modern Egyptians as timid, passive, and indifferent, and their rulers as barbaric and superstitious. Seen thus, Egypt would benefit from French conquest and rule.[40]

The despoiling of European art works for the glorification of Paris reflected another instance of Napoleonic appropriation of the past. A different use of history was seen in his deployment of terms and images from the Classical world when developing and expounding his image. From First Consul (1799) to Emperor (1804), Napoleon followed a Roman pattern, and the past thus provided a relevant iconography. In turn, celebratory works were produced, notably by David, including *Bonaparte Crossing the Great St Bernard Pass* (1800), *The Consecration of the Emperor Napoleon and the Coronation of Empress Joséphine on December 2, 1804* (1805–1807), and *The Distribution of the Eagle Standards* (1810).

CONCLUSIONS

In part a matter of selecting examples and models, history was also an example and explanation of political choice. Despite Classical imagery and interests, the French Revolution and Napoleon helped in the

West to awaken and strengthen an interest in modern – as opposed to ancient – history.[41] This interest was strongly related to political commitment and concern. Academics wrote on recent and current politics, the British theologian Herbert Marsh producing a *History of the Politics of Great Britain* and *France, from the time of the conference of Pilnitz to the declaration of war against Great Britain* (1799), an account of 1791–1793 that presented France as the aggressor. In 1800 he followed with *An Examination into the Conduct of the British Ministry relating to the late Proposal of Buonaparte.* His work praised by George III,[42] Marsh became Lady Margaret Professor of Divinity at Cambridge in 1807, his opening course of lectures devoted to "The History of Sacred Criticism." In 1816, March became a bishop. Much of the basis of the very diverse subsequent use of history can be seen in the French Revolution and the response to it. Yet, while focusing on this political dimension, it is also pertinent to consider the entrepreneurial world of publishing history that developed in eighteenth-century Britain and that is discussed earlier in the chapter.

FOUR

The Nineteenth Century

HISTORY AND COMMITMENT

The major overlap and close interaction of academic history and political engagement was amply seen in the nineteenth century. This was unsurprising, as commentators sought to mold and make sense of a period of growing change, of economic, social, political, intellectual, and cultural change, and at the global, national, regional, and local levels. This engagement was displayed both in favor of and against change. It was seen in countries at the forefront of new developments, notably Britain, Germany, the United States, and later Japan, and also in those not matching this process.

From the outset of the century, continuing the theme in the previous chapter, commitment was readily apparent in Europe as historians responded to the challenge of the French Revolution, which, to a degree, prefigured the different need for non-Western commentators later in the century to respond to the threat posed by Western expansion. The situation in Britain is of considerable interest, as this country was at the forefront of economic growth, imperial growth, and intellectual debate. Moreover, the freedom and size of its publishing industry provided plentiful and profitable opportunities for historians. There is a tendency to focus on liberal and Whig commentators, both at the time of the Revolution and subsequently, for example, Thomas Babington Macaulay (1800–1859). However, there was also an important conservative tradition. For example, Edward Nares exemplified the attitudes to history seen with Edmund Burke, and carried them forward. Like many

British and Continental writers, Nares combined a nationalistic perspective with an interest in history. In his case, his perspective was born of Protestant zeal and hostility toward foreign political developments, notably French radicalism. Having defended religion in the Bampton lectures of 1805, Nares held the Regius Chair of Modern History at Oxford from 1813 until his death in 1841. This was a post gained through his connections with the leading conservative politician, Robert, 2nd Earl of Liverpool, the Tory Prime Minister from 1812 to 1827.[1]

Nares's historical perspective continued unchanged after the end of the Napoleonic Wars in 1815. In 1828, his major historical work appeared, a massive biography of Elizabeth I's leading minister, William Cecil, Lord Burghley (1520–1598), a work that was to be criticized by Macaulay. In the preface, Nares clearly stated his methods, his commitment to particular principles, and, with them, an avowed partiality:

> He has not sought to qualify himself for an historian in the negative manner
> prescribed in a motto prefixed to the Memoirs of Horace Walpole: "Pour être
> bon historien, il ne faudroit être d'aucune religion, d'aucune pais, d'aucune
> profession, d'aucune parti." Believing such negations to be no securities against
> dangerous prejudices, but perhaps quite the contrary, he acknowledges that
> he prides himself upon being an Englishman, an English Protestant, a Church
> of England man, a Divine.

Thus, Nares rejected the skepticism of Enlightenment writers. Instead, he used his account of Tudor England to defend the establishment of the Church of England, which, in a reiteration of Tudor themes, was presented as "Catholic Christianity restored,"[2] in other words the revival of an obscured historical truth. In his last work, *Man as Known to us Theologically and Geologically* (1834), Nares sought to reconcile theology and geology and, criticizing some of the conclusions drawn, to ensure that the discoveries of the latter did not invalidate the historical framework of the former.

It is difficult for many today to appreciate the suppositions of Nares's world, because the intertwining of historical consciousness, historical examples, and political argument, while still normal, is generally now, in the West, different in tone and far less urgent. In part, this change is because the religious providentialism that inspired Burke and Nares, and that can be seen in the account of the advancement of society in the

1792 edition of the *Encyclopaedia Britannica*,[3] has largely lost its traction or ready applicability. Indeed, an aspect of this latter development is apparent in the tendency to present nineteenth-century history in terms of secular themes, or themes presented in a secular fashion, notably the rise of nationalism. This reading permits an understanding of the nineteenth century in modern Western terms, but at the cost of downplaying the continued relevance then of religious themes. For example, a consistent pattern in the thought of Sir John Seeley, Regius Professor of Modern History at Cambridge from 1869 to 1895, a scholar who believed that history should help solve present problems, was provided by "the vital link between religion and the state." Christianity indeed was a key context for Western history writing in the nineteenth century.[4] It offered an explanation of national destiny. Thus, James Anthony Froude (1818–1894), in his *History of England from the Fall of Wolsey to the Defeat of the Spanish Armada* (1858–1870), presented the English Reformation as providential. Froude became professor of modern history at Oxford in 1892.

This is not a view that would be taken today. It would be mistaken, however, to suggest that Christianity did not continue to play an important role for Western historians in the twentieth century; although it is important to note the complex evolution of what intellectuals meant by Christianity and Christian. In some hands, British Christianity, for example, has been defined almost out of existence. Others have been more consistent with earlier understandings. Herbert Butterfield (1900–1979), who became Regius Professor of Modern History at Cambridge, was both a devout Methodist and wrote a book on *Christianity and History* (1949). Butterfield also tried hard to extend the study of historiography to non-Western sources.[5] Another leading Cambridge historian, Maurice Cowling, produced a major work titled *Religion and Public Doctrine in Modern England* (1980–2001). Alongside those who are the opposite, many more recent historians, notably in the United States, have been devout, which often affects their work.

At the same time as the emphasis on religious themes in nineteenth-century Britain, there was contemporary criticism of the interpretations advanced by, and associated with, Burke and Nares. This criticism was particularly expressed by Whig writers and politicians. For Whig commentators, history both provided warning and meaning, offering an account suggesting that the Whigs would be vindicated, whatever the extent of their apparent political irrelevance in the Tory-dominated present. Whiggery was historically rooted, in large part with reference to the seventeenth century, but with the Whigs, who had been the "establishment" under George I (r. 1714–1727) and George II (r. 1727–1760), subsequently the critics, in the 1760s–1820s, of a Crown and governmental system that they felt had betrayed its legacy, largely due to George III (r. 1760–1820), who was presented as an authoritarian reverter to Stuart themes. This legacy made it necessary for the Whigs to offer an alternative historical account to that of the "establishment," when the latter was in what they saw as Tory hands, as was the case for most of the period from 1760 to 1830. Accordingly, the Whigs wrote history as a vindication and as a point of catharsis, with every contemporary situation placed in an historical context. The tone was dramatic, and the style drew on the development of the novel in the eighteenth century: "The Whig account is a penny dreadful story with virtue wrestling with wickedness, cliffhanging crises and the ultimate triumph of good."[6] In this neo-Gothic panorama, the Stuarts were to the fore among the villains, while Whigs could find heroes among their predecessors, indeed, ancestors. Furthermore, the present was coined into historical myth, as with their leader Charles James Fox, who, as soon as he died in 1806, gained iconic status. This legacy was seen in christening names as well as annual dinners. Liberty was thus asserted and carefully grafted onto Whig family trees.

Visually, the Whigs placed themselves before visitors in appropriate settings. In John, 6th Duke of Bedford's Temple of Worthies at his stately home (in other words, country palace) of Woburn Abbey, Fox was present with Francis, fifth Duke (1765–1802), and the sixth Duke (1766–1839), as well as the Elder and Younger Brutus, as remembrances of heroic virtue. A pediment by John Flaxman depicted Liberty and a frieze by Richard Westmacott on the march of Progress. Westmacott was also to produce the ornamental group representing the Progress of Civilization for the pediment of the portico of the British Museum, a work finished in 1847. The third son of the sixth Duke, Lord John Russell, 1st Earl Russell (1792–1878), was to be a Whig Prime Minister (1846–1852, 1865–1866) and an eminent Victorian historian producing

Memoirs of the Affairs of Europe (1824), *Causes of the French Revolution* (1832), *Letters of the Fourth Duke of Bedford* (1842–1846), and the *Life and Times of Fox* (1859–1867). Russell served as president of the Royal Historical Society in 1872. Family interests and honor were also expressed in paintings. Thus, Charles, 11th Duke of Norfolk, acquired Mather Brown's painting *Thomas Earl of Surrey defending himself before Henry VII after Bosworth*, a 1797 work referring to a 1485 episode involving the later 2nd Duke. The 600th anniversary of Magna Carta was commemorated by Charles, a staunch Whig, with an octagonal Great Hall built at Arundel Castle and dedicated to "Liberty asserted by the Barons in the reign of John."

The account of history as offering a clear prospectus of improvement, in ideas and in material culture, was to provide the key element of the Whig interpretation of history. This interpretation extended to include a liberal account of imperialism in terms of spreading progress,[7] although the situation looked less benign from the perspective of the colonized. There was also a stronger interest in the long term than is the case today, notably with constitutional development and foreign policy. Thanks to education and reading, historical memory went back to the Classics, while including a good grasp of national history. Thus, in 1861, Russell, then foreign secretary, replied to pressure from Richard Cobden, a prominent radical politician, about what the latter saw as unnecessary government expenditure on the Royal Navy and coastal fortifications. Russell noted that French diplomatic approaches to Cobden, who had negotiated a trade treaty with France in 1860, reminded him of the French effort, after the Peace of Ryswick of 1697 brought conflict between Britain and France in the Nine Years' War to a close, to weaken Britain by encouraging parliamentary opposition to the maintenance of a standing [permanent] army. Instead, the need for continued vigilance was indicated by the two powers going to war again in 1702, in part because Louis XIV was unwilling to help implement the partition of the Spanish Habsburg inheritance he had accepted earlier. Russell had read about this episode in Macaulay's *History of England* (1848–1862), a work that significantly began with the Glorious Revolution of 1688–1689, as a result of which the Stuart James II had been overthrown.[8] Macaulay provided classic Whig history, comparing what he presented as the backward England of 1688 to the more progressive present that had been created as a result of the Revolution Settlement. Macaulay's early death ensured that his coverage only reached 1702.

There was also a global scale for this presentation of history. A close relationship with Rome was provided by the Classically inspired civilizing ethos employed by the British to justify empire as a progressive imperial mission,[9] and by Americans to help justify expansion in North America. This account was linked to a critical account of developments in other civilizations. Nares in the third volume of the *Elements of General History, Ancient and Modern* (1822) by Alexander Tytler, Lord Woodhouselee, (1747–1813), Professor of Universal History at Edinburgh from 1780 to 1790, the volume written after Tytler's death that brought the compilation down to 1820, claimed: "Civilised Europe is the only part of the world that can claim the credit of all that has been done towards the advancement of knowledge since the commencement of the eighteenth century, and only a few parts after all of civilised Europe itself."[10]

The model of Classically inspired British civilization was linked to an account of social value that made sense of the expansion of the franchise in contemporary Britain. Thus, the Oxford-educated London barrister Edward Quin (1794–1828), in his posthumously published *Atlas in a Series of Maps of the World as Known in Different Periods* (1830), associated progress with the rise of the middle class, writing of Europe in 1100–1294: "Notwithstanding the gross superstition which prevailed, the undefined state of regal power and popular rights, and the many atrocious acts which were perpetrated, Europe was fast emerging from the state of barbarism in which it had been sunk for several centuries. In England, France, Germany, and Italy, the Commons or third estate, began to be recognised and respected; industry and commerce were acquiring their due weight and estimation, and through the study of jurisprudence, the rights of persons and of property were better understood." Subsequently, "the darkness of the Middle Ages was dispelled and the way cleared for the progress of the Protestant religion by the light of science, literature, and commerce."[11]

The examples varied in individual Western states, but the themes and tone were similar. In particular, science and industrialization contributed to a sense of change that encouraged people to trace their current and historical course.[12] Interest in change was related to the prominence of historicism, the belief that human nature is not trans-historical or universal, but rather is shaped by historical context.

EXPOUNDING THE MESSAGE

Whether written by Burke, Nares, or Russell, most history books were very much works produced for a wide and growing public. As such, they matched the situation across Western Europe and in the United States, where there was a presentation of history for a large market, at once interested in the past, politically engaged, and ready to spend money. The same was true of the arts, with reproductions serving to disseminate images produced on canvas. History painting was particularly popular in the first half of the century and could serve to provide apparently instructive parallels. For example, Paul Delaroche, a leading French painter (1797–1856), professor of painting at the École des Beaux-Arts in Paris from 1833, provided paintings of royal victims from English history – *The Princes in the Tower* (1828), *The Execution of Lady Jane Grey* (1834), and *Charles I Insulted by Cromwell's Soldiers* (1837), references respectively to events in 1485, 1554, and 1649. These apparently prefigured the royal martyrs of more recent French history.[13] Delaroche also painted *The Death of Queen Elizabeth* (1828).

History painters ranged across time for their subjects, as with Benjamin Robert Haydon (1786–1846), a less talented painter than Delaroche. He depicted Edward, the Black Prince (1330–1376), a hero of the Hundred Years' War with France, as well as the Duke of Wellington. Haydon produced *The Burning of Rome by Nero* as well as *Alfred and the First Trial by Jury*, images of bad and good monarchy.[14] The demand for an exemplary visual national history was seen in the Irish-born Daniel Maclise's grand frescoes of military triumph, *Wellington and Blücher at Waterloo* (1861) and *The Death of Nelson* (1864), painted for the new Palace of Westminster that was built after Parliament burned down as the result of an accident in 1834. Maclise (1806–1870) also painted *Alfred the Great in the Camp of the Danes* (1852). Alfred, King of Wessex (r. 871–899) provided England with a distinguished ancestry for notions of valiant liberty. John Rogers Herbert (1810–1890), a Catholic convert who painted religious and Shakespearean themes for the new Palace of Westminster, also painted a number of historical works, mostly on religious topics, including *St Edmund, King of East Anglia, on the Morning of his Last Battle with the Danes, Sir Thomas More and his Daughter observing from the Prison Window the Monks going to Execution, Assertion of Liberty of Conscience by the Independents in the Westminster Assembly of Divines, 1644,* and *The Acquittal of the Seven Bishops.* The last was very much an episode in the standard Whig account, but each of these paintings was about the conflict between position and power, a conflict that enabled British Catholics to position their own emancipation in the nineteenth century as a praiseworthy theme in secular as well as religious history.

The process of exposition, seen in both books and arts, included that of deliberately forgetting, or drawing exemplary lessons from, causes and episodes of past disunity, such as the St Bartholomew's Massacre of Huguenots (Protestants) in 1572 in France. The resulting choices of what to include or omit could be contentious. In Walhalla, the neo-Classical pantheon in which Ludwig I of Bavaria (r. 1825–1848), a German nationalist, sought to commemorate German worthies in order to help demonstrate an exemplary national-cultural past and, thereby, Catholic Bavaria's role in representing Germany, there was a vexed debate as to whether to include the Protestant Martin Luther among the worthies. He was accepted as worthy as a translator of the Bible into German, and not as the founder of Protestantism.[15] It is a sign of a very different public culture of history, that Walhalla is now an impressive architectural curiosity.

The exposition of the past linked the world of scholars to more broadly based currents of public interest. Indeed, in the context of a Europe in which the French Revolutionary and Napoleonic period (1789–1815) had ruptured a sense of continuity and thus created a crisis of identity,[16] historians sought to democratize the content, medium, scale, and audience of their historical writing, which was a departure from the practice of their predecessors.[17] Considered from a different angle, such democratization was an extension of a privileged narrative into new mass media markets, thus hoping to corner them.

SCHOLARLY METHODS

A different current was that of the rise of the research university where knowledge was produced.[18] Founded in 1810, Berlin University was particularly significant. The methods of documentary exegesis emphasized by Leopold von Ranke (1795–1886), Professor of History at Berlin from 1825 to 1871, in his positivist source criticism, proved especially important. Ranke's focus on documents, and on the skills necessary to use them, contrasts with the far lesser emphasis on such texts and skills today, let alone the only limited extent to which similar skills have been developed in order to use audio-visual and electronic documents.

Ranke had clear political and historical preferences in the shape of the development of a strong Prussia. Yet, he subordinated the teleology of his preferences to the weight of empiricism, and thus maintained not only the academic structure but also the rigor of research. The tone of professionalism he encouraged, and that was advanced and justified with reference to him, was seen in the periodicals established in the period, notably the *Historische Zeitschrift* (1859), but also the *Revue Historique* (1876), the *Rivista Storica Italiana* (1884), the *English Historical Review* (1886), and the *American Historical Review* (1895). Alongside scholarly periodicals was the spread of the research university, notably in Germany, and the increased importance of graduate, as opposed to undergraduate, education.[19] These changes, which crucially included the emergence of the doctoral thesis, were to influence the nature of choices and priorities in university education, not least moving toward expertise, rather than general knowledge and universal history.[20]

Moreover, the growth of academic history at university level enhanced the prestige and position of scholars, and the self-consciousness and organizational structures of the profession,[21] and also, with related consequences, greatly increased the public weight of the subject. This was not least because those trained there frequently went on to play prominent roles in politics, government, and education.[22] Secularization, professionalization, and the pressure of the expansion of government bureaucracy on the expectations placed upon academia were all linked.

The weight of empiricism had already been commented on by the writer Philip Sidney (1554–1586) when he referred, in sixteenth-century England, to "the historian . . . laden with old mouse-eaten records." Indeed, it is already for that Tudor period that a later prominent historian wrote, "It was, no doubt, inevitable that the price of a more scientific attitude to historical writing would be the forfeiture by historians of a wide public: the critical study cannot easily be a work of art."[23] This view does not account for eighteenth-century writers who enjoyed a large and wide-ranging audience, such as Edward Gibbon, or for some of the major writers of narrative in the nineteenth, such as Macaulay or, indeed, for some of the fine writing of recent years; but it did capture a significant tension, and one that continues to be important.

More positively, Western scholarship in the second half of the nineteenth century challenged the interweaving of the legendary and historical or, at least, the conventional and the uncritical, still apparent in so much Western historical writing of the early decades of the century. This was seen for example in accounts of the Spanish conquest of Granada in 1491–1492, a key moment in Spanish history, as marking the end of the *Reconquista* from the Moors. The first scholarly account of the episode based on a wide range of appropriate sources to appear in English, that by Henry Coppee, the president of the Smithsonian Institute in Washington, did so in 1881.[24] Sources, indeed, were repeatedly deployed by scholars in a critique of each other and also of works that were defined and disparaged as non-scholarly. The emphasis on archival sources posed a radical challenge for cultures where the presentation of the past was not traditionally based on this method.

ACCOUNTS OF HUMAN DEVELOPMENT

In contrast to Ranke, there were German writers, such as Alexander von Humboldt (1767–1835), who did not make the nation-state central to their vision of historical development. Indeed, many intellectuals were concerned to demonstrate the long-term validity of their particular vision of human development; and the role of the past proved especially important to this approach. In particular, the French philosopher Auguste Comte (1798–1857), in his *Système de Politique Positive* (1851–1854), advanced the theory of a multi-stage approach in which sciences, including history, moved from a theological stage to a metaphysical one, and then to a positive or experimental stage in which rational enquiry would open the way to understanding. The idea of a progressive presentation of the absolute in human history joined secular interpretations to religious counterparts, and also allowed the latter to be reinterpreted in a new and rapidly changing context.

Comte gained a hearing in Britain and the United States thanks to John Stuart Mill (1806–1873) and Henry Adams (1838–1918), respectively. Mill, a utilitarian and liberal philosopher, who proclaimed the utilitarian value of liberty and the need for government by a virtuous elite, saw in Comte a fellow radical and rationalist reformer. The two men corresponded warmly in the 1840s and, although Comte drove Mill away by arrogant and imperious behavior, Mill remained an intellectual admirer and disseminator of a version of positivism. The influence of Mill and Adams translated Comte into British radicalism and into American Gilded Age and Progressive-era liberalism. Educated at Harvard, before study in Berlin and Dresden, and serving as the secretary to his father when he was envoy in London, Adams taught at Harvard from 1870 to 1877, introducing German seminar methods. His large-scale *History of the United States during the Administrations of Jefferson and Madison* (1870–1877) sought a monumental status.

From the 1860s until World War I, a number of American liberal reformers were deeply influenced by Comtean ideas. The early American Comtists, who had tried to live out the weird quasi-religion formulated by Comte in his failing years, dispersed by the end of the 1860s, but intellectual heirs took up the more substantial content of Comte's thought and shaped it to fit their circumstances, in responding to, and seeking to shape, America's phenomenal growth. In particular, the sociologist Lester Frank Ward (1841–1913) and the journalist and publisher Herbert Croly (1869–1930) worked to define American liberalism in Comtean terms. From their influence, for example of Ward's *Dynamic Sociology* (1883) and Croly's *The Promise of American Life* (1909) and *Progressive Democracy* (1914), came the American impulse for technocratic social interventionism, the faith in a scientific elite, a belief in the susceptibility of society to programmatic, scientifically formulated reform, and, finally, the statism and corporatism that became ingrained in American liberalism.

Charles Darwin's *On the Origin of Species by Means of Natural Selection* (1859) affected American intellectual circles already attuned to positivism and Mill's liberalism. Ward particularly developed the idea that human intervention had made evolution teleological whereas it had not previously been so. Creation now apparently lay in the hands of Man, who had become both object and goal. Only the cataclysm of World War I shook the foundations of this Comtean faith, and, even then, there was no return to the traditional order, but only heightened attempts to formulate new policies including, from some, comprehensive social plans.

Comte's emphasis on a stadial (stages) approach to time, on the rise of progress, and on a future path illuminated by the past, was also seen with Karl Marx (1818–1883), who found history a convenient source of lessons. His was an account that emphasized historical materialism and saw the central theme as the history of class struggles. Marx offered a response to the unprecedented pace and scale of Western economic growth, and sought to shape an understanding of it for political purposes so that the future could be both understood and directed.

With fewer trappings of formal theory, but also confident that history was a progressive process that moved in the direction of human hopes, many Anglo-American writers offered a clear account of development, one that would be described as Whiggish. This confidence, ethos, and method could be applied to all forms, scales, and themes of history, for example that of merchant shipping by the British ship-owner and MP William Schaw Lindsay published in 1874–1876.[25] However, the focus was on the progress of civilizations. Thus, just as later German writers were to look back to Greece, particularly Macedon and Pergamon,[26] the British Empire was presented as the apogee of the historical process, one founded on the ancient civilizations of the Middle East and Mediterranean, and also looking back to the Holy Land. This linkage implied not only a powerful theme of continuity, indeed another version of the medieval *translatio imperii* in which the transfer of rule kept the dream of Rome alive, but also a diffusionist model of cultural history, with Classical Rome and modern Britain each shaping the world.

In an essay on colonies published in the *Rambler* in 1862, John, Lord Acton (1834–1902), presented colonialization as a necessary prelude to the spread of Christian civilization: "We may assume (as part of the divine economy which appears in the whole history of religion) that the conquest of the world by the Christian powers is the preliminary step to its conversion." Parallel arguments were offered elsewhere in Western Europe, not least as both France and Italy also lay claim to the mantle of Rome. This was particularly so as both sought to justify imperial expansion in North Africa.

Similarly, in the United States, there was an attempt to claim a link with Classical civilization, not only with the constitution, but also, for example, with public architecture. The range of the Classical world provided an appropriate frame of reference, as the United States looked to Classical republicanism, for example, in the naming of the Senate, in order to establish a clear break with the Europe of monarchies. They, in turn, sought a prestigious echo by reference to the Roman emperors.

The Classics continued to be a key source of historical reference, for example, for painters and for how their works were perceived. Thus, Eugène Delacroix's dramatic painting *The Death of Sardanapalus,* hung at the Paris Salon of 1827, depicts a mythical Middle Eastern tyrant, both cruel and weak, who chose to die surrounded by his slaughtered possessions (including slaves) as his state succumbed to rebellion. This painting was not regarded as offering a positive impression of monarchy at a time when the reactionary Charles X of France was facing considerable opposition.[27] He was overthrown three years later. Novels were also set in the Classical past, for example Bulwer Lytton's hugely popular *Last Days of Pompeii* (1834). A politician, he subsequently produced an epic poem, "King Arthur" (1848–1847).

NATIONALISM

Looking back to the Classical past did not prevent attempts to find an exemplary recent history, one moreover that was specific to the state or people in question, and frequently advanced accordingly in terms of a partisan politics. The emphasis, thereby, was on particular developments, indeed on national exceptionalism, and, thereby, on a wider

scale, national exceptionalisms, indeed competing national exceptionalisms. Thus, in the United States in the second quarter of the century,
Transcendentalist thought, combining Romanticism and Deism, and
associated with writers such as Ralph Waldo Emerson and Henry David Thoreau, reflected a strong American optimism and was seen as a
declaration of independence from church control and traditionalism.
Emerson presented America as a visionary poem, a country of young
men who, in 1775, had fired at Lexington on 19 April "the shot heard
around the world." While the American focus was on a new country and
people separate from the old world of Europe, in practice there was also
a history created to exemplify this divide.

The abandonment by many educational systems in Europe and the
United States over the last 150 years and, in many countries, over the
last half-century, of religion as the key context and a leading subject for
history and as a central aspect of historical analysis and explanation, is
not the sole instance of substantial change. There is also, with nationalism, another disjuncture, in this case between the commitment of the
nineteenth and early twentieth century to the growth and interests of
the nation-state, and the disengagement frequently shown today, at least
by the standards of past engagement, a disengagement that is particularly pronounced in Western Europe. Most academic history in the
West is not now written from an overt nationalist perspective. Moreover,
although national politics is still grounded in a measure of historical
awareness, this grounding owes relatively little to historians, particularly
academic historians.

In contrast, there is an important continuity between the late nineteenth century and the situation today in the case of the public provision
in education. Furthermore, despite the distrust of government by some
historians, such as Acton in Britain, the state played a leading part in the
development of academic history in the nineteenth century.[28] That development owed much to a utilitarian drive for education and training,
and to a commitment on the part of academics to the state, that were at
variance from much of the liberal Western academic culture of the late
twentieth century – although not so from modern governmental concerns. The nature of this academic commitment to the state varied in the
nineteenth century, not least due to opposition in some cases to imperial

rule. However, the value of history and of specific historical models was understood to be ideological and functional.

The nation and the state were not only increasingly realities for universities, not least in the emphasis on the vernacular rather than on Latinity. More generally, both liberal and conservative political, intellectual, and cultural themes and concerns were readily transferred into the nationalist agenda of state concern as well as the nationalism provided by print culture, other media – notably music and the visual arts – and leisure activities. Governmental concern was particularly seen with state educational systems, systems that encouraged schoolteachers and academics to think in terms of national identity, however defined. There were always some commentators who rejected this agenda in favor of an allegedly impartial dispassionate approach.[29] There were others who pressed for a more nationalist state and society.

There were also rival interpretations of the past, interpretations joined to current political movements, such as the longstanding struggle in nineteenth-century France between republican, Bourbon and Bonapartist (Napoleonic) visions of France,[30] the related rivalry between secular and clerical accounts, or the call – there and elsewhere – for a conscript nation in arms rather than a professional army.[31] Opinion and memory played major roles in these competing accounts, which very much sought to elicit public backing. As a result of this drive, there was a use of a range of available mediums: the artifacts of popular politicized history were far more prints, songs, and popular stories, both factual and fictional, than works of scholarship, although the latter were also highly important, and notably if deliberately presented for a popular market.[32] In France, republicans and their rivals sought to re-work their recent history in order to provide acceptable accounts for the present, for example of the French Revolution shorn of Jacobin extremism. In turn, these accounts provided ammunition for current differences, both in France and elsewhere. For example, warnings from the past, including concerning the very violent and eventually successful slave rising in Haiti in the 1790s, were deployed in America in the run-up to the Civil War.[33]

In empires, notably the Austro-Hungarian and Russian, but also the British, nationalism could represent, especially on the part of the

Czechs, Poles, and Irish, respectively, a rejection of imperial rule. Accordingly, the presentation of history owed much to a determination to develop and assert an independent national culture, one, moreover, presented in the national language.[34] For example, national institutions provided historical paintings of exemplary episodes, as with the National Gallery in Oslo, the setting for paintings such as Oscar Wergeland's *Nordmennene lander på Island* (1877). With its depiction of the brave Vikings who sailed the North Atlantic, this painting provided a reminder of past Norwegian resolution and activity. Norway was then ruled by Sweden, from which it broke away in 1905. Not only paintings, music, and literature was involved; there were also more specific approaches to the past. For example, historic preservation played a role in the depiction of a national inheritance, with such preservation shaped in terms of national narratives.[35] The process of proto-nations establishing a history extended to Jewish intellectuals advancing a call for Zionism.[36]

A nationalist political agenda was compatible with high academic standards, although the relationship was not without tension.[37] Nationalist historians looked back to previous writers, making them figures in a nationalist historiography of a long pedigree. Vjekoslav Klaić (1849–1929), a "founding father" of modern Croatian historiography, wrote in 1913 a study of Pavao Ritter Vitezović (1652–1713). The book was published by Matrix Croatica, a nationalist cultural institution. Vitezović had indeed published works providing a glorious account of the Croatian past, but it was all too easy to overlook the multiple purposes of his writing, notably of serving the interests of the contemporary Habsburg emperor, Leopold I (r. 1657–1705) under whom Croatia was ruled from Vienna.[38] The assertion of independent national cultures in the eighteenth and, even more, nineteenth centuries looked toward the similar situation under imperial rule in the twentieth century.

Nationalist historians could bridge the gap between the universities and the public, both the expanding and assertive middle class and the newly educated working class. Charles Kingsley (1819–1875), a clergyman who was Regius Professor of Modern History at Cambridge from 1860 to 1869, wrote a number of historical novels glorifying heroes from the English past. These included *Westward Ho!* (1855), an account of the Elizabethan struggle with Philip II of Spain, in which the Inquisition and the Jesuits appear as a cruel inspiration of Spanish action, a work that was especially significant given the restoration of the Catholic hierarchy in Britain in 1851. *Hereward the Wake* (1866) provided an inspiring account of resistance to the Norman Conquest. Such, however, was not to be the path followed at Cambridge or in other universities, and a gap opened up, with popular writers, such as G. A. [George Alfred] Henty (1832–1892), fulfilling the interest in historical fiction and much (but far from all) of the interest in readily accessible history. Henty's adventure stories, such as *Under Drake's Flag* (1883) or *With Clive in India* (1884), which dealt with war in the 1750s, did well in the United States as well as Britain.[39] These novels were still widely available in British public libraries in the 1960s.

THE NEW SCALE OF HISTORY

More generally, the late nineteenth-century emphasis on state development, the rise of publication in most European languages, the more widespread growth of the publishing industry, the development of national school systems publishing works in the vernacular (as opposed to Latin and wide-ranging "cosmopolitan" languages), and concern about social change and tension, including urbanization and immigration, all encouraged the appearance of historical works, and thus the transfer of historical and historiographical understandings into print. One clear instance was provided by the nomenclature employed, as the spelling of names helped proclaim identity and longevity. Nomenclature was an aspect of the fixing of knowledge through classification and categorization that was particularly significant in the late nineteenth century, as efforts were simultaneously made to respond to the explosion of information, the intellectual development of new subjects, and the need to offer an organizational structure for the purposes of teaching at school and university level. Thus, Dmitri Mendeleev (1834–1907), professor of chemistry at St Petersburg from 1866, devised the periodic table that grouped chemical elements.

The teaching and research of history shared in this process and also proved a means of intellectual organization. Thus, manuals for historical study were produced, notably Johann Droysen's *Grundzüge der Historik*

(1868), Ernst Berheim's more successful *Lehrbuch der historischen Meth-ode* (1889), and Charles-Victor Langlois and Charles Seignobos's *Intro-duction aux études historiques* (1898).[40] Such works were the counterparts of the establishment of national archives and related archive schools. At the same time, historical work could challenge established accounts, including significant national accounts, as the use of source-criticism overturned existing authorities and narratives.

The appearance of large numbers of relatively inexpensive books reflected not only the opportunities of the market arising from the rise in literacy, but also the results of technology and development, in the shape of the greater ease of moving timber thanks to railways and steamships, the development of wood-pulp papermaking, the mechanization of the casting of metal type, and lower printing costs, as well as the impact of entrepreneurial publishers.[41] "Modernity" therefore eased the path for history. Another aspect of the juncture of technology and entrepreneur-ship in creating expanded markets for history was provided by public spectacles, such as panoramas, which were circular canvases depicting historical episodes, phantasmagorias, in which images were created by moving lanterns, and wax displays. Both London and Paris proved sig-nificant for the development of those spectacular histories,[42] which, by the end of the nineteenth century, helped lead to cinema.

Such developments as photography, the telephone, and the cinema were aspects of the extent to which traditional concepts and divisions of time and space, indeed of reality, were challenged, reconceptualized and replaced.[43] Photography encouraged the idea of authenticity, of an accurate – or apparently accurate – scientific account that was separate from the impressionism of painting, however realistic.[44] This authentic-ity was also the goal of scholars who emphasized academic precision. At the same time, photography offered a tool for enthusiasts throughout society, comparable to the freedom gained through reading.

ADVERSARIAL HISTORY

The phrases used to describe change, such as "encouraged the appear-ance," seem benign, as there was much that was adversarial in this use of history to affirm states and/or nations. As an aspect of a widespread struggle over its character and presentation, nationalism frequently changed from being regarded as progressive and liberal to being presented in a "blood and soil" character, and increasingly so in the last decades of the century. By its very nature, this process hit against those who could appear to challenge such an affirmation, or, rather, an affirmation in particular forms. Other states and nations were the prime target of nationalist history, but there was also a process of discrimination against groups who might offer contrasting values, as well as against citizens who could be presented as different. Thus, the age of nationalism, in the closing decades of the nineteenth century, saw opposition to international movements with national local representations, such as trade unions and the Catholic Church. There was also the rise of an anti-semitism, notably in Russia, Austria, France, and Germany, that presented Jews as a foreign people, and that was concerned about Jewish immigration as well as Jewish cultural movements. At the same time, traditional anti-semitic ideas were advanced – notably the (unfounded) charge of ritual murder, which was revived by August Rohling, a professor of Catholic theology at the German University of Prague, whose *Der Talmudjude* (*The Talmud Jew*) was published in 1871. In such literatures, historical fictions published in the guise of fact overlapped with crude sensationalism. The "scare" literature of the period served to contest, as well as to affirm, identity, and was also seen, for example, in anti-Chinese literature, notably in America and Australia.

In France, the recent past provided an opportunity to contest ideas of the nation: constructions of national identity interacted with political contention about the entire period from the Revolution on.[45] Catholic legitimists actively challenged the anniversary of the Revolution in 1889 as part of their assault on the Third Republic, the constitutional system from 1870 to 1940;[46] and both prejudice and the past were mobilized in order to provide Catholic politicians with a platform, notably with the *Union Nationale,* founded in 1892 by Théodore Garnier, a priest. This populist, corporatist party argued that Jews, Freemasons, and Protestants were running the Third Republic and ruining France. Historical resonance was found in Joan of Arc's struggle against the English in the early fifteenth century, a theme later used by the Vichy regime of 1940–1944.[47] The statue of Joan in the Place des Pyramides in Paris was a key point for mass demonstrations by right-wing nationalists in 1896–1897. Moreover, Garnier frequently referred to a (non-existent) secret plot devised in 1846 by Henry, 3rd Viscount Palmerston, the British Foreign Secretary and, according to Garnier, a Jew and a Freemason, which would have surprised the Viscount; a plot seeking to use Jews and Freemasons to destroy France and Catholicism. Historic movements were presented as at war, not least when Garnier spread the inaccurate idea, advanced in France in 1881 in the Catholic journal *Le Contemporain,* that a Jewish conclave the previous year had decided to take vengeance for their historic oppression. The French Revolution came into play with the emancipation of the Jews by the Revolutionaries in 1791 presented as a deliberately anti-Catholic step.[48] Thus, a vision of France drawing on an established pattern of historical responses was offered. This vision was tremendously important in the Dreyfus Affair, which began in 1894 with the unfounded conviction of a Jewish officer for treason, and was to influence politics in the early twentieth century, notably with the Vichy regime during World War II.

In turn, this issue has had a resonance in more recent times, with the question of the French Church's relationship to anti-semitism in the 1890s clearly seen by some as prefiguring the similar question, for both the French Church and the Catholic Church as a whole, of the response to the Holocaust. Catholic historians have tended to underplay the role of priests in the anti-semitism of the 1890s, although, in 2005, the beatification of Abbé Léon Dehon, a prominent Social Catholic of the 1890s, was stopped by the Vatican once his strident anti-semitism came to widespread attention. The Vatican's attempt, for example in the 1998 report "We Remember: A Reflection on the Shoah [Holocaust]," to distinguish between its role in an earlier anti-semitism and what it claimed was a different nineteenth- and twentieth-century racial (rather than religious) anti-semitism, understates the role of some clerics in anti-semitism in the later period.[49]

CONCLUSIONS

The presentation of the past by the Catholic Church suffered in Europe and Latin America in the nineteenth century as a result of secularism, nationalism, and the rise of state power. In contrast, where religion, nationalism, and the state could be readily linked, there was no such division in the account of the past. In Japan, state Shinto developed as an amalgam of a longstanding animist religion with a new authoritarian form of government, and was significant in the creation of the new Japan in the late nineteenth century. Militarism and the new past played a role with the foundation in 1869 of Yasukuni as a pre-eminent shrine that was a symbol of nationalism and a site where the war dead were commemorated. Time itself was reordered as part of the state-driven account of Japan's past and present. Whereas each new reign had begun a new sequence of years, in 1869 a parallel dating system was introduced. This took 660 BCE, when Jimmu, the mythical first emperor, had begun his rule, as year 1. Thus, an invented account served a modernizing state. In part, this was designed to bring Japan into line with the West, a process also seen in the adoption of a related periodization of history.[50]

The development of new national accounts of past, present, and future in the late nineteenth century was one of the important links between that period and the early twentieth. Continuity at the level of many states also ensured that nineteenth-century historical themes played a major role in the politics of identification in the first half of the twentieth century.[51]

FIVE

The Twentieth Century

THE STATE, THE MARKET, AND THE ACADEMY

This chapter serves as an historical introduction to the themes covered in chapters 6 to 9, where the focus is on recent decades and the organization by types of states. The varied, often clashing, concerns of the state and the market, of officials and entrepreneurs, come to the fore in this account. However, these concerns differ quite conspicuously from the views of many cutting-edge thinkers on the purposes of history and on historical method, and notably so in the twentieth century and the twenty-first. Officials and entrepreneurs offered an assessment of history that was, understandably, far less affected by advances in theoretical developments or in other intellectual disciplines. Instead, the needs of state identity and the very different exigencies of the market took a greater role. It would be difficult to imagine many popular writers joining Jacques Le Goff, the influential director of studies at the *École des Hautes Études en Sciences Sociales* in Paris, who wrote, in 1992, that "banal, reactionary modes of history – narrative, the history of events, biography, and political history – continue or stage comebacks."[1]

Indeed, the vitality and self-sufficiency of populist accounts of the past throw doubt on Eric Hobsbawm's claim that "What goes into school textbooks and politicians' speeches about the past, the material for writers of fiction, makers of TV programs and videos, comes ultimately from historians."[2] In practice, such material does come ultimately from historians, but often from outdated or amateur historians, rather than the scholars to whom Hobsbawm referred.[3] Moreover, far from there being clear-cut links with scholarly accounts, the representation of the past offered to the public has captured, and sought to mediate between, many constituencies – as public memorials amply displayed (and display).[4] Confidence by the academic leadership about the exposition of the past, *their* exposition of the past, might have been the perception for some when the history made available to the public was dominated by governments that at least paid lip service to (compliant) academics, as in Communist regimes, or was otherwise presented in top-down fashion, as in Britain, and to a considerable extent the United States, before its society became less deferential and more independent beginning in the 1960s.[5] Thus, in 1947, the prominent historian G. M. [George Macaulay] Trevelyan (1876–1962), Regius Professor of Modern History at Cambridge from 1927 to 1940,[6] spoke for an hour on the BBC's Third Programme on "Society in Roman Britain," offering an appreciation of the Victorian intellectual Thomas Carlyle later in the year, while, in 1948, this radio channel broadcast a series on "Ideas and Beliefs of the Victorians."[7] At that time, there were only three radio channels in Britain.

The focus has since greatly changed in Britain with the move toward a more demotic culture. However, even earlier, there were influences scarcely traceable to academic pressures. For example, the historian William Lecky (1838–1903) had emphasized the importance of "childish recollections of the more dramatic conflicts of the past," writing: "We are Cavaliers or Roundheads [a reference to the Civil War of 1642–1646] before we are Conservatives or Liberals. . . . Language which grew out of bygone conflicts continues to be used long after those conflicts and their causes have ended."[8] Moreover, as the last two chapters indicated, entrepreneurial drives and popular interests created a world of publications in which academic accounts were of limited significance.

This contrast between academic and non-academic history remained relatively pertinent throughout the twentieth century, but it would be mistaken to put either category too clearly in a box and to imply that there were no overlaps. Indeed, in the United States, Britain, and other countries, there was to be considerable popular, and thus commercial, interest in certain historians and some historical works that could be regarded as academically sound, even cutting edge. Nevertheless, there was a clear trend: the increase and diffusion of wealth in most cultures was such that the balance between state and market tilted toward the latter as far as publications were concerned. As for science,[9] publication and programming reflected the identity of those who paid for popularization; and in the West, this increasingly became the market. This trend was not new, but it became more pronounced and prominent. The focus on the market challenged the consequences of the large-scale expansion in higher education across the world after World War II, and notably from the 1960s, and the consequent growth of the academic constituency. Indeed, one aspect of the discussion of historical method and historiography was that, in practice but without acknowledgement, it represented an attempt by academics to fix and deploy methods, standards, and narratives of development in the face of a situation in which the academic approach was becoming less potent, and, indeed, less relevant.

AUTHORITARIANISM AND IDEOLOGY

If the rise of the market is regarded as of long-term significance, there was a series of more particular and often contrary episodes and movements, political and intellectual, through which this process was mediated in the shorter term. In particular, those episodes and movements that emphasized the role of the state led to a focus on its historiographical concerns. This was the case for all states. It was most obvious, however, with authoritarian political movements, notably Communism and Fascism, and with the need of newly independent countries to create new histories. In the case of both authoritarian political movements and newly independent countries, there was a tendency to present a clear developmental and "moral" account of progress in time that reflected the strictures of a specific ideology. Independence from the past was, at least in part, an explicit rejection of former governmental systems and intellectual and moral norms. The process of offering accounts of the past was at once complicated and simplified by the extent to which governments also sought to focus on visions of the future. Embracing the latter necessarily affected the presentation of the past, not least due to the affirmation of continuity or discontinuity. However, there was a common process of choosing aspects of the past that seemed most convenient for the narrative of the individual regime. The process of creating an appropriate new history, historiography, and historical consciousness was to extend to new supra-national bodies, such as the European Union (see chapter 9), albeit with only limited success, leading indeed to what was termed a "European memory crisis."[10]

The creation of new histories and new futures was repeatedly seen as independence was obtained. In a process that was to be commonplace, the successor states that became independent from the Habsburgs after the defeat of Austria in 1918 employed history to help forge national identities and to respond both to the legacy of imperial control and to subsequent developments.[11] Those seeking independence did the same, albeit not always with success.[12] Anniversaries served the cause of identity, state affirmation and, therefore, political calculation. Thus, in 1926, on the 400th anniversary of the destruction of the Hungarian army by the invading Ottoman Turks at Mohács, Miklós Horthy, the regent of Hungary from 1920 to 1944, delivered a speech at the site suggesting that a common interest linked the fate of Hungary and Yugoslavia, a neighbor the alliance of which it was seeking to win. Similarly, the authoritarian Ulmanis regime in Latvia used the country's history both to affirm its separate identity and to provide settings for the dictator, Kārlis Ulmanis, president from 1934 to 1940. In 1934, he spoke at each of the three performances in the Festival of Rebirth, a pageant presenting an account of Latvian history. Such activity was part of a wider process in Latvia and elsewhere. In Courland, part of Latvia, though historically semi-independent, Ulmanis was greeted with speeches focusing on Courland's greatness in the seventeenth century.[13]

States that created a new political order through revolution, such as China, Iran, Mexico, the Soviet Union, and Turkey, established and staged a new public history, one focused on recent events.[14] In China, dynastic history lost its relevance with the end of the Manchu (Qing) Empire in 1911–1912 and the creation of the republic. Moreover, the Confucian order, once the dominant intellectual and moral model, was historically relativized.[15] The fashioning of a new history exploited intellectual and political developments in China in the late nineteenth and early twentieth centuries. China, hitherto a poorly defined concept, was presented as a nation-state inheriting the position of the Manchu dynasty and coterminous with it territorially. This account was then read back into Chinese history, annexing the dynasties to the new state. This process linked state and nation as each was defined in terms of the other.[16]

IDEOLOGY AND COMMITMENT

Ideological commitment took on potency when linked to state policy. Indeed, as a consequence of the diverse, but often highly assertive, role of governments, there are significant chronological and geographical variations to the rise of market-driven history. These variations also affected academic trends, not least with the careers of scholars owing much to the state or being affected adversely by political changes. Some historians were prominent in politics. Mykhailo Hrushevsky, a history professor at Lvov, became president of the Central Rada, Ukraine's new parliament, in 1917, only to flee Ukraine when the government was overthrown in 1918, and to be the target of Soviet police activity.[17] Seeing themselves as public figures, historians sought to influence the official world in many states, including Britain. In a lecture to the Imperial Defence College on 24 October 1938 that was circulated to the Cabinet, Sir Ernest Llewellyn Woodward, a prominent Oxford historian, argued in favor of postponing a confrontation with Nazi Germany and pressed for a reliance in Britain on naval supremacy. He also feared that war with Germany might create more problems than it solved.[18] The government had just negotiated the Munich Agreement with Germany. Woodward's career indicated the interrelationship of academe and politics. After serving in World War I, Woodward (1890–1971) was attached to the historical branch of the Foreign Office and employed to write a history of the Congress of Berlin (1878) as a briefing paper for the 1919 Paris Peace Conference. An interwar academic, Woodward considered standing for Parliament and warned about the threat from Hitler. Woodward's stance serves as a reminder that institutional positions and cultures have to be handled with care. Not all fellows of All Souls, Oxford, were supporters of the Appeasement of the dictators. During World War II, Woodward worked first in Political Intelligence and then in the Foreign Office, editing diplomatic documents.[19]

Many historians were victims of political circumstances and developments. In some cases, this was a matter of missing out on appointments or promotions due to various political factors, which, in part, were often a variant on the commonplace politics of academic appointments, a politics that is far more affected by national politics than many academics will accept. However, there were also more active state policies of appointment and removal. These reflected ideologies that could be political, social, racial, or religious in character. The discriminatory and, later, genocidal treatment of Jews by the Germany of the Third Reich (1933–1945) was particularly important. Large numbers of academics suffered, not only in Germany, but also in the countries allied to Hitler, such as Romania, or occupied by his forces, for example, France. Conversely, many historians backed the Nazi regime.[20] The net effect of Nazi rule and expansion on intellectual life was considerable and extremely negative, although there were also some beneficial consequences. German academic emigration to Britain and the United States was important to all three countries, and helped to stimulate new work in those two countries,[21] as well as to increase interest there in Continental history. Conversely, German scholarship lost much of its quality.

Totalitarian regimes with a clear ideology politicized the presentation of history as part of their attempt to direct both national life and history as a whole. This usage of history was a product of the utilitarian view toward universities and knowledge adopted by such regimes. There was scant interest in disinterested research and teaching, and this approach encouraged the purging of academics. Both processes were aspects of the legitimating of new regimes. In Communist states, Marxist-Leninism became a major field of study, while control over education was enhanced by moving research from universities into national academies.[22] Yet, at the same time, left-wing regimes sought to profit from nationalist themes, and, in doing so, annexed them to their ideology or, at least, politics. In Sarajevo, the site of the assassination of Austrian archduke Franz Ferdinand and his wife in 1914 was marked, initially, by a memorial to the victims, taken down in 1918 when the Austrian Empire collapsed and then, under independent Yugoslavia, by a memorial to the assassin, erected in 1930. In turn, this was removed in 1941 when the

Germans conquered Yugoslavia. The plaque was presented to Hitler as a birthday present. Next, when the Communists eventually triumphed in World War II, a new plaque was erected, annexing the assassination to the purposes of an exemplary revolution: "From this place on 28 June 1914 Gavrilo Princip with his shooting expressed the people's protest against tyranny and the centuries-long aspiration of our peoples for freedom."[23] "Our peoples" was a reference to the Communists' idea that Yugoslavia was not an expression of Serbian nationalism, which, in fact, was the key element in the assassination.

While drawing on German history, the Nazi regime sought a comprehensive manipulation of the past in order to offer a totalizing account of the present, one that covered the mobilization of German society in what was seen as an existential struggle to overcome what were presented as the challenges of Communism and Judaism, and to create a Nazi future. The use of history was part of a presentation of the past in which the Aryan race was a key player,[24] but with history given particular note as it appeared to prove meaning in time and to point the way. Other movements and regimes shared an account of the past in which ethnic groups were presented as key players.[25]

World War II (1939–1945) led to an upsurge in historical references as a key aspect of the mobilization of domestic public support, and also as a means to seek foreign backing. National heroes were deployed accordingly. In the Soviet Union, Stalin supported reference to Aleksandr Nevskii, an opponent of German invasion in the thirteenth century. The Vichy regime in France turned to Joan of Arc (c. 1412–1431), a national heroine canonized in 1920, who had an appropriate anti-English pedigree. She had led a French army to victory over the English at Orléans in 1429, a victory that proved a turning point in the Hundred Years' War between the two. In turn, others were attacked. For example, Enlightenment figures were criticized under Vichy. They were seen as secularists who had helped cause the French Revolution. The Abbé Grégoire (1750–1831) had played a major role in late Enlightenment French thought, pressing for equality notably on behalf of Jews and slaves. The occupying Germans destroyed his statue at Lunéville in 1942, while later, under the Fifth Republic, Jean-Marie Le Pen's far-right National Front was to attack his legacy.[26]

In the search for allies, as in their efforts to mobilize public opinion, the Axis powers sought to strike historical notes that would secure support. For example, in Inner Mongolia (part of China), much of which it occupied, Japan encouraged the building of a large temple to Chinggis Khan (d. 1227) in Ulanhot. Japan's prime opponent, the Nationalist Chinese government, protected the sacred relics of the Khan held at Ejen Khorooo in Inner Mongolia, moving them to Kansu, and Mao Zedong, the Communist leader, conjured up the example of Chinggis Khan in calling on the Inner Mongolians to resist Japan. Stalin supported reference to the Khan in the independent state of Mongolia. The situation changed after World War II, with a move away from such nationalist heroes in China and the Soviet Union. Under Soviet influence, the government of Mongolia dismissed Chinggis Khan in 1949 as a feudal reactionary whose warfare had exploited the people. However, the Communist regime in China followed a very different tact, restoring the Temple of Chinggis Khan in Ulanhot, and, in 1954, returning the Khan's relics to Ejen Khoroo, where a massive mausoleum was built in 1956. Celebrations in Mongolia in 1962 of his 800th birthday led to Soviet complaints, and the Mongolian government then became more cautious.[27]

Anniversaries, more generally, served as a way to annex history, as in 1983 when East Germany celebrated not only the 100th anniversary of the death of the founder of Marxism, Karl Marx, but also the 500th anniversary of the birth of Martin Luther. Luther was presented as a progressive German, and thus as a figure worthy of memorialization. The Reformation and, thereby, Protestantism were annexed to the Communist state. At the same time, by allowing the public to assemble, anniversaries represented threats, as in East Germany in 1988 when, at the anniversary celebration of the murder in 1919 of the revolutionaries Rosa Luxemburg and Karl Liebknecht, there were protests by those seeking to leave the country, a clear demonstration of the rejection of Communism.

Anniversaries were part of the ordering of the past. This was more generally an aspect of periodization. Thus, under Mao Zedong, dictator from 1949 to 1976, the beginning of China's modern history was dated to the humiliating Anglo-Chinese Treaty of Nanjing in 1842, and recent history to the anti-imperialist protest movement of 1919. Radical Maoist intellectuals in China in the early 1960s argued not only for the primacy of class struggle but also for the need for historical research to serve present-day politics.[28] These attitudes contributed to the Cultural Revolution that Mao instigated in 1966, a revolutionary assault on all aspects of non-revolutionary behavior that included a deliberate attack on continuity in the shape of culture, customs, ideas, and habits. As a result, books seen as "capitalist" were destroyed, and museums and temples were attacked.

A different assault on both the past and present was seen with the Soviet attack on the Jewish heritage. Without any reason, the post-1945 Soviet Union presented Jews as unpatriotic cosmopolitans. Moreover, the support shown to Israel by the United States from 1967 and, conversely, Soviet backing for Egypt, Syria, and pan-Arabism, strengthened Communist anti-semitism. In the bizarre word of Soviet propaganda, Zionists were accused of cooperating with the Holocaust in order to give birth to Israel. Linked to this was a downplaying of the extent to which Nazi atrocities were aimed at Jews, as seen in memorializations at the extermination camps. For example, Auschwitz in Poland, a country where there was much anti-semitism, including an anti-semitic purge in 1968, was presented as a symbol of Christian, Polish resistance. Jewish victims were not mentioned, and the museum there, on which work began in 1947 as a memorial to the "martyrdom of the Polish nation and other nations," was used to disseminate a Communist view of events. This was also the case with the International Auschwitz Committee established in 1954. Polish and Soviet publications made mention of the large numbers killed, without identifying the fact that many were Jews. In part, this reflected the argument that Communism, a movement that supposedly was axiomatically opposed to religious or racial prejudice, took precedence over other identities. In this light, Jews should not be treated as separate. Thus, Babi Yar outside Kiev, where 33,771 Jews were killed by the Germans in three days in 1941, was presented as the site of the slaughter of "peaceful Soviet citizens." The inscription there did not mention Jews.[29] Auschwitz I, not Auschwitz II, the site of the killing of most of the Jews, was for a while the only part of Auschwitz that could be visited. The *Historical Atlas of Poland* (1981), a state-approved work, claimed that over six million Polish citizens were killed during the war, without giving a figure for the Jews. It also stated that in Auschwitz, people "of various nationalities" perished, which overlooked the very large numbers of European Jews transported there to be slaughtered.[30]

Alongside the destruction of the past and the devastation of academic life and principles due to totalitarianism and war, came the creation of new networks due to both. German and Soviet expansionism led to such networks, with compliant historians appointed and promoted accordingly. War strengthened the scholarly networks within the British Empire[31] as well as leading to a growth in personal connections between British and American historians and between each and the country of the other. This led to an historians' Anglosphere as part of a wider intellectual, cultural, and political affinity. This historical Anglosphere was linked to a serious weakening of former intellectual and academic ties with Germany, and remained strong until the 1960s saw in a new intellectual world. In this new world, ideas of history linked to French scholarship, initially the *Annales* school, were to the fore, while the coherence of the Anglosphere was affected by generational change, anti-Americanism in the era of the Vietnam War, and the declining role of Britain in its former empire.

Of all the academic subjects, history, throughout the twentieth century and across the world, proved particularly important to government, and subject to government intervention, because history was so bound up with presentations of national interest. This was true of right-wing regimes, which tended to look to the past as a framework of reference. Their left-wing counterparts were concerned to annex the process of change to their ideology, and presented the past, accordingly, as a demonstration of the need for, and nature of, change.

At the same time, political pressure on academics did not only come from governments. Within the academic community, there was frequently a marginalization of unfashionable opinions, which was a long-standing process. For example, Charles Beard (1874–1948), a prominent American historian of the Progressive Era, was vilified by prominent liberal historians such as Samuel Eliot Morison and Arthur Schlesinger Jr. for 1944 and 1948 studies that were critical of President Franklin Delano Roosevelt (r. 1931–1945). By systematically trying to destroy his reputation they, allegedly, blatantly disregarded his academic freedom.[32] The same process can be seen today. Work that is unfashionable and unwanted is frequently slighted or ignored, not least by resting unreviewed; and this process undermines the self-presentation of the academic community and academic practice as meritocratic. In the case of the United States, the attack on Beard reflected, in part, serious problems with his work, but the attack also arose from the cult of the American consensus that characterized the dominant strand of liberal history.

Socio-economic changes were also important in the changing response to the past. For example, Reba Soffer has suggested that support for conservative historical perspectives was weakened by austerity after World War II. Moreover, in the subsequent prosperity of the 1950s, the future became more attractive than the past to great numbers of people whose past was not nearly as comfortable as their present.[33]

Many historiographical arguments were played out with reference to political controversies of the day. This was particularly so with the intellectual struggle between Marxist and non-Marxist interpretations, which was often (although far from invariably) an adjunct of the Cold War between the Communist bloc and its opponents. Marxist readings tended to be offered by those who were on the Left, although not all were members of the Communist Party, or at all sympathetic to the Soviet Union. The reading of the French Revolution very much reflected this tension. French Communist scholars, such as Albert Soboul, professor at the Sorbonne from 1966 to 1982, were keen advocates of a Marxist interpretation of the Revolution, seeing it as a bourgeois victory over, first, the old order of the *ancien régime* and, then, popular radicalism. In contrast, revisionists, such as François Furet, contested this interpretation, both by challenging the Marxist account and by arguing the need to move away from a socio-economic account of the Revolution.

Whatever the faults of the academic world in the West, the situation was far more dire in authoritarian societies, notably because there was room for considerable debate in the West over how best to study history – debate that continues to the present day.[34] The impact of totalitarianism was such that the overthrow across much of Europe of Fascism in 1943–1945 was a major step, as was that of Southern European right-wing authoritarian dictatorships in Greece, Portugal, and Spain in 1973–1976, and of Communism in Eastern Europe and the Soviet Union in 1989–1991. The overthrow of Fascism did not bring liberty to Eastern

Europe, which, instead, came under a Communist tyranny for over four decades, but, elsewhere, the overthrow of totalitarianism brought a freedom that proved highly conducive to debate over history. This freedom was in part expressed, indeed contested, in such debate. These were not the sole political developments that were of significance, but they were highly important.

The significance of these developments can be grasped by assessing the situation in China, where a Communist dictatorship remains to this day. China's inability to cope with its recent history is striking. In particular, there is a determination to hide the Tiananmen Square massacre of 1989, with the state using force to end pro-democracy uprisings. As such, the episode was a historical crux of the legitimacy of rule by the Chinese Communist Party, one that led Bill Clinton to argue that this party had forever put itself on the wrong side of history. The reports of the unrest were highly misleading, and rewriting was followed by excising the episode. This proved particularly effective for cities outside Beijing, where there were foreign journalists; for example, Chengdu, where the unrest and its brutal suppression long remained hidden. Moreover, no public discussion is permitted – a situation enforced by Internet censors in order to reinforce collective amnesia. Thus, in 2013, Li Weiguo, an activist who applied for permission to hold a candlelight vigil, was detained and interrogated by the police, while, in 2014, a private symposium held in Beijing to commemorate the 25th anniversary led to interrogations and detentions. Most students today cannot identify the iconic photograph of a man standing in front of a column of tanks near the square. Moreover, most young Chinese know nothing about the massacre or understand it solely in terms of the party's propaganda about its role and past.[35]

Outside the context of Communism, there was, from the early 2000s, a revival of authoritarianism in post-Communist Russia, and this affected the presentation of history. For example, the end of Communist rule in 1991 had been followed by the establishment of a museum covering the *gulags*. Located on the site of a Stalin-era labor camp, Perm-36 recorded the fate of the dissidents incarcerated there until the end of Communism. After 2012, when Vladimir Putin became president again, a supporter, Viktor Basargin, was appointed the local governor. Having cut regional finances and raised taxes, he removed funding altogether in 2014, and the museum, without water or electricity, closed.

AFTER AUTHORITARIANISM

The fall of authoritarian regimes, whether domestic or foreign in origin, provided an opportunity not only for rewriting the past but also for re-thinking history and its presentation as processes. The symbolic potency of history was exemplified in the fate of statues, for example those of the imperial powers, most of which were rapidly removed.[36] Moreover, there was a challenge to move on, from redressing the picture offered by such regimes, to offering a new account that incorporated the authoritarian and post-authoritarian regimes as part of a larger story.

Contested narratives, and the complexities involved in the con-struction of historical reputation,[37] emerged in all states, and not only in countries where authoritarian regimes had recently collapsed. They were also the case in states with a longer experience of democratic practice, with contested episodes of the past providing opportunities for the ex-pression of political tensions. Indeed, this led in many cases to the propa-gation of inaccurate views that expressed these tensions. The German massacre of 335 civilians outside Rome on 24–25 March 1944 provided an instance, as hostility on the part of some commentators to the Re-sistance led to a tendency to blame it for German reprisals, an approach that underplayed the viciousness of German policy. Historical engage-ment also plays other roles. Alessandro Portelli wrote his analysis of the episode and the subsequent response in reaction to the painting – on the day in 1994 that Silvio Berlusconi, the right-wing candidate, was elected Prime Minister – of a swastika across the memorial to others massacred by the Germans on 4 June 1944.[38] At a far less consequential level, my choice of the word German rather than Nazi to describe the massacre and reprisals reflects my view that use of the word Nazi in some way lessens the role of German society and the German Army as a whole in World War II, including in the murderous policies pursued by Germans, many of whom were not members of the Nazi Party.

Would-be nations and states also sponsored histories underlining their distinctive character, especially with reference to the nations and states they were trying to reject. This process continues, for example with Catalonia and Scotland, both would-be states for much of their populations, and East Timor, a state that gained independence only in 2002. However, the intensity of the process also varies, not least with relation to political developments.[39] The same was true of the response of the other nation/state in the relationship, as with shifting English views of Scotland.[40] Moreover, as in Ireland, notably with its Nationalists and Unionists, competing senses of identity offered room for different narratives of the past, while present developments provided opportunities for restating accounts of the past.[41] Whatever the circumstances, the call to make history was as one with an annexation of it for political purposes. Thus, in Greece during the European elections in 2014, Alexis Tsipras, leader of the radical-Left Syriza Party, opponents of austerity, declared at an election rally: "The will of the Greek people will sweep away those who are selling out our country. Our people are going to make history!"[42]

ACADEMIC HISTORIOGRAPHY

Compared to developments such as the fall of Communism, the issues that dominate conventional accounts of historiography, for example the rise from 1929 (and subsequent decline) of the *Annales* school,[43] or, later, of post-modernism, appear of only limited significance, and certainly so outside academe. Post-modernist assertions of the lack of objective and authoritative truth mean as little to most people as the idea of an absence of intrinsic meaning. That historians write and, therefore, create does not worry (or surprise) most readers. However, at the theoretical level, this process of creation leads to continuing disputes over the nature of evidence and the possibilities of recovering the past.[44] Objectivity is only one of the battlegrounds. Furthermore, an argument for the lack of objective and authoritative truth does not prevent historical work by means of the testing of ideas and the advancing of judgments.

In contrast to an earlier tradition, bypassing theoretical reflections and explicit engagement with issues of explanation,[45] a tradition readily apparent in much nineteenth-century academic work, many of the cutting-edge historical thinkers of the twentieth century engaged explicitly with theory and, linked to this, were greatly affected by developments in other disciplines. As a result, historiography came to appear as a branch of modern intellectual history. This process gathered pace in the profession from the 1960s. Even prior to that, the methodological professionalism that was so important to academic historians was often open to developments in other subjects, as with the application by Lewis Namier (1888–1960) of his interest in psychology to his work on eighteenth-century English high politics, notably with his books *The Structure of Politics at the Accession of George III* (1929) and *England in the Age of the American Revolution* (1930). Similarly, economic historians were greatly influenced by economic theory.[46] Namier's life and career reflected the role of politics. Born in Russian Poland to a Jewish family that had become Catholic, Namier left Poland in part due to anti-semitism. He was educated at Oxford, but, in 1911, failed to obtain both a fellowship at All Soul's and posts at the University of Toronto because he was Jewish. In contrast, Ernest Llewellyn Woodward, a Protestant, was a fellow at All Soul's from 1919 until 1944. An expert adviser at the Foreign Office during World War I, Namier argued in favor of the subject nationalities within the Austrian Empire, publishing *The Case of Bohemia* (1917) and *The Czecho-Slovaks: an Oppressed Nationality* (1917). An active Zionist, he acted as a liaison officer between the Jewish Agency and the British government during World War II. From 1931 until retirement in 1953, Namier was professor of modern history at the University of Manchester.[47]

The disciplines affecting historical method in the 1960s included economics, sociology, psychology, and anthropology, the last two encouraging a focus on collective feelings and related views of culture. The journal *Annales: Histoire, Sciences Sociales,* the self-consciously innovative exponent of new ideas in French historiography founded in 1929, published sociologists, geographers, and economists as well as historians. Reacting against the previous positivist historiography, with its focus on the accumulation of facts and its dominant concern with the political elite, the *Annalistes* pursued what they presented as a "total history" based on an understanding of the interactions of geographical, social, economic, and cultural contexts and developments. In the preface to the first edition of his path-breaking study of the Mediterranean world in the late sixteenth century, published in 1949, Fernand Braudel described the history of events as the "crests of foam that the tides of history carry on their strong back," while his preface to the second edition, written in 1963, asked "Is it possible somehow to convey simultaneously both that conspicuous history which holds our attention by its continual and dramatic changes – and that other, submerged, history, almost silent and always discreet, virtually unsuspected either by its observers or its participants, which is little touched by the obstinate erosion of time?"[48]

In the *Annalistes'* approach, the conditions, lives, and beliefs of the bulk of the population were of central importance. The concern of the *Annales* school with the idea of *mentalités* led to an interest in psychology and anthropology, both of which provided a guide to the collective unconscious.[49] For example, folktales and legends became topics of research affecting the study of witchcraft and other topics.[50] This process underlined the extent to which changing notions of meaning provided opportunities as well as challenges for the process of historical research. As a result, the objectivity of myth, its existence as a subject at once real and different, posed problems for the myth of objectivity.[51] In the case of French politics, the role of myth and belief was strongly demonstrated in the reputation of General de Gaulle, the president from 1958 to 1969,[52] although most scholarly work by the *Annales* school did not display a direct engagement with contemporary politics.

The shift to a social history focused on *mentalités* reflected the social history of the profession, notably the rise of younger scholars with a culture and ideology different to that of their forbears. There was more than one iteration of this process, but the expansion of the university sector in much of the world in the 1960s proved particularly significant. That episode brought together factors often seen as in a complex and sometimes competing relationship, notably structure, culture, and agency. The net effect was of a major change in historiographical content and method.

NEW CULTURAL HISTORY

The new social history was followed by the new cultural history.[53] This drew heavily upon developments in linguistic theory and employed them to probe issues of identity, power, and meaning, both of what happened and of how it was to be understood. Prominent Western theorists

whose insights were employed and works cited included Jacques Derrida, Michel Foucault, Clifford Geertz, and Jürgen Habermas; and theory itself was pushed to the fore in much, but by no means all, Western
academic historical scholarship. Information as an objective ideal and
progressive practice was affected by the problematizing of meaning and
power by Derrida (1930–2004) and Foucault (1926–1984), respectively.
Each emphasized the subjectivity of disciplines and categories, and the
extent to which they reflected and sustained social norms. Ironically, in
critiquing power, these critics and their supporters gained and deployed
considerable academic power of their own. This movement encouraged
a degree of intellectual introspection and skepticism, notably in terms
of the values of the categories used by historians, such as nations.[54] In
turn, cultural history, like social history, has been affected by fresh theoretical ideas.[55] Few have translated well to non-academic audiences.

Cultural approaches came to play a major role in other fields, for example military history. Culture is a much-employed term there; for, aside
from the culture of society as a whole, including why people fought and
how they responded to the issues and experience of conflict, on which
there has been excellent work for the American Civil War,[56] there is also
the organizational culture of particular militaries, a topic that overlaps
with sociology. This category, which includes issues such as hierarchy,
discipline, and the responsiveness of subordinates to responsibilities,
illustrates the widespread applicability of the concept of culture and
of related terms and vocabulary.

There is also the concept of strategic culture, employed to discuss
the context within which military tasks were "shaped," a concept that
overlaps with that of strategic landscapes, and a topic that interacts with
issues raised in international relations studies.[57] For example, it has been
argued, notably from the 1970s, that China's strategic culture was primarily defensive and focused on protecting its frontiers, but there has
also been a critique of the notion of a defensive, Confucian, strategic
culture, seeing instead longstanding expansionist themes in Chinese
strategic culture, notably at the expense of steppe peoples. This issue is
regarded as of considerable pertinence at present, although it may also
be asked how far a discussion of Chinese war making in, say, the eighteenth century is of relevance today, in what is a very different political

context, both domestic and international, as well as with regard to the nature of war. In this context, it is clear that there have been significant changes before, notably the contrast between early and (more defensive) late Ming war making, and that between late Ming and (more aggressive) Manchu attitudes. Scholars debating Islam as a strategic culture raise a host of similar points, notably, for the early twentieth century, the tension between pan-Arabism and pan-Turkish ideas. The use of culture as an argument for essentialism, and as a vocabulary suggesting a core identity, can therefore be misleading. Its use approximates to earlier and current discussions of distinctive ways of war, in particular the notion of an American culture of war. This notion draws on the longstanding presentation of an American exceptionalism,[58] an approach, however, that can be misleading and can serve to justify a lack of knowledge of events elsewhere, by both students and academics.

More generally, there is a danger that culture becomes, like technology, an overused term. Such usage would be another aspect of a more general poverty of historiography in the field of military history, a poverty highlighted by the ethnogenesis apparently offered in some cultural interpretations of warfare. Moreover, it is valuable to draw attention to the culture of military history itself. Dennis Showalter noted in 2002 that "military history is arguably the last stronghold of . . . the 'Whig interpretation' . . . [it] sees the development of warfare as progressive."[59] In practice, culture is dynamic as both a reality and an analytical process. A key development in cultural history has been the rise of scholarly interest in collective memory.[60] This has become both a significant theme and an important method. Broadly conceived, cultural influences notably emerge clearly in the writing of history, including military, political, and economic history. Culture also overlaps with other types of history as with the discussion of the chivalric society of medieval Europe in terms of the history of masculinities. Thus, culture needs to be tackled as a dynamic and problematic phenomenon, whereas the standard approach in history is to employ less refined concepts of culture as an overarching, one-dimensional, and fixed set of objective ideas, a practice long challenged within the social sciences. Furthermore, in history, not everything is cultural, much as not everything cultural is of relevance to specialists in other fields.

CONCLUSIONS

Alongside these thematic developments in historiography came partly related geographical ones, especially a greater focus on areas that had hitherto been largely neglected by outside historians, notably Africa where the first generation of Africa's professional historians came to the fore with independence in the 1950s and 1960s.[61] These areas posed distinctive methodological problems, in part due to the nature of the sources, not least the role of oral history and the difficulty of establishing chronology. This process involved the need to reconcile the approaches taken by African historians with those taken by non-African scholars, as well as the need to bring together regional and continental perspectives.[62] There was also the problem of responding to ethnicity, which was, in part, created by politicians through the manipulation of collective identities.[63]

The rise of analyses of global power, notably the world's systems theory advanced by Immanuel Wallerstein, was also significant. This economic account was to be followed by the use of globalization as a setting for discussion of a range of social and cultural topics, particularly race and migration. Sub-sets of the global dimension were offered by other areas in which transnational themes could be probed, for example the so-called Atlantic world. That ocean and its surrounding lands became a setting for accounts of race,[64] gender, and class. In contrast, conventional scholarly parameters and aspects of imperial activity, for example military and high political, were discarded or dramatically rewritten. Globalization as a topic, approach, and mentality also offered means and cause for historiographical controversy over purpose in history, in particular with debates over the value of Western expansion, the British Empire, and liberal economics. These debates were directly linked to engagement with modern world politics. They certainly proved a way, for both supporters and critics, to contest the American role, notably in the 2000s and 2010s.[65]

As far as non-academic history was concerned in recent decades, key changes in the media have been significant. In particular, the shift from literary to visual history was important, with the rise of cinema and television followed by internet games. Visual sources, such as photographs and films, can readily create false memories.[66] History through film, often inaccurate,[67] helped provide different accounts, leading to contrasting readings, a stress on other issues, and, indeed, challenges to ideas of historical progress.[68] As a separate point, the rise of the visual has redefined the nature of the generalist, for to be able to perform on television has in recent decades, and notably from the 2000s, been increasingly significant for commentators on history, in appearing to offer validation as well as to secure public attention. Looking to the future, this rise of the visual – at least on screen – will be of growing importance for historiography. A key element will be the greater understanding of the extent to which the nature of the visual media, and the relevant institutional and commercial imperatives, all play a role in what appears.[69]

SIX

New States and the Possibilities of Lineage

THE MUSEUM OF DESIGN IN LISBON OCCUPIES THE CENTRAL site of the former bank that handled the currencies of Portugal's colonies, its extensive African Empire. In the former bank's lobby, there is a colorful and large wall mosaic from 1962 depicting Portugal's colonization of Africa from the fifteenth century. This colonialization is presented in benign terms, with friars teaching natives, other natives farming, and the Portuguese soldiers not shown engaged in any violent acts. Ethnic harmony, progress, and Christian proselytization under Portuguese leadership are the key themes. Attractive, misleading, but convenient for Portugal which, in fact, in 1962, was confronting the outbreak the previous year in its major colony, Angola, of a revolutionary war for independence from colonial rule. One-time imperial powers have to respond to a loss of empire, as Portugal did from 1975. The mosaic is now a curious decoration, one that possibly would have been swept aside were it not fixed in position.

However, new states, such as Angola from 1975, face the very different problem of replacing earlier histories and establishing a workable past. This process is designed to help provide both identity and legitimacy, and is seen as an aspect – generally a crucial aspect – of the winning, and sustaining, of independence, not only nominal independence but also an independence from former links. The workable past that is presented is exemplary in a partisan fashion. Episodes that reveal a different reality are ignored. Thus, in Angola, the Popular Movement for the Liberation of Angola (MPLA), a Marxist insurrectionary movement supported by the Soviet Union and Cuba, which gained power in 1975, was opposed by the American and South African–backed National Union for the Total Independence of Angola (UNITA), but also faced opposition from dissidents within the MPLA who were against the dictatorial rule of Agostinho Neto. In 1977, the regime crushed a demonstration, presenting it as an attempted coup by MPLA "factionalists." Between 2,000 and 90,000 Angolans were then slaughtered as Neto consolidated his control, with Cuban forces playing a role in the carnage. The resulting culture of silence was linked to this becoming a massacre that was remembered by Angolans but lacked any public attention. With foreign commentators largely supportive of the MPLA because they were critical of UNITA (and, in many cases, left-wing), the massacre failed to attract foreign attention until very recently.[1]

Between 1945 and 1975, much of the world, especially in Africa, South and South-East Asia, and Oceania, gained independence from imperial rule. This change meant that the states in these regions had to create public histories. The task was made more difficult by the repeated attempt, as part of this process, to substantiate, indeed establish, a lineage that spanned the period of Western imperial rule so as to link newly independent states to pre-imperial predecessors and thus to expand their history. This chapter looks first at Asia, and then at Africa, where independence was (largely) won later, before offering some general conclusions.

As in Europe earlier in the century, the creation of public history did not begin with a clean slate. Indeed, there was often a fatal intertwining between the creation of this history, the winning of independence, and the justification of the position of the new governing regime. The regime tended to regard these processes as the same, so that the political purpose of the public history did not strike it as illegitimate. Far from it. Indeed, there was a clear-cut pattern of involvement in this history by public intellectuals who benefited directly from their links to the regime. A major aspect of this commitment was an exemplary and extensive account of the process by which independence had been obtained. This can be seen, for example, in states as varied as India, Indonesia, Israel, and South Africa. The role of particular individuals and groups in this process was employed to justify their subsequent prominence in national life.

INDIA

Thus, in India, the Congress Party could be presented as both cause and end of independence. There was an emphasis on the Congress Party's "Quit India" campaign in 1942 in leading to British withdrawal five years later. In practice, this was a disingenuous account, however, that greatly underplayed the role of British governmental policy in leading to independence. So also with the emphasis on Mahatma Gandhi and his non-violent resistance to British rule.

Not only was recent history presented anew in India. There was also a far more critical account of India's history under British rule, as well as an attempt to argue that India had a cultural unity that predated British rule – an account that is highly flawed. The criticism entailed minimizing the value and creativity of British rule, as well as applauding those who opposed it and ignoring the many who cooperated, not least by serving in the army. Thus, aside from arguing that Indian resources were used to help Britain expand its empire, empire was presented in India as a vehicle for British plunder and economic exploitation, and therefore as an economic burden that delayed the development of the country and affected subsequent views of it. In place of the British emphasis on progress toward modernity under colonial rule, came criticism of the latter.

This criticism was linked to a rewriting of episodes in the conflicts of imperial conquest, in particular, Indian atrocities, which had been discussed by the British in part in justification of their claim to be superior, and, therefore, as an excuse to justify imperial rule. A prominent instance was the Black Hole of Calcutta, in which Siraj-ud-daula, the Nawab of Bengal, had, in 1756, imprisoned with fatal results British captives from the East India Company base at Calcutta.[2] So also with the treatment of British women and children during the "Indian Mutiny" of 1857–1859, particularly the massacre at Kanpur. Now, the emphasis has moved, instead, to British atrocities, as with the treatment of captured sepoys (Indian soldiers) during the Mutiny. The latter itself was reinterpreted and renamed as a rebellion that was intended to begin a war of independence. The role of religious sectarianism in this rebellion was downplayed. Calcutta itself has been renamed Kolkata.

Twentieth-century Indian history was a matter of contention from the outset, with disagreement over how far, and how best, to present Indian pressure for autonomy and, subsequently, independence. The perception of this pressure, and of the response to it, was an aspect of the politics of the period and subsequently. For example, Udham Singh, a Sikh living in Britain, was executed for killing Sir Michael O'Dwyer, the former governor of the Punjab, in 1940 as a response to the Amritsar Massacre of protestors in 1919. He was treated as a hero by many Indian contemporaries, and has since been seen in the same light. Indeed, an annual conference is held in his memory. At a different scale, the failure to prevent famine in World War II Bengal in 1943 was castigated,[3] without adequate attention being devoted to the logistical problems facing Britain as well as the disruption to the rice trade arising from Japan's conquest of Burma (Myanmar) in 1942. In addition, positive attention focused on Indian politicians who advanced the cause of independence, and not on those who cooperated with the British against Japan during the war. Moreover, Indian state-building, in the 1940s and subsequently, was in part based on a suppression of rival nationalisms, a process often neglected, underplayed, or misrepresented in India. This was done on a variety of scales: within India, at the level of India as a whole, and in South Asia, where Pakistan in particular suffered.[4]

INDONESIA AND MALAYSIA

In Indonesia, as in India with the British, the winning of independence from the Dutch in 1949 after an insurrection was followed by praise of earlier opposition to the Dutch. Indeed, Dutch rule was presented as an occupation. As with other states, there was also felt to be the need for a historical backing for unity. Achmail Sukarno, the nationalist who became president in 1949, was convinced that history had a crucial role in the assertion of Indonesian identity. Because the state was, in practice, the product of a brief period of Dutch imperialism, and the word Indonesia was only coined in the nineteenth century, there was a need for a unifying ideology when that imperial control was removed. As part of this ideology, the longevity of the concept of Indonesia was asserted, and misleadingly so, with precursors sought, such as the fourteenth-century Javanese empire of Majapahit.

As with other newly independent states, there was also a stress in Indonesia on national history, rather than on the regional dimension. The latter was particularly unwelcome given episodes of regional separatism which, in Indonesia, occurred in Sumatra, Sulawesi, Indonesian Borneo, and West Irian. Indeed, Indonesia was in part a greater Java that adopted a convenient identity and sought to deploy a history accordingly, a process also seen with other states. Over a much longer time-scale, this included Western states, notably Brazil, France, Spain, Scotland, and, back to the tenth century, England.

In Malaysia, the emphasis, again, was not on the separate historical identities of its constituent parts. Instead, efforts were made both to assert unity in Malaya and to find common strands with the Malaysian part of Borneo. This process involved underplaying other historical links, notably within Borneo and between northern Malaya and Thailand. In both Indonesia and Malaysia, the attempt to overcome regional consciousness was linked to the multi-ethnic and multi-religious character of these far-reaching states. Thus, a new national identity was not simply a matter of justifying the state but also of creating a new commitment that moved beyond these real and potential divisions.

THE PHILIPPINES

In their commemoration of the past, states frequently focused on the experience of oppression and conquest. A Spanish colony, at least in part, from the 1560s, the Philippines became an American colony after Spain was defeated in 1898. The Filipino nationalist movement was suppressed by America, as was regional separatism, notably in the Islamic south. In turn, having been a semi-autonomous commonwealth, the Philippines became fully independent in 1946, but it was long in the shadow of American power. As a result, it proved easier and less contentious to provide an appropriate image by focusing on opposition to Spanish rule. The situation would have been different had there been a successful rebellion against American rule or influence.

The stress on opposition to Spain is particularly apparent in the capital, Manila, with a focus there on the fate of José Rizal, a nationalist writer who had denounced Spanish rule, only to be executed in 1896. The site of the execution is now part of Rizal Park, which houses the Rizal Memorial and another commemorating three priests executed for their alleged role in the Cavite uprising of 1872 against Spanish rule. Prior to his execution, Rizal was held in Fort Santiago, the seat of colonial power. Part of this much-visited site is devoted to his imprisonment, notably with the Rizal Shrine, where he spent his last hours. Visitors to the National Library see one of his original works. Elsewhere in the city are the Rizal Memorial Complex, Rizal Street, and so on. In addition to Spanish oppression, evidence of the cruelty of the Japanese occupation of the Philippines in 1942–1945 is not hidden. Both periods serve to provide an appropriate basis for national identity, as with the references in the Chinese Cemetery in Manila to the sufferings of the Chinese-Filipino community during the Japanese occupation and its role in resisting Japan. These episodes underline the role of the community as good Filipinos.

KOREA AND TAIWAN

Thus, it was not only Western imperialism that was at issue. The collapse of the Japanese Empire in 1945 meant the withdrawal of Japanese troops from China and the end of Japanese control over both Taiwan and Korea – although neither had an uncomplicated passage toward sovereign independence. Korea was initially divided between rival nationalists who led a Communist north and a capitalist south. After a Communist insurrection in the south, and then the full-scale Korean War (1950–1953) begun by an invasion by North Korean forces, Korea was more fixedly divided between a Communist dictatorship in the north and a pro-Western south. Each struggled to define both an acceptable account for themselves and also one that would work for the whole of Korea, which each claimed to represent. Present-day purpose was to be vindicated in part by the use of history. This process led to opposition to China over the latter's claim on part of what both North and South Korea saw as their history. They agree that the Koguryo Kingdom (37 BCE–668 CE) was one of Korea's founding kingdoms, and that its territory included part of northeast China. However, in 2002, the Beijing-based Centre for the Study of Borderland History and Geography took forward Chinese academic claims that Koguryo was in essence a Chinese state. This was unacceptable to both North and South Korea, and the resulting contention saw the customary range of sites of dispute. These included contested monuments as well as natural sites, specifically Mount Paektu, a key icon of Korean history, as well as textbooks. In the latter, South Korea argues that the Kojoson kingdom started much earlier than its Koguryo counterparty, a backward extrapolation of distinct Korean history designed to make the Koguryo issue less central.

This dispute related not solely to the question of the longevity of Korea as a separate culture and political entity, but also to its extent. The context was one of the longstanding Korean effort to maneuver for position between the two stronger, and competing, regional powers, China and Japan. In the absence of any system akin to the Western practice, derived from the Peace of Westphalia of 1648, of accepting the full claims to sovereignty of all states, Korea had had to struggle to advance a claim to full sovereignty – the latter understood in terms of legitimacy. The result was an acute sensitivity to the content and presentation of the historical legacy. Japan's conquest of Korea in the 1890s made relations with Japan particularly difficult.

Taiwan was returned by Japan to China in 1945, only for the Nationalist Chinese regime of Jiang Jieshi to flee there four years later when it was driven from mainland China. The Nationalists then faced the problem of presenting a different account of Chinese history while only controlling a small portion of it. Eventually, there was the contrasting issue of reaching out toward the establishment of a national historical tradition for Taiwan itself. The latter led, in the 2000s, to a rejection not only of rule from Communist Beijing, but also of the Nationalist legacy, not least the previous hero status of Jiang Jieshi. His statues were removed, for example from military bases, and there was a widespread process of renaming, which included streets as well as the international airport.

As so often, anniversaries also proved a key issue. In this case, the 228 Incident is central. On 28 February 1947, protests in Taiwan against rule by the Nationalists were violently suppressed, leading to the slaughter of possibly 28,000 people. The sixtieth anniversary commemoration in 2007 provided an opportunity for the Democratic Progressive Party, the pro-independence government, to criticize Chiang and the Nationalists, whose Kuomintang Party remains powerful. The latter were portrayed as an outside force suppressing a popular movement in 1947. Indeed, tension in Taiwan over rule from Beijing had been an important feature before the period of Japanese rule. Marking the anniversary in 2007, the government changed a key site of national memorialization, the Jiang Jieshi Memorial Hall. Renamed the Taiwan Democracy Memorial Hall, its perimeter wall was removed in order to underline its democratic accessibility. These and other moves symbolized a break with the past that was also a rejection of the link with Chinese identity and, thus, with mainland China. This is a contentious theme and policy that plays a key role in Taiwanese politics. The contrast with the Chinese failure to recall the 1989 Tiananmen Square uprising is readily apparent. History is only one of the elements that is affected in Taiwan. So too is language, not least the system used for Romanizing Chinese words. Hostility to employing the system used in China is an aspect of opposition to reunification with China.

ISRAEL AND PALESTINE

A distinctive instance of Asian post-colonial history was presented by Israel; not that Israelis, who regard themselves as part of the West, generally appreciate being placed geographically in Asia. Similarly, Estonians regard themselves as Western European, although geographically part of Eastern Europe. In Israel, the focus was not on a long period of anti-imperial struggle, because it was the British who had driven out the Ottoman Turks in 1917–1918, ending an imperial rule that had begun in that case in 1516 (replacing the earlier, Egyptian-based, Mameluke empire), while the key opposition to the British in the 1930s, the Arab Rising, had been led by the Palestinians and not by Jews.

Furthermore, much of the Jewish heritage and claim were European in origin, rather than unambiguously Asian. Although much is made of the Biblical status of the Jews in modern-day Israel, with independence in 1948 seen as the reestablishment of a Third Jewish Commonwealth, the Holocaust also plays a central role in Israeli self-identification. This was notably so with the establishment in 1953 of Yad Vashem in Jerusalem as "The Memorial Authority for the Holocaust and Heroism," a Holocaust Memorial, museum, and archive, and with the seizure and trial of Adolf Eichmann, a major Nazi war criminal, in 1960–1962. The foundation of Israel is widely seen as a key episode in Jewish escape and recovery from the Holocaust. All Jews killed in the Holocaust were granted "memorial citizenship" in Israel in 1953. Israel itself was presented as the safeguard against another Holocaust, as it was to be the safe haven of all Jews and a land in which, under the "right of return," all Jews could become citizens.

In the Israeli context, the Holocaust was given a distinctive historical context. The theme of Jews as fighting back linked the brave, but doomed, defense of Masada against the Romans in 73[5] to the Warsaw ghetto uprising in 1943. This theme sought to counter the feeling, not least in Israel where there was criticism among Zionists from the Diaspora,[6] that, due to passive acquiescence, not enough had been done by Jews to resist the Holocaust, and that the Jews, and therefore Israelis, appeared in some fashion weak. Designated in 1951, Holocaust Day marks the anniversary of the 1943 uprising and is actually Holocaust and Heroism Day, a reflection of the stress on the need to fight back. In the Yad Vashem museum, armed resistance to Nazism is seen as an exemplary episode.

The extendable meaning of the Holocaust was also indicated when it was used as a symbol of the travails of the Jews through history. For Israel, this ensured that an account of the Holocaust that had most meaning for the large numbers of Jews who had emigrated there as refugees from Europe in the late 1940s, and that had played a key role in Israel's early history, could also be a crucial identifier for the large number of Jewish refugees from Muslim countries who became proportionately more important in the 1970s and 1980s. Similarly, in France, the large number of Jewish immigrants from the former colonies of Morocco, Algeria, and Tunisia, who arrived in the 1960s, absorbed the travails of the Jews of metropolitan France during the Vichy years as an aspect of their history. Israeli pressure on behalf of persecuted foreign communities of Jews, such as those of Ethiopia, reflected not only the traditional obligation and practice of helping fellow Jews, but also the impact of Holocaust consciousness.

In the face of the hostility, from 1948, of Arab states, which, at the least, intended the ethnic cleansing of Jews, if not genocide, the Israeli emphasis on the sufferings and endurance of the Jews was not matched by adequate consideration of the plight of the roughly 760,000 Palestinian refugees, or of the extent to which, in what the Palestinians called the *nakhba* (catastrophe), they had been forcibly driven out of their homes in what is now Israel. This provides an alternative account of grievance about Israel to that which focuses on the Israeli territorial gains in the Six Days' War in 1967, and one that is less subject to apparent compromise than the 1967 gains, which are apparently easier to reverse, as when Israel evacuated first Sinai and then the Gaza Strip. The Palestinian claim to a "right of return" has proved particularly problematic, and has directed attention to the circumstances in which the refugees left. The contentious nature of the historical legacy of Arab-Israeli relations was illustrated by the controversies caused in Israel by historians who exposed "ethnic cleansing," sometimes murderous, by the Israelis in 1948, for example in the town of Lydda. At the same time, the relatively liberal nature of Israel was indicated by its ability to conduct such a debate.[7] In contrast, in its illiberal neighbors, there was no such willingness to consider similar episodes; for example, Egypt's treatment of its Coptic minority. As part of the competitive process of grievance, Jewish settlers in Hebron refer to the massacre of their predecessors by Arabs in 1929.

As a related point that focused on an apparent ranking of achievement by ethnic groups, as well as on a teleology based on performance, the Israeli position was defended by the association of progress with Zionism, specifically the paternalist argument that Jewish settlers had made fertile land that had been neglected and mishandled by the Palestinians. This argument depended on an account of environmental development that was historicized by reference to alleged earlier neglect.

Aside from the true nature of the *nakhba*, another lacuna in Israeli history was the sometime reluctance to consider the role of terrorism in the process by which Zionists challenged the British Mandate, for example the bombing of the King David hotel in Jerusalem in 1946. This point was more pertinent because, from 1976 to 1983, the Prime Minister,

Menachem Begin, had been the head of the *Irgun Zwei Leumi,* the military wing of the Revisionist Zionist Movement, while Yitzhak Shamir, his successor as Prime Minister (1983–1984, 1986–1992), was a member of the more radical *Lohamei Herut Yisrael,* which was called by the British the Stern Gang. Streets were named after members of the group, and Yair, the *nom de guerre* of Avraham Stern, served as a name for Kochav Yair, a West Bank settlement, as well as for the sons of prominent right-wing figures.[8]

The Holocaust provides a potent historical frame of reference for considering Israel's predicament in the face of Islamic hostility, one that has an existential character. The Holocaust leads to a call for perpetual vigilance. Reference to the Holocaust also acts against suggestions of compromise. Thus, pressure for action against Iran in the 2000s and 2010s as it developed its nuclear capacity made reference to Nazi policy, as with Prime Minister Binyamin Netanyahu's "It is 1938, and Iran is Germany." This was a pointed reference to the Appeasement of Nazi Germany, which apparently served to locate Iran as well as those in the West who did not share Israeli views or match its pressure for action. The reference was not accepted by the Obama administration in the United States. However, Mahmoud Ahmadinejad, the president of Iran from 2005 to 2013, scarcely eased the situation by referring in 2005 to the Holocaust as a "fairy tale" serving Israeli ends. This claim echoed the ludicrous argument that Israel or the United States, or a combination thereof, was responsible for the 11 September 2001 attacks on New York and Washington. To refer to these totally unfounded claims as mad is to be unfair to the insane, but these claims are frequently repeated. Indeed, in Naples, Italy, in 2014, I was amazed to hear otherwise intelligent people express them.

AFRICA

Israel looked back to a biblical past of Jewish statehood. On a very different timescale, in Africa, the dissolution of European empires led to the creation of new states that sought to appropriate a pre-colonial past in order to establish an exemplary history. This was a contrast to the position taken by Latin American states after they gained independence in the nineteenth century: their ruling elites did not identify with the bulk of the population, much of which was descended from indigenous people or African slaves; but, instead, with Europe. In Africa, the search for history directed attention to powerful civilizations and states such as Ghana (northwest of modern Ghana) in the eleventh century, Mali from the 1240s to the mid-fifteenth century, and thirteenth-century Zimbabwe. Thus, the names of these states were used by new countries created in the late twentieth century.

Earlier European attempts to explain such African civilizations as the work of Mediterranean peoples moving south were rejected. This rejection was in accordance with academic shifts, but also fitted the new political mood with its stress on African achievement and, thus, on the absence of need for European intervention. Moreover, the historical consciousness of pre-colonial societies was recovered by work on oral history. Research indicated that the earlier notion of tribes was a misleading aspect of Western categorization that was designed to aid classification, if not control, and, due to the pejorative connotations of tribalism, to demean African society. Alongside an emphasis on Africa as not following "behind,"[9] a more complex account of ethnogenesis could therefore be offered. Such research created issues for the presentation of the past, not least because the territorial scope, and thus ethnic composition, of states was the work of Western conquerors, and therefore relatively recent. However, a similar point could be made about states in Asia and Europe; for example, Poland. In addition, alongside criticism, Western territorialization, as well as concepts of identity and political authority, were themselves used to particular ends by African nationalists. At the same time, Africans invented and developed their own notions of race and did not just take them from Western imperial rulers.[10]

The rethinking of the colonial period in Africa led to a stronger emphasis on resistance to colonial rule, in part in a deliberate "appropriation" of resistance for the cause of nationalism and thus for the legitimation of the subsequent regime. This was particularly useful in Guinea in West Africa, where Ahmed Sékou Touré, the long-serving first president of the state from 1958 to 1984, which gained independence from France in 1958, was the grandson of Samori Touré, the leader of the Mandinke people who had fought the French in the 1870s and 1880s. As was generally the case, reference to him ignored the extent to which he had been a tyrant and had oppressed other peoples. This omission was part of a more general pattern of treating African states prior to European conquest in a benign fashion, a practice particularly apparent with the blaming of the slave trade on Western purchasers, and not also on the African rulers who enslaved and sold captives. Ironically, Ahmed Sékou Touré ran an authoritarian state with frequent purges, known as the "Tropical Gulag."

Consideration of the colonial period in Africa and elsewhere was itself politically problematic, as it posed a question mark against the limited success of post-colonial governments in improving living standards and maintaining stability. Such consideration also directed attention to current relations with the former colonial power.

There has been a major increase in those being trained in Africa in historical graduate programs and working on regional history. These individuals offer much that is lacking in Western scholars, not only because they speak a range of local languages and make good use of oral history, but also because they are in a position to bring academic scrutiny to bear on the popular conceptions with which they have been raised. A less optimistic formulation of that relationship can be offered, but the common element is one of a strengthening of local perspectives in the presentation of history. The rejection of imperial rule that continues to influence the presentation of past and present across much of the world can, however, lead to a misleading division between "collaborators" and "resisters," a division that fails to understand the contingencies, compromises, and nuances of the past, not least the way in which people then understood their position.[11]

SOUTH AFRICA AND CYPRUS

The situation in South Africa was different to that across most of Africa. To South Africa, imperialism was seen not so much in terms of Dutch and, even more, British rule, as with regard to the Afrikaners. Of Dutch descent, they dominated the white settler society that did not disappear like European imperialism elsewhere in Africa, but, instead, ruled South Africa until 1994 when the apartheid system and white minority rule came to an end. This situation ensured complex issues from 1994 over how best to handle not only the presentation of South African history but also the role within it of the Afrikaners. As the latter remained in South Africa, the extent to which they should be able to maintain a different history was also a problem, for their cultural heritage and sense of identity was bound up in such a history. The resulting pressures at the national level were seen in such problems as naming, public celebrations, and school curricula. Thus, the ANC (African National Congress), which came to power in 1994, rewrote the history syllabus in order to reflect its views.

The general theme, however, was reconciliation, as in the designation of a Day of Reconciliation: 16 December, when in 1838, during the Afrikaner Great Trek, there was a key victory over the Africans. At the same time, there is an emphasis on different histories seen, for example, in 2007 with the success among Afrikaners of a song about Koos de la Rey, a Boer general who fought the British. The black response to the ANC approach depended in part on whether the black politicians supported distinctive voices of their own – most obviously the Zulu heritage, which was the key element for the Inkatha Freedom Party.

The general context in South Africa is far more positive than in most of Africa, as the Truth and Reconciliation Commission provided a good means for defusing anger, not least by insisting that truth and amnesty were joined in a synergy. The example, indeed cult, of Nelson Mandela, the imprisoned freedom leader who became the country's first black president (1994–1999), played an important role in this process. Moreover, there have been other policies to redress peacefully the impact of apartheid and, before that, white and colonial rule: both black economic empowerment and land reform. Each starts from a sense of unfairness that has an historical dimension, but that sense is essentially based on an understanding of the situation today.

A different form of multi-ethnic, post-colonial history was seen in Cyprus, which gained independence from Britain in 1960, having been transferred from Ottoman (Turkish) rule to British control in 1878. The Ottomans had conquered Cyprus from the Venetian empire in 1570–1571. Thus, there was a long imperial legacy for Cyprus. This created serious problems in formulating a new history but so, more directly, did the fact that the island had two major communities: a Greek majority one and a Turkish minority. They had contrasting identities and histories, the two being mutually supporting. *Enosis,* reunion with Greece, was the goal of many Greek Cypriot nationalists. In 1955, EOKA, a nationalist movement, launched bomb attacks on the British authorities, beginning, depending on one's perspective, an insurrection or a terrorist movement. As with Ireland, the British response provided fresh material for the nationalist cause. Those killed by the British were memorialized as Greek national heroes, with their photographs prominently displayed. The Greek Cypriot account, which treated Greece as the motherland and taught a love of Greece, left no positive role for the Turkish Cypriots, who were treated as interlopers under the rule of the Ottoman Empire who then cooperated with the British Empire.

After independence from Britain, fighting between the communities broke out in 1963. Whereas Greeks and Turks had lived in villages together under colonial rule, now there was an ethnic consolidation with refugees fleeing to ethnic strongholds. In 1974, matters came to a head, as an attempt at *Enosis,* encouraged by the military regime in Greece, was countered by a Turkish invasion. The victorious Turks drove the Greek Cypriots from the north and carried out a partition, establishing a state of North Cyprus that otherwise lacked international recognition. Turkish Cypriots were told to forget the idea of a united Cyprus. Regarding them as insufficiently Turkish, the Turkish government deployed a public memorialization intended to inculcate identity with Turkey. Flags and statues, notably of Kemal Atatürk, the founder of modern Turkey, were prominent. In turn, under the AK government in power in Turkey from 2002, there was a view that Turkish Cypriots were insufficiently religious, which led to the building of mosques in northern Cyprus.

Meanwhile, in the remainder of Cyprus, still the Republic of Cyprus, there was an emphasis on the territory and individual properties that were lost, and the relatives who had been killed. The slogan "I don't forget" is printed in textbooks that show the north as part of Cyprus. This was a living history that helped drive modern politics, and conspicuously so when Cyprus opposed Turkey's accession to the European Union, playing a role, alongside Greece, Austria, and France, in blocking accession. A Christian view of European identity and history was and is to the fore, with the Turks regarded as barbarians, past and present. The prospects for reunification are affected by these competing histories. External attempts to attribute blame do not help. In 2014, the European Court of Human Rights ruled that Turkey must pay 90 million euro in damages for its invasion, the largest compensation order in history. 30 million euro were to the families of those missing or killed in the invasion, and 60 million euro for the suffering of Greek Cypriots living in an enclave in the north. The Turkish Foreign Ministry responded that the ruling was unfair and inconsistent.

DEMANDS FOR RESTITUTION

More generally, interest in pre-colonial lineage as an aspect of identity led to demands for restitution, not least the repatriation of material acquired by Western powers. The process of acquisition of this lineage and material, whether by research (for example, archaeological or anthropological), purchase, or looting,[12] mattered less than the fact that it had been lost. The symbolic value of such loss became a prominent theme, and was linked to the expression of grievances, and, indeed, at times, their manufacture or manipulation. Thus, Ethiopia complained about the consequences of two Western invasions by Britain in 1868 and Italy in 1935–1936. In 1868, a British force, successfully sent to rescue imprisoned hostages, stormed the fortress of Magadala, the base of the Emperor Theodore, and seized both secular and religious treasures there. The loot included crowns, shields, crosses, and manuscripts, as well as tabots, sacred carved blocks of wood or marble. In response to these complaints, the eleven tabots in the British Museum were moved aside for special treatment and only made accessible to priests; but the museum's position in this and other cases is that, under its charter, it is not permitted to return accessions.

This, for example, is the response to the longstanding demand from Greece that the Elgin Marbles be returned to Athens, a demand that reflects the determination of modern Greeks to bask in the reflected glory of Classical Greece. The descent from Classical to modern Greeks and Greece is, at best, very indirect, but it is important to the identity of modern Greece, not least to the claim to be civilized, notably as opposed to the "barbarians" in Turkey and the Balkans. The case of the Elgin Marbles indicated that the demand for returns does not always arise directly from imperial control, in that Britain was not the imperial power in Greece, although the sale in 1816 took place because there was an imperial power, Turkey. Instead, there is a sense that power was misused at the expense of the complainant, combined with anger about the loss of history; this is seen as a fundamental challenge to identity.

Peru's demand for the return of Incan treasures provides an example of the assertion of identity. The Peruvian government of the 1910s agreed the dispatch to Yale University in the United States of the Inca treasures discovered at Machu Picchu, but its modern descendant claims that they were only loans and should be returned. This effort reflects in part Peru's present-day determination to emphasize an Inca heritage that it had earlier cared little about, when the emphasis, instead, was on descent from Spanish conquerors. A similar nativist emphasis can be seen with neighboring Bolivia.

Demands for the return of antiquities and remains do not always relate to imperial powers. There are also disputes between other states. Thus, in 2000, Afghanistan, Iran, and Pakistan disagreed over the mummified remnants of a Persian princess discovered in the Pakistani region of Baluchistan and deposited in the National Museum in Karachi, Pakistan. Modern Iran lays claim to the longstanding legacy of Persia. Moreover, there has also been the deliberate destruction of monuments, as by the Taliban in Afghanistan. The great statues of the Buddha at Bamian were regarded as sacrilegious and were therefore blown up: earlier Islamic conquerors had removed their faces.

RE-NAMINGS

The issue of lineage and colonial status was also shown in re-namings. The patina of Western rule was, it was hoped, removable, as the names of countries, towns, and landscape features were changed. Thus, the French colonies of Dahomey and Upper Volta became Benin and Burkina Faso, the British colony of Nyasaland became Malawi, the Portuguese colony of East Timor became Timor-Leste, and so on. Each of these changes provided an opportunity to reject the colonial legacy and assert a new identity.[13] This is generally that of the country in question, although a different and distinctive internationalism may also be sought. Thus, in Kolkata (Calcutta), the Marxist local government renamed Harrington Street as Ho Chi Minh Sarani, after the leader of the North Vietnamese opposition to American-backed South Vietnam during the Vietnam War. In Britain, left-wing councils named streets and buildings after international figures deemed praiseworthy, such as Nelson Mandela.

BLAME AND CREATION

Other forms of history were also reconceptualized. King Mohammed VI of Morocco, paid sixty percent of the budget of the film *Indigènes* (2006), which threw light on the major role of France's North African soldiers, including Moroccans, in World War II. The film was released in Britain as *Days of Glory*.

Africa is still very much in this process of rejecting the colonial legacy, but this rejection helps ensure a difficulty in addressing problems other than through a prism of blaming outsiders. An extreme example is provided by Zimbabwe (formerly Southern Rhodesia) under Robert Mugabe from 1980. This regime tends to see its difficulties as derived from the legacy of British imperial control and the continuing reality of British economic presence, rather than addressing serious issues in its government policies and structures. Aspects of the British legacy that might indeed help greatly in economic regeneration, for example the security of contract that encourages investment, have been neglected.

In rejecting the West, nationalist state-builders in the Third World have also borrowed heavily from it. The extrapolation of the Western model of the nation-state has indeed been of great value for nationalists elsewhere, although it may well have been a very misleading application. Indeed, it is possible that the states and, especially the political identities, particularly across much of Africa, that were first charted in any detail in the nineteenth century have had their longevity exaggerated by Western assumptions, as well as by the agendas of ethnogenesis that lie at the heart of proximate cultural nationalism. Some revisionist archaeologists have thrown doubt on the extent and even existence of certain pre-colonial states. Furthermore, modern concepts of nationality have been misleadingly employed in Africa to interpret the polities and politics of the past. Instead of the image of lasting national units, the basis for modern claims for historical lineage, there appears to have been considerable migration for centuries in almost every sphere of human activity across what have since been constructed as national boundaries. Linked to this were multiple civil and sacred identities. Thus, borrowing Western concepts may be a poor guide to past realities. However, this ahistoricism appears necessary, negatively, to the regimes that run many states, and, more positively, to the attempt to create a new nationalism. This process is not solely seen in Africa. Thus, the comment about migration can serve more generally. Indeed, historical interest in this process is reflected in the development of the idea of transnationalism.

It is scarcely surprising that governments seeking to position themselves and to frame a public history have charted paths that suit their political purpose. In this process, nationalism and ethnicity have played major roles. Paradoxically, in light of the rejection of the imperial legacy, the major emphasis is on the continuation of colonial boundaries and an opposition to ethnic and regional consciousnesses that challenge the stress on unity – which generally means government control. The decision by the Organization of African Unity to support the maintenance of colonial frontiers is a product of this emphasis. For example, the public history of Nigeria, a state created by British imperial rule that ended in 1960, supports federalism and is very hostile to separatism. This provides the context within which the civil war of 1967–1970 that stemmed from Biafran separatism is considered, as is Biafra's defeat. There is a different narrative in the one-time putative state of Biafra; but more clearly now in the Muslim north, where fundamentalists press variously for a different Nigeria and for a Nigeria that is part of a larger Islamic state. The latter represents an opposition to colonial-era borders, rather as does the idea of an Islamic union of Iraq and Syria.

Opposition to separatism could overlap with the brutal treatment of regions of opposition support. This was the case with Zimbabwe, particularly in the *Gukurahundi* [Early rain that washes away the chaff], the brutal treatment of Matabeleland in the early 1980s. Such episodes bring up another issue of the weight of history – namely, the extent to which punishment for such misdeeds should be a goal and, indeed, an aspect of politics. Thus, whether President Robert Mugabe should be tried for such action became an item in the broader question of how to ease him from power.

The ability to manage, even define, a peaceful transition of power is an issue in many African states. By extension so is the problem of offering a critical, indeed objective, account of earlier periods of activity by the regime or its progenitors. In Morocco, an Equity and Reconciliation Commission was established by Mohammed VI, after his accession in 1999, to consider human rights abuses under his predecessor and father, Hassan II. However, although they have become more common, such processes are not invariable and face serious problems, a theme addressed in other sections of this book, for example the coverage of Northern Ireland.

Much of the use and presentation of nationalism and history in postcolonial Africa was familiar from the earlier use of history in the West in the nineteenth century. However, such a stadial account of history (development through historical stages), an account seen with many branches of progressive and teleological thought, including Enlightenment and Marxist, was not welcome to most African states. The suggestion that they were passing through stages reached earlier by others was regarded as disparaging and also as failing to appreciate the specific cultural traditions and needs of particular regions. Moreover, the creation of new states and constitutions in Europe in the twentieth century, including in the second half of the century, underlined the extent to which this process was not restricted there to the nineteenth.

Alongside the attempt by former colonies to define a new lineage has come the effort by the imperial powers to come to grips with the legacies of imperialism. These legacies include not only the often-critical views of the former colonies, but also the ambivalent attitudes of immigrants from them, as well as the debate in former colonial metropoles over imperialism and how it should be presented. This was seen in Britain and elsewhere, for example, with the response to the slave trade, and also in France with the reaction to the bitter Algerian War of Independence of 1956–1962. The bicentenary of the abolition of the slave trade in Britain in 1807 led to a commemoration that was different from that of a century earlier. There was a stress on the Africans, rather than on the white abolitionists. In 2007, this emphasis led to the proposal to erect a national memorial in Hyde Park to commemorate the enslaved Africans; although that idea did not come to fruition. The French reaction to the Algerian War became more controversial during the mid-2000s. On the one hand, in 2006, there was controversy over legislation intended to prescribe the teaching of a positive treatment of French imperialism in the school syllabus. On the other, there was pressure for a more critical account of this imperialism and, conversely, a rehabilitation of the Algerians. In 2005, President Jacques Chirac, who, a decade earlier, had apologized for France's role in the deportation of Jews during World War II, did so for the "inexcusable tragedy" of the massacre of Algerians at Sétif in 1945, which followed an unsuccessful rebellion against French rule. This was a marked variance with the earlier policy of ignoring the occasion. Indeed, greater engagement with a troubled past became a characteristic of French government after François Mitterrand ceased to be president in 1995. This engagement was challenged by fresh episodes; for example, France's permissive, if not supporting, role, under Mitterrand, in the Rwandan genocide of 1994. The global scope of human rights law ensured that this issue became one for the French courts in 2013–2014. In 2014, the twentieth anniversary of the massacres made them newly controversial.

Sensitivity over colonial links was stronger in former colonies than in their one-time European rulers. In Algeria, there was anger at apparent echoes of French colonial attitudes. In December 2013, a joke by President François Hollande about the security situation in Algeria was interpreted by the Algerian media as scorn for a former colony. *El Watan,* a prominent Algerian newspaper, claimed that the joke reflected the racism and stereotypes that had been seen in 1930 when France celebrated the centenary of the colonization of Algeria. It was not only the imperial experience that was at stake in former colonies. There was also, in these states, a revival, outside the parameters of imperial control, of other historical themes. These themes ranged in accordance with the specific nature of societies and cultures. For example, in Lebanon, strong divisions grew anew in intensity after French control ceased following World War II. These divisions led to a number of historical narratives, each focused on the claims of particular communities. One that is of contemporary importance is that of the Lebanese Shi'a, which was developed in the 1960s and 1970s by Sayyid Muse al-Sadr, who created the Supreme Islamic Shi'a Council. He focused Shi'a history on the travails of the Lebanese Shi'a, which was to be important to the evolution of Hezbollah ideas.

CONCLUSION

Lebanon suffers in particular from the combination of warring communities and a weak state. However, more generally, the variety of historical themes that could be developed, and their, real or potential, cohesive or divisive, consequences or connotations, helped explain the emphasis on national historical accounts for new states or for new regimes in old states, such as Egypt after the overthrow of the monarchy in 1952.[14] The need for a cohesive account appeared readily apparent in the face of possibly divisive rival nationalisms or other ideologies, and their related historical vistas.

SEVEN

The Historical Dimension
of Manifest Destiny

THE UNITED STATES

The United States had gone through its own process of creating history in the wake of independence. The presentation of history, indeed, notably the history of winning independence, was an important aspect of American state-building and nation-forming. More recently, this presentation has played a central role in what the Americans see as culture wars. History wars proved an important component of these, although the term is a misnomer as fatalities scarcely match levels seen elsewhere in the world when such contests over identity are waged.

COMPETING OVER THE CONSTITUTION

From the outset of American independence in 1776, the past was not only celebrated, but also contested as an aspect of debates and disputes over the nature and role of political authority. Particular controversy focused on the rights of federal and state authorities. These concerns affected interest in the history of other countries. This history, notably of countries when under republican governments, such as the Netherlands in the early-modern period, Classical Athens, and republican Rome, was scrutinized in order to provide constitutional guidance and political ammunition. The strong interest in history shown by the Founding Fathers focused on how to save republics from succumbing to foreign attack, domestic discord, or the rise of tyranny. James Madison, later fourth president, wrote a study of previous attempts at confederation. Thomas Jefferson, the second president as well as the founder of the University of Virginia, wanted modern history taught in order to show what he saw as the folly of the opposing Federalists.

Jefferson was also concerned with creating history. Knowing that his letters would be used as historical sources, he was very self-conscious about them. Jefferson also encouraged John Trumbull to paint a series of works to depict American history, for example the presentation of the Declaration of Independence. These and other paintings were frequently reproduced as copies and as engravings.

Much was involved in the question of how best to interpret the Constitution, with cleaving to the past seen as the way to prevent the United States from falling prey to the hazards of history – more specifically the cyclical rise and fall that had brought down Athens, Rome, and other countries. At the same time, developments affected the perception of the Constitution and, more generally, the political trade-offs involved in American history. When, for example, in the Nullification Crisis of 1832, South Carolina claimed that the tariff was unconstitutional as well as unfair, and that individual states could protect themselves from such acts by interposing their authority, and thus nullifying the federal law, the terms of the Constitution were up for debate.

THE LEGACY OF CIVIL WAR

The Constitution was not the sole source of controversy in which the interpretation of the past played a crucial role. Later developments offered a rich crop for further debate, most conspicuously so with the Civil War (1861–1865), and its aftermath in terms of Southern Reconstruction. The Civil War provided, at the same time, a myth (generally misleading) of Southern honor, the so-called Lost Cause, and also the basis for a new attempt at national unification. Northern politicians and public opinion came to support reconciliation with the South, from which the final post-war garrisons were withdrawn in 1876. The senior Confederate commander, Robert E. Lee, received good obituaries in the Northern press after his death in 1870, and, in 1898, it was acceptable for surviving Confederate generals to be made US generals. In 1913, at the fiftieth anniversary of the Battle of Gettysburg, President Woodrow Wilson declared there that the Union and the Confederacy had "found one another again

as brothers and comrades in arms." Wilson was a Democrat and South-
erner, rather than the choice of the Republicans, the party of Abraham
Lincoln who had led the struggle against the Confederacy. This reconciliation, however, was at the expense of the African Americans of the
South whose rights were infringed by a resurgent Southern racism that
overthrew the Reconstruction governments. Southern attitudes, as well
as concern about the South that also reflected a more widespread racism,
affected commemoration at the national level. It was only in 1998 that
the "Spirit of Freedom," the African American Civil War Memorial, was
unveiled in Washington.

The Civil War also brought forward the issue of national greatness.
While primarily a prospectus for the future designed to cast light on
the present, national greatness was also highlighted by the search for
an appropriate past. This was seen at the battleground of Gettysburg,
where, on 19 November 1863, the day of Lincoln's famous speech commemorating the victory, Edward Everett, Professor of Greek Literature
at Harvard, who spoke for much longer, compared the site with that
of Marathon in 490 BCE. In doing so, Everett provided an echo of the
glorious defense of liberty by the Greeks against the invading Persians,
and an account that cast Greek civilization as the progenitor of modern
America. This was a comparison that the listeners could be anticipated
to understand. It annexed the Classical past for the Union cause and
sought to deny it to the Confederacy, whose commentators had made
much of the role of slavery in the Classical world.

THE IDENTITY OF AMERICA

Despite the emancipation of slaves in 1865 with the Thirteenth Amend-
ment to the Constitution, American identity and history continued to
be focused on whites. The nature of this identification, however, was
challenged by successive waves of immigrants, each of which appeared
to offer a different identity and historical frame of reference. Nineteenth-
century American concern about the Irish was followed by anxiety about
Poles and Italians, while, on the West Coast, Chinese and Japanese immigration became a major issue. The response was xenophobia, an emphasis
on an exclusive sense of national identity, restrictions on immigration,

and a conscious fashioning of historical accounts. In the 1910s and 1920s, the fall of the Roman Empire at the hands of "barbarian" invaders was used as a motif for American developments by commentators concerned about foreign challenges, whether immigration or Communism. There was no comparison between the two cases, but the use of Rome as a historical model meant that the example of its decline had to be faced.

In the 1920s, there was also a major cultural emphasis on the British basis of American culture. This was, in part, a political project, but was also seen in the material culture of the period, notably in John D. Rockefeller's attractive sponsorship of the presentation of the colonial period in the shape of Colonial Williamsburg. Aside from offering a reaffirmation of the British origins of America, this emphasis was designed to teach new immigrant groups the allegedly true nature of America. Thus, history served to provide an incorporating model, but, at the same time, it left the new immigrants second-class and bore no relation to what would subsequently be termed the melting pot theory of America. The presentation of a nation-state in which new whites were accepted provided they conformed to the standards of the old whites was seen as necessary not only in response to immigration, but also as a result of the apparent challenge from far-left politics inspired by the Communist Revolution in Russia, a concern that was strong in the aftermath of both world wars. By treating left-wing solutions as un-American, however, not only foreign models but also the once powerful American Progressive tradition was marginalized. This conceptualization of the United States remained potent until the 1960s. In 1957, to celebrate the 350th anniversary of the foundation of Jamestown, the first English settlement, it was reconstructed near the original site. The reconstruction was benign, with scant emphasis on the slaves who would be brought to Jamestown soon after its first settlement. Instead, a pleasant village was presented. This was a site that did not challenge visitors such as Queen Elizabeth II of Britain.

In the 1960s, the WASP (white, Anglo-Saxon, Protestant) view of America was challenged both by economic, social, cultural, and political pressures and by calls for a more diverse United States. This challenge and the response provided the basis for the subsequent "culture wars." Such conflicts concern how memories and events are shaped in terms of longstanding assumptions about identity and value. They are a major theme in the perception and ordering of social developments, as well as in the framing of political debates.

In the 1960s, new gender and youth expectations and roles commanded attention across the world, and there was a widespread questioning of authority. Hedonism focused on free will, self-fulfillment, and consumerism. The net effect was a more multi-faceted public construction of individual identities, and a more fluid society. The challenging, in the counter-culture, of earlier norms was, in turn, opposed by a backlash characterized by conventional morality and patriotism. Tension between the radicalism of the counter-culture, and the backlash led to the "culture wars" of the last half-century.[1] These were an acute instance of the more common process by which the past was represented in collective memory.[2] At the same time, there are significant variations in "history wars" within and between countries. Some are more national in their orientation; others devote more attention to the international dimension. A national focus was/is certainly the case of those in the United States. Indeed, the insularity of its "history wars" was, and is, one of their distinctive features. This was in part a reflection of America's history, one in which the country has not had its continental landmass invaded since 1815.[3] Moreover, the pattern of American politics and religion has been more insular and distinctive than that of most countries. The absence of an established (state) church is significant, as is the fact that America's political parties have been restricted to that country.

"Culture wars" were not the sole context for the expression and integration of new accounts of America's past. The regional dimension was also acute in the case of understanding the Civil War. Resistance to civil rights was affected by this historical memory in the South, and vice versa. In turn, episodes of prejudice encouraged pressure to obtain civil rights.[4] Moreover, alongside resistance in some areas to civil rights constituting a key theme in American history came a widespread acceptance of its significance as such a theme.

AMERICA AND THE HOLOCAUST

It proved easier, eventually, to incorporate the Holocaust into the history told in the United States, in large part because the villains in this case were not Americans. The history of Holocaust reception in the United States, however, is highly instructive as it shows the extent to which attitudes can change, and the range of factors involved in this. The Holocaust had not played a role in American policy during the conflict or a significant part in earlier public debate about the move toward confrontation with Germany in 1941. Moreover, this theme was subdued immediately after the war itself, and for over three decades thereafter. The Holocaust certainly played a role within American public discussion in the late 1940s, not least in encouraging support for the foundation of Israel, which the United States was the first to recognize, but it was not a central subject or theme in recent history, neither for public education nor for reference in discussion. A toxic effect of the early stages of the Cold War was that, at this stage, US intelligence was recruiting Germans who had been involved in the Holocaust.[5] Concentration camps and the treatment of Jews played a role in films, including Orson Welles's *The Stranger* (1946), which contained footage of the camps, George Stevens's *The Diary of Anne Frank* (1959), Stanley Kramer's *Judgment at Nuremberg* (1961), and Sidney Lumet's *The Pawnbroker* (1964), but the Holocaust was not a major theme. The focus for wartime horrors was on cruelty to American prisoners of war, for example the Bataan Death March at Japanese hands in 1942 and the German massacre of prisoners near Malmédy in 1944. In the mid-1950s, the integration of German forces into Western defense structures encouraged American leaders to become more favorable toward Germany and the reputation of the *Wehrmacht* (German Army).

The Holocaust became more significant in American public consciousness from the 1970s, not least with six important television miniseries: *The Holocaust* (1978), *Playing for Time* (1980), *The Wall* (1982), *Wallenberg: A Hero's Story* (1985), *Escape from Sobibor* (1987), and *War and Remembrance* (1988–1989). The last depicted Auschwitz and the slaughter of Jews at Babi Yar outside Kiev. It has been argued that "the Holocaust had become an effective moral catharsis for American viewers after the Vietnam war," not least because the Americans emerge by extension in a heroic and unproblematic light as opponents of the Nazis.[6] This approach, however, is overly reductionist and ignores the wider re-evaluation of the Holocaust across the West.

Marvin Chomsky's series *The Holocaust* (1978), which won an American audience of 120 million viewers, was particularly important, both for Jewish viewers – for whom it asserted, demonstrated, and underlined the centrality of the Holocaust – and for non-Jewish viewers. The use of a soap-opera format, focusing on a particular family, helped make the series more accessible. It followed Chomsky's series *Roots* (1977), which had had a similar impact for African Americans. The *Holocaust* series also helped establish the term as the normal one in the United States. Moreover, aside from the Holocaust, the Nazis came to play a greater role in Hollywood as an existential threat to humanity in touch with occult forces, not least with Steven Spielberg's hugely successful films *Raiders of the Lost Ark* (1981) and *Indiana Jones and the Last Crusade* (1989).[7] This approach captured the idea that the Nazis were not simply, even largely, a threat to Jews.

Closer relations with Israel from the late 1960s were also significant, as was the degree to which American evangelical Christians became actively pro-Israeli. That the Holocaust became more prominent in American public memory was an extraordinary departure, as it related to events in foreign countries that did not involve Americans as perpetrators or victims. As such, the only real comparison for Americans was with the New Testament account of suffering and fortitude.[8]

This prominence, however, helped ensure that the Holocaust was drawn into America's "culture wars," with claims by counter-culture critics that the Holocaust was detracting attention from varied ills – current and historical – attributed to the United States, such as slavery, the fate of the Native Americans, and the Vietnam War.[9] A lack of comparability, however, made this a poor argument, and it was weakened further by the intemperance of the polemic.

There was also a significant change in the stance of America's Jewish community, the largest in the world. This change underlined the extent to which sub-national groups, whether international or not, both had a historical dynamic of their own and could play a major role in framing the historical understanding of the nation as a whole. Initially, America's Jewish community was reticent in drawing attention to the Holocaust or pressing for support for Israel in the late 1940s and 1950s. Instead, it focused on integration and combating domestic anti-semitism and did not associate closely with the victim status of European Jewry. Attitudes changed in the 1960s, not least as the Holocaust was increasingly incorporated into American consciousness, but also contributing to that end and outcome. Growing activism on the part of American Jewry, which, in part, reflected the degree of their integration already into American society, as well as their confidence following Israel's victory in the Six Days' War of 1967, led not only to increased public pressure on behalf of Israel, but also to a focus on the Holocaust. This pressure and focus also reflected fears about the security of Israel, not least because the Six Days' War was followed by renewed Arab pressure that culminated in the Arab attack in the Yom Kippur War of 1973. As a reminder of the contentious and complex nature of naming, that is the Israeli name for the war; other names are used by Arabs, including the October War and the Ramadan War.

Among the American Jewish community, memorialization of the Holocaust in part reflected collective mourning. It was also a response to concerns about the challenges to Jewish identity in the liberal culture and society, both of the United States and of American Jewry. Commemoration of the Holocaust underlines an international quality to, and consciousness of, Jewishness that is under challenge from the powerful assimilationist tendencies in American society as well as from the reality that America's Jews come from different traditions and countries. Thus, the Holocaust is seen as a cohesive experience of Jewishness and one that should serve as a living memory, even though most American Jews are not Holocaust survivors, nor are their descendants.[10]

"CULTURE WARS" AND RELIGION

More generally, history provided a key theme in America's "culture wars," although much of the history was not that considered in many history courses. Instead, in a pointed reminder of the role of religion in ordering the past and linking it to the present, religious concepts of time and development could play a significant part in disputes. In particular, fundamentalist Christians had rejected the theory of evolution from the outset, and this opposition continued, and continues, to be a potent force. In 1925, John Scopes was convicted for teaching evolution in Tennessee, where it was forbidden. Thereafter, the Scopes Trial was kept alive in popular culture. It was the basis of *Inherit the Wind*, a Broadway hit of 1955 that was made into a Hollywood film, and of *The Great Tennessee Monkey Trial*, a radio play of 1992, updated in 2005.

The issue was treated as a litmus test by liberals who, in turn, had their own paranoia, or at least rhetoric. This was shown by Edward Kennedy, a member of the Senate Judiciary Committee, when, in 1987, he opposed President Reagan's nomination to the Supreme Court of Robert Bork, a conservative jurist. Kennedy offered a nightmare vision that joined past realities to fears for the future, when he anticipated "a land in which women would be forced into back-alley abortions, blacks would sit at segregated lunch counters, rogue police could break down citizens' doors in midnight raids, [and] children could not be taught about evolution."

At the level of some school districts, the teaching of creationism (the Biblical account) was the issue of dispute. In 1987, the Supreme Court determined, in *Edwards v Aguilard*, that teaching creationism in the science classes of public schools was an unconstitutional erosion of the boundaries between church and state. This decision encouraged the formulation of the thesis of intelligent design, which argued that an intelligent being shaped development. This was a form of creationism that did not mention God and that was seen as the form most likely to survive legal challenge. The struggle went back and forth, with public debate and the democratic mandate playing a role alongside judicial decision. In 1999, for example, the Kansas Board of Education decided that creationism should be taught alongside evolution, although the guidelines were repealed in 2001 after considerable public protest had led to changes in elections in 2000. The topic, nevertheless, remained a live one. A creationist majority was put back in place in Kansas in 2004, and, in 2005, it voted to introduce criticism of evolution into science lessons. Attention also focused on Dover, Pennsylvania, where the school board required that teachers explain intelligent design alongside evolution. This led to a federal court case brought by parents claiming that this decision violated the constitutional separation of church and state. In 2005, most of the board was voted out in a local ballot. The issue continued to play a major role in local politics in parts of America into the 2010s.

THE BOSTON TEA PARTY

Less distant history could also be a source of historical contention and reference, most prominently, in the 2000s, with the Tea Party movement. This conservative, anti-governmental movement drew on a key moment that was part of the foundation account for America but, because it focused on that account, also had a particular resonance in terms of modern American society. Multiculturalism in America in 1773 was very different than today. Most blacks in the British colonies were slaves. The historical Tea Party occurred on 16 December 1773 when the Sons of Liberty seized 340 chests of tea[11] from three British ships in Boston harbor and threw them into the water. The episode is worth considering because it illustrates how groups use the past (often in distorted form) to establish a current identity. Tea Party supporters invoked an event from the past – without fully understanding it historically – to advance a particular agenda in the present.

It is fruitful to turn from the highly partisan modern-day use of the events in order to understand the differing viewpoints that led to the action in the first place. In the Seven Years' War (1756–1763), the British had conquered the French territories in modern Canada with some assistance from their colonies, an assistance emphasized in accounts of what, to the Americans, is known as the French and Indian War of 1754–1763. This war, however, had left Britain with an unprecedented national debt, as well as with pressing questions of imperial governance. Transatlantic economic and political links between Britain and its colonies entailed and registered pressures, which were exacerbated by legislation that, if not inappropriate, was designed for different purposes than keeping the colonies happy.

This legislation rested on the principle of parliamentary sovereignty over the colonies. In 1767, the British government imposed, by a revenue act, customs duties in the colonies on a variety of goods, most valuably tea, at that time a luxury commodity only available by import from China. This act was designed to pay the costs of civil government in the northern colonies, such as Massachusetts, which would end the dependence of officials and judges on the colonial assemblies. The measure was unwelcome in North America, but served the needs of strengthening the empire as it helped the finances of the British East India Company, which bore the burden of Britain's position in Asia, even while it exercised a monopoly of British trade with China. The taxation of tea was scarcely new, having been included in the very first Excise Act, of 1660, but the tea duty symbolized Parliament's right to tax, and this duty led to a boycott of tea by many Americans. Subsequently, from the 1780s, British opponents of the slave trade and slavery were to boycott sugar, the key product of the slave-labor plantations in the West Indies.

The taxation of tea was complicated because smuggled Dutch tea, also from East Asia, challenged the British East India Company's sales in North America. As a result, the government, in 1773, passed a Tea Act that abolished British duties on tea re-exported to America and allowed the Company to sell the tea directly to consignees to the American colonies. This was a measure designed to cut the cost of tea there, thus boosting sales and helping the Company. The Americans, however, would still have to pay duty on the imported tea. This was condemned by activists, unwilling to accept Parliament's right to impose direct taxes on the colonies and fearful of the political implications of the government enjoying a larger revenue in America. Such a revenue would enhance government power. The Americans also rejected the monopolistic structuring of the trade around the Company and the consignees. The legalization made tea cheaper for consumers, but imposed a monopoly that cut out American importers who did not smuggle their goods at ports. It was the merchant class, which was well represented in the colonial assemblies and within the Sons of Liberty, that felt victimized by the Act.

Opposition to the Act led to the resignation of intimidated consignees and to the departure of tea ships without having landed their cargo; and this opposition culminated in the Boston Tea Party. In throwing the tea into the harbor, colonial protestors fashioned a powerful symbol of resistance, one that dramatized the breakdown of imperial authority for at least some of the colonists. The process of reaching, and endlessly redefining, a consensus that underlay and often constituted government, including colonial rule, in this period, had broken down.[12] The drama of the Boston Tea Party, however, is a very poor model for politics within a modern civil society. Moreover, the events of 1773 do not describe modern America. In addition, these events do not match the simple assumptions of Tea Party supporters. The role of colonial Boston as a slaving port undercuts the pretensions of patriot assertions of liberty.[13] Yet, conversely, such an undercutting tells us more about modern sensitivities than about the views of the age, as an ability to reconcile apparent contradictions is part of every political culture. This reconciliation also requires an ability to engage with the contrast between universal values and freedoms that are applied in a more specific fashion. Slavery was seen by (white) Americans (and Britons) as a state to be resisted if applied to them by an allegedly authoritarian government in Britain, but one that could be applied legitimately and profitably to Africans. A critical notion was that of "property." The rights of property, including over slaves, were thus justified. The Anglo-American liberal-revolutionary impulse had not yet focused on all people rather than on some people and property.

MULTICULTURALISM

The apparent relevance of the events in Boston in 1773 has seemingly been lessened by population changes within America. This was part of the process by which the debate over American history was affected by a marked change in the demographic balance, and will be more so in the future. In 1960, whites made up 159 million of the population of 179 million, but by 2000 they were only 211 million of the 281 million. In the early 2000s, the issue of American identity became increasingly prominent. Books such as Victor Hanson's *Mexifornia: A State of Becoming* (2003) and Samuel Huntington's *Who Are We? The Challenges to America's National Identity* (2004) warned about a change of consciousness and a challenge to American-ness as a consequence of large-scale immigration. Critics of multiculturalism in history lessons referred to a fragmentation that denied any sense of national unity, and that made it difficult to produce more than a series of histories of minorities. In contrast, supporters of multiculturalism focused on recovered voices. This contention, which could be seen in other countries, was linked in America (and some other countries) to the debate over the value of bilingual education; in America's case, English and Spanish.

NATIONAL HISTORY STANDARDS

The debate over multiculturalism also acted as a background to the controversy over the release, in 1994, of the draft National History Standards. These were intended to act as a voluntary system of guidance to state boards of education and other bodies. Instead, however, of providing – as intended – readily accepted outlines and study guides for teaching American and world history, the draft Standards led to a controversy over alleged political correctness and anti-Americanism. The Standards also ignored the established pantheon of American and world heroes, because the authors contested the interpretations that led to these choices and were opposed to the emphasis on great men in history. This emphasis had caused a storm in 1992, with disagreement over how best to commemorate the anniversary of Columbus's "discovery" of the New World in 1492 and, in particular, whether it should be presented as a background to expropriation, slavery, and genocide.[14]

The controversy over the National History Standards was politicized, with two Republican senators introducing amendments to ban the employment of federal money for the implementation of these draft Standards. They also required that such money should be spent only on those who "have a decent respect for United States history's roots in Western civilization," which was a critique of the search for other roots, for example African-American ones, and also of cultural relativism. Eventually, after the Standards were revised under the auspices of the Council for Basic Education, not least to provide a different account of the Cold War, and then released in 1996, the controversy became far less heated. Nevertheless, its legacy was divisive, bolstering the convictions of both sets of protagonists.

THE POLITICS OF HISTORY

Such controversies were played out in terms of existing cultural and political tensions, with a downplaying of the autonomy of disciplinary issues and the past. This downplaying was an aspect of a more general process in which both liberalism and conservatism are, in part, shaped as monoliths by outsiders. In doing so, they offer a false coherence (matching that of polemicists within each tendency), which fails to address the gradations and divisions of these tendencies. This is but part of a more general false consciousness of agglomeration, seen, for example, in the treatment of "the 1960s" as a unit, both by those who see whatever the phrase is taken to imply as inspiration, and by those who are appalled by it or by some aspects of it. The same is also true of other periods of time and of individual presidencies, for example "the Reagan years," as if 1981–1989 were a coherent unit.

The self-conscious political presentation of the past came to play a greater role in the United States from the 1990s, notably, but not only, in the National Standards controversy. The governmental and political emphasis on the need for, and content of, history, however, could detract attention from the problems posed by the subject, not least the extent to which history involves questions as well as answers. A grounded understanding of the process of history, indeed, is only offered by narratives and interpretations that are alive to contrasting interpretations and to the problems of using evidence. This, however, is of scant interest to those who seek to use history to support the allegedly manifest destiny of their particular political interpretations.

An interesting vignette on the extent to which history could play a role in the discussion of policy at the very top of American politics came from an article in the *Sunday Times* of London of 4 March 2007 by Irwin Stelzer, a conservative journalist. This article offered an account of a lunch at the White House to discuss Andrew Roberts's *A History of the English-Speaking Peoples since 1900* (2006), a lunch held because, according to George W. Bush, president from 2001 to 2009, "history informs the present" and his goal was to see what history could teach him. Those present included Roberts and fellow conservative historian Gertrude Himmelfarb. In the account by Stelzer, Roberts offered a number of alleged lessons from history:

> First: do not set a deadline for withdrawal from Iraq. That led to the slaughter of 700,000 people in India when the British left in 1947, with the killing beginning one minute after the midnight deadline. Bush wondered if there were examples of occupying forces remaining for long periods other than in Korea. Roberts suggested Malaysia where it took nine years to defeat the Communists after which the occupying British troops remained for several years. And

Algeria, added Bush, citing Alistair Horne's *A Savage War of Peace: Algeria 1954–1962* for the proposition that more Algerians were killed after the French withdrawal than during the French occupation. Second lesson: will trumps wealth. The Romans and other rich world powers fell to poorer ones because they lacked the will to fight and survive. Whereas the Second World War was almost over before Americans saw the first picture of a dead soldier, today the steady drumbeat of media pessimism and television coverage are sapping the West's will. Third lesson: don't hesitate to intern your enemies for long periods. That policy worked in Ireland and during the Second World War. Release should only follow victory. Lesson four: cling to the alliance of the English-speaking peoples. Although many nations are engaged in the coalition in Iraq and Afghanistan, troops from Britain, Canada, Australia and New Zealand are doing the heavy lifting. The closing note was more somber. Roberts told Bush that history would judge him on whether he had prevented the nuclearization of the Middle East. If Iran gets the bomb, Saudi Arabia, Egypt and other countries would follow. The only response was a serious frown and a nod.

Dick Cheney, vice president from 2001 to 2009, who was also at the lunch, was observed carrying Roberts's book when he visited Kabul. In his memoirs, *Decision Points* (2010), Bush referred to his presidency as "reading history, and making history," also writing, "I know a lot of history. I know how lessons work. I hope people come to understand how history works." Bush read fourteen biographies of Lincoln during his eight years in the presidency (2001–2009). Bush's concern with history and legacy was also shown by his plans for his presidential library, which outlined the establishment of an institute designed to present his views. President Barack Obama continued the practice of discussing matters with historians, while Gordon Brown, British Prime Minister from 2007 to 2010, was also interested in history (he had a doctorate in the subject) and historians.

The habit of reference to the past is at once encouraging and dis-couraging – encouraging as it indicates the extent to which the present is understood as part of a continuum, and discouraging as all too often history is treated in a nonlinear and ahistorical fashion: lessons are drawn, as in the example of the White House lunch, without sufficient care to consider alternative expositions and the impact of particular contexts. Indeed, the very unpredictability and specificity of context that ensures multiple discontinuities in the past, and between past and present, tends to be underplayed.

The nature of America's past provides plenty by way of emotive issues and therefore references. Race is a key issue because it is one that can be extrapolated to encompass many other disputes across the world, irrespective of the appropriateness of such extrapolation. Thus, when the position of Arabs in Palestine in the mid-2000s was compared to the earlier segregation of African Americans by Condoleezza Rice, the secretary of state from 2005 to 2009, herself an African American, this remark was powerful in American terms.

The presentation of past conflicts is another source of controversy in the United States, notably the Vietnam War, but also World War II. The exhibition planned for 1995 by the Smithsonian Institution's National Air and Space Museum on the fiftieth anniversary of the end of the war was designed to center on the *Enola Gay,* the plane that dropped the atomic bomb on Hiroshima, but excited fierce controversy over the conclusions of the exhibit narrative and the issue of culpability for the bombings.[15] In 2010, in the United States, the National Endowment for the Humanities (NEH) was criticized for its sponsorship of an academic conference, "History and Commemoration: The Legacies of the Pacific War." This conference was presented by critics as "publicly supported anti-American revisionist history," and the criticism served to attack the NEH.[16]

More continuously, the existence of a two-party tradition has left different American histories to provide appropriate references. Thus, on 1 January 2014, the formal inauguration of Bill de Blasio, a Democrat, as mayor of New York, was conducted using a Bible once owned by Franklin Roosevelt, an iconic Democratic president linked with the idea of a new start in the shape of the New Deal. There is every sign that such symbolism, and the related contention over historical references and symbols, will continue. This contention contributes greatly to the controversies over America's identity, and these play a powerful role in its politics.

AUSTRALIA

Australia provides a parallel instance of "manifest destiny," although there are contrasts, not least in the far lesser role of religion in Australian public discussion. Furthermore, the Aborigines, who were dispossessed of Australia by the British settlers, are not equivalent to African Ameri-

cans, descendants of involuntary (slave) immigrants who became a dis-
criminated-against group. A conservative position on Australia's history
was strongly advanced by John Howard, the Prime Minister from 1996
to 2007. He was concerned that a positive interpretation of Australian
history should be propagated. Howard wanted this version to replace
what he saw as a liberal multiculturalism that, under the goal of offering
an account that accepted Aboriginal perspectives, was negative about
Australian achievements. In this continuing debate, academic, political,
and public crosscurrents play a major role. As in other settler societies,
land rights are a particularly charged issue, not least as they bring into
contention Aboriginal and non-Aboriginal views, as well as questions
about past meanings, specifically in the case of the interpretation of legal
judgments. In 2008, Howard's Labour successor, Kevin Rudd, apologized for the treatment of the Aborigines. This was in line with a pronounced trend from the 1960s, in which, through legislation and judicial
rulings, discriminatory practices were abandoned, land rights conceded,
and original occupancy recognized.[17] There was bitter controversy over
whether the treatment of the Aborigines was genocidal. This varied controversy was central to Australia's experience with "history wars."

Reconsideration of the position of the Aborigines was linked to a
more general rethinking of Australia's history. In place of beginning it in
1788 – with the arrival of the British "First Fleet" and the establishment
of a penal colony – has come an interest in the long human occupancy
of the country. Moreover, there has been a presentation of this occupancy as more sophisticated and adaptable than in terms of a simple and
static designation of the early inhabitants as "hunter gatherers."

Changes in historical interpretation were not limited to this contentious issue. There was also a movement away from a focus on the imperial background and British origin of modern Australia, a move that is
partly a response to a rise of Asian identities and concerns for Australia.
A comparable move away from such a focus, albeit in different contexts,
was also seen with America, Canada, and New Zealand. In each, strategic, economic, and demographic interests all affected public history. The
contrast between the public history of the United States and Australia
can be readily expanded by considering Canada and New Zealand. In
each case, the "manifest destiny" at issue was different, not least because,

in these former colonies, the British legacy played through different historical processes. Moreover, the ethnic and legal consequences of the settlement process varied greatly.

There was, however, a common background in the shape of the seizure of "new lands" for cultivation and the dispossession of the existing population, followed by the development of a society and economy that was more complex. The public history that was offered became more distinctive and different in the former British colonies as the colonial experience receded. Nevertheless, owing in large part to a much longer colonial experience, major contrasts to American public history remained.[18]

CHINA

The location of discussion of China in a book on this subject indicates the problems created by typology and the resulting positioning of states. China might have presented itself as moving to a new stage with Communist success in 1949; but, in the 2000s and 2010s, the state chose to focus on its long-term heritage. Thus, chapter 6 is an inappropriate home for a discussion of China. The major changes since the death of Mao Zedong in 1976 might appear to suggest a degree of post-Communism, but democracy has been resisted, and China is still a one-party state. Thus, chapter 8 is an inappropriate home. Instead, and ironically so, given that this chapter is otherwise occupied by democracies, China may appear more properly located among states convinced that they have a manifest destiny. Yet, its character is very different to those already discussed.

EIGHT

Post-Communism and the New History

THE FALL OF THE COMMUNIST REGIMES IN EASTERN EUROPE in 1989 and the collapse of the Soviet Union in 1991 brought together a number of post-war trends that provoked new histories, particularly the collapse of imperial rule, the creation of new, as well as newly independent, states, for example Croatia and Ukraine, and sweeping political changes. The fall of the Communist regimes had reflected the difficulty of grounding authoritarian regimes in the absence of popular support – however much the people were told that there was a dialectical necessity for the success of these regions and one located in a clear historical continuum. A lack of popularity, particularly in Eastern Europe, made it difficult for the Communist governments to view change and reform with much confidence. Rather than vindicating the Communist prospectus, the passage of time made more apparent the sham character of Communist progress.

Far from having being made redundant by the advance of Communism, nationalism reemerged publicly as a powerful force, in Eastern Europe and the Soviet Union, as well as in China, which ostensibly continued to be Communist. Nationalism, which became a more central political issue in the former Communist bloc from 1989, apparently offered identity, freedom, and a route to reform freed from a sclerotic imperial structure. Nationalism also entailed the rejection of Soviet and Communist history and, instead, an emphasis on the histories subordinated by both. This process led at once to a searching reevaluation of recent history and to an often-strident consideration of earlier episodes. For example, in the Baltic Republics, Estonia, Latvia, and Lithuania, there were complaints about the Soviet annexation in 1940, complaints that led to a focus on the Nazi-Soviet Pact of 1939 under which the annexation had taken place. This was a pact that the Soviets had done their best to ignore. Moreover, nationalism could be readily combined with the revival of public religiosity that was also prominent in Eastern Europe and the former Soviet Union. Indeed, this revival helped give a particular character to nationalism in specific contexts, most obviously with Polish Catholicism.

The fall of the Iron Curtain thus meant not the "end of history" as was fashionably suggested from 1989 by Western commentators – notably the originator of the concept, Francis Fukuyama – but its marked revival. "Blank spots on the map of time" were filled in.[1] Across the former Soviet Bloc, the new governments opened archives, such as those of the East German *Stasi* (security police), and lifted bans on books, which people could now read and debate publicly. The opening of the archives also shone revisionist light on the history of other states affected by Soviet policy, for example showing how Stalin manipulated the Spanish Civil War to his own ends, not least to gain Spanish gold from the Republicans he supported and to destroy Trotskyist critics on the Left.[2]

In many states, the key emphasis from 1989 was no longer on Nazi killing but on Communist and Soviet oppression. Thus, in Belarus, the mass graves at Kuropatny, where the Soviet NKVD (Secret Police) had slaughtered at least 100,000 people between 1937 and 1941, were exhumed from 1988,[3] reviving and popularizing Belarussian nationalism in the crucible of anger.

There were, and still are, larger questions of how best to present the national narratives of formerly Communist states. The same is true for German history as a whole: the fall of the Berlin Wall in 1989, and the subsequent reunification of West and East Germany in 1990 lent energy to earlier academic suggestions about rethinking the German past,[4] as well as ensuring a new national narrative. With reunification and the end of the Cold War, Germany's geographical and political positions within Europe changed. There was talk of Germany being in the center of Europe, not part of the West, and consideration of what this would mean for its history. At the same time, new issues were thrown into prominence, notably the treatment of the Communist years and of sites of memory created then. Thus, in former East Germany, there have been disputes over whether the memorialization of the victims of the Third Reich (1933–1945) should take precedence over those of the Communist years (1945–1989) in sites where both were held, such as the former military prison in Torgau.

As Eastern Europeans came to regard themselves as victims of Communist rule who had played no role in the regime (a frequently misleading view), while Communism was presented as a foreign ideology, so the twentieth-century sufferings of others, such as Jews, were neglected. Moreover, the tendency seen earlier in the twentieth century to link Communism with Jews, a tendency very much pushed by Nazi Germany and its allies, was revived in the 1990s, with anti-semitism playing an explicit or implicit role in populist nationalism. Furthermore, the long-held tendency to emphasize Christian victims of Nazi persecution as much as, or more than, their Jewish counterparts continued. This was seen, for example, in the contest between Catholic and Jewish interpretations of Auschwitz.[5] Across much of Eastern Europe, there was also a reluctance or failure to acknowledge the degree of local complicity in the Holocaust. In Lithuania, the process of exonerating anti-Communists extended to include celebrations of "heroes" who fought with the ss, and in 1992, a general pardon was given to wartime collaborators.[6] Across Eastern Europe, the extent of anti-semitism, especially participation in the Holocaust, became an issue. Doing so entailed recovering a local memory that had been neglected or suppressed.[7] In Poland, the Institute of National Remembrance, a government agency, was instructed to ascertain the role of Poles in the killing of Jews ordered by the Germans.

In contrast, anti-semitism during the Communist years was largely ignored in Eastern Europe. It was rarely deadly, but was part of the history of these years. A key aspect of the alleged legitimacy of the Communist regimes had been based upon their role in replacing governments that had been pro-Nazi, and complicity in the Holocaust had been an important aspect of this support, particularly in Romania. In practice, there had been a fair amount of anti-semitism during the Communist years, part of it under the guise of anti-Zionism. The situation was transformed after the fall of the Communist regimes, as wartime regimes, such as those of Ion Antonescu in Romania, Ante Pavaelic in

Croatia, and Jozef Tiso in Slovakia, were rehabilitated. Antonescu, dictator of Romania from 1940 until 1944, had actively persecuted Jews and collaborated with Hitler. He was executed for war crimes in 1946. However, in the 1990s, Antonescu was proclaimed as an anti-Soviet nationalist, and cities rushed to name streets after him. Although not seen as anti-semitic, this process was an aspect of the expression of traditional themes that included anti-semitism. In part, this anti-semitism was a reflection of religious tensions, in part the ethnically exclusive concept of nationalism, and in part hostility to what were seen as cosmopolitan pressures. Thus, nationalist opposition politicians in Hungary in 2006–2007 actively pushed anti-semitic themes in an attempt to discredit the government. The coalition that ran Poland in the mid-2000s included a party with anti-semitic inclinations. All too often, there is alignment between a xenophobic nationalism and ecclesiastical bigotry or self-interest, as with the close link between government and Orthodox Church in Romania, or government and the Catholic Church in Poland.

The rehabilitation of past regimes was linked to present politics. For example, Franjo Tudjman, the president of Croatia, not only (in the 1990s) praised Ante Pavaelic, denying that his *Ustasha* regime had killed as many, principally Serbs, but also Jews and Roma (Gypsies), as was in fact the case, but also supported brutal policies of ethnic aggrandizement against Muslims and Serbs. The *Ustasha* were presented as Croatian patriots, and their hostility to Communism was emphasized. It was not until 2004 that the Romanian president, Ion Iliescu, made the first official acknowledgement of the country's role in the Holocaust – as opposed to the earlier tendency to blame the Germans. The previous year, he had established an international panel to report on the subject, which did so in 2004. This report made the Romanian role clear. Iliescu was an ex-Communist, and it is unclear whether a right-wing leader would have made the same decision. Indeed, it is improbable, while Iliescu had scarcely been eager to take the step. In 1996, it was an ex-Communist, Dariusz Rosati, who, as Polish foreign minister, apologized to the World Jewish Congress for anti-semitism and the postwar Kielce pogrom. Only in 2004 did the Polish president officially acknowledge that maltreatment by Poles was an aspect of the wartime devastation of Poland's Jews. This was followed in 2006 when President Lech Kaczynski joined Jewish leaders in breaking ground for the Museum of the History of Polish Jews in the heart of what was once the Warsaw ghetto.

The determination of ex-Communist states to win international agreement, not least in order to provide a degree of protection against a resurgent Russia, led them to face up to the international significance of the Holocaust, especially in the United States, the key to NATO membership, and Western Europe, the key to European Union membership. Thus, in 1995, Algirdas Brazauskas, the president of Lithuania, addressing the Knesset (Israeli parliament), publicly apologized for the Lithuanian role in the Holocaust. In May 2007, seeking to make all the correct gestures at a time of great sensitivity about memorialization, the Estonian Prime Minister, Andrus Ansip, attended ceremonies at a Holocaust memorial outside Tallinn, as well as at a cemetery commemorating soldiers who had died in Estonia fighting for the Soviets and the Germans and at the recently, and controversially, moved monument to Red Army casualties in World War II.

Aside from the relevance of the Holocaust to continuing anti-semitism against surviving Jewish communities, there was the issue of ethnic violence and alleged genocide in Eastern Europe in the 1990s. The end of Communism had led to an upsurge in national consciousness. This highlighted the role of ethnicity in national narratives and thus the position of minority groups. The use of ethnic considerations to advance nationalist territorial assertion and aggressiveness in the former Yugoslavia led to ethnic cleansing and massacres.

These events encouraged Western intervention, and there were direct references to the Holocaust on the "never again" theme. President Bill Clinton pressed people to see the film *Schindler's List* (1993). There were also arguments that the massacres in Bosnia were different to the Holocaust, not only because of the organized nature of the latter, but also because Bosnia was more in the pattern of brutal ethnic cleansing.[8] This interpretation was contested by the argument that a systematic murder that amounted to genocide was being carried out.[9]

The rethinking of history is not simply a matter for academics and governments. Thus, in Germany, Hungary, Russia, and, indeed, across Eastern Europe, the legacy of Communism has been considered since its fall in terms of political contention, with chauvinistic nationalism playing an important role. In Ukraine in 2008, controversy erupted over the television series *Great Ukrainians,* which was launched on the model of BBC's successful *Great Britons.* Victory for Yaroslav I the Wise (r. 1019–1054), Grand Prince of Kiev, represented a triumph for the pro-Russian east of Ukraine, as Kievan Rus was presented as not only the cradle of Russian civilization but also as the demonstration of the Russian destiny of Ukrainian history. In contrast, Stephan Bandera (1909–1959), a leading Ukrainian nationalist who had proclaimed Ukrainian statehood in 1941 and been assassinated by the Soviets, was the candidate of the nationalist west. He came third, and it was claimed in the west that the victory for Yaroslav was fraudulent. The choice of exemplary historical figures was also important elsewhere. In Kazakhstan, formerly a republic in the Soviet Union, the search for past heroes led to the presentation as Kazak nationalists of figures who had not obviously displayed that characteristic.[10] Once Mongolia had broken free of Russian/Soviet control in 1990, Chinggis Khan was depicted as the father of the nation and as a highly favorable figure.

The revival of history was a matter not only of the contents of the presentation of the past, but also of its form. There were new museums and monuments as well as a transformation of those already there.[11] Thus, in Latvia, there is a Museum of Occupation, covering both Soviet and German rule from 1940 to 1991, as well as a Museum of Barricades that deals with the opposition to the re-imposition of Soviet control in 1991. The same change was true of sites of commemoration and celebration, and, indeed, of the entire process of public education. The statues of Communism have been largely discarded, although the issue remains a live one, as seen during disturbances in Kiev (Ukraine) in 2013 when a statue of Lenin was knocked down by opponents of the pro-Russian regime. What has replaced the Communist statues has also been a source of controversy. In 1997, in Moscow, a statue of Tsar Nicholas II was blown up and a fringe body looking back to the Communists, the Revolutionary Military Council of the Russian Soviet Federative Socialist Republic, claimed responsibility for an attempt to blow up one of Peter the Great. The fate of statues was highly symbolic

There is an instructive contrast between the uses of the term "history." In Western Europe, when someone says, "That's history," it means it is a matter of no current, topical interest, and, indeed, something anti-quated. In contrast, in Eastern Europe, for example in Hungary, Poland, and Russia, this phrase means that troubles are now ahead in the discussion and as an issue, as many historical conflicts there are still unsolved and of great importance to current political affairs. Aside from national-ism, there was the need on the part of post-Communist states to face the legacy of the recent past and the pressure created by the politicization of this legacy. The previous century, and, even more, the years from the 1940s, were dissected in order to allocate responsibility, and thus blame, and to castigate rivals. Thus, in place of the longstanding Communist focus on Eastern European Fascist, or authoritarian, collaboration with Germany during World War II, came a focus on the cruelties and iniqui-ties of the post-war era as a way to condemn the Left. For example, the Polish government of the Kaczynski brothers and their Law and Order Party, in 2007, opened secret police files from the Communist era. This process was linked to moves against the WSI, the military intelligence service, and, with an obvious extrapolation of the past into the present, to an attempt to use vetting to remove the alleged secret system of pro-Communist agents of influence in public life. Thus, the politics of the period were fought out in part in terms of the real and alleged legacy of the Communist years.

In Romania, the issue of the relationship between the Ceausescu regime and post-Communist governments was a matter of controversy, with claims that there was more continuity than there should be, not least by the renamed Communist Party. There was also a determination to draw attention to the crimes of the Ceausescu regime, which included the memorial established in 1992 at Sighet, where opponents had been imprisoned. An attempt to discover information led to scrutiny of the *Securitate* (secret police) that was not welcome to its successor, the SRI. A National Council for the Study of the *Securitate* files was established in 1999, in part with the help of the comparable East German body. The sensitive nature of history was indicated in 1990, when Ioan Petru Cu-lianu, a prominent Romanian historian, was murdered.

In some states, the issue of continuing Communist influence played a greater role than elsewhere, which, in turn, helped direct attention to the Communist years. In former East Germany, the role of the *Stasi* (secret police) did not become a political issue comparable to that of the secret police in Poland. For example, despite the large-scale oppressiveness of its policies and attitudes, the *Stasi* was never declared a "criminal organization," unlike the Gestapo. Many *Stasi* members were reemployed in the police, and benefited from an effective support network. In opposition, the Association for the Victims of Stalinism sought to direct attention to the plight of those who had been jailed in East Germany. The use of former prisons as museums contributed to this process.

In Hungary, emphasis was on the reevaluation of the 1956 Hungarian Revolution, which had been brutally suppressed by Soviet forces. This reevaluation was part of the very challenging, and then rejection, of Communist rule in 1989, as a new public identity was vigorously asserted. In June 1989, the remains of Imre Nagy, Prime Minister in 1956 who had been executed in 1958, were dug up and ceremonially reburied. The eulogies provided a criticism of the suppression of the rising, and a large crowd of about 100,000 attended. Ironically, in an attempt to garner support in the face of popular outrage shortly before the Revolution, the hardline Communist regime had, on 6 October 1956, reburied four victims of Stalinist repression including Lazlo Rajk, a Communist interior minister, in a public funeral. Instead, the funeral itself became an opportunity to demonstrate widespread pressure for change. Statues and other memorials had also played a role in the events of 1956. Demonstrators then focused on monuments to nineteenth-century opponents to Habsburg rule, which could be seen as a precursor to the foreignness of Soviet domination. Thus, students marched to Batthyányi's Eternal Flame Memorial, while statues of Sandor Petöfi and Josef Bem served as displays of opposition. Petöfi was a major nineteenth-century nationalist poet.

Once the Communist regime had gone, and Hungary had become a democracy, the representation of 1956 and the Communist years gathered pace. In 1996, a statue of Nagy was unveiled near Parliament, part of a process by which the statuary in Budapest changed guard. Sculptures from the Communist era were collected and displayed as interesting relics of the past in a sculpture park that was deliberately located in a remote area. This proved less controversial than their destruction. The very large memorial to the Soviet Army that towers over the city from the Buda side of the Danube is now known as the Freedom Monument.

Also in Budapest after the end of Communist rule, a 1956 Institute was established; and, in 2006, on the fiftieth anniversary of the uprising, a memorial was unveiled where Stalin's statue once stood, and "cultural" events were organized by the government. The visit in 2006 by President George W. Bush, underlined the political dimension of the commemoration. The changing international context was also shown in 1992 when the post-Communist Russian government of Boris Yeltsin handed over Soviet documents from 1956. The most potent legacy in Budapest is the Museum of Terror on Andrassy Boulevard, in the very building where the secret police once did their worst. This museum preserves the cells and the torture and execution chambers. The oppression during and after the suppression of the 1956 revolution was brutal, but the Soviet Union kept news of the atrocities its forces committed secret.

The Communist era was not the sole period of controversy in Hungary. The very shape of the country has an iconic and symbolic potency. The use of the pre-1920 boundaries in maps, car stickers, and other forms represents a hankering after past glories and a rejection of the more limited boundaries decreed by the Treaty of Trianon in 1920, after participating, as Austria-Hungary, on the losing side in World War I. This issue remains a live one. The nationalist government of Viktor Orbán introduced a National Unity Day to remember these losses, and granted citizenship to ethnic Hungarians living in the lands lost then to what are now Romania, Slovakia, Serbia, Croatia, and Slovenia. In 2011, there was controversy over the use of the pre-1920 boundaries on a carpet sent to Brussels to lay in the atrium of the Council of Europe during Hungary's six-month tenure of the EU presidency.

Across the former Communist bloc, the preservation and destruction of the physical remains of oppression were sometimes controversial, as with local opposition in 2000 to the demolition of the last of the watchtowers of the Berlin Wall. At the same time, the language of the Communist years was discarded. Counter-revolutionaries have become heroes. Yet, as democratic politics have created and revealed fault-lines, so the memorialization of the past has become more complex. This is particularly so in Hungary, as there remain unanswered questions about actions and responses in 1956.

More generally, the issue of actions during the Communist years became an apparently key test of integrity, and thus a source of rumor and dissension. This affected the Catholic Church in Poland in 2007, with the resignation of Stanislaw Wielgus, the archbishop designate of Warsaw. The Wielgus resignation provided an opportunity for the expression of historicized hatreds. To some, the charges against Wielgus of active collaboration with the Communist secret police indicated the work of Jews, foreigners, and liberals concerned to disparage the Church. The issue brought up questions of contrition and forgiveness that reflect the complex relationship with conduct under a totalitarian past as well as the relationship between religion, history, and redemption. Pope Benedict XVI (r. 2005–2013) had declared in Poland in 2006 that nobody should "sit in judgment on other generations," but that approach covers a multitude of sins. Commissions for Reconciliation offered a governmentally directed alternative to religious conspectuses of confession, forgiveness, and redemption. The former took the country as the relevant unit, whereas the latter tended to emphasize the role of the individual, although social activism by churches could add a different dimension. A reminder of the complexity of religious references was provided by the controversial visits of Japanese Prime Ministers to the Yasukuni Shrine.

Competing views on the Communist past were given a different twist in Yugoslavia as the key issue there became the creation of new states and their attempt to justify their territorial and other pretensions by reference to the past – both recent and more distant. The Communist state had sought unity under, and through, its control by emphasizing a united wartime struggle against Nazi Germany as its foundation account. However, as a federal system, especially once decentralized, the Communist era saw the development of distinctive accounts that not only disaggregated Yugoslavia but also provided competing interpretations of World War II. These came to include bitter wartime rivalries between ethnic groups and the related massacres. In the 1990s, the assertion in what had been Yugoslavia of newly independent or autonomous territorial identities overlapped with the feuding characteristics of some ethnic protagonists to provide a particularly chilling instance of the weight of the past. One-sided histories focused on the cruelties inflicted by others.[12] As under the earlier Communist regime, the relationship to the past included the attempt to disrupt, if not destroy, the historical consciousness of opponents. This led, for example, to the bombardment of historic monuments that were culturally important. Given the religious divides in former Yugoslavia, it is unsurprising that this destruction extended to churches and mosques. Indeed, at a far smaller scale, the situation replicated the Nazi assault on Jewish cultural continuity, as well as the Jewish role in history, that had been such an insidious aspect of the Holocaust.

The Yugoslav crisis also saw the looting of history for example and admonition that is such a key feature of its use. Serbian nationalists looked back to the struggle against the Muslim Ottoman Turks, particularly the heroic, but unsuccessful, battle of Kosovo of 1389, in order to provide historical reference and resonance, notably Christian resonance, for their opposition to the Muslims of Bosnia and Kosovo. Dirges and other songs sought to make the battle, and the loss it represented, relevant to the circumstances of the 1990s.[13] This was an aspect of the degree to which in the Balkans it was necessary to negotiate not only the Communist legacy, but also the legacy as conquered subjects of the Ottoman Empire.[14] Like the Serbs, Croats, Slovenes, and others sought heroic resonances from the past. History provided opportunities for assertion through symbols, as in 1989 when the remains of King Nikola Petrovic of Montenegro (r. 1860–1918), who had died in exile, were returned to the Montenegran capital, Cetinje.

Political issues were also presented in terms of historical references from elsewhere. Aware of the near-universal use across the West of the Munich Agreement of 1938 as a craven and foolish appeasement of Fascism, the spokesmen of Vojislav Kostunica, the Serbian Prime Minister, in 2007 rejected the proposal by the UN representative for independence for the former Serbian province of Kosovo, by arguing that this step would be akin to the 1938 loss by Czechoslovakia of the Sudetenland with its majority German population. The comparison was totally misplaced, not least because the harsh Serb treatment of Kosovo was very different to that of the Sudetenland, but that was scarcely going to stop it. As elsewhere in Eastern Europe, the legacy of the Communist years was a major issue, but in the former Yugoslavia the particular historical concern was also that of the conflicts of the 1990s, notably the war of 1992–1995, which focused on Bosnia. With Muslims, Croats, and Serbs convinced that they were victims, charges of mistreatment served to underline differences and to lessen chances for cooperation. These charges were contested not only within the former Yugoslavia but also more generally, as in the eventually unsuccessful Bosnian case before the International Court of Justice that Serbia was responsible for genocide, although the Court did decide in 2007 that Serbia had failed to stop the genocide that did occur.

In the former Communist bloc, and more generally, the end of the Cold War discredited Marxism as an official creed and greatly lessened its influence as a basis for analysis. The impact of the two was a major shift in the understanding of society, which was linked at the international level to the expression, revival, or rise of national grievances, notably within the Communist bloc. In Ukraine, independence brought public attention to the Soviet government's complicity in the mass famine that began in 1933, and led to pressure for its recognition as a genocide. In 2010, Stalin and colleagues were indeed convicted posthumously of genocide in a Ukrainian court.

There was also a shift in some academic work toward a more critical attitude to Communist regimes. In 2010, *Stalin's Genocides* by Norman Naimark presented Stalin's mass killings of the 1930s as genocide in a work published by a major press, Princeton University Press. In doing so, Naimark, Professor of East European Studies at Stanford, offered a work that is significant not only for the understanding of Soviet history but also for the assessment of genocide. In particular, Naimark pressed for discussion of genocide as a product of Communist societies. Stalin was presented as a malevolent and murderous leader, and attempts to extenuate his character and policy were dismissed. The treatment of Ukrainian peasants as enemies of the people who deserved to die led Naimark to conclude that the Ukrainian famine was genocide. So also with the treatment of allegedly dangerous and traitorous Poles and Germans in the Western borderlands of the Soviet Union in 1932–1933, most of whom were soon killed. A similar approach could be adopted to the murderous treatment both of the peasantry and of those deemed "right deviationists" during Mao Zedong's attempt to transform the Chinese rural economy. This attempt led, in 1959–1962, to the deaths of between twenty and forty million people, mostly due to famine. Naimark's comparison of Hitler and Stalin noted that de-kulakization and the Ukrainian famine were attempts to eliminate "a class of people," while the nationalities most brutally attacked by Stalin were "slated for elimination, if not physically, then as self-identifying nationalities." Naimark concluded that both systems were genocidal by their very character, not only their ideological motivations, but also their Promethean transformative aspirations. This approach was also taken by the Russian writer Aleksandr Solzhenitsyn. Naimark presented the Holocaust as the worst case of genocide in the modern era, but made it clear that Stalin was also guilty of genocide.

Revisionism remains a powerful element in the political culture of the region, and history provides more episodes for revision and debate. As in the nineteenth century, loss of land is an issue. So, too, is disruption and loss of possessions resulting from the compulsory movement of people, especially after World War II. Thus, in Hungary, the right-wing Fidesz party has won support by pressing for what it terms justice for the Hungarians deported from Czechoslovakia, Romania, and Yugoslavia from 1945. A historicist sense of identity and interest was also important to relations between the newly independent countries, as well as between them and the major states of the region, Germany and Russia. This was a particular problem for Poland, for which historical resonances were pressing in its relationship with each power. This situation contributed to tension and made cooperation difficult. Thus the Kaczynskis' government regularly insulted Germany in the mid-2000s.

Equally, the governments of Germany and, even more, Russia found it difficult to abandon a sense that their views ought to prevail. In large part, this sense reflected their inherent strength, for example that of Russia in energy supplies, but the resonances of past concepts of intrinsic influence also played a role. The attitudes of Vladimir Putin, Prime Minister or President of Russia from 2000, toward Ukraine, Belarus, and the Baltic Republics of Estonia, Latvia, and Lithuania very much demonstrated this role. For Russia, there was, under Putin, an unwillingness to abandon the sense of natural dominance over Eastern Europe that had developed during the Cold War. A rethinking of the relationship on the basis of the equality of sovereign states akin to the post-1648 Westphalian system in Western Europe, proved unwelcome. Indeed, the keenness of the Putin government to reverse Russia's relative decline extended to include rethinking recent history. Thus, in Munich in 2007, Putin argued that, far from losing the Cold War, and thus being weaker than the United States, the Soviet Union had voluntarily ended it. There was also a reconsideration of public commemoration in Russia that drew on atavistic impulses that could plunder history for supporting examples. For example, to replace 7 November, Revolution Day, 4 November became a new national holiday. It was intended to mark the expulsion of the Polish garrison from the Kremlin in 1612, a key episode in bringing the Russian Time of Troubles to an end.

In turn, pro-Russian elements in what had formerly been part of the Soviet Union, but was now independent, drew attention to historical episodes that supported their case. In Ukraine, these episodes included the Treaty of Pereiaslav of 1654, under which the Cossacks had turned for Russian protection.

Within Russia, a search for distant and recent memory, or rather the use and misuse of it, focused on Russia's international standing. There was far less concern about the past domestic situation, under the Romanov Tsars or the Communists, and unsurprisingly so as most of it offered little to a Russia that was experimenting with democracy. Thus, Putin does not want attention directed to the role of terror in supporting Communism, not least because he was a KGB officer. There is no state museum dedicated to the *gulags,* and the wealthy Russian oligarchs have also failed to institutionalize this powerful experience and memory.

In 2014, when Putin annexed Crimea from Ukraine, the theme was of history reversed. This was literally the case with the reversal of Nikita Khrushchev's handover of Crimea to Ukraine, then a Soviet republic, in 1954. There was also a more profound reversal of what was seen as the humiliation of Russia over the previous quarter-century. Both themes were present in the speech Putin delivered to Russia's parliament on 18 March 2014 when, in the Kremlin, he signed a treaty to annex Crimea. Putin referred to the dissolution of the Soviet Union as a mistake, and added a theme of blood-right: "Crimea has always been and remains an inseparable part of Russia. This commitment, based on truth and justice, was firm, was passed from generation to generation. There are graves of Russian soldiers on the peninsula whose courage enabled Russia to make Crimea part of the Russian Empire in 1783." Later, he told crowds in Red Square: "Crimea and Sevastopol are returning to their home shores, to their home port, to Russia! . . . Glory to Russia."

The crisis, in turn, led to the creation of an "instant history," in which opponents were vilified. Thus, Russian commentators and supporters claimed that Ukrainian nationalists were Fascist and anti-semitic, and that Ukraine was not really a country and lacked its own history. In turn, these claims were denied and presented as pro-Russian. The killing of violent pro-Russian separatists in Odessa in 2014 was illustrated in part by photographs of a very different episode: a massacre by the pro-German Ukrainian Insurgent Army in 1943.[15]

The theme of historical links was also taken by Russia's allies and would-be allies. On 12 May 2014, the "People's Republic of Donetsk" in eastern Ukraine proclaimed its unilateral declaration of independence from Ukraine and then asked to join Russia. Denis Pushilin, the chairman of the Presidium, declared: "People of Donetsk have always been part of the Russian world, for us, the history of Russia is our history. Based on the will of the people and the restoration of a historic justice, we ask the Russian Federation to absorb the Donetsk People's Republic into the Russian Federation." This republic was not recognized by Ukraine, the international community, or even Russia.

Putin's account of Russia's part was linked to recent international developments in which he discerned an American-led unilateralism. The NATO air attack on Serbia over Kosovo in 1999 was cited as evidence. This instance was also used by an ally of Putin, Gerhard Schröder, chancellor of Germany from 1998 to 2005. As an instance of the politics of historical reference, Angela Merkel, Schröder's successor, told Germany's parliament that this was a "shameful" comparison, as in Kosovo NATO had intervened to prevent atrocities. In turn, a very different frame of reference was offered by Mikhail Saakashvili, former Prime Minister of Georgia, a state attacked by Russia in 2008. He argued that the situation was "very, very similar" to that in 1938, that "We saw where it led before," that there was the danger of "a new Munich" and, in response to the question, "Are you seriously comparing Putin to Hitler," replied that Putin was attacking neighboring people in a similar fashion.[16]

A common theme in what has been discussed so far is that, far from the end of Communism leading to a liberalization of practices and a de-politicization of history (and much else), there has, in fact, been a tendency to maintain practices of state control, albeit without the directing ideology of Communism and in a context of active public debate. This situation, of the state playing a role but without a directing and international ideology, has ensured that nationalism has come to play a greater part. Yet there has also been a degree of freedom not possible under Communism. This has included the ability to debate the Communist years and to represent them fictionally, notably, but not only, in the former East Germany, as in Florian Henckel von Donnersmarck's film *The Lives of Others* (2007) about the *Stasi*. Such debates were challenged by ex-*Stasi* demonstrators, while there were also attempts to alter Wikipedia entries on East Germany, but at least there was debate while Germany is now a democracy and has a democratic culture.

The post-Communist experience does not only relate to Eastern Europe and Russia. There is also the case of the post-Communism in former republics of the Soviet Union, both in the Caucasus and in Central Asia, where the reconceptualization of history in part reflects a rejection of Russian and Soviet imperialism. In the case of Mongolia, there is a parallel process, although Mongolia was part of the informal (not formal) Soviet empire. The net effect is of a variety of post-Communist experiences, and, thus, histories. This variety is matched by the range of historical discussion offered in the remaining Communist states: China, North Korea, Vietnam,[17] and Cuba.

THE NORTH KOREAN CONTRAST

In the case of North Korea, there has been no letup in the deployment of history to support the personality cult of the ruler. In a state totally controlled by the government, there are state historians and approved works, iconography and terms, alongside incessant censorship.[18] At the same time, the fall of Communism in Eastern Europe, the Soviet Union and Mongolia acted as an historical lesson about the lack of inevitability in current arrangements. Moreover, Germany offered a more specific instance of the possibility of reunification between capitalists and Communists, a reunification, furthermore, that suggested that North Korea could only have a transient existence as a separate state. Thus, in March 2014, it was in a speech given in Dresden, in the former East Germany, that Park Geun-hye, the president of South Korea, outlined proposals designed to ease the reunification of Korea. History as a cumulative process, one in which the past provides a source of new examples and arguments, is exemplified by this episode.

Western Europe

"LE NATIONALISME, C'EST LA GUERRE" ["NATIONALISM IS WAR"], declared François Mitterrand, president of France from 1981 to 1995, in a speech to the European Parliament in 1995. On the one hand, this statement captured the variety of tensions between national and supra-national identities in Europe, and notably the disruptive legacy of nationalism. On the other hand, supra-nationalism, especially in the shape of the European Union, contested the search for renewed patriotism and the sense of national identity in many European countries. Moreover, this supra-nationalism was not readily compatible with an emphasis on cultural diversity and political pluralism.

From a related, but different, perspective, there is a ready tension in contemporary Europe between two uses of history, a tension amply demonstrated in 2014 as Scotland debated independence from Britain and, thereby, separation from England. The first use is the attempt to fashion new myths intended to serve as the basis for a new prospectus of power. The second is the assertion of more longstanding national accounts that, in part, act as a critique of such a new prospectus. The key new myth is that of Europe as an integrationist project resting on a common history and culture – although that is not the sole level of such new history. At the national and regional levels, there have also been attempts to fashion new myths. However, in many senses, these attempts relate to longstanding tensions and debates at these levels, for example over the status of Catalonia within Spain, and are not comparable to the European myth.

A COMMON EUROPEAN HISTORY?

The latter myth draws heavily on the European Union (EU), an active sponsor of such arguments; but the feasibility of this myth has been greatly challenged by the expansionism of the Union since 1973. The original six members of the European Economic Community (France, West Germany, Italy, Belgium, the Netherlands, and Luxembourg) could pretend to a degree of historical as well as geographical and political cohesion, and made reference accordingly to historical figures, notably Charlemagne and Erasmus. In practice, this cohesion was undermined historically by religious and political divisions derived from the Protestant Reformation, which had shattered the unity, first, of the Burgundian inheritance in the Low Countries and, then, of the German-centered Holy Roman Empire.

Accessions of new member states, after the original six, began in 1973, but lacked any logic in terms of cohesion. The contrasts in economy and culture between Britain and Greece, or Finland and Portugal, were matched by a lack of common historical experience, a situation that was exacerbated after former Communist states became members. This lack was disguised by talk of a deep history that looked back to the supposed common characteristics of European culture. However, this interpretation faced serious drawbacks. The idea of a common base was flawed as an analysis of the development of European societies that, in fact, revealed major contrasts and discontinuities.

Moreover, if the emphasis was to be on European culture, it was unclear how this was supposed to exclude the European settler cultures, such as those in the Americas and in Australasia. Lastly, such an interpretation underlined the problem of how best to treat the large immigrant populations in Europe, many of whom did not display these supposed cultural attributes and inheritance. Such issues were pushed further to the fore when the European Union sought to "deepen" and extend in new directions from the mid-2000s, and then to respond, from 2008, to an unprecedented fiscal and economic crisis that opened up strains within the Union.

This deepening involved the attempt to draw up a constitution. As with similar attempts, the search for a common purpose in fact encouraged dissension over this purpose. This occurred in particular over the question of whether the European Union was to be taken to have a Christian character, a character that was held to be historically rooted in European culture. The issue was accentuated by the effort to expand the European Union to include Turkey, a state that was certainly not Christian and which was scarcely European. This effort encouraged a serious questioning of the extent to which the European Union had in fact lost direction. Thus, an argument of identity and difference that owed something to past rivalries, particularly between Christian Greece and Cyprus, and Muslim Turkey, fed into a debate over the future of the European Union. The nature of Turkish development in the twentieth century, as well as more recently, played a role in the discussion of this particular issue. The latter has been especially contentious in the case of Turkish unwillingness to confront the Armenian massacres, while there has been European criticism of both the nature and legacy of Atatürk's regime, the foundation of modern Turkey, and the public culture of its rival, the AK, the Islamicist Justice and Development (Adalet ve Kalkinma) party that has wielded power since 2002.

Spurious claims about Europe were the case for both near and distant history. For example, it was argued that the European Union had kept the peace in Western Europe since 1945. This oft-repeated remark was an all-too-typical instance of the preference for assertion over reason that is an aspect of myth-making, whether national or international. The claim totally underplayed the role of NATO (the North Atlantic Treaty Organization, founded in 1949) and of American military ascendancy in keeping the peace.

In 2007, when Germany held the presidency of the European Union, the German Chancellor, Angela Merkel, suggested a standardized history textbook across the European Union. No such textbook was produced. Indeed, emphasis on a common European core leads to a repetition of a small set stock of figures and episodes. Erasmus, the early sixteenth-century Dutch Humanist writer, is uncontroversial, but some of these figures and episodes have more complex resonances. Thus, Charlemagne, who in 800 CE became the first of the revived Roman emperors, launching what was to be called the Holy Roman Empire, was also a brutal opponent of the Saxons, responsible for the death of large numbers of them. His legacy was called on during World War II when the SS fielded the Charlemagne division of French collaborators. The recent, more positive, use of Charlemagne therefore is an aspect of the rewriting of the past. The set stock includes the Holocaust, presented as a formative episode for contemporary Europe, specifically as a key aspect of the Nazi regime, against which the European Union was established. This account underplayed the extent of widespread complicity in the Holocaust, both in Germany and by Germany's allies.

In 2007, Germany also utilized its presidency of the European Union to ensure the passage of race-hate laws for the entire Union. The German government saw these as an historic obligation, and also an opportunity to exercise leadership. German legislation provided a background, as Holocaust denial was already a crime. However, German hopes of replicating this on a Union-wide scale and thus of enacting a specific ban on Holocaust denial failed. Instead, the EU agreed to criminalize "publicly condoning, denying or grossly trivializing crimes of genocide, crimes against humanity and war crimes," although only where "the conduct is carried out in a manner likely to incite violence or hatred." Estonia, Lithuania, Latvia, Slovenia, and Poland tried, but failed, to have included in this criminalization, a crime of denying, condoning, or trivializing atrocities committed in the name of Stalin.

CONTESTING NATIONAL HISTORIES

Alongside the European myth has come the bitter contesting of national histories. In part, this contesting reflected social and economic changes that led to the weakening or collapse of previously potent social identifiers. These were linked to a more general lack of confidence in hitherto powerful cultural projects for unity through assertion. There was also a breakdown of postwar political consensuses. The challenges were varied, being particularly potent from regional political groupings that embraced autonomy or separatism, for example Catalan and Scottish nationalists. There was also a greater assertiveness on the conservative part of the political spectrum, notably the far Right. Much of this assertiveness was directed against dominant left-of-center, or, at least, corporatist accounts, as well as against immigration and other aspects of globalization. Most of the challenge to consensus was not a matter of historical debate. Instead, the end of the long boom in the early 1970s, followed by the immobility and corrupt elitism of long-standing governments in the 1980s and 1990s, helped lead to anger and to a questioning of conventional nostrums. It was possible to criticize the Kreisky government in Austria, or its Mitterrand (France) or Kohl (Germany) counterparts, without having any particular views on history; although, in 1984, I had the experience of being entertained in Vienna by a senior opposition parliamentarian who was convinced that the best way to understand the position of Bruno Kreisky, chancellor of Austria from 1970 to 1983, was to understand that of Sir Robert Walpole in Britain in the 1721 to 1742, another first minister known for his skill at political manipulation.

At the same time, anger and opposition could be grafted onto long-standing differences and disputes. Indeed, there were "history wars" in each country that had political resonances, "history wars" that looked to the continuation of old rivalries in competing and contested identities. In part, this was a question of names, with the Greens and Whites of Montenegro, the rivals in 1918–1919, over unification with Serbia or autonomy, becoming names that continue into its modern politics. Names carry historical weight as well as present content.

GERMANY

For Germany, the challenges of recent history were very different to those confronting France. As an overseas imperial power, Germany had been more brutal than France or Britain, as the treatment of the Herero tribe of Namibia in 1904–1945 indicated, but Germany's colonies had been lost in World War I before there could be any significant immigration from them to Germany. As a result, the legacy of transoceanic empire is not highly contentious in German public history. This situation is helped by the extent to which Germany did not play more than a minor role in the Atlantic slave trade. The major immigrant community in modern Germany, that from Turkey, is kept separate by the definition of German nationality, and is also in effect in large part segregated into different living areas. Although very important to contemporary discussions about German identity, this community does not play a significant role in the German historical memory, or in controversy about the past.

Instead, it is a community that has largely disappeared that plays a major role: the Jews. This is because they were destroyed by the Germans. The extent to which "ordinary Germans" were involved in this process has been a matter of major contention. The scale of the German killings did not become public knowledge until the liberation of the concentration camps in 1945. The victims, however, were not generally initially differentiated as Jews. Genocide, a term coined in 1944 by the Polish jurist Raphael Lemkin, was not a charge used in the Nuremberg trials of German leaders, "Holocaust" was not a term employed in the trials, and Jewish survivors were not called as witnesses. Nevertheless, the "mass murder" of Jews was an aspect of Count Four of the indictments at Nuremberg, while, in 1948, genocide was made into a crime by a United Nations Convention. The war was followed by a series of trials of those directly responsible for the Holocaust, especially the commandants of concentration camps.

The Holocaust, however, then receded from attention, as efforts were made to forget the war, and as Germany was reconceptualized with the Cold War. Trials were downplayed or abandoned. The desire first to get occupation zones to work and then to "normalize" West and East Germany ensured that, although the Nazi system was rejected, other issues were stressed. Partly as a result, relatively little attention was paid to the Holocaust in the 1950s. This also reflected the nature of the earlier prosecutions, which had focused on proving a Nazi conspiracy to aggression, and thus war guilt, rather than on detailing the actual Nazi crimes. With the emphasis on Nazi perpetrators, and not on their victims, the notion of the collective Jewish suffering was downplayed.[1]

The West German government preferred to ignore the Holocaust and to downplay the Nazi era. One of the first laws passed by the newly constituted *Bundestag* (legislature) in 1949 was a widespread amnesty. The government paid compensation, with the first Federal Compensation Law with Israel being passed in 1953, but there was considerable reluctance to do so, and American pressure was important to securing the measure. Underlining the political character of the treatment of the past, the Social Democrats were readier to engage with the issue of Jewish reparations, whereas the more reluctant Christian Democrats, who were the governing party, tended to emphasize aspects of what they saw as German victimhood. Many West Germans were inclined to criticize what they saw as the Allies' verdict on the war, not least complaining about what they claimed was the "victors' justice" of the Nuremberg and other trials. As with Japan, this was a key aspect of the self-serving presentation by Germans of themselves as victims of the war. Issues of widespread German responsibility were generally shunned. Instead, Hitler and the Nazi regime were held accountable for World War I. Polls indicated that many Germans thought the Jews partly responsible for what had happened to them.[2]

Many Germans, moreover, developed a longstanding account of victimhood that looked back to defeat in World War I and its aftermath, and then to the experience of being bombed by the Allies in World War II,[3] and, subsequently, to the brutal postwar driving of Germans from Eastern Europe. Not only individual German responsibility was shunned, but also the damage done by Germans to others, most blatantly the Holocaust. In explaining the neglect of the Holocaust, this reluctance deserves as much attention as the repositioning of Germany (West or East) as an ally in the Cold War.[4] During the chancellorship of Konrad Adenauer, from 1949 to 1963, many former Nazis were employed in responsible positions in West Germany, while few were tried for war crimes, and the even fewer who were convicted received very light sentences. Reintegration and amnesty were key themes in government policies that enjoyed much public support. Most West Germans proved very willing to ignore or downplay the evidence of the extermination camps, which were now in Communist-run Eastern Europe.

European integration was popular in West Germany as the way back into the international community. In pledging to work for "an ever closer union of the peoples of Europe," the Treaty of Rome of 1957 did not leave room for the recollection of German popular support for Hitler. Meanwhile, East German accounts tended to neglect the Holocaust or to mention it either as a product of capitalism, specifically needs for labor and capital, or of an attempt to divert attention from the failings of capitalism and the Nazi system. Compensation was not paid to Jews. This was because East Germany perceived itself as an anti-Fascist state, and not in the tradition of previous German states, whereas West Germany saw itself explicitly as the legal successor of the German Reich. In East Germany, the victims of Nazi killing were presented as opponents of Fascism and not as Jews.[5]

The situation subsequently changed. The attempt to contain the effects on Germany's image by blaming the atrocities specifically on the Nazis, and thus presenting the bulk of the population as victims, was eventually challenged in West Germany. The pressures on the collective myth of general social and cultural changes were important; specifically, the rise, from the 1960s, of a generation that did not feel responsibility for Nazism, the decline of deference toward the former generations, and the need to explain what had happened during the war to those who had not lived through it as adults. The political and cultural agenda was no longer shaped by the pressures of post-war reconstruction, as well as by the evasion of responsibility by presenting wartime conduct as that of uninformed bystanders. Indeed, an aspect of the critique by the generation of 1968 of their predecessors was the charge that the latter did not mark a break from the wartime cooperation with Nazism and had not accepted individual responsibility. The radical Left accused the previous generation of being the "Nazi generation." It was now argued that coming to terms with the past was an aspect of anchoring democracy in Germany. Human rights became increasingly important in the political agenda. This argument also reflected the rise of the Social Democrats who, from 1969 to 1982, occupied the Federal Chancellery. Visiting Warsaw in 1969, the new chancellor, Willy Brandt, knelt before the Ghetto Monument, a powerfully symbolic gesture of official atonement.

In part, the shift in German attitudes was due to a growing awareness of the atrocities committed by the Nazi regime, not least the trial that opened at Frankfurt in 1963 of 23 men involved in Auschwitz. Witness statements left no doubt of what had occurred and also provided an opportunity for public testimony by survivors. A wall of silence was broken. In December 1964, members of the court made an official visit to Auschwitz. The trial had a strong Cold War dimension, with Friedrich Kaul, the lawyer for the East German civil plaintiffs, being instructed by the East German government to use it as a propaganda opportunity; while the visit to Auschwitz was encouraged by the Polish authorities.

Both despite and, because of, this dimension, the West German authorities and the court did not allow the trial to be used to discredit the idea of trying war criminals, as the key defense lawyer, Hans Laternser, wanted. However, in what, in some respects, proved an unsatisfactory outcome, it proved difficult to bring together collective responsibility and individual guilt.[6]

While there was increased focus on the Holocaust from outside Germany, within West Germany there developed an influential determination to treat the Holocaust as the defining moment of public responsibility. In place of the notion of the Germans as in some way victims of the Nazis[7] (an idea that continued to be pushed especially hard in Austria for the Austrians), came the view that the Germans had collaborated. Recognition of this version was seen as important to the health of German democracy and as crucial to public education. From 1962, the *länder* (provinces) extended the teaching of history to cover the Hitler years, including the Holocaust. Becoming effective from 1967, this was a major step in a process of public education over the Holocaust and one that ensured that the Germans became better informed on the Holocaust than other Europeans, although there were still important lacunae and a lack of agreement about how best to interpret the information. Moreover, there was a reluctance to commemorate key sites. The Bavarian provincial government was opposed to spending money to maintain Dachau as a memorial, and the same was true of the local council.

On the extreme right, Holocaust deniers were active, such as Wilhelm Stäglich, author of *Der Auschwitz-Mythos* (1979). The presence of such deniers and, more generally, of neo-Nazis, who were responsible for acts such as the desecration of Cologne synagogue in 1959, as well as the electoral success of the far-Right NPD during the 1960s, led to support for an emphasis on the need for public education about the Holocaust. This also encouraged a more positive response to foreign representations of the Holocaust. Crucially so in 1979, when the American television series of that name was broadcast to an audience of about twenty million, over half the adult population of West Germany.

Alongside growing interest in, and reference to, the Holocaust were disputes about it – aside from the denial that became central to the mythology and discourse of the extreme Right.[8] In the *Historikerstreit* (controversy among historians) of 1986–1987, there was a dispute about the relationship between the Nazis and the longer-term trends in German history. This had direct relevance to heated debates over the legitimacy of the West German political system and was linked with challenges to the dominant conservative (and, to an extent, gerontocratic) character of post-war West German historical scholarship. The controversy was played out in a very public fashion, with many articles appearing in prominent newspapers. In part, this was a product of the attempt to normalize German history made by historians close to Helmut Kohl, the Christian Democratic chancellor from 1982 to 1998. This normalization was taken to mean making German history more acceptable in order to ground national identity and seek inspiration. Kohl saw such normalization as a necessary basis for patriotism, national pride, and spiritual renewal, a theme taken up more generally by the Christian Democrats. Kohl himself had earlier voted against abolishing the statute of limitations for murder, an abolition that left ex-Nazis vulnerable to prosecution. As a related, although different point, the exceptional focus of the earlier Prussian state on war and the military was downplayed in the major exhibitions devoted to Prussian history, notably under Frederick the Great (r. 1740–1786), those of 1981, 1986, and 2012.[9]

In the *Historikerstreit*, the degree to which Nazism could be seen as an historical episode, rather than inherent in longer-term trends, and to which the Holocaust arose from specific German characteristics, rather than being an aspect of more widespread violence, were debated. So also was the extent to which the German state had an historical mission – specifically to resist advances from the east, the Soviet Union. This approach, pushed by conservatives such as Andreas Hillgruber, led to the claim that German iniquities had to be considered against this background, with Ernest Nolte arguing that the Nazis were a reaction to Communism and that their actions in part emulated those of the Communists. The argument that the Germans had to fight on to resist the Soviet advance was also that of German generals in the final stage of the war. This self-serving argument did not stop them from also mounting fierce resistance to Anglo-American forces, including directing the reserves involved in the 1944 Battle of the Bulge counter-offensive against them, rather than against the Soviets. Fighting on also provided more time for the Holocaust. An essential issue in the *Historikerstreit* was that the Holocaust was seen as implying the problem, indeed issue, of the legitimacy of West Germany. Kohl's attempt at a re-evaluation was unsuccessful in that it led to much criticism, both within Germany and internationally. Nolte and others were attacked by a number of prominent scholars, including Jürgen Habermas. They argued that Nolte was trying to relativize or historicize Nazi activities and thus limit them and reduce the collective and individual responsibilities of Germans. Instead, the Nazi regime was presented as unique in its criminality.[10]

In 1985, Kohl had successfully pressed Ronald Reagan, the American president, on a state visit to West Germany, to visit the military cemetery at Bitburg. The controversy arose because the cemetery contained the graves of forty-nine members of the *Waffen-ss*. They were not ss concentration-camp guards, and, by the time they died, the *Waffen-ss* was no longer a volunteer army. Only fifteen of the forty-nine were registered in the ss personnel files. Nevertheless, the *Waffen-ss* was a vicious organization (indeed, a criminal one in clear breach of international law). Reagan, who had been advised not to visit Bitburg, described the soldiers as being as much victims of the Nazis as those who had suffered in concentration camps, a bizarre remark, but one that reflected the sense that he had to say something about the camps.[11] Reagan also visited the former concentration camp at Belsen.

Especially from the 1990s, new sites of memorialization were opened. In Berlin, the Jewish Museum, opened in 2001, was followed in 2005 by the opening of the Memorial to the Murdered Jews of Europe, which was designed to represent a Jewish cemetery. A large work, the size of two football fields, built close to the Brandenburg Gate and the site of Hitler's bunker, the memorial was presented not simply as a response to the past, but also as a warning. In 2004, Wolfgang Thierse, the speaker of the parliament, praised the memorial for being also "about the future: a reminder that we should resist antisemitism at its roots."

Rivalry for historical attention was prominent in the case of sites. Thus, there was competition over funding between former concentration camps, such as Buchenwald, Dachau, and Ravensbrück, and sites in East Germany that commemorate the victims of Communism. Within the Christian Democratic Party, there is pressure for equivalent treatment, as all those commemorated were victims of political dictatorship. This was the argument of Bernd Neumann, the head of cultural affairs in Angela Merkel's chancellery. The Central Board of German Jews rejects this equivalence, arguing that it diminishes the Holocaust. Furthermore, it was necessary to rely on Stalin's forces to end the Holocaust.[12]

The murderous treatment of the Jews was the key section of a more generally shameful set of German policies between 1931 and 1945. Subsequent controversy over them has reflected political and social changes in Germany. For example, the extent of German resistance to the Nazi regime has been discussed in a fashion that was greatly affected by postwar politics. Seeking to integrate West Germany into the West as the front line against Communism, there was a tendency during much of the Cold War to emphasize the role of the resistance and also to downplay the part of Communists within it. There was a linked positive presentation of the *Wehrmacht,* which was contrasted to the ss, to provide the idea of good and bad Germans. This approach proved particularly convenient given the major role of the *Bundeswehr,* the West German army, in NATO, and the extent to which part of the membership and identity of the *Bundeswehr* derived from the *Wehrmacht.* This approach did not encourage scrutiny of the actual conduct of the army.

Subsequently, in contrast, there was a growing, but contested, willingness to note the extent of popular complicity in the Nazi regime. This process extended to a far less positive account of the *Wehrmacht.* Its complicity in the brutalities of the Nazi regime was brought out. The greatest controversy was caused by the *Wehrmacht* exhibition arranged by the Hamburg Social Research Institute, which toured Germany and Austria from 1994, drawing 800,000 visitors in thirty-three cities by 1999. The photographs of *Wehrmacht* soldiers involved in atrocities had a major impact on the public and led to much discussion and contention, including hostile demonstrations in Dresden and Munich and a terrorist attack by right-wing extremists at Saarbrücken in 1999. The thesis that the army, instead of only the ss, had been active in the Holocaust cut across the argument that they were patriots fighting for their country.[13] There was a corresponding reinterpretation of other institutions, such as the judiciary, emphasizing their active role in the Nazi regime.

At the same time, there was a major emphasis on the role of the German resistance, which was presented as demonstrating a line of continuity in German history beyond Nazism. The annual state ceremony to commemorate the July 20, 1944, bomb plot against Hitler was important to this commemoration.[14] In practice, these plotters were scarcely democratic, but they were important for the construction of an acceptable German identity.

In the 2000s, stress on the Germans as victims reemerged with the treatment of the Third Reich in films, a downplaying of the role of "ordinary Germans" in support of Hitler,[15] and an emphasis on suffering at the hands of Anglo-American bombers and advancing Soviet troops. These themes were also much pressed in the 2010s. The idea of the Germans as victims was deployed not only to make a convenient sense of the past but also to make political points.

By the 2000s, the issue of surviving Nazis ebbed as they died out, but, earlier, that had been a key topic. The career of Hans Filbinger (1913–2007) was symptomatic: Minister-President of Baden-Württemberg from 1966 and a critic of the Left, Filbinger was named in a newspaper article in 1978 as a wartime military judge who sentenced deserters to death. Filbinger responded by denial, suing for libel, and claimed that "what was lawful then cannot be unlawful now." Filbinger was forced to resign that year, and his rehabilitation in the 2000s was controversial. Revelations remained contentious, including, in 2006, in the autobiography of Günther Grass, that he had spent several months in 1944 in the *Waffen-ss*. Grass had long pressed for an honest appraisal of the German role in World War II without mentioning this war service.

More recent history was also a matter of contention, not least the degree to which West Germany should be seen as a continuation of earlier periods in German history, and therefore of the authoritarian, aggressive regimes that had run Germany in 1871–1918 and 1933–1945. In part, this issue was a revival of the controversies that focused on the left-wing activism of 1968. That activism was more charged than in many European countries because of the legacy in the shape of the violent Red Army Faction (Baader-Meinhof Gang); again, the choice of terms can be significant. Whether its members should be released thus became an aspect of an ongoing engagement with the recent German past, which, in the case of the activities of the Red Army Faction, reached its height in 1977. The Italian and British equivalents are discussion about the Red Brigades and the Provisional IRA, issues that relate, especially in the case of the latter, to present politics as much as historical discussion. As elsewhere, the debate in Germany focused also on issues of symbolism. Thus, in 2007 there was controversy over whether Kochstrasse, the Berlin headquarters of two leading German newspapers, including the right-wing *Bild Zeitung*, should be renamed Rudi Dutschke Strasse after a prominent radical of 1968. The residents voted yes, but the *Bild* went to court to oppose the measure as overly expensive.

ITALY

The contentious nature of Italian politics ensured that, as with other Mediterranean states, it proved impossible to advance an account of the national past that captured support across the political spectrum.[16] Indeed, hostility to the established account became more intense as a full-fledged separatist party developed in the shape of the Northern League, the very title of which was a reference back to medieval episodes of urban leagues in northern Italy.

The *Risorgimento*, the struggle for national unification, had been the central narrative in the history of the Italian state. This struggle was largely achieved in 1861, when Naples and Sicily were brought into the state by conquest. That verdict was inscribed in street names and statues across Italy, with streets and squares named after the rulers of the House of Savoy, now kings of Italy, and after the ministers and figures who had furthered the *Risorgimento*, notably Cavour and Garibaldi. At the time of the fiftieth anniversary, in 1911, these themes were to be fore under the Liberal governments of the period, which were descendants of those that had secured the *Risorgimento*. The situation was to be different for the centenary in 1961.

By then, Italy was a republic and the role of the House of Savoy was scarcely to the fore. Moreover, the Left, notably in the person of Antonio Gramsci, had denounced the *Risorgimento* as a Liberal movement that had neither sought, nor brought, social justice. Instead, the emphasis on the Left was on the Resistance to Germany and Italian Fascism in 1943–

1945, a resistance in which the Left, notably the Communists, had been prominent. In 1961, the commemoration of the *Risorgimento* was pushed by the Christian Democrats who dominated the Italian government. Emphasizing the *Risorgimento* meant countering the view of the Left and also affirming an honorable tradition of, and for, Italian nationalism.[17]

By 2011, the situation was totally different. A Left in which Communism was far weaker was ready to embrace the *Risorgimento* as a progressive nationalism. Conversely, the right-wing government under Silvio Berlusconi was somewhat embarrassed by the anniversary in large part because the governing coalition included the Northern League, a separatist movement for which union with the South in 1861 was a mistake. Indeed, the Northern League had sponsored its own history involving an emphasis on Northern Italian distinctiveness. At times, this was highly problematic, as in attempts to argue that there was a Northern Italian political identity prior to the Roman conquest.

FRANCE

In France, the key debate was over the Vichy legacy. This debate related in particular to France's behavior during World War II, one that also looked to the more distant past of France as well as to its current politics. Established in 1940 after France's defeat by Germany, the Vichy regime ran the part of France not under German or Italian occupation, and cooperated with the Germans. As such, the regime was opposed by the Resistance, which existed within France and was given leadership by the Free French movement led, in exile in London, by Charles de Gaulle.

The merits and popularity of Vichy proved contentious subjects after World War II. Debate was patchy, often a matter of private discussion, but with some public consideration. For long the role of Vichy was underplayed, notably by the French government. For example, in the Memorial to the Martyrs of the Deportation in Paris inaugurated in 1962 by Charles de Gaulle, president from 1958 to 1969, there was no mention of the major role taken by Vichy. This remained the case for the information displayed at the entrance there in 2014. De Gaulle's attempt to create a collective memory involved sidestepping, indeed ignoring, many of the complexities of the war.

However, these complexities became more prominent from the 1970s. Discussion encompassed an assault on the myth that most of the French had supported the Resistance against German occupation in 1940–1944. This discussion was linked to longstanding contention over the political complexion of the Resistance. Such contention led to rival, indeed contested, commemorations of episodes and of heroes such as Jean Moulin, a major Gaullist Resistance figure, responsibility for the capture of whom by the Germans was bitterly disputed.[18] At the same time, scholarship and the publication of memoirs threw additional light on the Resistance.[19] False accounts, however, circulated in France, notoriously that by Louis Darquier, Commissioner for Jewish Affairs under Vichy,[20] who told the journal *L'Express* in 1978 that the Holocaust was a "hoax" and that "only lice" were gassed in Auschwitz. His self-interested lies were only different in scale to those voiced by many other Fascists, both French and others.

The presentation of Vichy has been the main theme in "history wars" in France since the 1970s and, even more, 1980s.[21] Tarnishing the Resistance, or questioning its popularity, served the interests of those who looked back to Vichy, as well as compromising the nationalist historical account outlined for the Fourth and Fifth Republics. Indeed, the government still memorializes the Resistance with considerable zeal. The sensitivity of France's wartime conduct was increased, first, by the ambiguous approach to Vichy taken by François Mitterrand, President from 1981 to 1995, and his failure to condemn the regime, and, secondly, by the use of Vichyist themes by Jean-Marie Le Pen's far-right-wing *Front National* (FN) movement. Le Pen was also charged with denying the Holocaust. Mitterrand proved a particularly ambiguous figure, adamantly refusing to apologize for the Vichy regime, being a friend to Vichy figures, and sending wreaths to the tomb of Marshal Pétain, the head of the Vichy government. One of Mitterrand's friends, René Bousquet, wartime chief of police in the Occupied Zone of France, had allowed the use of French police in arresting Jews and had pressed for the deportation of foreign Jews to Eastern Europe. Bousquet was assassinated in 1993, just before he could be tried for his role in rounding up Jewish children for deportation to slaughter.[22] Maurice Papon, the wartime Secretary-General at the Prefecture of the Gironde, who had played the major role in the deportation of Bordeaux's Jews, before having a distinguished post-war career as a minister and official, was only arrested after Mitterrand's death. In his refusal to accept collective responsibility, Mitterrand shared the attitudes of his friend and political ally, Kohl.

In contrast to Mitterrand, Jacques Chirac, the president who succeeded him in 1995, serving until 2007, was at great pains to apologize and commemorate the victims, as was his successor, Nikolas Sarkozy. On 16 July 1995, the anniversary of the major round-up of Jews in Paris in 1940, Chirac accepted national responsibility for the wartime treatment of Jews. In 2004, as part of its attempt to combat anti-semitism, the Education Ministry distributed to schools DVDs with excerpts of *Shoah* (1985), Claude Lanzmann's film about the Holocaust (in Eastern Europe, not France).[23] Also that year, Chirac sought an appropriate historical context for a call to act against a rising wave of anti-semitism and racism. He travelled to Le Chambon-sur-Lignon, a village in the Massif Central that had sheltered Jews from the Holocaust, in order to declare: "Faced with the rise of intolerance, racism and antisemitism . . . I ask the French to remember a still recent past. I tell them to remain faithful to the lessons of history, a so-recent history."

De Gaulle's role in public history in France rests largely on his rejection of surrender to Germany in 1940 and his leadership of the Free French, a key body in the resistance to German occupation. This history therefore looms heavily in the background when French politicians seek to appropriate his legacy, as in 2010, the fortieth anniversary of the President's death. Sarkozy used the commemorations to claim the mantle, employing de Gaulle's phrase "If France has called me to serve as its guide, it is certainly not to preside over its sleep," as a way to claim a pedigree for his own deeply unpopular attempt to raise the retirement age. Earlier in 2010, Sarkozy had visited London to commemorate the seventieth anniversary of de Gaulle's BBC broadcast of 18 June 1940, urging continual resistance. In turn, Sarkozy's critics, such as Dominque de Villepin, a former Prime Minister and a bitter rival on the Right, denied the linkage between Sarkozy and de Gaulle, not least by referring to the Anglo-French defense agreement of 2010 negotiated by Sarkozy as contrasting with the general's robust national self-sufficiency. The fortieth anniversary of de Gaulle's death led, in November 2010, to a public opinion poll in France surveying what event linked to him seemed the most remarkable. Compared to the poll in November 1970, there was a marked rise in those who answered with the call to resistance made on 18 June 1940. The differences in the two polls, and further information on current views provided by the age-breakdown of respondents,[24] indicates the extent to which history, in the sense of the understanding of the past, is protean and is changed by, and through, the public, as much as by other bodies. Moreover, the commemorative role provides instances of what was seen as significant. Thus, in 1958, de Gaulle presented his new constitution establishing the French Fifth Republic to the nation in a speech delivered on 4 September, the anniversary of the proclamation of the Third Republic in 1870, and therefore an affirmation of continuity with the republican past, rather than, as his critics claimed, as an authoritarian alternative.[25]

In France, apologies and commemorations are used to try to still controversy or signal unity around a particular consensus, as in 2006 when Chirac praised the vindication a century earlier of Alfred Dreyfus, a Jewish army officer wrongly sentenced for treason amid much controversy and publicity in 1894, and subsequently cleared. In doing so, Chirac, a figure of the Right, signaled his opposition to more toxic and long-lasting aspects of the right-wing legacy. This approach drew a line between the established Right and the extremist *Front National*, and showed that the established Right was the appropriate custodian of the republican legacy, a point long contested by the Left. The approach to World War II provides particular instances of this approach, as both Chirac and Sarkozy strongly dissociated the republic, the Right, and themselves, from the Vichy regime and from collaboration with German occupation – episodes that have led to repeated crises of memory in France.[26] In 2010, Sarkozy unveiled a plaque at the Arc de Triomphe commemorating the Parisian students who demonstrated on 11 November 1940, against the decision taken by the German authorities and the collaborationist prefecture of Paris to downplay the commemorations of the Armistice ending World War I, a demonstration that was violently suppressed. The role of commemorations was exemplified in this issue, as the Armistice commemorated France's earlier defeat of Germany.

Also in 2010, the SNCF, the state-owned rail company, expressed remorse for carrying Jews to German concentration camps. In part, this step was taken to ensure a better chance at obtaining well-paying contracts for high-speed rail lines in the United States. In 2011, this step was followed by a formal public apology directly to Holocaust victims, while the company handed the station of Bobigny over to local authorities in order to create a memorial to the Jews transported from there to the concentration camps.[27]

Supported by the French republic as an aspect of its commemorative process, the politics of apology is reasonably successful in asserting norms of behavior. National identity provided not only a means to link past and present, but also to justify particular policies. In 2009, Sarkozy and the Prime Minister, François Fillon, wrote to Eric Besson, the new Minister of Immigration, Integration, and National Identity, announcing a clear prospectus: "La promotion de notre identité nationale doit être au coeur de votre action" [the promotion of our national identity must be at the heart of your action]. At the same time, the use of history by the government in the cause of identity was criticized from within the French academic community. The "Maison de l'histoire de France" that Sarkozy announced in 2010 was criticized for being Franco-centric and ideological, and for focusing on the state. The signatories of a critical piece in *Le Monde* on 22 October 2010 were major historians, including Roger Chartier, Arlette Farge, Jacques Le Goff, and Daniel Roche; but there was also an air of unreality about their wish to dilute the national, etatist (state) account.

Differing views on Vichy resonate with contrasting accounts of France and French history as a whole; and, in turn, these validate current political preferences. Challenges to an acceptable French historical nationalism came from a variety of directions. Part related to the conduct of France abroad, specifically the character of French imperialism, especially in North Africa where France was the colonial power in Algeria from 1830 to 1962. This conduct was politically sensitive because of contention over the consequences of large-scale immigration from the region, not least the extent of disorder in areas dominated by immigrants. Riots in Paris, for example, in 2005, made the issue more acute. The result was a controversy over the nature of French imperial policy that ended up in legislative debate and public contention. In 2006, there were bitter quarrels about the treatment of Algeria when a colony. The issue also had a cultural manifestation with *Indigènes* (2006), a major film discussing the role of the Algerian soldiers who fought for France in the two world wars and then were largely ignored, not least in terms of their war pensions. The entire episode underlined the difficulty of creating an effective historical account in a state with an imperial past where a major legacy of that past is a substantial immigrant population with a sense of grievance, unless that grievance is openly confronted. Assimilation confronted resistance to incorporating accounts.

Moreover, political contention about historical episodes did not slacken with time; however, there could be changes in emphasis. Marine Le Pen, who succeeded her father as head of the FN in 2011, offered a different historical focus, concentrating on immigration rather than World War II. She faced charges in early 2014 for comparing the spillover of Islamic prayers into the streets to the Nazi occupation, an approach, implicitly criticizing Vichy, which, to a degree, dissociated her from her father's favor for Vichy and his association with anti-semitism. A rift between the two over the latter became public later in 2014.

The ability of the past to provide issues and symbols that resonate ranges widely across the political agenda in France, but is particularly significant when popular agitation plays a significant role, because of the historical legacy of popular action. Thus, in the region of Brittany in 2013, a fiscal revolt against a new "eco-tax," which was to be a charge on large trucks using main roads in an effort to discourage road freight, led to large-scale demonstrations as well as to attacks on toll sensors. The demonstrators waved Breton flags and wore *bonnets rouges,* red woolen hats, an echo of the headgear worn in a 1675 uprising in Brittany against taxes imposed by Louis XIV. That uprising was unsuccessful, but it was an act of large-scale, armed Breton resistance, and provided an unwelcome parallel for the unpopular Socialist government of President François Hollande, which abandoned the tax in 2013. In this case, as in many others, the echo of the past provides a resonance that is not related to the particular issues at stake.

The same could be seen with the dispute in early 2014 over the Hollande government's attempt to revise terminology and laws in order to ensure legal parity between men and women. The Right, in response, evoked a range of references, not only Orwellian language, but also the attempts of the Revolutionaries to transform French society in the 1790s. The Minister of Women's Rights, Najat Vallaud-Belkacem, was referred to as an indefatigable Fouquier-Tinville of familial practices and personal habits. This was a reference to a bogey of the French Revolution, Antoine Quentin Fouquier-Tinville, the public prosecutor before the Revolutionary Tribunal during the Terror of 1793–1794. The comparison, which was ridiculous, had no meaning outside France, but showed the range of possible reference. The government backed down.

SPAIN

In the case of countries ruled into the 1970s or beyond by authoritarian right-wing regimes, such as Chile, Greece, Portugal, South Africa, and Spain, the legacy was different from that of the former Communist states. Once these regimes had fallen, the new governments and the liberated publics did not have to address so insistent and comprehensive an ideology as Communism, in part because, however authoritarian, these right-wing states did not have a regime as powerful and insistent as the Communist ones. In part, this reflects the continuation of a liberal dimension to society during the years of conservative ascendancy and its ready return to influence once the latter ended. Moreover, despite the significance of American support for these states during the Cold War, there was no equivalent then to the dominant power of the Soviet Union. Nevertheless, the weight of the past has still been addressed. This need reflects a drive for justice, in part the attempt to exploit the past for political ends, if not revenge, and, in part, the attempt by conservatives to adapt to newly democratic times. Reference to truth and reconciliation, in short, does not capture the varied cross-currents in such situations, nor the extent to which only some of these currents tend to be, often can be, expressed in truth and reconciliation processes.

In Spain, the right-wing dictator Francisco Franco, who had seized power as a result of his success in the Spanish Civil War of 1936–1939, died in 1975, after which his authoritarian system came to an end. During his regime, there was a determined attempt to present the type of history that the Vichy regime in France would have applauded. There was an emphasis on unity and the central role of Catholicism, and an exclusion both of regional perspectives and of the important role of Jews and Muslims in Spanish history. The harsher aspects of the Francoist approach were, however, moderated from the late 1950s as the divisions of the Civil War, while still stressed, were replaced. Instead, there was a memorialization linked to an attempted national reconciliation. This reconciliation was designed to secure the stability of the new order, a new order that adopted a more technocratic character. Indeed, in order to pursue reconciliation, there was at times a conscious omission of the Civil War; rather as Communist China was to underplay the Chinese Civil War (1946–1949) when seeking reconciliation with Taiwan. The university curriculum under Franco frequently stopped the teaching of Spanish history in the nineteenth century, or quickly moved through the 1930s, presenting them as a lesson about the dangers of liberal rule. Critical accounts of Franco and of the Nationalists in the Civil War of course were not published in Spain. Thus, a Basque translation of George Steer's *The Tree of Gernika: A Field Study of Modern War* (1938) had to be published by exiles in Caracas in Venezuela in 1963.[28] The Spanish government also took measures to stop the investigation of many episodes, notably the Civil War, not least by closing the archives. The situation abroad was not much better, as many relevant archives, particularly those of the Soviet Union, were also closed, which made it difficult to follow the politics of intervention in the Civil War, and, indeed, the extent to which each side received foreign assistance.

After Franco's death, there was a determination to move beyond his legacy as an aspect of the creation of a new, democratic Spain. This was the Pact of Forgetting, and it was maintained during the centrist government of 1976–1982, and its left-wing and right-wing successors of 1982–1997 and 1997–2004, respectively. The last, the Aznar government, in particular, tried to present a consensus view of the past. There was also a failure of novelists and filmmakers to consider the Civil War, especially in the 1970s. The anniversaries of key events in the 1930s were left to private discussion rather than to public memorialization.

There were, however, cracks in the edifice. An anti-Francoist intellectual consensus developed with, for example, a discreet revolution in the Spanish universities in the 1980s. Moreover, a Civil War archive in Salamanca was organized in the 1980s. Ironically, most of the material was originally by Republicans and had been compiled under the Francoists in order to try Republican leaders. The opening or, at least partial opening, of foreign archives was also instructive. The end of the Cold War and the fall of the Soviet Union were important, as they clarified much about Stalin's policy, not least his manipulation of the Republican government. There was also an opening up of non-Soviet material, including in Italy.

In the 2000s, the uneasy consensus within Spain about the Civil War collapsed. In part, this collapse was a result of political pressure, especially from regions striving for proto-nationalism, particularly Catalonia. The more general assault on the Castilian, centralized account of Spanish history helped lead to reconsideration of the Civil War, in part because of the prominent role of Catalonia in the resistance to Franco. There was also an attack in Spain at the popular level on the Pact of Forgetting, an attack that proved an aspect of the loss of control by the politicians in a more democratic society. The *Asociación para la Recuperación de la Memoria Histórica* (ARMH), established in 2000, sought to recuperate the historical memory of the Republicans. Novelistic accounts of the large-scale slaughter of Republicans during, and after, the Francoist takeover were published in the 2000s in what became a widespread cultural movement. These books became popular, and many were published at the local level. Moreover, the internet was extensively used to discuss the issue. Much of this discussion and pressure focused on the bodies in the large number of mass graves across Spain. The families of Republicans were insistent that their forbears be exhumed, identified, and reburied. This pressure coincided with advances in DNA testing and forensic science that made such identification a stronger prospect. Furthermore, the age of the children of the victims lent a sense of urgency to the situation, with pressure for the identification of their parents before they themselves died. The grandchildren proved the main champions. The first exhumation occurred in 2000, and, by 2003, there were exhumations at Francoist concentration camps. The search for truth was linked to memorialization, with plaques now explaining how people had died. This process paralleled that in France where plaques came to emphasize the role of Vichy in the fate of France's Jews. As with similar campaigns elsewhere in the world, Spain came under pressure to grant restitution of property and for the return of children that had been seized. After the Civil War, such children had been given to the families of Francoist officers, as also happened in Argentina under an authoritarian conservative military rule in the 1970s.

Politics played a role. The Aznar government opposed what it saw as left-wing pressure for action, not least for a judicial process to investigate the cause of all deaths. After the government fell in 2004, its replacement, under the Socialist José Luis Rodríguez Zapatero, was keen not only to reverse Aznar's policies but also to win political capital thereby. Funds, political backing, and legal support were provided for the ARMH. The left-wing pressure led to a backlash from the Right, with writers who restated the old Francoist view and attacked the re-evaluation of the history of the 1930s finding an eager public. In 2006, 30 percent of the respondents in a poll in the newspaper *El Mundo* argued that the Francoist uprising of 1936 had been justified. Thus, the recall of history reflected and sustained persisting cleavages in Spanish society, and, indeed, beyond. The Civil War, moreover, continued to be part of the vocabulary of Spanish politics. In 2007, Jesús de Polanco, the head of media empire Grupo Prisa, accused the conservative opposition People's Party of wanting "to go back to the Civil War" because of its criticism of left-wing media opinions. This reference to the past provided an easy way to say that something appeared unacceptable, a more general tendency. However, the comparison was misguided, not least because Spain was in a very different situation to that in the 1930s, in part because in the 2000s it was part of international systems, most obviously the European Union. The bitter debate continued into the 2010s, with revisionism on behalf of Franco criticized from the Left. Tales of atrocities by both sides were recounted in a partisan fashion.[29]

Controversies in Spain are, at once, as is common elsewhere in the world, an instance of the truth and reconciliation process and also an example of present politics. The first has become normative as a result of what is held to be the positive instance of such a process in post-apartheid South Africa. The political dimension operates in part as a cross-current to that of truth and reconciliation, as political capital is sought, although this process can also be regarded as central to the entire idea of truth and reconciliation.

In Spain, the role of politics was seen in 1998 when a Spanish judge arranged for the arrest of General Augusto Pinochet, dictator of Chile from 1973 to 1990. This was a move very much opposed by a Spanish government that was keen on reconciliation within Spain. Pinochet was regarded on the Left as a substitute for the dead Franco. Contradiction in Spain between the impossibility of arresting any member of the Franco government and the possibility of acting against Pinochet was brought into the open in a way intended to embarrass the Aznar government.

The complex process of marking Spain's recent past was seen in 2014 when the anniversary of an attempted right-wing military coup in 1981 was marked. Lieutenant-Colonel Antonio Tejero Diaz of the Civil Guard was dismissed for organizing an unauthorized lunch at a Civil Guards barracks for his father, the leader of the attempted coup, and other plotters.

PORTUGAL

In Portugal, the legacy of the authoritarian right-wing Salazarist *Nova Stato* dictatorship from 1932 to 1974 was not, subsequently, a key element in political dispute. In part, this was because there was, in effect, a pact of forgetting between the political parties, but also because there was no political movement of weight looking back to the Salazar dictatorship. There was no past on offer that was attractive, not least because Portugal's imperial position, which had been significant to the ideology of the *Nova Stato,* was totally gone. The post-dictatorial governments did see a degree of restitution, notably for the reputation of Humberto Delgado, a one-time figure in the regime who had become a democrat and stood for President in 1958, only to lose in a rigged election. In 1965, Delgado was killed by the secret police in circumstances that are contentious, notably as to whether he was plotting against the regime or had been entrapped. Marío Soares, the Socialist Prime Minister from 1976 to 1978 and 1983 to 1985, had supported Delgado, and had his remains interred in the National Pantheon. Delgado was also retrospectively promoted to field marshal.

However, in the early twenty-first century, dissension over Portugal's economic-social crisis led some historians on the Right to praise Salazar, a parallel to the revisionism on behalf of Franco and Mussolini already seen in Spain and Italy. In contrast, on the Left, there was criticism of the failure of Portugal to modernize during his regime. Academic and popular interest in the regime rose. The future role of the Salazar regime in Portugal's politico-historical consciousness is unclear.

BRITAIN

The situation in Britain has varied considerably over the last three decades. Again, political partisanship has played a role, and there has been a conscious process of revisionism. This was particularly seen on the Right. Under the Conservative governments of Margaret Thatcher (1979–1990) and John Major (1990–1997), there were efforts to argue a continuation with the past, not least in terms of a robust patriotism that was particularly asserted by Thatcher and linked to her wish to revive appreciation of pre-1945 values and achievements, particularly those of the Victorians. Thus, in 1986, Conservative MPs criticized *The Monocled Mutineer,* a BBC drama about an alleged mutiny by British troops during World War I, as inaccurate and as deliberately designed to mock authority. In an article published in the *Daily Mail* on 3 January 2014, Michael Gove, the Conservative secretary of state for education from 2010 to 2014, cited the program as an instance of the distorted view of the war as a "misbegotten shambles."

In academic circles, Thatcher's call to reconsider national history was related to a positive re-evaluation of the Conservative leaders who preceded Churchill and the strand of Conservatism that was displaced by him. This reevaluation was certainly not linked to Thatcherism in foreign policy as her effort to increase ideological commitments and to push the bounds of possibility clashed with the pre-1940 policies of appeasement. In domestic policy, however, there was a clearer parallel in terms of a self-conscious rejection of elements of the big government of 1945–1979. Thus, Correlli Barnett's book *The Audit of War: The Illusion and Reality of Britain as a Great Power* (1986) argued that Labour's expenditure on welfare compromised the economic and military future of the country. This sense of betrayal drew on another historical work, Martin Wiener's *English Culture and the Decline of the Industrial Spirit* (1981), which appealed to Thatcherite critics of Conservative "Wets" (liberals) with its argument, or what could be constructed as its argument, that the economic past (and therefore future) had been betrayed by elitist liberal opposition to entrepreneurism. Far from seeking to preserve the past, Thatcher was happy to reject what she saw as its responsibility for decline, and notably so in the case of the recent past, which she saw as a betrayal of a deeper past. Indeed, drawing a parallel to radicalism in China, her cabinet colleague John Biffen referred, as a result, to "Tory Maoism."[30]

The continuing contentiousness of the Thatcher government was apparent in 2013 in the divided response to her death, and also, each year, as documents from the period were released to public view in the National Archives. The controversial character of what was recalled was seen in 2014 as some commentators focused on documents indicating that there had been a government plan to close coal mines – a plan denied at the time – while others noted government concern about the links between the National Union of Miners and both the Soviet Union and Libya, in short a location of the bitter 1984–1985 miners' strike in terms of the Cold War. There was also division within the Right over the Thatcher legacy, with critics of David Cameron, Conservative Prime Minister from 2010 to 2015, contrasting him to what was presented, somewhat misleadingly, as a degree of greater ideological coherence on the part of Thatcher.

Alongside the ritual obfuscation of the faults of the deceased and the skullduggery linked to their rise and maintenance in power, obituaries became a way to contest recent history and, in doing so, to probe values. The memorialization of Thatcher provided an instance, and so did that of one of her opponents, the veteran left-wing politician Tony Benn, who died in 2014. There was much praise for Benn across the political spectrum, but also a biting piece in the *Times* by the former Conservative MP Matthew Parris, who referred to Benn as "a deluded left-winger . . . notorious old twister . . . [with] poisonous beliefs . . ." Parris continued by making a broader point about the role of memorialization and "uncritical legacies" in helping to shape myths that made "a 'sensible reading of history'" harder to explain. That doubtless would be a widely accepted view, although it raises the question of what constitutes such "a 'sensible reading.'" Parris went on to criticize Clement Attlee, the Labour Prime Minister in 1945–1951:

> Attlee's takeover of the coal and steel industries began a series of nationalizations that pointed post-war economic policy in wholly the wrong direction and helped to cripple our recovery.... The slow-burn catastrophe of putting health into the hands of a central state monolith was one of 20th century Britain's most far-reaching mistakes. Do we find it hard to come to terms with the mistake because of misplaced deference to the "nobility" of their venture . . . ? Demythologizing the leaders of the Left in Britain since 1945 would be a useful first step towards thinking straight about modern political history . . . Anthony Crosland is lauded as an intellectual: he was a destroyer of our education system.[31]

The details and tone of this critique can of course be contested. However, its significance is clear, for Parris and those who disagree with him understand that contesting the recent tradition of a political party is an aspect of the politics of today. And so, also, as this book argues, with earlier history. The notion of an autonomy from the political process is of limited value in so far as the implications of historical works are concerned.

Under Labour, in power from 1997–2010, there was a transformation in historical consciousness. The espousal of new policies under the self-conscious New Labour platform was linked to a process of asserting a new identity that included a different historical consciousness to that which had hitherto prevailed. Class-based analyses and trade union sentiment were pushed aside, as Tony Blair, Labour leader from 1994 to 2007 and Prime Minister from 1997 to 2007, made a pitch for the middle ground. In doing so, he deliberately broke with the past and embraced the idea of the new, as in his references to "New Britain." Indeed, in 1997, Peter Mandelson, a key ally for Blair and the ideologue for New Labour, declared, "We are defining ourselves by the future." Similar platitudes were frequently offered. This policy had immediate implications with the provisions for new government in Scotland and Wales, and for changes in the House of Lords. The Northern Ireland settlement, the Good Friday Agreement in 1998, also led to an avowed break with the past, with Blair urging that the legacy of sectarian bitterness be ditched.

In part, in 1990s Britain, there was a rejection of the past and, in part, a response to the multiplicity of narratives of the past being offered in an increasingly openly diverse society. These included narratives of ethnic and religious difference and distinction, as well as specifically gendered narratives, for example "queer history."[32] This approach was very apparent at the time of the Millennium in 2000, with the emphasis being very much on present and future, rather than the past, which, indeed, was largely neglected in the events depicted in the Millennium Dome in London, the most prominent (and expensive) commemoration of the Millennium. Underlying assumptions continued. In July 2003, Blair told the American Congress "a study of history provides so little instruction for our present day."

A different approach, however, was increasingly taken by the mid-2000s, largely in conscious reaction to what was seen as the modishness of New Labour and, in particular, to its negative consequences for a sense of national identity, indeed popular nationalism. The 2005 London suicide bombings by British-born citizens contributed to a sense of crisis about an apparent failure of collective consciousness. As a result, Labour politicians, most obviously Gordon Brown from 2006, and, even more, while Prime Minister from 2007 to 2010, reached out for an assertion of nationalism that included a positive embrace of the past. This approach reflected civic purpose as well as political calculation, the latter how best to sell a Scottish-dominated Labour Party to an England increasingly concerned about developments and to a Scotland greatly affected by nationalist separatism. Holding UKIP (the United Kingdom Independence Party) and, even more, the far-Right BNP (British National Party) at bay, by ensuring that nationalism was not annexed to xenophobia, was also an issue.

More than Labour calculations, however, were at stake. Indeed, the pressure for a more public history in large part sprang from a reaction against earlier Labour neglect under Blair, which, in some non-Labour cases, was compounded by concern about the direction of Labour's interest when roused. The latter certainly underlay Conservative discussions prior to, and after, the 2005 election about the need to assert a positive account of national history. There was, for example, disquiet about *Life in the United Kingdom: A Journey to Citizenship,* the Home Office-sanctioned summary of British history that was seen as part of the process of naturalization, and also about the content of the citizenship studies advocated by the government. Other circles and constituencies also called for more national history, not least in response to school curricula dominated, or apparently dominated, by discussion of the Third Reich. These calls affected the new National Curriculum, introduced in 2013.[33]

There is a tension in Britain between positive integrative history and disparate traditions, and, in essence, Labour switched position from the second to the former in the 2000s. Initially, the Labour failure to endorse national history to any extent was linked to its greater accessibility to, and for, the disparate approach. It was as if there was a vacuum, with history as a national cause being anachronistic and associated with the Conservatives. Subsequently came history-building by national government, first Labour in the late 2000s, and then the Conservative-dominated coalition established after the 2010 general election. In 2014, David Cameron, the Prime Minister, pressed the case for teaching national values, in part in response to concerns about Muslim influence in some schools. His definition of national values was grounded in an account of British history that was contested by critics who adopted a more critical approach and one that made more of an allowance for a variety of accounts.

In seeking to establish praiseworthy and integrating values by looking to the past – in short, a benign national identity – government, however, necessarily offers a partial account of both national identity and national history. By its nature, this approach, moreover, clashes with that of disparate views, as these views frequently presuppose a malign, hostile, or, at least, indifferent national culture against which they exert themselves. Thus, in 2004, the Labour Home Secretary, David Blunkett, at the first "citizenship ceremony" for immigrants, provided a positive account when he declared, "Britain has a great tradition as a tolerant and welcoming nation." While correct in comparative terms (compare Britain to Germany or Japan), this view did not find favor with critics advancing the disparate views approach. For example, the head of the NUT rejected it at the annual conference held in Belfast in 2007.

In 2014, at a time of contention over alleged Islamic penetration of British secondary education, the Prime Minister, David Cameron, ordered that every school pupil be taught the "British values" enshrined in Magna Carta, a key constitutional document of 1215. Cameron added that the charter's principles "paved the way for the democracy, the equality, the respect and the laws that make Britain Britain," and that he would make the 800th anniversary in 2015 the centerpiece of a fight back against extremism. This account ignored the extent to which Britain did not exist in 1215: the terms of the charter did not apply in Scotland, which was independent. Magna Carta has become a substitute for a written constitution, a document that is important because Britain does not have one. Also in 2014, at the time of the rejection in Scotland of a referendum of independence, Cameron referred to "the strength and stability of our ancient constitution."[34]

The centenary in 2014 of the outbreak of World War I provided both need and occasion for the employment of history and for discussion about its relationship with national identity and nationalism. Governments, media, and public each struggled as how to best express their views on the conflict. The theme was commemoration, not celebration, but that still left unclear how best to commemorate and, indeed, how far commemoration might equate with celebration. In France, François Hollande, the President, declared that "to commemorate is to renew patriotism." The French government planned about 1,500 events, providing the largest national celebration since the 200th anniversary of the French Revolution in 1989. To a degree, Hollande's theme was also adopted in Britain as ministers and historians sought to respond to earlier criticism of the conflict as futile as well as deadly. Thus, on 3 January 2014, Michael Gove, the Conservative Secretary of State for Education, published "Why does the Left insist on belittling true British heroes?" an article in the *Daily Mail* refuting the satirical critical approach to the war taken first in the film *Oh! What a Lovely War* and then in the *Blackadder* television series.[35] The British government plans to spend £50 million for events, from battlefield visits for schoolchildren to preserving warships. Commemorative paving stones are to be placed in the home towns of men who won the Victoria Cross. The BBC established a special unit to coordinate 2,500 hours of programming about the war. In Germany, there is much less governmental commitment to the commemoration of the war.

The books on the war that are favored form an instructive contrast. In Britain, the most popular in 2013–2014 was Max Hastings's *Catastrophe* (2013), which blamed the Germans for the war, a reasonable view as long as the Germans are linked to the Austrians. In contrast, in Germany, Christopher Clark's *The Sleepwalkers: How Europe Went to War in 1914* (2013) proved more popular, not least because it blamed the international system, and thus the powers as a whole.

In his article in the *Daily Mail* on 3 January 2014, Gove argued that the challenges faced today were also faced a century ago: "Great power rivalry, migrant populations on the move, rapid social upheaval, growing global economic interdependence, massive technological change and fragile confidence in political élites." Gove claimed that the war was justified: "The ruthless Social Darwinism of the German elites, the pitiless approach they took to occupation, their aggressively expansionist war aims and their scorn for the international order all made resistance more than justified . . . for all our mistakes as a nation, Britain's role in the world has also been marked by nobility and courage." To demonstrate the politicized nature of the issue, the *Observer*, as its lead item on 5 January 2014, carried a piece about an article, published in that issue, by Tristram Hunt, Labour's shadow education secretary, accusing Gove of crassness, citing Clark's *Sleepwalkers*, and arguing the case for patriotism on the Left. A key theme in the coverage of the war was that of commemorating and honoring the dead, rather than entering into the politics of the war. However, that approach ignored the extent to which such commemorating and honoring required engagement with why men volunteered, fought, and faced the practical, moral, and emotional challenges involved in killing and being willing to risk death.

While most of the discussion of World War I that attracts political attention is at the national level, much historical activity is at the local. It is there that memorialization arises from the textures of life and recollection. This situation throws considerable light on the processes by which history is lived and "created." For example, as an instance of the role of individuals, the range of activity, the impact of new technology, and the place of anniversaries, in this case the centenary of the outbreak of World War I, it is possible to consider www.pinterest.com /TimeRemembrance. This aims:

to archive as many images of timepieces belonging to those associated with all conflicts locally, nationally and internationally. The timepiece may have been worn by your great-grandfather in the trenches in WWI, saved the life of a Tommy [British soldier] at the Somme [1916], been worn by one of the Land Girls ... We are inviting visitors to our website to post their pictures and stories or leave contact details in order to grow the archive and compile the greatest and most diverse compilation of timepieces associated with wartime or conflict ever achieved. This is a unique concept, and driven not only by our love of horology but also in an awareness that fewer people seem inclined to "remember" our heroes than used to be the case.

The emphasis on remembering is particularly instructive.

Local engagement with the past in part benefits from public funds. At the same time, this engagement is not free from political commitment. As an instance of a wider process, the Heritage Lottery Fund provided support for "Telling our Stories, Finding our Roots: Exeter's Multi-Coloured History," a project, produced by Devon Development Education, that, in 2013, offered a very different account of the city's history to that with which its inhabitants were familiar. The self-guided tour drew attention to longstanding ethnic minorities, and to less comfortable links with the past. For example:

Bishop's Palace. Henry Philpotts, Bishop of Exeter, received a share of £12,729 4s 4d, which was a portion of the £20 million paid to compensate slave owners for the loss of their human property, following the Abolition of Slavery Act of 1833. The Bishop's Palace was also the site of one of Exeter's sugar processing factories linking Exeter to the plantation economies.

Royal Clarence Hotel. Well-known Black British singer Leslie Hutchinson (Hutch) visited the city during WWII and was not allowed to stay in the Royal Clarence Hotel.

Tensions in discussing the past will continue whichever party is running the government. These tensions underline the problems of formulating history as a national project in a democratized and disparate modern society. In the context of cultural flux, it is difficult to win uncontroversial support for a historicized concept of national values and for the idea of a trust between the generations. Looked at differently, this trust between the generations has been altered: whereas a Burkean strand of the relationship between the generations focuses on that of past and present, the emphasis, in recent and current politics, is of that of present and future. This contrast, between past-present and present-future, can be approached in both philosophical and pragmatic lights. In the case of present-future, the nature of identity can be perceived as resting on aspiration, rather than legacy; or rather, aspiration can be seen as stemming from present hopes and not the continuing impact of past goals. Indeed, present hopes for the future may be based, in part at least, on the rejection of the past. This re-conceptualizes history away from constraints and toward a stage in which hopes are played out. This process, however, can lead to an ahistorical failure not only to understand the past, but also to engage with society and the world as they are, because they are not located in an historical context.

At the same time, the context selected can be partisan and misleading. This was amply demonstrated in 2014 as Scotland debated independence, a debate that involved a highly misleading account on the part of the separatists of the origins and course of the Union begun in 1707. This was an aspect of a longstanding invention of Scottish history,[36] one given particular cinematic force in the error-strewn Hollywood blockbuster *Braveheart* (1995), a film that encouraged separatist feelings. Nationalists argued that the Scottish Parliament had simply been adjourned in 1707, but, in fact, the 1998 Scotland Act declared, "There shall be a Scottish Parliament," an assertion of creation, not continuity. The debate over the Union between England and Scotland provided a prime instance of the argument that countries are synthetic constructs. The added argument was that, as the factors that had led to their construction ebbed, so they might dissolve. Britain was presented by critics as a product both of contingent relations between its constituent parts and of conflict with Europe, and its national myths as less relevant in an age of weaker nationalism.[37]

A more difficult instance of the problems of approaching the past, not least the trust between the generations, was provided by the retrospective treatment of the "Troubles" in Northern Ireland from the 1960s to the 1990s. The 1990s peace process did not see agreement on a reconciliation process to cover the crimes of that period. In the 2010s, there was controversy, notably over the legal treatment of former Provisional IRA members, as well as of British soldiers. The brief detention for questioning in 2014 of Gerry Adams, the president of Sinn Fein, the former IRA political wing, exacerbated the issue, not least because

Sinn Fein is now part of the power-sharing government in Northern Ireland. Adams was questioned about the torture and murder in 1972 of Jean McConville, a widowed mother of ten children, who was falsely accused of being an informer for the British. The Provisional IRA long denied involvement in the murder, but subsequently admitted it. However, members of the McConville family were threatened when seeking to find out who was responsible. The episode raised the question of how far crimes should be punished, and whether creating a new political system that at least worked was more important and at least an acceptable definition of reconciliation. These points, debated in the British press in April 2014, are of more general significance.

The episode also raised the related question of how far material gathered for purposes of historical research could and should be used for legal purposes. The key evidence over the McConville killing came from the taped testimonies of Provisional IRA veterans gathered by Boston College as part of a research project designed to create an oral history of the Northern Ireland Trouble. This testimony was not given for legal purposes and was given on the understanding that accounts would not be released without permission or until after their deaths; but in 2013, the Police Service of Northern Ireland won a legal battle to force Boston College to release the records relevant to the McConville murder.

NATIONAL HISTORY AND EUROPE'S NEW STATES

Comments about contingent statemaking and weak national myths can also be made about other states. Nationhood, therefore, emerges as weaker than might be anticipated. Alongside contestation of history at the national level within Western Europe came the assault on that level from advocates for regional autonomy, if not nationalist separatism. This was seen with Scotland and Wales within Britain, and also in Spain, particularly with Catalonia and the Basque Country. In 2007, a new charter of autonomy for the Spanish region of Andalusia declared that it had a "millennium-long" history and a "nationality." A separatist emphasis could certainly be seen in much of the history produced in such regions. Anniversaries proved especially significant. The planned date of independence selected by Scottish nationalists – 24 March 2016 – is the anniversary of the 1603 Union of the Crowns and the 1707 Act of Union. Catalan nationalists transformed the commemoration of the end of the War of Spanish Succession in 1714 into an attempted denunciation of "Spain against Catalonia."

A new history was taken further in states that had won independence. Ireland from 1922 provided a key example, more so than for Belgium or Norway, neither of which centered its historical account on grievance. The Belgian revolution of 1830 against Dutch rule, and the Norwegian break from Swedish rule in 1905 are not controversial. Slovakia's independence from what had been Czechoslovakia in 1994 also led to a new history, but one that was not dominated by ire. In contrast, the nationalist fervor of Irish history is notable, in the public and popular dimension, and this fervor links Ireland to the Irish diaspora. The Great Famine of the 1840s is the crucial episode in public discussion and provides an agenda of grief and blame. Earlier episodes, such as the 1641 rebellion, have been overshadowed and tend to leave only a faint impression in folklore and popular culture.[38] Another key episode in such public discussion is the Easter Rising of 1916. The emphasis is on the executions of resistance figures after the suppression of the Rising, and not on the fact that Britain was then at war, that the rebels had links with the Germans, and that those they killed included Irishmen. Indeed, if the term "rebels" is replaced by "terrorists," then a different impression is created.

More generally, the relationship between public discussion and scholarly assessment is far from clear. The survival of the Irish union in the nineteenth century might be "the great elephant in the room of modern Irish historiography,"[39] but public attention to this point is less striking. This contrast is also true of the particular episodes referred to. The Eastern Rising was in part a case of Irish-on-Irish violence, but that is not an echo seen much in public. At the same time, the narrative of Irish distinctiveness was in part reconciled with the British connection by means of the symbolism and rhetoric surrounding the first ever state visits of a British monarch to Ireland since independence and of an Irish President to Britain, in 2011 and 2014, respectively.

CHANGING IDENTITIES

The nature of changing identities is significant. It is indicated, for example, by developments in the British population in the early twenty-first
century. Polls in the early 2010s indicated not only that the percentage
of the population from ethnic minorities was due to rise to nearly a third
in 2050, but also that its sense of national identity and pattern of political allegiance were very different from those of the indigenous white
minority. In particular, minorities were less likely to vote Conservative
and were more prone to see themselves as British, rather than English.
This had consequences in terms of the historical frame of reference. This
Britishness came from the experience of the empire and from an identification of the far Right with Englishness. In neither case was this a
Britishness focused on an approach to the history and politics of the British Isles. A more diverse British society will probably encourage a more
varied treatment of the past, as on the American pattern. The extent to
which the range of commemoration currently extends may ensure that
this process can be relatively easily accommodated. Indeed, the same
date and event may serve differing purposes. Thus, Norway's Constitution Day on 17 May celebrates the split from Denmark and the writing
of the Norwegian constitution in 1814, but has been given greater resonance by also marking the end of German occupation on 8 May 1945.
Similarly, literary references, images, and sites can be used to support a
wide range of assumptions.[40]

The varied messages that can be gained, both from the past as a
whole and from particular episodes in it, does not, however, make the
discussion of history less contentious. Instead, it has become newly so
in Europe since the end of the Cold War because the ideologies that
were to the fore then no longer appear relevant. This is particularly so in
Europe as it struggles, in issues of identity and interest, over the respective weight of globalization and transnationalism on the one hand, and
a sense of place and continuity on the other.

TEN

Contesting the Past,
Claiming the Future

IT IS TIME TO PULL TOGETHER SOME OF THE THEMES OFFERED in the last four chapters while stressing anew the variety of ways in which history is presented in public, and the range of resulting contentions. As a reminder of the extent to which this is not simply a debating exercise, it is appropriate to begin with controversies related to two appalling losses of life.

ARMENIAN MASSACRES AND TURKISH HISTORY

In 1939, Hitler added an accompanying remark in his exhortation to his generals to be murderous: "Who, after all, speaks today of the annihilation of the Armenians?" The answer now is far more people than in 1939, and not solely Armenians and scholars. In the event, Hitler's own genocidal policies toward Jews and Roma understandably guaranteed a new audience determined to remember, through public and popular history, all cases of historical mass brutality.[1]

The treatment of the Armenians by the Ottoman authorities during World War I was murderous and, in many eyes, genocidal. In a process that had begun prior to the war, Turkish nationalism became more important in the Ottoman Empire. The Christian Armenians were seen as a pro-Russian fifth column and were brutalized.[2] Aside from the large-scale killing of men, women, and children, including the burning alive of children,[3] many Armenians were driven into an arid region where they died. About 1.5 million were killed or died. Their property was seized.

This became the most famous, but only one, episode in the process by which the nineteenth-century Ottoman Empire was transformed into Turkey, a state with a clearly proclaimed ethnic identity, and one that broke with the multiple ethnicities and intercommunality of the far more cosmopolitan Ottoman system. Thus, the substantial Greek population in Asia Minor, over a million strong, was brutally driven into exile.[4]

In Turkey, criticism of the events of the 1910s and 1920s was, and is, unacceptable. Such criticism is seen as a direct challenge to the integrity and cohesion of the state and to the Kemalist tradition of Mustafa Kemal Atatürk, who had established the modern Turkish state by defeating the foreign forces seeking to impose the 1920 peace settlement. Although not in power during World War I, he did not acknowledge the treatment of the Armenians by his predecessors. The Armenian cause was, and is, also regarded as a Trojan Horse for the Kurds, who also challenge Turkish nationalism. As a result, legal measures were, and are, taken against those who discuss the Armenian Massacres, while nationalist thugs also took direct action.

Different accounts were offered outside Turkey. In 2006, it was made illegal in France, where there is a significant Armenian minority, to deny that the massacres occurred. This legislation did not improve relations between France and Turkey. It was not motivated simply by a historical dispute, for there was a clear political dimension. Aside from the domestic politics, there were international angles. French critics of America found it useful to condemn one of its major allies, Turkey. Moreover, those unhappy with the prospect of Turkey in the European Union focused on an issue in which the possible member state readily appeared in a poor light. More commonly, this critical approach focused on the present politics of Turkey. Indeed, in this case, the weight of history has to be seen as an aspect of a broader disengagement with, and criticism of, Turkish politics.

A minor aspect of the general tension is the question of the care of the part of historic Armenia that is a section of modern Turkey, a sentence the phrasing of which itself reveals the problems of addressing such issues. The area includes key Armenian archaeological sites that are significant to the Armenian collective historical consciousness, for

example Ani, which became the capital in 961. Armenians allege that
Turks neglect their sites, a charge that can be related to the more general
issue of a lack of Turkish interest in the cultural heritage of non-Turks
that is located in Turkey, for example of Greeks. Turkish officials, such as
the culture ministry, in contrast, claim to be mindful of such sites. In the
specific case of Ani, they argue that damage to the site is coming from
the use of explosives in a quarry across the border in Armenia.

The Armenian issue gathered pace as the anniversary of the mass
slaughter in 1915 neared. More specific political pressures played a role in
the controversy. For example, the rise in Islamic political fortunes within
Turkey, where the Islamicist Justice and Development (AK) has wielded
power since 2002, increased tension. In 2003, the Turkish refusal to allow
the United States to use Turkey as a base from which to invade Iraq led
to American anger. This was accentuated when, seeking to be an Islamic
regional power, Turkey put out feelers in the 2000s to Hamas, Iran, and
Syria. The result was pressure in the United States, leading in 2007 to a
Bill in Congress for declaring the Armenian slaughter a genocide. American military figures pointed out that such views had consequences for
cooperation with a NATO ally. Not only Turkey refused to accept that
genocide had been committed, but also Israel, both because it sought
cooperation with Turkey and so as not to detract attention from the
Holocaust. The uniqueness of the Holocaust was, and is, a major theme
in Israel.

Within Turkey, meanwhile, nationalist pressure increased. Article
301 of the penal code, which criminalizes insulting "Turkishness," was
used to take action against intellectuals such as the leading writer Orhan
Pamuk. In 2007, Hrant Dink, the Turkish-Armenian editor of the weekly
newspaper *Agos,* was murdered by a teenage nationalist for such an "insult." There was also tension between the nationalism offered by the secularists on the Atatürk tradition and that of the AK. The latter attacked
the military, a key element in the Atatürk regime and tradition. Thus, in
2014, a court jailed for life the two surviving leaders of the 1980 military
coup for "crimes against the state": one of the men, Kenan Evren, the
chief of staff, served as President until 1989. Defending what was presented as the national honor is significant in the political maneuvering
in Turkey. More generally, the Kemalists and the AK offered different

emphases in their accounts of Turkish history. The Kemalist stress on Atatürk was joined from 1953 by a popular emphasis on the 1453 capture of Constantinople by Mehmed II. However, the AK has taken interest in the Ottoman legacy much further. It is presented as a source of national fame and an example of a heroic Islamic past. Moreover, there was an ability to portray Turkey as a wide-ranging regional power, as with public maps depicting the extent of the Ottoman Empire. The neo-Ottoman approach affects public commemoration, sport, fiction, films, and museums. The 1453 Panorama Museum in Istanbul is the most popular in the country for Turks, but not for foreign visitors.

In turn, views that could be regarded as critical were castigated. In 2011, the *Magnificent Century,* a television series about a major and highly successful Ottoman ruler, Sultan Süleyman the Magnificent (r. 1520–1566), resulted in complaints and street protests. The emphasis on the sultan's womanizing and drinking aroused anger, and attracted viewers. The controversy was politicized, with prominent members of the AK leading the charge, at the same time as they restricted the sale of alcohol. Recep Tayyip Erdogan, the pugilistic Prime Minister, linked the controversy to the strength of an historically grounded culture, declaring: "The privacy of historical figures is important. We are not a nation or a state without roots; we are a nation that built civilizations." Similarly, RTUK, the media regulator, claimed that the series failed to show "the necessary sensitivity to the privacy of a historical figure," thus breaching a law that broadcasts "should not violate society's national and moral values."[5] Sensitivity was not limited to Süleyman and conservatives. In 2008, a documentary displaying the human weaknesses of the "Father of the Republic," Atatürk, led to complaints from secularists.

JAPAN AND CHINA

Another legacy of violence much affecting current attitudes is seen in East Asia, notably as Japan considers how best to record its role in 1931–1945. Nationalists have both downplayed Japan's responsibility for the warfare of the period and presented a seriously misleading account of its brutality. Anger with this approach has focused on two issues in particular. The "Rape of Nanjing" in 1937, in which large numbers of Chinese civilians were cruelly slaughtered after the city, which had been the Chinese capital, was captured is the most prominent. The enforced prostitution and harsh treatment of large numbers of "comfort women," especially, but not only, in Korea, in order to provide sex for Japanese troops, is also a major issue.

The Japanese were apt to downplay both issues, omitting them from textbooks, and denying the plentiful evidence about the brutality involved. Advance word that the 2005 edition of *The New History Textbook*, created by the nationalist Japanese Society for Textbook Reform would remove "any reference to matters associated with . . . 'dark history' [issues such as the comfort women or the 'Rape of Nanjing'] that might make Japanese schoolchildren uncomfortable" prompted angry Chinese to stone the Japanese Consulate in Shanghai. In 2007, the Chinese Foreign Ministry responded critically when Satoru Mizushima, a nationalist Japanese filmmaker, proposed to make a documentary "The Truth about Nanjing" that would deny evidence of Japanese atrocities, not least by querying the evidence. In turn, the "Group to Study the Truth of the Nanjing Incident" formed by eighteen young Japanese MPs was eager to use the language of national honor. One, Yohei Matsumoto, declared, "To clarify the truth of the history is to recover our national honor. We need this so that Japanese can feel proud of themselves in years to come." Another, Eiichiro Washio, stated, "We have to pass on true history to young people. We must fight this information war against the rest of the world."

History was therefore central to an "information war" conceived in nationalist terms. The role of honor was underlined by the controversial nature of the visits by Japanese politicians to Yasukuni, the war shrine in Tokyo commemorating 2.5 million Japanese war dead, but one that includes memorials to fourteen Class-A war criminals from World War II. Junichiro Koizumi, Prime Minister from 2001 to 2006, visited the shrine six times then. His successors did not do so until Shinzo Abe, who had not visited the shrine while Prime Minister in 2006–2007 (but had as a MP), did so as Prime Minister on 26 December 2013. Aside from the issue of honoring the dead, this visit was seen as important in strengthening Abe's political position as he sought to push through his domestic political agenda.[6] However, there was criticism of the visit from other powers, including Singapore and the United States, and fierce complaints from China and South Korea. Seeking wider global resonance, Chinese government spokesmen referred to the war criminals remembered at Yasukuni as "the Nazis of Asia." Moreover, the issue was linked by this spokesman to the crisis over competing territorial claims in the East China Sea by claiming that Abe's visit amounted to beautifying aggression. In April 2014, the Yasukuni issue was revived when Abe sent a ritual offering to the shrine. His decision to do so, rather than to visit in person during the Spring Festival, was regarded as a concession to the United States, but was still criticized in China.

The limited character of the coverage of this subject within Japan helps explain why so many Japanese do not understand foreign perceptions. These controversies also reflect historically grounded domestic differences. Thus, the Liberal Democrats, the mainstream conservative party, are traditionally linked to the Japan Association of War-Bereaved Families, while the more moderate New Komeito party is supported by the Soka Gakkai. This is a Buddhist organization that was persecuted during World War II by leaders of state Shinto, for which Yasukuni was the foremost shrine and a focus of nationalism.[7]

Japanese attempts to underplay their role in 1931–1945 are unacceptable to the Chinese. For the Chinese government, Japanese atrocities also provide a useful aspect of nation-building, one that distracts attention from the brutalities of the Communist regime. National Defense Education Day provides an annual highpoint for such reminders. References to past Japanese aggression, moreover, are employed to try to pressure Japan into publicly renouncing any intention of reverting to an interventionist military posture. At the same time, such an instrumentalist interpretation is inadequate as complaints about Japanese accounts also draw on a deep well of anger in China, one that is more frequently expressed with the spread of the internet there.

The continuing controversy will be kept alive by anniversaries of the conflict. On one hand, these can be regarded as extraneous to "realist" disputes focused on the issues of the here and now, particularly the political and economic manifestations of regional dominance. On the other, tensions over the past can be seen as encouraging distrust and rivalry when addressing these issues. Joining both is an aspiration to

assert what are presented as national interests. This means a more robust stance, both politically and in terms of identity. In large part, the
two cannot be separated. For example, in the case of Japan, military
deployments and an interest in missile-defense systems are related to
ideological transformation, not least the demand for a revision of article
nine of the constitution, which commits Japan to pacific policies. Such
a demand draws in large part on developments in the international system, particularly a more aggressive China. Historical factors also play a
role, notably accounts of World War II that do not present Japan as an
aggressor. These accounts, instead, claim that Japan had to act in 1941 in
response to American pressure, particularly restrictions on the supply
of oil.

Japanese assertion is within an international political context that
in part draws on differing responses by other powers. Thus, Japan's post-
war government and political culture was molded by the American victors and occupiers. Subsequent relations with China proved far more
difficult. The experience and nature of Japanese occupation was clearly
part of the equation as China was brutally treated, whereas the United
States avoided occupation. This contrast was also seen in 2007, when
Japan and Australia were able to negotiate a security pact. Australia had
been briefly bombed by Japan in 1942, but had otherwise not had its territory attacked.

In 2007, the Prime Minister of China, Wen Jiabao, raised the issue
when he spoke to the Japanese Diet (parliament), acknowledging Japan's
official regret and apology for its actions in the war, but also asking that
its government act on those attitudes and promises. This was understood to mean that Japanese Prime Ministers not visit Yasukuni. Wen
noted that the invasion of China was the cause of "indescribable pain
and wounds in the heart of the Chinese people." He also commented
that the Japanese were victims of "a handful of militarists," a conciliatory view designed to lessen tension. This view reflected the standard
left-wing account, of the bulk of the population having shared views
across international lines that defied the aggressiveness of ruling elites.
This approach was also adopted by the Communist East Germans when
discussing relations with the Soviet Union. Wen continued by meeting

Emperor Akihito and drawing to his attention remarks Akihito made in a birthday speech in 2005 emphasizing the need for "history to be handed down in a proper manner."[8]

Tension over this difficult shared history continued and became more prominent in 2013. A stronger nationalism was offered by the Abe government. In turn, China displayed a more assertive and more strident nationalism under Xi Jinping, the new President. This nationalism is represented in China as an attempt to reverse a malign history, going back to the 1830s, when China was weak as a consequence of Western and Japanese pressure and assumptions. Thus, in April 2013, the Shanghai Maritime Court ordered the seizure of a Japanese ship in a ratcheting up of an historical legal claim that indicated the potential significance of such claims for current relations. By their nature, legal claims are historic and backward-looking. In this case, in 1936, Daido Kaiun, a predecessor of Mitsui OSK Lines, the owner of the ship, rented two freighters from the Chung Wei Steamship Company. In turn, these ships were taken over for the Japanese navy and then sunk during World War II. From 1964, the descendants of the owners of the Chung Wei Steamship Company pursued lawsuits against the Japanese government and Daido Kaiun. In 1972, China had renounced further claims to Japanese war reparations, but, in the 2010s, Chinese courts accepted lawsuits filed by private individuals seeking compensation from Japanese companies for forced labor. These cases contribute to initiating Japanese opinion against China.

In 2013–2014, Sino-Japanese tension over the East China Sea led to much talk, notably in the Western press, but also by Abe at the World Economic Forum in Davos in 2014, about the extent to which the situation risked a repeat of World War I. Such a reference had also been made at the time of the Cuban Missile Crisis between the United States and the Soviet Union in 1962. The past was believed significant, not least as a potent example. The appropriateness of the weight of the past in these cases is problematic, partly because there are no indications that any of the powers in 1962 or 2013–2014 sought war, whereas in 1914 the Austrian and German general staffs certainly did so. Thus, for considering later crises, historical analysis of the situation in 1914 can prove instructive. Moreover, reference to the use of historical examples throws light on the question of how, and how far, the past plays a role in the culture of decision making. That is not the same as saying that the past is crucial to the decisions taken.

The weight of the war and of past imperial control was also seen elsewhere, notably in Japan's relations with South Korea. Despite a shared capitalism, there was (and is) considerable tension largely based on Japan's colonial rule of Korea. Historical commemoration provided a way to mark this. Museums portray the period of Japanese rule as one of the suppression of Korean culture. For example, in 2013, Park Geun-hye, President of South Korea, on a visit to China, requested that a monument be built to honor Ahn Jung-geun, a Korean nationalist executed by Japan in 1910 for the assassination, in the Manchurian city of Harbin, of Hirobumi Ito, Japan's colonial governor in Korea. Unveiled in 2014, this monument was greeted with anger in Japan where Ahn is regarded as a terrorist. The President wished to be seen as a nationalist, not least because her father had been regarded as pro-Japanese. In turn, Japanese revisionism raised tensions in relations with South Korea in the 2010s. In March 2014, Park Geun-hye made goodwill dependent on Japan agreeing not to reopen issues of history while also displaying sincerity over the "comfort women" forced into prostitution for the Japanese army. In response, Abe adopted a conciliatory stance.

There is a tendency to treat all states as akin in such discussion, but it is necessary to note that Japan and South Korea have far more pluralistic public politics and freedom of publication than China. For example, the Tiananmen Square Memorial Hall, a museum opened in Hong Kong in 2014 by pro-democracy activists, highlighted that the episode was still taboo elsewhere in China. Moreover, the opening of the museum had faced difficulties and delays.

The contentiousness of 1931–1945 does not prevent the presentation in Japan of differing accounts of these years, but it can encourage a focus on earlier periods. Thus, in 2010, NHK, the state broadcaster, produced a series dramatizing the life of Ryoma Sakamoto, a key figure in the Meiji Restoration of 1868. It was followed from December 2010 by a series on the Russo-Japanese War of 1904–1905, in which Japan had been victorious. These were acceptable topics, unlike past wars with China.

TERRITORIAL CLAIMS

A key difference between China and Japan in the 2010s focused on competing territorial claims in the East China Sea. This dispute brought together many of the contrasting issues raised by such claims. *Revanche* for past historical wrongs is a key element in the pursuit of such claims. China seeks the reversal of what it claims was foreign oppression from the 1830s to the 1940s. Other states also seek to reverse nineteenth-century setbacks. Thus, Evo Morales, the President of Bolivia, has demanded that the International Court of Justice should order talks over Bolivia's access to the sea, lost to Chile in the War of the Pacific (1879–1883). Alongside discussion of historical wrongs, the past provides insight in the shape of the rules developed in the discussion of international disputes at sea.

PUBLIC DISCUSSION

The sheer length of the list of redress sought for past wrongs underlines both the diffuse character of engagement with the past and the extent to which this engagement suffuses public discussion and debate. These points, however, do not ease the problem of deciding how best to organize any such assessment of the role of history. The key point is that, in the public sphere, contesting the past is explicitly a matter of debating both present and future, whereas academic historical culture frequently tends to resist the extent to which there is a link; although there are other academic subjects that are happier to engage on this scale.

Historians of course do not own the past, but, because they spend their time studying the subject, they are in a better position than most amateurs to make reasoned judgments. More particularly, although each historical event is unique, a study of history provides warnings about possibilities, gives both context and example, and aids in formulating questions.[9] However, the historical profession has largely turned inward in the last half-century, with the result that much historical study today is self-referential. This criticism is certainly true of Britain, and owes much to the interaction of the dominant academic culture with government policy, in funding universities via a research "excellence" largely pursued in terms of specialization. In the United States, in contrast, there is no unified national education policy at the level of higher education. However, history curricula at the level of high schools are decided state by state by elected boards of education, which poses serious problems when fundamentalists win seats and alter educational standards.

AN INSTANCE OF TELEVISION HISTORY

In practice, even for academic history, there are overlaps with the public sphere, and most notably when academics appear on the television, a practice that became more common in the early twenty-first century. For example, Simon Schama's *The American Future: A History* (2008), a BBC television series and book, intercut past and present, and showed how competing views about the American future have played a central role in the identity disputes that have been so important to American politics. This was very much an account by a fluent historian who, in the fashion of the period, put himself center-stage. Thus, the presidential election campaign of 2008 was presented through the perspective of authorial journeys and interviews, and with throw-backs to his early visits to America. In part, this is the television dictating, the present providing access for the camera, while Schama's account of having been at the Democratic Convention in 1964 brought the narrator in as a central observer. Given the very engaged character of the enterprise – the narrator as Obama champion – it is not surprising that there is such an emphasis on the individual travelogue. To that extent, the dictates of both camera and prose are as one. Schama personalized the role of the historian in terms of his own views and experience,[10] and was happy to mix historical narrative with more partisan reflection. This is a well-established position for some historians. In Britain, the Whig writer Macaulay did the same in the early nineteenth century, as did the mid-twentieth-century academic, television historian, and popular writer, A. J. P. Taylor. Whatever the deficiencies of television history, it reflects a desire for clarity and moralizing that is well-developed in the public sphere.

In 2009, Schama followed with a two-parter on BBC2 to mark the first anniversary of the Obama presidency. This provided a stark juxtaposition of Main Street and Wall Street in the exposition of America's present socio-economic condition and plight. The television showed the bleakness of factories and run-down residential districts in the Rust-Belt, notably in the city of Cleveland, a one-time industrial center; and linked this poverty directly to the policy of the banks. There was no suggestion that the problems were longstanding and historic, that there had been a movement of employment and prosperity to other parts of the United States, notably in the car industry, and that there were also highly relevant global economic trends, especially the focus on manufacturing in China. Looked at differently, the complexities of history in this case were politicized, with the historical component put to one side. The simplicity of the analysis was matched by the historical analogies: Obama and Afghanistan was discussed in terms of President Truman and the Korean War (1950–1953), while Roosevelt (FDR, not Teddy) provided the key background for the critical discussion of the contemporary bankers. This approach offered the opportunity to retell easy stories, for example that of Truman and General Douglas MacArthur, but the analogies were not helpful because the circumstances were very different. Afghanistan, for example, was scarcely central to America's geopolitical confrontation with China, whereas the Korean War was the front line in a Cold War that was only cold in the temperatures experienced in the Korean peninsula. So far, the Korean War is the sole conflict since 1945 in which the modern superpowers have fought each other, although, at that time, China was not a super-power while the Soviet Union made sure it was not on the front line.

REDRESS AND THE END OF THE COLD WAR

The frequency and range of historicized grievances and calls for justice are notable, although there is the question of whether they have become more frequent or simply more prominent with the role of the media and, in particular, the internet. There is no ready measure of historicized grievances and calls for justice, but they appear to have become far more common in public and political discussion over the last two-and-a-half decades. Indeed, these grievances are a characteristic content for post-Cold War history as various partisan groups (and nations themselves in an international context) have adopted a strategy of historical grievance in the service of their political goals. The reasons for this are varied and in large part have to be extrapolated by the observer, which is always problematic. The most significant factor appears to be the extent to which, earlier, the narratives of the Cold War structured or super-seded much public history-telling, notably in the authoritarian societies of the Communist bloc, while agenda linked to economic concerns were to the fore. The rise in historicized grievances, in part, is a response to the end of the Cold War and the resulting weakness of the narratives relevant to it.

However, this was not the complete story. There was also a response to the shifting perception of societies. Class-based accounts had offered an account of society, its structure and dynamics, focused on wealth-linked criteria and encouraged a search of the past for ideas and images of economic oppression. Thus, in 1989, protesters against the Poll Tax in Britain were likened to those rebelling in the Peasants' Revolt of 1381, and were happy with the parallel, one that drew on a potent tradition of English radicalism,[11] even though the 1381 revolt was unsuccessful. In part due to the difficulties of providing an attractive and accessible ac-count of the social politics of medieval societies, references this distant were relatively uncommon in Western Europe, other than in asserting nationalism on the part of would-be states such as Scotland. However, in 2000, the Belgian city of Ghent affixed to its ancient walls the names of citizens whom the ruler, the Emperor Charles V, had executed in 1540 after the city's long rebellion came to an unsuccessful end. Irrespective of the end of the Cold War, class-based analyses already, by the 1990s, seemed less than appropriate for increasingly complex societies, in which ideas of ethnicity, gender, sexual preference, and age were all deployed in a vocal fashion, while democratization, environmentalism, and multicul-turalism were asserted as key goals. These ideas and interests conformed to the trend in academic history toward a concern with social analysis that did not draw on economic fundamentals.

HISTORICIZED GRIEVANCES

Both domestically and internationally, historicized grievances, whether well-founded or more questionable, provided the easiest way to mobilize identity and expound policy; and the use of grievance in this fashion by one party encouraged its employment by another. Specific grievances are by their nature self-absorbed, and those who assert them frequently are not interested in finding common cause with other complainants, not least because they are concerned that reference to other grievances will dilute their own. Moreover, casting a wider span will probably draw attention to explicitly contrary arguments.[12] Indeed, the copycat nature of public history has become very apparent, as in rival Chinese and Japanese demonstrations, for example those touched off by disputes over the East China Sea. Grievance thus became a way both to interrogate the past and to deploy the past to present effect. Grievance also offered clear guidance to the future, because it provided a warning about what could happen or was happening, and thus prefigured what could recur or continue.

This approach lent itself to the democratization of politics seen in many countries from the 1990s, as societies adapted not only to democracy but also to a practice of accountability and responsiveness that was far more frequent than that of elections. Indeed, the Tea Party movement in America clearly fits into this development. Populism was least fixed by existing constitutional forms and political practices in countries suddenly developing as democracies, notably those of Eastern Europe. Nevertheless, mobilizing popular, specifically electoral, support by reference to history was not only an issue in such states. The rise of historical reference was also linked to the emergence of political parties that owed little to the traditional class-based divide of left and right. This was particularly the case with the rise of additional parties that had to find a different resonance, and notably with those of the far Right.

These parties sought to use historicized notions of identity to mobilize popular support across a wide range. Such mobilization was directed against the pressures of globalization, as with the National Front in France and UKIP in Britain. References to the past thus provided both a sense of identity and a rationale for policy. The "Blood and Soil" ideas employed in the late nineteenth and early twentieth centuries were given a new lease on life. At the same time, these far-Right parties faced a troubling historical legacy due to their being associated (fairly and unfairly) with the far-Right parties that had collaborated with Hitler.

Thus, in a variety of ways, history was important in the language of political contention. The pattern of grievance and retribution works in part at the international level because states are treated as nations and anthropomorphized in terms of supposed characteristics. As a result, good is found on one hand and bad on the other. At the national level, such an approach can leave little space for divisions over identity and policy.

Whether commentators approve of particular manifestations of the presentation of the past, the habit of state direction in this presentation is a powerful one. Moreover, the lack of ready alternatives to history as a means for national identity appears clear across the world. The decline in ideological or party political commitment across much of the world is an important aspect of this stress on history. Religion does not provide a comparable civil politics in most states, not only because of the decline in some (but far from all) popular religious observance, let alone conviction, but also as a result of the weakness of the concept and practice of state religious institutions. Yet, the mushrooming of religious sects shows that religion is actually growing outside of the established institutional framework and, at this level, provides a sense of clear identity.

Religion also offers narratives of the past, including from the perspective of grievances. Visiting Spain in 2010, Pope Benedict XVI, a critic of the social liberalism in that once strongly Catholic country, warned of a "strong and aggressive secularism" similar to that seen in the 1930s. This was a highly contentious reference, as the violent attacks on the Church prior to the Civil War were used by the Nationalists as a pretext for their eventually successful rebellion against the Republican government in 1936. The role of religion exemplifies the extent to which historical accounts were presented from a variety of backgrounds with statehood conceptualized accordingly. In the 2010s, both in sub-Saharan Africa and in the Middle East, there were attempts to create new states based on far-reaching Islamic aspirations. Thus, an al-Qaeda splinter group, ISIS, the Islamic State of Iraq and al-Sham, sought to establish a Sunni state in Iraq and Syria. Its online magazine, the Islamic State Report, presented ISIS as seeking to reverse a longstanding Western attempt to divide the Muslim world. The 1916 Anglo-French Sykes-Picot agreement to partition the Ottoman Empire was presented as a key episode:

> It was 98 years ago that the Allies of WWI forged a secret agreement to carve up the territories of the Muslim lands. They would form a symbolic precedent for subsequent partitioning of Muslim lands by crusader powers. Years after the agreement, invisible borders would go on to separate a Muslim and his brother, and pave the way for ruthless, nationalistic *tawaghit* [idolatry] to entrench the *ummah's* [Muslim world's] division rather than working to unite the Muslims under one iman carrying the banner of truth.[13]

This served as a blunt reminder of the number of historical contexts, as well as interpretations, that were not only on offer, but also being enforced. In 2014, ISIS fighters taunted captured Iraqi soldiers they were taking off for killing by calling them Safavids. This was a reference to the Persian (Iranian) empire of the sixteenth to eighteenth centuries that had contested the control of Iraq with the Ottoman Empire. The Ottomans, like ISIS, were Sunnis, while the Safavids were Sh'ites. ISIS was therefore providing a sectarian account that was supported by a longstanding sense of grievance.

NATIONAL VARIATIONS

Aside from differences over content, tensions over historical method can be seen. In France, the style of most academic history is framed in terms of the conceptualization and methodology of recent decades, whereas the public has a much greater zest for narrative. Indeed, *L'Histoire du France pour les nuls* [*Dummies*] has sold 800,000 copies. In France, however, there is also a willingness by many academics to write both biographies and general synoptic works designed for a large readership, and not all of them are on the history of France. For example, there is a creditable literature in French on the history of England, one that British scholars would profit from reading.

National variations in the presentation of history reflect both longstanding differences and also the way in which new developments are experienced and handled. The impact of the global economic and fiscal problems seen from 2008 on the public discussion of history is an instructive example. This impact has been more muted than might have been anticipated. In part, this was because the recession was not played through in terms of divisive strategies of goodies and baddies, other than with reference to bankers. There was only a relatively limited recurrence of earlier patterns of ethnic stereotyping, notably the anti-semitism that played a role in the critique of bankers, particularly on the part of the far-right, indeed neo-Nazi, Golden Dawn party in Greece. Instead, the Wall Street Crash of 1929 and the Depression of 1930s was held up as a warning, as by David Cameron, the British Prime Minister, when he claimed, on 12 November 2010 at the G20 summit in Seoul, that the global economy risked a return to the 1930s: "The fear we should all have is a return to what happened in the 1930s: protectionism, trade barriers, currency wars, countries playing beggar-my-neighbor policies – trying to do well for themselves but not caring about the rest of the world. That is the danger."

The election of governments presenting themselves as modernizers, for example those of Nicolas Sarkozy and François Hollande in France (2007; 2012), Barack Obama in the United States (2008, 2012) and David Cameron in Britain (2010), was another cause of a more muted discussion of the distant past than might have been anticipated. In each case, there was a willingness to talk about the past, sometimes in a misleading fashion, as when Obama told a Pittsburgh audience in 2008 that the American Revolution came about when the people rose up to demand "their independence from British tyranny." Nevertheless, the predominant theme for these governments was of new beginnings, if only, as in the United States and Britain, in response to the alleged serious failings of the previous administration. Continuity was not the theme that was stressed. In looking for new beginnings, the grounding was not on another history, but rather on what was presented as necessary.

Immediate history provided a key element of current political debate, with the reputation of the previous government serving as the basis for the rhetoric of present contention. Just as Margaret Thatcher, British Prime Minister from 1979 to 1990, drew on the "Winter of Discontent," the semi-anarchic trade union disruption of 1978–1979 under the Labour government of James Callaghan, and Cameron on the failures of Gordon Brown, Labour Prime Minister from 2007 to 2010; so Obama criticized his predecessor, George W. Bush, President from 2001 to 2009. In these and other instances, memoirs, partisan history, moralistic viewpoints, and public opinion elide each other, and are employed in the creation of competing historical memories. Moreover, history was – as is to be expected – employed in an *ad hoc* fashion, one in which expediency played a key role. Thus, in November 2010, when Britain and France signed treaties on defense cooperation, there were references by Cameron to alliance in the two world wars, but no real attempt to look at the long-term relationship between the two powers, both cooperative and hostile.

The slackening or foreshortening of historical resonances in some cases is not the same as denying their role. Moreover, such resonances remain potent across much of the world. They are, however, changing with demographics as well as politics. In particular, with the passage of time, an ever-smaller percentage of the population has any involvement in, or recollection of, the key divisive issues of the 1930s and 1940s, such as the Spanish Civil War (1936–1939), the Vichy government (1940–1944), and the pro-German Salò Republic in Italy (1943–1945). As a result, the impact of these issues in modern politics commonly becomes less direct or less effective. In 2014, Charupong Ruangsuwan, the interior minister in the Thai government overthrown in a military coup, invoked World War II resistance against the Japanese when forming an opposition group in exile. The resonance of such a reference was weaker than it would have been even twenty years earlier.

However, as indicated in chapter 9, distance can also lead to a willingness to engage with episodes that had proved difficult or that had been shelved in an attempt at reconciliation. More generally, there is a shift in historical resonances at present as a result of the rising percentage of the population that grew to political maturity after the Cold War, or indeed the post-Maoist reforms in China. The movement into the new millennium in 2000 also affected the frame of historical reference for the bulk of the population. Yet, a slackening in the current divisiveness of much of the political agenda of the twentieth century does not mean that central episodes, notably the Holocaust, have come to lack resonance. Moreover, this twentieth-century agenda still has continuing impact for many states, such as (differently) Cuba, North Korea, South Korea, and Israel, as well as for many communities, notably émigrés, for example Cuban Americans.

A slackening, in some cases, of the divisiveness of what might be seen as middle time, that which is remembered directly only by the elderly, and thus only indirectly by the young, does not mean that "deep history" and its grievances have lost their echo. In the case of these grievances, there is a tendency to move across large periods of time in order to assemble a cast of episodes, such as the Crusades (1095–1292),[14] the medieval Spanish *Reconquista*, the Anglo-Chinese Opium Wars (1839–1842, 1858–1860), the American Civil War (1861–1865), or the Armenian Massacres (1915), that can serve to provide explanations and calls for action. There is no sign that this situation will cease.

For example, in 2010, calls for Muslim worship in the Spanish cathedral of Cordoba, earlier a major mosque, or for the cathedral to be signposted as a cathedral-mosque, led in Spain to contention in which themes from the *Reconquista* were echoed. Anxieties about the extent to which immigration from North Africa was affecting the character of Andalusia (*al-Andalus*) gave a current focus to the politics of the issue. Moreover, the Muslims demonstrating in London in 2010 against the NATO intervention in Afghanistan called themselves "Muslims against Crusades." There is no real comparison between the two, but Osama bin Laden and his supporters attached great importance to the idea of Western "Crusader" aggression toward the Muslim world; and this term has proved resonant among young Muslims internationally. At the trial of the terrorists responsible for the murderous bombing of a Bali nightclub in 2003, one of the accused shouted "Jews: remember Khaibar. The army of Muhammad is coming back to defeat you," thus bringing the defeat and enslavement of Jews in 626 into the modern age. Such a frame of reference is very different to that employed in the West.

Movements and groups seeking a religious resonance are likely to range widely through time in their search for examples, in part because they wish to position the present as an aspect of a revived sacred history. For states that do not pursue such an agenda, and that have a modern, consumerist public, the frame of reference is generally more recent. However, what is perceived, fairly or otherwise, as humiliation in relatively recent years can encourage resorting to more distant times, and notably so when, as with Japan, this means moving from a focus on aggression and defeat, in this case, World War II.

Deep history of a different type is presented with the emphasis on establishing national museums as signs of identity. This resonates on the international scale as with the demands in 2010–2011 from the Egyptian government for the return of historical remains, such as the Rosetta Stone from the British Museum for the projected Grand Egyptian Museum. Museum-building has been used in post-Communist Europe to try to assert, and thus create, a new consensus.[15] The same process can be seen in Scotland.

CONCLUSIONS

The role of collective memories, and of the stories and/or myths that play a major role in their content and expression, remain a key reason why history takes a leading part in public life and popular culture.[16] Adopting the male-centered approach particularly characteristic of the Classical world, the Roman historian Tacitus (c. 55–120 CE) began his *Agricola,* a life of his father-in-law, by writing, "To hand down to posterity the works and ways of famous men was our fathers' custom."[17] Anniversaries provide an obvious instance of this handing down, although one that may fade if the me/now generation fails to note this process of continuation. However, states do not tend to share this ostentatiously presentist attitude. Instead, their sense of identity requires just such a continuation. Thus, on 15 May 2014, in dedicating a museum that commemorated the events of 11 September 2001, President Obama declared: "Here we tell their story so that generations yet unborn will never forget," adding that the museum was a "sacred place of healing and hope." Moreover, national leaders continue to claim their place in destiny, in part because they are interested in history and read history books. The validating role of anniversaries therefore not only has been significant, but also continues to be important, notably as an assertion of identity. Identity requires assertion and differentiation. It is an active pulse, for, without feeling and expression, there is no identity. Moreover, among the range of possible feelings and expressions on offer, there is competition; and the presentation of identity is a key aspect of this competition. The assertion of nationalism can be compatible with other, sub-national identities, but they can also compete and, indeed, even be part of a zero-sum situation, with one becoming more prominent only at the expense of another.

ELEVEN

Historiographies of the Present

MANY HISTORIANS OFFER, ALONGSIDE THE SENSE OF HISTORY as a continuing process, a defense of its value that at least implies that it will provide clarity, answers, and solutions. If both past and present can be seen as part of a process of continual change, then an understanding of the past has obvious value for the present. For example, in *The Dragons of Expectation: Reality and Delusion in the Course of History* (2004), Robert Conquest noted the contingent nature of historical judgments, but also presented the subject as a means for education, with a particular emphasis on the recent past: "History is that part of the Humanities which enables us to look back with a real perspective and so, also, to look forward as well-briefed as we can be. We need the whole accessible past to give us a deep perspective. We need the history of the twentieth century because it contains, if sometimes in vestigial form, the elements of the present – and the future."[1]

To move, however, to specifics in terms of learning lessons is far less easy. This is a problem that has also occurred when advice is formally sought from historians, including those in government service. The track record here is poor, as with the British use of official historians after World War II. The ability to draw lessons from the past does not mean that these lessons are applicable. Moreover, there is a tendency for those seeking to draw lessons to offer contrasting answers. There are also problems in the use of history in non-official arenas. Aside from academic disputation, there is the issue of public knowledge when references are made. This is an aspect of the current situation in which the frequent use of historical resonances is clear, but their impact less so,

whether considered in terms of understanding the references or of being persuaded by the reference to history. Take the letter in the *Times*
of London on 10 November 2010 from prominent former naval figures
criticizing cuts in the Royal Navy and warning that they endangered the
safety of the Falkland Islands, a British colony threatened by Argentine
claims. The letter referred to the risk of "a national humiliation on the
scale of the loss of Singapore [to Japan in 1942]" and, later, "The Government has, in effect, declared a new 'ten-year rule' that assumes Britain
will have warning time to rebuild to face a threat. The last Treasury-
driven 'ten-year rule' in the 1930s nearly cost us our freedom, faced with
Hitler." Clear enough to some, but only a portion of the general population would understand the reference. As a reminder of the selective
use of history, Matthew Parris felt able, in that paper on 27 November
2010, to discuss Britain's possible response to a crisis in Korea without
mentioning the Korean War of 1950–1953 in which Britain had been
heavily involved.

Again demonstrating the extent, as well as range, of historical references, the same newspaper, in its lead editorial on 18 November 2010, offered a confused account of the wider social placing of the forthcoming
marriage of Prince William and Kate Middleton. To see the marriage as
resolving a historical tension between the social elite and the upwardly
mobile, the "mill owners" of the nineteenth century, and to take the discussion back to the 1830s, was far-fetched. Yet, again, the use of history
revealed more about the present. In this case, the hope of the editorial
writer was that it would be possible to create a more benign environment
for economic enterprise and, in particular, disrupt what was seen as an
unhelpful alliance between the elite and the workers, an alliance supposedly directed against enterprise. Setting this discussion in an historical
context was unhelpful.

THE REACH OF POLITICS

The extent of debate over the presentation of history in Britain or the
United States is not typical, for, in much of the world, there is less of a
range of publicly held views while there is a stronger attempt to produce
a coherent national narrative. Indeed, the reach of politics and the state

in education and the public discussion of history can be truly disturbing. To teach in Madagascar or Uzbekistan is to be part of a governmental system in which there are assumptions about the loyalty of public servants to the system that greatly compromise their independence. The situation is bleak in most of the Islamic Middle East.

The situation is also grave in the former Soviet Union, including Russia. There is still greater freedom there than prior to the collapse of Communist rule in 1991, but the situation in some of the former republics of the Soviet Union is disheartening. In Belarus, academics are required to attend weekly ideological orientation (i.e., policing) sessions, and all universities are directly under the minister of education. Comments by British academics suggest that some feel they face a similar control with "staff development," "quality assurance," and a barrage of controlling acronyms. This managerialism indeed may have Orwellian and authoritarian implications and dimensions, while, in other contexts, political correctness of some form or other reduces or affects the range of opinion that can be offered. However, the situation in dictatorial Belarus is totally different. Public history in Belarus very much emphasizes the country's affinity with Russia, notably due to liberation from German control by the Red Army in 1944. The dictator, Aleksandr Lukashenko, had his former history teacher, Yakov Treshchenok, write the school history textbook. Pre-Soviet history was largely ignored, while Catholics and Jews were written out of the history, and a pro-Russian account of the rising of 1863–1864 was offered.[2] Such accounts came in a potent tradition of nationalism recast through ideology.

Alongside cases like the continued role of the Communist Party in China and the revival of authoritarianism in Putin's Russia in the 2000s and 2010s, many of the states that emphasize control by government are poor and lack resources for their educational system, *let alone* for higher education in the humanities, *let alone* for research in the latter. This situation encourages a focus in historiographical work on the more affluent countries. That is understandable, but, before pursuing this commonplace approach, it is important to underline the degree to which the approach has limitations. In particular, there is often a mismatch between many countries that receive insufficient attention, even though they have a contested official history, let alone official history as a whole across the world, and, on the other hand, Western academic educational systems whose intellectual cultures and strategies are deemed more worthy of attention.

The situation in much of the world also poses a question-mark to conventional confident remarks about academic history. For example, Richard Evans, Regius Professor of History in Cambridge, wrote in 2006: "Controversy is an indispensable means of advancing historical knowledge, as the rough edges are rubbed off implausible or exaggerated interpretations, and reasoned debate consigns the unsupported argument to the dustbin of discredited hypothesis."[3] Such an argument appears not only somewhat complacent as an account of the situation in the West, but also misleading, often highly misleading, for that elsewhere.

At the same time, there is a need to avoid the extremes possibly suggested by Belarus and Britain. In many parts of the non-Western world, notably much of Latin America and South Asia, there are fairly lively communities of historians, even if the relationship of academics to government departments of education or their equivalents is generally much more direct than in Britain.

ACADEMIC PRACTICE

In the West, historiography is still greatly affected by the long-term rise from the late nineteenth century of the influence of academic practices and professional standards. It is also deeply influenced by the broadening of the intellectual agenda centered on the 1960s. This was a broadening out of both content and method, including the somewhat questionable assumption that scholarly endeavor can be assessed by "locating it" in the "discourse" of the subject's literature. The new social history of the 1960s, a social history that hit hard at previous emphases on the material environment, both Marxist and *Annaliste*,[4] continues to play a central role. Indeed, this social history, notably so with gender studies, has become more prominent because those who were doing doctoral research have risen to be prominent figures in the academy. In turn, they have been appointing the next generation of academics. As a result, what, at one stage, was radical and avant-garde has become rather establishment and often complacent. This is certainly the case in the United States and Western Europe.

Alongside topic has come method, with particular interest shown in disinterring episodes that supposedly illustrate processes of social engagement at work. In addition to this so-called "thick history" is an emphasis on oral history. Methods drawing on the social sciences also encourage comparative historical approaches that undermine the distinctiveness of earlier traditions, for example that of the history of China.[5] As a whole, historians operating in the modern Western academy are supposed to be sensitive to gender, sexual orientation, ethnic, and other key issues; and this sensitivity and prospectus affects the understanding of other topics and sources. Moreover, the shift to social history, broadly interpreted, has had an effect of diverting attention from formerly key aspects of academic history. In particular, there has been a marked decline in the practice of constitutional, diplomatic, legal, military, and high political history, and notably for periods prior to 1900. Micro-history, the detailed practice of much social history, does not lend itself to the narrative tradition of political history. Even more, the shift in social history, away from a socio-economic focus and toward cultural issues, has diminished the role of narrative altogether.

There have also been significant changes in other branches of history. In particular, economic history has been transformed. There is far less of an emphasis, certainly in "post-industrial" societies, such as Britain, on production and, instead, a greater stress on consumption. This approach turns economic history into a branch of social history. As a result, the standard account of the British Industrial Revolution no longer focuses on inventors and entrepreneurs.[6] Military history has been pushed toward a "war and society" approach. Shifts of emphasis in the teaching of history have become an important aspect of the so-called "culture wars" in the United States. The resulting trend has produced the decline of military and high-political history, and the deliberate move away from a focus on the West, on states and on power, toward, instead, the non-West, the disempowered, and the treatment of authority as a form of exploitation and power as an abuse.

BRITISH CULTURE WARS:
THE CASE OF MAURICE COWLING

Discussion of history in terms of "culture wars" is frequent, although, alongside some such episodes, there can also be what may be more appropriately termed "culture antagonism." Moreover, institutional and professional pressures and culture may operate to moderate tensions. Yet, there are, and were, academics who can be seen as political, for example, in Britain, Maurice Cowling, a Fellow of Peterhouse College, Cambridge, from 1963 to 1988. He offered powerful and competitive studies that challenged received wisdom and sought to undermine the nostrums of the Left. *Mill and Liberalism* (1963) presented liberalism in the person of John Stuart Mill as totalitarian in intention, his secularist utilitarianism a harsh elitism in practice. It was a potent undermining of standard views and an iconic figure; while, in *The Nature and Limits of Political Science* (1963), Cowling challenged an increasingly fashionable subject. Cowling's three major political histories – *1867: Disraeli, Gladstone and Revolution: The Passing of the Second Reform Act* (1967), *The Impact of Labour 1920–1924: The Beginning of Modern British Politics* (1971), and *The Impact of Hitler: British Politics and British Policy, 1933 to 1940* (1975) – were masterpieces of high political analysis. Their focus on political wheeling and dealing, the gaining, retention, and use, of power, was a marked contrast to the habitual emphasis in British historical scholarship on progressive forces and standard interpretations, including the extension of the franchise and the rise of the Labour Party.

Focusing on Conservative politicians in the recent past proved particularly attractive to Conservatives fascinated with politics, and Cowling was held to be especially influential in molding the intellectual ideas associated with the government of Margaret Thatcher, Conservative party leader from 1975 to 1990 and Prime Minister from 1979 to 1990. He did, indeed, play some important roles. In 1978, Cowling was a founder of the Salisbury Group, and he taught or influenced a number of subsequently prominent Conservative politicians and writers, including, as was made much of in the 1990s, when he was seen as a potential party leader, Michael Portillo. Yet, much of this association between Cowling and Thatcher was made by non-Conservative commentators. Indeed, it is striking how far Cowling's approach was different to that of Thatcher. He did not share her commitment to fiscal policy. Moreover, his emphasis on calculation as a means of political action was not conducive to a leader who sought to reshape public culture and transform Britain, and who was uncomfortable with a clubland approach to politics, namely it being crucially decided by small numbers of the elite. In many respects, Thatcher was a populist rejoinder to this world, and Thatcherism an attempt to move beyond it. Moreover, Cowling devoted the Thatcher years to writing a three-volume *Religion and Public Doctrine in Modern England* (1980–2001), a work well removed from her clarity. In emphasizing, in this study, the need for a Christian conservatism, Cowling produced a massive piece of scholarship, the arguments of much of which would have suited Conservative moralists. The recovery of Christian conservative writers, most of whom had been ignored by progressive scholars, and several of whom had influenced Cowling as a young student at Cambridge, was particularly impressive, but their more general impact has been limited.[7]

Cowling's case is instructive in part because it reflects a period when the tensions of British academic history could appear important to politics, rather than being separate from it, or a reflection of it. At the same time, and here change plays a role alongside personality, there seems a clear contrast between the means of historical influence in Britain in the 1980s and those of the present-day. Today, television is far more prominent, and, with it, metropolitan and international interests and trends, while the internet has brought a form of democratization to the transmission of knowledge and opinion. In contrast, much of the British academic profession appears less prominent than in the past. Television plays a particularly transformative role. The historians who appear most frequently are those who are best able to play the contact systems that influence commissioning. They tend to be fluent, sometimes facile, assertive and, often, personable, if not attractive. This represents a different range of criteria to those seen with the senior figures in the academic hierarchy. The latter are more prominent in the world of scholarly books, but that is a world of declining influence as far as the public, including the interested public, is concerned.

CONTESTING WORLD WAR II

Particular subjects attract television history, notably the drama of modern warfare, especially World War II. Separately, the prominent role of World War II in the historical narratives of many modern states and the recovered memory of their publics helps ensure that controversies over the war attract great attention. These controversies relate to the causes of the war, to its conduct, and to its consequences.[8] The treatment of civilians has proved especially contentious. In part, this was because that has become a key way of defining war guilt, a change from the emphasis on actually beginning hostilities which had been the major theme in previous conflicts. This new focus not only accorded with the idea of citizen-societies, but also offered a way for modern societies to look back and make sense of the experience of their forbears, a sense that also relates to them.

The resulting emphasis was seen in the controversy of the Anglo-American bombing campaign against Germany. As an indication of the national differences that are so important to the treatment of the war, this campaign caused far more controversy in Britain than in the United States. This contrast largely arises because discussion in the latter focused on the air attacks on Japan, culminating in the dropping of two atomic bombs in August 1945. The controversy in Britain is instructive because it brought together a number of themes. These included public commemoration, academic re-evaluations, popular writing, the views of the public, and the impact of current affairs. The last may be the most influential because the criticism of the wartime bombing became a major theme, and drew energy from successive campaigns against bombing after 1945. Thus, the British Campaign for Nuclear Disarmament in the late 1950s and early 1960s, and again in the early 1980s, was one source of criticism. So, too, was opposition to area bombing during the Vietnam War. An instance occurred with a letter to the *Times* on 25 November 1969 in which the writer attacked both the Vietnam War and World War II for making it acceptable to carry out the "wholesale slaughter of women and children."[9] Again, controversy in the 1990s and 2000s played a role, with critics of the use of air power against Serbia and Iraq and in Afghanistan playing a role in discussion of World War II, and vice versa.[10]

The pressure of current events was matched by that from more general social and cultural trends. Here, the focus was on a less deferential society and a less nationalistic culture. Related to this came a conviction that morality, rather than national interest, was the key context and that national interest could not define morality. Opposition to area bombing and to bombing that involved civilian casualties played a major role in this cultural shift. Accordingly, there was much criticism of the wartime bombing campaign from the 1960s, a period in which society became more self-consciously liberal. An anti-war component was an important aspect of this.

Linked to this shift came academic assessments initially suggesting that the wartime bombing, while causing heavy civilian casualties in Germany, had been ineffective. This was notably the case with the British official history, Charles Webster and Noble Frankland's *The Strategic Air Offensive against Germany, 1939–1945* (1961). The criticisms were picked up in the British press as a major news story, and, in turn, led to claims in letters to British newspapers and other sources that the bombing was immoral. More popular works criticizing area bombing followed the official history, and had a similar impact.[11] Particular controversy focused on David Irving's *The Destruction of Dresden* (1963), which became an international bestseller. Claiming that 135,000 civilians died in the 1945 raid on Dresden, an exaggeration, Irving attacked area bombing as criminal.[12] The book had considerable impact, and led to newspaper discussion of the raid as a "holocaust" and a "massacre."[13] Although the casualty figure was disproved, and, indeed, retracted by Irving in a letter to the *Times* on 7 July 1966, it has continued to influence public attitudes.[14] Thus, Irving's casualty figure was used in a House of Commons' debate on 12 December 1989 about the ethics of area bombing.[15] This usage reflected the extent to which Dresden served as a benchmark for commentators. It was also cited by the Soviet Union during the Cold War in order to castigate the wartime record of Britain and the United States. German victimhood became a theme intended to link the East German workers to the Soviet Union.[16]

Aside from the focus on Dresden, there was a broader pattern of criticism of the bombing as disproportionate and immoral.[17] These arguments made the memorialization of Bomber Command, and the 55,000 men in it who died in active service during World War II, controversial. For a long period, this commemoration was limited, and notably in contrast to Fighter Command, which enjoyed a good post-war coverage due to its key role in defeating German air attack in the Battle of Britain (1940). Thus, it proved easier to commemorate the underdog and the defender of 1940, even though the individual bombers that attacked Germany were highly vulnerable. It was not until 1992 that a memorial was unveiled in London, in the shape of a statue of Sir Arthur Harris, the controversial commander-in-chief of Bomber Command. Intended to commemorate both Bomber Command and Harris, this was seen by some, both in Britain and in Germany, as an untoward step. The statue was defaced with red paint by protestors that year. In contrast, the unveiling by the Queen in 2012 in Green Park, London, of a national memorial to Bomber Command was regarded as a less contentious step. The focus was on reconciliation not least with the inscription "We remember those of all countries who died in 1939–45" and with a tree donated by Germany as part of the memorial. This case exemplifies the capacity of war memorials to encompass a variety of themes.[18]

In Germany, there was a related, but also different, direction in the discussion of the bombing. After decades in which suffering from Allied bombing was overshadowed by German war crimes, there was an emphasis, notably from the 2000s, on German casualties,[19] and thus on the alleged inequities of Allied bombing. This was an aspect of a broader presentation of Germans as victims. This presentation was different to that which had focused on German refugees from Eastern Europe, after the war, not least because those refugees had been closely aligned with the Right and were widely seen as seeking an element of *revanche* in the shape of regaining territory. However, there was a degree of similarity in practice, with victimhood characterizing both the refugees and the later discussion about the impact of bombing.

The political context, domestic, and international, was different after the Cold War. A focus on the bombing offered a way to deal with the legacy of Nazism, as well as to provide a history for a new, reunited Germany. In 1995, the 50th anniversary of the raid was marked by a commemoration in Dresden in which the mayor criticized Harris as a "hangman."[20]

In part, the current approaches in official memorialization in Britain and Germany are joined by an emphasis on remembering and honoring the dead, rather than debating the morality of the policy itself. That, however, does not capture the range of private and academic discussion, or the point that engaging with the issue of morality is an aspect of the remembrance and honoring of the dead. Many (although not all) Germans are disinclined to consider Germany's wartime role in beginning terror bombing, its willingness to move to use rockets simply fired against civilian targets such as London, and the vicious nature of the wartime German state and the extent to which it enjoyed popular support.

The context of such popular trends can be considered when focusing on the more academic aspects of controversies. It is instructive to consider a spat in 2009 when a prominent British popular historian wrote a major work on World War II that was widely praised by many reviewers, only for it to receive a highly critical review from one of the leading British academic historians. That was the fate of Andrew Roberts's *The Storm of War: A New History of the Second World War* in the *Times Literary Supplement* of 28 August 2009 at the hands of Richard Evans, then Regius Professor of History at Cambridge, a distinguished scholar of modern German history. The entire episode invites discussion at a number of levels, but let us start with this episode as a case study of historiography in action. Evans's review provided an opportunity because it sets up an apparent contrast of popular history with academic scholarship. That certainly was the tone of the review: "Roberts approaches his topics in a kind of *Boy's Own* spirit, filling his pages with acts of derring-do by heroic, almost invariably British troops." *Boy's Own* was a popular British comic. Evans presented the book as a version of a type of "hastily written potboilers, widely criticized by reviewers for their inadequacies and inaccuracies," and wrote of the "many other inaccuracies or errors," and so on.

So far, apparently so clear: academic standards versus popular mendacity. However, most academic reviewers were far less harsh. In the *Observer* of 9 August 2009, Robert Service praised "a sparkling addition," and noted, "The thread binding the book together is the question of historical contingency." The complaint, instead, from academic reviewers was about a lack of originality, which is of course a persistent problem with writing on the subject of the war, but not one that prevents academics from tackling the familiar. Secondly, not all the non-academic writing about Roberts was positive. Instead, there was a degree of political critique, notably with a harsh assault in the *Independent* of 31 July 2009 by the journalist Johann Hari. As another strand, Hari, like Evans, is on the Left; Roberts on the Right, as were some of the journalists who praised him, such as Simon Heffer. Evans, indeed, devoted a certain amount of attention to his subject's political resonances: "Roberts is an unabashed apologist for the British Empire . . . an unapologetically Conservative historian."

Evans also argued that disproportionate space was devoted by Roberts to the British, an accurate point. In particular, there was room, as in other histories of the war, both British and non-British, for far more attention to the Sino-Japanese War, begun in 1937. It had already, by 1939, provided a clear indication of why Germany would lose, notably with the Japanese failure to turn victory in the field into a successful end of the war by offering the defeated Chinese terms they could accept.[21] This was a key instance of the contrast between output, in the shape of people killed or territory conquered, and outcome, in the form of a satisfactory close to the conflict. Evans's objection to Roberts's national coverage is pertinent for most scholarship. Thus, American treatment of the war against Japan consistently underplays the role of China, Britain, and Australia. So also for Germany. Evans criticized Roberts for failing to consult the *Germany and the Second World War* volumes produced by the Military History Research Office in Germany, volumes from which he made good use in his own *The Third Reich at War* (2008). Yet, although the global dimension is addressed, for example in volumes VI and VII, this series is heavily focused on the German war and underplays that involving Japan. Moreover, in criticizing Roberts, Evans cited Karl-Heinz Frieser on the battle of Kursk of 1943. However, Frieser is all too typical of much German scholarship in presenting defeat as a result of being beaten in "the production battle in the factories,"[22] and as minimizing or ignoring the extent to which the Germans were eventually outfought. The last is a key point, and one about which academics are divided in their emphasis. In a repetition of work on World War I, Germanists tend in their account of World War II to underplay the battlefield in favor of the Home Front and the struggle for production. Thus, again, the academic versus popular approach only works up to a point. In practice, each constituency is highly diverse.

With the issue of the popular world of history comes its exploitation by the practices and ethos of trade history. Such exploitation is particularly apparent for topics that sell well, such as World War II. For example, press coverage is symptomatic of a wider situation in which big publishers have a lock on some of the reviewing, not least due to advertising buy-through-the-paper deals, and thanks to the lobbying of review editors. Moreover, bookshop placements of display copies are frequently purchased. In addition, publishers pay often substantial advances to works they have contracted with agents, and, when these books arrive, the review process is frequently perfunctory. Alongside personality, politics, and publishers, period plays a role. The politics of the 1930s and World War II inspire not only controversy but also, as has already been indicated in this book, animosity; and writing on the period can reflect this. There are many controversial issues involved in the presentation of World War II, for example the role of Pope Pius XII (r. 1939–1958). He has been attacked for failing publicly to denounce the Holocaust in 1941 and 1942. In the 2000s and 2010s, this topic led to criticism over delays in the declassification of records and over the Vatican's failure to take up observer status at the Task Force for International Cooperation on Holocaust Education, Remembrance, and Research.

CONTESTING CONTENT

In so far as content is concerned, historiography owes something to academic politics, whether personal, sub-disciplinary, disciplinary, or institutional. Yet, factors that are non-political also play a role. For example, the balance of academic appointments is related to the emphasis both on teaching and on research, which is not a balance struck largely in political terms. As far as institutional politics are concerned, the state of history as a subject in part reflects the tensions arising from fiscal pressures, and thus the competition for resources between disciplines. In such battles, history suffers from being unable to raise significant research income. On the other hand, the discipline benefits not only from being relatively cheap to teach, such that a true market of costs for courses in various disciplines would make it attractive to students, but also because, even when subjects are charged at the same level, there is much demand for undergraduate history courses. As a result, there is, in this respect, a close relationship between public interest and the academic world. However, this relationship does not generally extend to the content of the teaching. Indeed, there is frequently a striking mismatch between what students wish to study on history courses and what they are usually offered. This mismatch is a component of the historiographical world at the university level and echoes a wider failure of most professional historians to satisfy "a mass thirst for knowledge."[23] That situation casts an ironic reflection on the pledge, in the prefatory note of 1886, that the *English Historical Review* would be devoted to general readers as well as scholars. The call for history teaching to serve as "inspiration"[24] finds relatively few echoes within the academy, which helps to explain the limited wider relevance of the latter. The profession has turned inward. Historians go to enormous trouble to unearth interesting things, then bury them in books and periodicals that nobody (except other professionals) ever reads. The collection *À quoi sert l'histoire aujourd'hui?* (Paris, 2010), responses by forty historians, scarcely offers encouragement about the situation in France, but, at least, it could be found in bookshops there.

More generally, the pseudo-scientificization of academic history poses a serious problem as far as the popular resonance of this history is concerned. This longstanding tendency reflects a loss of confidence in the liberal arts and began with liberal education reformers who assaulted the models of Classical education in the nineteenth century. The cult of science played a major role, as did intellectual-cultural-political developments in particular countries, such as American Progressivism. The more recent tendency to locate history in the social sciences rather than the humanities and, in particular, the development of particular types of social history, has contributed to this situation. The funding, certainly in Europe, of research on a group basis does not generally result in publications that are attractive to read. However, the popularity of more traditional forms of history also varies. Ironically, it is often historiographical courses and those on historical method that are of least interest to undergraduates, although the situation is different at the postgraduate level. The relative lack of popularity of courses on historiography and historical method (and there are, of course, variations by institution) can be seen as arising in part from the subject matter as a whole, but, in part, from the way that these courses are commonly taught. There is usually an emphasis on theory, rather than practice, and on self-conscious theoretical texts, instead of on the nature of historiography and historical method in society as a whole.

Undergraduates tend to prefer outline courses, the "big picture," and to be particularly interested in what relates to the issues of the present day. Thus, the prominence of relations between the West and the Islamic world in the 2000s and 2010s led in Western universities to greater interest in past episodes, notably the Crusades. There has also been a rise in interest in relations with China. The broadening out of the classic agenda is shown in the treatment of history in encyclopedia. Take *The Encyclopedia of World History, Ancient, Medieval, and Modern,* a work that derives originally from Karl Ploetz's *Auszug aus der alten, mittleren und neuren Geschichte,* a successful, multi-edition fact book, which was published in the United States from 1883, first as *An Epitome of Ancient, Medieval, and Modern History.* The sixth edition of the *Encyclopedia,* published in 2002, offered a greatly expanded coverage of the world outside Europe and North America, notably the sections dealing with Africa, the Middle East, South Asia, and Latin America. However, to keep down the size of the book, much of the European material was cut. There is a parallel tendency toward a global approach in historiographical studies,[25] although this development has had less impact hitherto than should be expected.

Alongside institutional pressures, the practice of the profession is more significant for historiographical development at the university level than is suggested by the usual stress on intellectual trends and leading thinkers. Indeed, it is striking, when responding to questions about "developments in history," to consider the degree to which the profession is atomized, with dynamic specialisms and sub-specialisms taking the bulk of attention. In practice, most historians feel a sense of identity in terms of these fields. Thus, there are eighteenth-century historians, or medieval economic historians, and their knowledge of, or concern for, other specialisms is limited in the extreme. The same is even true of the relatively new subject of world history. This limitation has been exacerbated by the extent to which teaching has become narrower in focus, while the growing size of the profession and the rising volume of output makes it very difficult to keep up with work in subspecialisms, let alone elsewhere in the subject. Individual sub-disciplines have suffered greatly from a concern with professional interests and assertion within the discipline, rather than with reaching out to a wider audience.

There has also been a significant cultural change. The image and self-image of the academic as a man (less commonly woman) of letters, an intellect abreast of wider currents, able to chat in the staff/common room on such topics and to read the *New York Review of Books* or the *Times Literary Supplement* (or, in scurrilous fiction, to drink and debauch), is now essentially redundant. First, there is no time; as teaching and professional duties rise, notably, in Britain, in response to greater student numbers, the energy is devoted to marking. Secondly, the domestic context of most academics' life has been transformed, leaving them less leisure for such activities. The "bachelor don" (less commonly spinster don) has long ceased to be the typical figure. Thirdly, and most significantly, the emphasis now is on scholarly development in terms of work in the particular specialism of choice, as is the case in both America and Europe. Thus, historians attend conferences, read books and articles, participate in internet sites, and advance their career through publications, but all in a specific field, generally a highly specific field.

From this perspective, general discussion of historiographical trends is irrelevant and appears inconsequential, and even subjects and approaches that are broad-ranging in theory, such as world history and transnationalism tend to become specialisms with arcane controversies, vocabularies, and historiographies. Indeed, to give a flavor of the situation reveals the limitations of the individual scholar because it is difficult to be sure of one's understandings of other fields, even if one has an interest in them. Historiography as a subject (rather than as a description of historical work) becomes not so much a prism through which to look at history as yet another specialization. In practice, historiography also becomes a specialization that has only limited resonance with the rest of the subject, and indeed one that frequently underplays the significance of political and social contexts and developments. This point is more generally true of the entire field of intellectual history, which partly explains why it often seems remote to scholars in other fields of history.

It is also striking that those who work on specific fields, such as military history or historical geography, usually work with a distinct historiographical literature that only indirectly interacts with standard works on historiography as a subject or with topics in the latter. There is no particular reason for this situation, but it reflects a sense of the irrelevance of these general works or, rather, their failure to reach out to offer insights that seem of interest to specialists in specific historical fields. For example, to take Chinese military history, the standard account of Chinese history, one that cites Confucian values, argues for an essentially pacific strategic culture. In contrast, there has recently been a strong body of scholarship in the West focusing on Chinese expansionism and arguing that the Chinese accordingly developed an offensive capability, one that led to the conquest of important territories to the west, notably Xinjiang and Tibet in the eighteenth century.[26] The debate raises more general issues, not least concerning the value of texts, and also the extent to which the historical profession had – and has – has a preference for accounts that do not stress warfare or the military. Nevertheless, it is difficult to see any strong relationship between work on Chinese military history and discussions about historiographical trends in the subject of history as a whole. In practice, this is a misleading approach. For example, Enlightenment thought on the nature of human development is of value to historical geographers dealing with that period.[27] Similarly, Karl von Clausewitz (1780–1831), the leading theorist of military affairs in the nineteenth century, is best understood in light of the general German intellectual life of the period.

Specialization, however, ensures that there are a range of historiographies. Within each one, historians think, read, and write with reference to past and present scholarship that prompts their work by stimulus, whether by complementing it, opposing it, or offering alternatives: counterfactuals or otherwise. The absence of a big idea or a set of big ideas means that this range of historiographies lacks coherence and, instead, is part of the general atomization of the discipline. This point is accentuated by the extent to which many specializations have distinct and different institutional or disciplinary formats. In Britain, "area studies," the classic form of teaching much non-Western history, are often separate from history departments, while ancient history is covered by Classics departments. The American system, in which non-Western and ancient history are both covered by history departments, offers a less bitty account of history as a discipline, but there is still, on the part of individual scholars, an absence of intellectual similarity with fellow-scholars working in different fields and, instead, a preference for the particular specialism. The use of the word "similarity" is instructive, as it could have been "coherence" or "conformity." The choice of words leads to different impressions, and this variation is instructive because, to the specialist, any similarity, coherence, or conformity with fellow-scholars might be potentially misleading. However, such characteristics might be more in demand for historians, then or later, seeking not only a shaping of the past for purposes of analysis and presentation, but also a shaping of the study of the past.

Variations between types of history can be extended if the situation is considered at the international level, because specialisms take on differing meanings and follow contrasting patterns in particular states. Thus, although China has moved greatly from the political and historiographical situation in the 1970s, there is still concern among its historians with economic issues and causes that is greater than that seen in the West. As a result, the character of political, and indeed economic, historical studies in China is different to that in the United States. Despite the decline of Marxist influence in historical analysis, the Chinese historical tradition also struggles with the tension between the universalism within Marxist theories and the nationalism that is so potent in Chinese accounts and that has become more prominent over the last decade. In paleontology, there is an emphasis on the Peking Man discovered in the 1920s as the ancestor of the modern Chinese, and therefore a resistance to the idea that the Chinese had a shared origin with the rest of humanity in Africa.[28]

TRANSNATIONALISM

An attempt at coherence in academic historical work has been provided by the rise in the 1990s of what is termed transnational history.[29] This approach, which moves beyond that of comparative history, an earlier and still active challenge to "nation-state-centered historiography,"[30] instead stresses the intensity, range, and importance of connections between societies, indeed their interconnectedness. Migration and international networks are key subjects in transnational history. As an explicit challenge to historical accounts focused on nations, this form of history can be related to the crisis of identity perceived in many states, not least because there was another academic critique that focused on the idea that nations were "imagined communities."[31] The last is certainly not true of national academic communities. Far from being "imagined communities," the differences between them in interests, conceptualization, methodology, and language pose challenges for both comparative and transnational history.[32] In some respects, transnational history echoes the wide-ranging stadial accounts[33] of Enlightenment writers such as William Robertson and Adam Smith as it revives interest in the dynamics of universal history and, indeed, is linked to the rise of global history as a topic and practice.[34] This kind of historiography is still, to an extent, in its making, and themes such as connectivity are in need of detailed scrutiny. Nevertheless, global history already has had a major impact.

CONCLUSIONS

This chapter has highlighted serious challenges facing the world of academic history. Some of these come down to issues of relevance and to changing focuses. It is sometimes difficult for the world of academic history to shift gears as quickly as students would like in order to meet the students' interests of the moment, let alone to respond to changes in government policy, but there can be related questions about the willingness and ability of academics to respond.

In terms of content, there are also major challenges, but empiricism as a foundation for the profession has persevered and remains a major focus of historiographical discussion. Despite the emphasis here on variations between national traditions of scholarship, there is a widespread commonality in the tension between empiricism, or fact-based research, and, on the other hand, the need to draw broader conclusions. This is a tension that overlaps with that between argument from evidence and the emphasis, instead, on theoretical understandings. Traditionally, history as an academic discipline has put the emphasis on research, notably in archives. The influence of nineteenth-century German ideas and practices on the development of the American university system was particularly important here. Moreover, academic historians have presented this characteristic as a means to draw a contrast with the use of the past by other specialists and subjects, for example by political scientists and sociologists, let alone with public myths. As a reminder that prestige and power also play a role, the emphasis on the scholarly skills linked to archival research has served as a way to accumulate intellectual prestige, and thus establish expertise and rank, notably at the expense of amateurs.

The academic stress on empiricism, the role of facts, took a battering in the late twentieth century from a number of challenges, culminating in post-modernism.[35] However, the stress on empiricism, albeit with a greater awareness of the multiple interpretations possible of those facts, remains characteristic of academic scholarship,[36] with "referentiality and historiography" marking the distance from fiction.[37] Therefore, empiricism is a key point of methodological and historiographical discussion. This is the case whatever may be the caveats of those with a turn to philosophy and to discussion about the nature of meaning. In so far as the practicalities of research and teaching are concerned, the interests and concerns of those engaged in these philosophical questions are shared by only a small minority of the academic profession, let alone popular historians.

TWELVE

Historiographies of the Future

HISTORY AS A SUBJECT MAY DEAL WITH THE PAST, BUT IT IS A living discipline and thus has a future. Historiography necessarily should consider this future, not least because it will help to establish the significance of the current situation and of earlier developments that already are the subject of historiographical discussion. This is the case not only for the content of history but also for its forms in the changing shape of historical method and of intellectual discussion of the nature of history. Moreover, official, public, and popular history considered in terms of "history wars" has a future that will help establish the significance of present developments. This passionate history sits in an uneasy relationship to the search for cold objective truth praised, for example, by the journalist Anne Applebaum in 2010: "If we remember the twentieth century for what it actually was, and not for what we imagine it to have been, the misuse of history for national political purposes also becomes more difficult."[1] In practice, as we have seen in earlier chapters, history has always been, and will continue to be, a battleground for politics, identity, and understanding.

As before in this book, there is no obvious priority in discussing these issues into the future; and to begin with one issue might suggest that it is particularly significant. That is not the intention here. Certainly, the idea of some sort of neo-Platonic hierarchy, with academic history to the fore, is problematic. This is particularly so because it is probable that the nature of academic teaching will be transformed, and this transformation may well have major consequences for the process of research. The vice versa linkage may also occur, although probably not to the same extent. The current model of universities as distinctive institutions for the face-to-face teaching of young people is already being replaced by a far more varied menu including distance learning through the internet, as well as shorter and sandwich courses, and most-age teaching, that is, for most ages rather than largely the 18–22 cohort. The net effect will be to challenge existing institutional provision and hierarchies. The particular consequences for any individual discipline are unclear. However, as history is a subject lacking a vocational structure or oversight, and a subject that is very much presented in the vernacular, so it will be especially prone to influence not only from the political questions of the day but also from the wider currents of social expectation. The former influence can be registered in the successive editions of books.[2] In countries with high rates of participation in higher education, such as Britain and the United States, social expectation from higher education will probably include a lower level of detail in explanation and exposition on the part of historians than was the pattern in, say, the 1970s, still more the 1950s, before subsequent periods of university expansion. The result is likely to be an expectation of a clarity that may seem like simplicity to many academic commentators.

This development will probably be taken further if history is increasingly taught as part of a general course of studies. Such a location for the subject encourages the broad-brush approaches of social scientists, with their emphasis on abstraction, generalization, and semi-automatic patterns of cause and effect, rather than any stress on contingency, the individual or individuals, and the moment. The second group of factors offers a perspective currently understood, accepted, and respected as valid by many historians, notably in the Western empirical tradition.[3] As another aspect of context, governments want all university activity to be considered in terms of output, with this output, including the graduates themselves, to be much more useable and employable for the benefit of the economy, and in the shortest possible term. Training is their ideal, not education.

A drive for simplicity in explication may well be furthered by a general decline of social deference that is linked to an attack on expertise and professionalism, both seen as inherently un-democratic and as constraints on accountability. Excess deference certainly is unhelpful to scholarship when it deters students from challenging their teachers' ideas. In some countries, students essentially are expected to reproduce the lessons of their teachers rather than to engage in independent research. This is the case, for example, in many Italian universities. However, in the contrary direction, in societies where views are validated by conviction and emotion, the expert will have a contested role, and his or her status will be challenged. There has also been the rise of the "secondary intellectuals," such as journalists, novelists, and television personalities, who supersede academic historians. This rise is an aspect of a general media-driven present-mindedness. It is accompanied by a shrinking of attention spans with a consequent demand for readily digested views of the past.

If academic institutions become less specialized, as they are increasingly doing in the post-industrial world, that is likely to have an impact on the research that is produced, not least because there will be a reduced need for staff qualified at the level currently judged appropriate. It may indeed be asked whether most undergraduate teaching in the humanities requires the level of expertise currently expected from the academics, or requires the small-group teaching that is widely taken to be the ideal state, but which appears to be in conflict with the logic of distance education in so far as the latter leads to large-scale provision. In each case, it is possible to see fiscal pressures triggering a pedagogic rethink, with institutions that have less money, especially new providers, challenging conventional wisdom about teaching methods in order to assert their market position. The net result of changes in higher education may well be less of what is called blue-skies research (research with no direct economic application) in the humanities, but that is not the same as a historiographical void. Instead, there is likely to be a growth in publishing short, accessible, general texts, such as the Italian series *Farsi un'idea* [*Getting an idea*], publishing of course understood to include the internet as much as, and eventually more than, hard copy. The appearance of these works may require a change in historiographical discussion so that greater attention is devoted to this form of academic publication; a form that will also ease communication between specialisms. Yet, such a change will test existing academic practices and hierarchies in a profession that, despite its frequent talk of radicalism, is often quite hidebound, or at least conservative, in its practices.

CHANGING WORLD POWER

A key topic for these general texts will be provided by rapid changes in the world, a process that encourages not only futurology but also the appearance of historical studies that range into the future.[4] Particularly important changes are likely to arise from the relative rise of East and South Asia, as well as from the decline of Europe, changes that were anticipated in some historiographical works of the late twentieth century.[5] The United States is likely to remain the leading world power in military, although, less clearly, in economic, terms. Yet it will be so in a world that is different to that of the late twentieth century, let alone that century as a whole. This relative decline may greatly complicate attempts to continue providing an optimistic account of American history. However, to refer to a crisis of American historical identity would be going too far and would be overly reductionist. It is important to recall that there have been past episodes of grave concern about America's position, for example in the 1970s in the aftermath of failure in Vietnam as well as of the Watergate Scandal. There are practical reasons in academic culture, notably its specialist research practices, for a disinclination to address broad and large-scale themes such as national decline, and these are often handled instead by more populist commentators.

It is also pertinent to note aspects of continuing American strength in the twenty-first century, notably the continuing role of America's cultural industries as a currency of American power in general. Thus, software brands are dominated by American products. This strength has a major impact in the politics of identity, notably in Europe but especially in Asia. The effort of China to stop Google, Facebook, Hollywood, and at the same time to push the Olympics, the World's Fair, and Confucius Institutes is a recognition of the force of the cultural confrontation. The extent to which culture adds value and values to power encourages the invention of traditions, as in Singapore, Taiwan, and China. This invention is an aspect of a serious cultural competition that is ever more self-consciously organized.

An instance of the sensitivities caused by different histories arose in 2010 when the British Prime Ministerial–led trade delegation visit-

ing Beijing was asked to remove the poppies they were wearing because
of the Anglo-Chinese Opium Wars of the mid-nineteenth century, conflicts seen both as a national humiliation for China and as the cause
of a far greater subsequent foreign intervention that gravely weakened
China. The British refused to put aside the poppies, worn in memory
of the war-dead. In fact, the British poppies, which symbolize French
poppies from World War I battlefields of Flanders, are very different to
those from which opium is derived.

More consistently, there will be pressure to devote greater attention
to the part China and India took in both of the twentieth century's world
wars. At the same time, revision of the wars' presentation will not only
relate to these powers. Instead, there is likely to be a more general response to the multitude of perspectives on the war, not least as Western
(and Russian) public histories lose their relative potency in other parts
of the world. For example, in New Guinea, the Australian account of the
war with Japan does not match that of the local peoples.[6] The world wars
will also be reinterpreted to make sense of changes in the world today, as
with the argument offered by Adrian Wooldridge, an *Economist* journalist, writing in the *Sunday Times* on 27 April 2014: "The first half of the
20th century was ruined by Europe's inability to come to terms with
Germany's growing power and ambitions. The same could easily be true
of the 21st century: China is already gobbling up resources across Africa,
much as imperial Germany once did, and engaging in sabre-rattling."
Wooldridge was trying to warn of the dangers of established powers
mishandling the rise of a new great power.

Aside from the coverage of specific episodes in Chinese and Indian
history, there is already a more wide-ranging presentation of Asian history designed to depict the West as in many respects long dependent
on initiatives from the East. This approach represents a rewriting of the
standard Western account of civilizational development and progress.[7]
This rewriting is not unprecedented. Indeed, Edward Gibbon, rather
than focusing solely on the decline and fall of Rome and the fate of its
successor states, already a big topic, extended his scope to a history of
Eurasia, and within these confines, he was particularly interested in the
displacement of the Greek and Syrian world of Byzantium by that which
is Arabic and Islamic. Indeed, while Gibbon was writing, the banners

of the Ottoman Empire still waved above the walls of Belgrade, Sofia, and Athens. In focusing on Byzantium and its invaders, Gibbon both therefore reflected an aspect of his contemporary situation, and, in more generally describing the triumph of barbarism and religion, sought to explain the world of post-Roman power, ecclesiastical authority, and scholastic philosophy against which modern civil society had been constructed.[8] Yet, although he toyed with the idea of the West succumbing to renewed attack, Gibbon did not devote much attention to the issue, and there was no reason in the 1770s to 1780s to fear such an outcome. To that extent, the rise of China and India presents a challenge to Western historians not seen in recent centuries.

Whether the Chinese or Indians will devote sufficient attention to the problems of their own histories is unclear. The lack of official acceptance in China of the disastrous and deadly consequences of Mao Zedong's Great Leap Forward in 1959–1962 is not encouraging.[9] Referring to the massacre of the Tiananmen Square protestors in 1989 as "putting down a riot" is linked to the misleading argument that, as a foreign ministry spokesman put it in 2014, China "does not have dissidents, only law-breakers."[10]

More generally, engaging in the West with non-Western histories at greater length will, in transforming historiography, also challenge established conceptualizations, notably simplistic views about the non-West. Such conceptualizations draw on a long history going back to the Classical Greek views of Persia, thus providing an account of Asia as despotic and backward, the origins of what in recent decades was decried by Edward Said and others as Orientalism. As an instance of present-mindedness, such an account, which anyway has serious historical flaws, is in large part undermined for the here and now by the rise of China and India.

Thus, established historiographical hierarchies and practices will be questioned not only because they are implausible in academic terms, but also if they fail to make sense of the world around. It is unclear whether a displacement of attention from Europe or the Western world will lead to a new hierarchy of national histories or to a transnational history with different priorities. The need to rewrite world history, already facing the challenge of providing post-Eurocentric hypotheses,[11] will be driven by this experience of change. This rewriting will move beyond the stage of presenting modern history in terms of the response to the rise of the West, the last understood as cause, course, and consequence of globalization.[12] It is unclear how far the greater global importance of China and India, and their stronger economic interaction with other countries, will lead to a commitment in these countries to world history akin to the spatial expansion and globalization in course designs that happened in the United States and Britain during the late twentieth and early twenty-first centuries.[13] There is unlikely to be an immigrant flow to China and India to encourage such an approach, although the size of the Chinese and Indian diasporas may be a factor.

The change toward a post-Eurocentric history in the West has implications for more detailed research as job appointments are made accordingly. Developments have led to a rise in the importance of Chinese historians and China specialists, and this process will continue. The significance of politics for international academic hierarchies can be considerable. For example, the primacy of German scholarship was greatly harmed by the Nazi period and by Germany's defeat in World War II.

CHINA AND THE CHALLENGE TO THE WEST

The extent to which the future of historiography is bound up with that of the West is uncertain. One prospectus would be that of the relative decline of the West in the face of a model of authoritarian statecraft focused on the Chinese domestic and international system. In such a model, the presentation of history is of great relevance. For China, presentist history is linked to a critique of liberal universalism, a critique that is highly significant to the ideology of the current government. In particular, the commercial nationalism of the present day that it sponsors is deliberately counterposed to a free trade order that is presented in terms of an historical pedigree including past Western pressure to open up the Chinese economy, pressure that is regarded as unacceptable. Anti-Western tendencies are encouraged by the degree to which earlier episodes of foreign rule by non-Chinese dynasties, most recently the Manchu (1644–1912), were made acceptable with the argument (now controversial) that conquerors were absorbed by Chinese civilization

and thus sinicized.[14] This argument, which greatly suits Chinese nationalists, encourages interest in the imperial legacy,[15] but cannot be
extended to Western or Japanese pressure. Instead, there is a critical account of the failure to resist Western pressure in the nineteenth century.
Such arguments reflect the more general process of presentist history
in China. Nationalist coherence is the goal, as also after the brutal suppression of the demonstrations in Tiananmen Square in 1989, which
were followed by a major effort to use nationalism to support the system. Flag-raising ceremonies became mandatory in schools, museums
were presented as "patriotic education bases," and, in 1991, the general
secretary of the Chinese Communist Party, Jiang Zemin, wrote that
patriotic education would "let the Chinese people, especially the youth,
enhance their pride and self-confidence in the nation and stop the rise
of the worship of the West."

Chinese nationalism was encouraged by the depiction of maritime
history. Gavin Menzies's tendentious theory that the Chinese circum-
navigated the world in 1421[16] was welcomed, with the *China Daily* happy
to claim in July 2004 that the Chinese did so well before Columbus
and Magellan. Furthermore, Zheng He, the great navigator of the early
fifteenth century, was commemorated in 2005. His voyages into the Indian Ocean, which were represented in the opening ceremony of the
2008 Olympic Games at Beijing, are regarded as prefiguring the present
situation of Chinese international influence by means of governmental
initiative. It is instructive to note no comparable attention devoted to
the very extensive Chinese diaspora of that period, a diaspora that, unlike Zheng He's voyages, was largely the product of independent action.

Particular anger in China is directed at the eight-nation international force that suppressed the Boxer Uprising of 1900, a force in which
the Japanese provided the largest contingent but that otherwise included
American and European troops. This anger is especially voiced by *fenq-
ing* (angry youth) whose nationalism is strongly tinged with xenophobia. Anger is directed not only against foreign powers, but also at those
Chinese seen as collaborators. Sensitivity over the latter led to rage when
sixty-six Chinese Catholics killed by the Boxers were declared saints
in 2000, a decision announced on China's national day, 1 October, and
treated by the Chinese government as a "gross insult."

A portrayal of past humiliation for China, notably in the nineteenth century, helps justify a resistance to liberalism; and the latter is seen not as offering universal values but as being a cover for particular interests, essentially Western interests. This approach entails a dethroning of a notion of liberal universalism by treating it as a culturally specific ideological preference with democracy simply one model of government. Moreover, this democratic model becomes apparently steadily less valid as a result of the process of history, which, in turn, can therefore demonstrate the greater success of the Chinese model. This situation has obvious implications for the "space" allowed for free debate, both in China and in other states that, at least in some aspects, subscribe to its model and are allied to it. The latter states do not have to provide an identical history, and, indeed, do not have a history of comparable longevity that can be readily recovered. Nevertheless, there is scarcely going to be an encouragement of criticism of China, a situation that extends to its past. Tiananmen Square is a term blocked on Sina Weibo, China's version of Twitter, as part of the "Great Firewall of China." Furthermore, the identification of liberalism with a universalism held to advance Western interests does not encourage debate or free enquiry in states that reject these interests.

Given the extent to which many (but by no means all) Western as well as non-Western academics criticize, if not condemn, aspects of the United States, notably its policy past and present,[17] and are also critical of Western culture and liberal universalism, it is worth appreciating the extent to which the academic "project," understood as free enquiry, rests on this culture and universalism. It is also necessary, in contrast, to note the degree to which the model of intellectual activity that has been dominant across most of history accords more closely to the Chinese one than to its modern Western rival. The pattern of religious activity for most of history was of authoritarian cults punishing heterodoxy and linked to government; a pattern in which the presentation of history was supposed to serve clear ideological interests. Many of the intellectuals in these societies were part of the religious establishment or linked to it. An alternative statist form of history developed from the nineteenth century as bureaucratic governments used an ideology of nationalism to provide coherence to states and content to new education systems. This was not an approach that encouraged debate.

The combination of authoritarianism and commercial nationalism now on display in China will probably be seen across much of the world in the future, not least if economic travails and environmental problems encourage other states to adopt all or part of these remedies. The result is likely to be an academic world that is brought into line with other aspects of government. Bodies such as the Chinese Ministry of State Security or the research institutions of the Chinese Peoples Liberation Army will have considerable influence on the future presentation of history. An element of control already underlies the Chinese establishment of an information infrastructure, notably with Chinese Central Television, the Xinhua news agency, and the Confucius Institutes.[18] The line taken by those Confucius Institutes located in British universities was criticized in 2014. China and Russia played a key role in the 2000s and 2010s in seeking to establish a new UN order to regulate the internet so as to lessen the ability to disseminate material judged unwelcome by governments. The growth in China in the number of new museums, with about 350 opened in 2011 and over 450 in 2012 alone, offers an increased coverage of the past, but mostly in the shape of artefacts. There is little to challenge the role of the Party.[19]

REWRITING EUROPE

While China and India will become more important as centers of historical work, they will not be the only states involved in this relative decline of the position of the West. The resurgence of nationalist history in Russia can also be seen in this light. This resurgence extends to defences of aspects of the Stalinist period, including the Nazi-Soviet Pact of 1939, which was condemned by the Soviet Parliament during the *Glasnost* era. The pact is now presented as an equivalent to, and consequence of, the Munich Agreement of 1938, which is a way to spread the blame to Western powers. Territorial aggrandizement and control in the name of national security remains a Russian goal, as has been shown in the Caucasus and Crimea, and historical arguments are deployed to support such action.

As discussed in chapter 6, the probable decline of the Western position in history will extend to include Third World countries as a result

of the receding role of colonial accounts of history. Political changes
will also affect the history of Europe itself. Despite its focus on practical guidance for policy, the role of the European Union as a paymaster
of historical research is significant, and contributes to an emphasis on
transnationalism – or what is also termed "histoire croisée."[20] For example, the European Science Foundation has devoted much effort to
a collective program on "Origins of the Modern State in Europe 1300–
1800."[21] There will also be a working through of the consequences of the
fall of the Iron Curtain. The combination of Communist ideology, the
wartime and subsequent destruction and disruption of records, and the
lower prosperity of Eastern Europe, affected the nature and extent of research. Moreover, in the Communist years, there was also a shutting
out of most Western scholarship, whereas in Western Europe detailed
archival research by foreign, including American, scholars made a major
contribution, not least to encouraging debate within national scholarly
traditions. These circumstances have not changed totally, and the potential impact of foreign scholarship will be constrained by language problems, while declining American interest in European history will also be
a factor. Nevertheless, an increase in knowledge about Eastern Europe
can be anticipated, and this will bring with it a breakdown in simple
theories that treat this area as a largely undifferentiated whole. In addition, general theories of European development will need to respond to
this knowledge. This situation will further challenge the habit of treating France as a paradigm, a treatment which has had an unfortunate
consequence for our understanding of early modern Europe. Instead, a
greater consideration of Eastern Europe, not least its diversity, alongside
recent work on German and Italian history, will underline the variety
of the early modern period. This may also affect perspectives on English/
British exceptionalism; an exceptionalism, moreover, that tends to echo
the French paradigm as a benchmark for comparison without adequate
consideration of the situation elsewhere.

SOURCES AND TOPICS

As far as historical method in the future is concerned, it is likely that
the primacy of literary-based evidence and analysis will be increasingly

matched by the consequences of the greater prominence and range of visual sources, although they can be very hard to work with. Access can be a major problem, while there is also the need for specific vocabularies, perspectives, and methodologies to cope with visual sources and convert them into instruments for the understanding of things other than just themselves. As an instance of the pace of change, it is worth reminding ourselves that the photograph and its later incarnations are only about 170 years old. Visual sources will probably play a greater role in the future in mixed-media forms of exposition. As a result of this rise in the visual element, the overlap between educational material and public history may well grow. There will also be a challenge to the intellectual discussion of history and, in particular, philosophical speculation about historical truth, because an emphasis on visual material and, crucially, perception will raise questions about established explanations of proof and accuracy.

Alongside such abstract points, will come the more concrete need to address the implications of change for public history and for existing or new "history wars." As mentioned earlier, alterations in the respective weighting of states will be of significance. There will also be major developments in the themes covered. In particular, there is the challenge of addressing environmental changes, a developing sub-discipline of note. Moreover, the likely impact of the rise of religious consciousness and issues may well make the relationship between secularism and religion a topic of particular note for research and teaching. There will probably need to be both a development of historiographical models to give greater weight to these issues, as well as changes in their specific historiographical methodologies. Church history has usually been written by the churches in order to justify their current agendas, whether political, economic, doctrinal, or liturgical.[22] Academic engagement offers a different approach. Moreover, social structure and dynamics may rise anew to prominence as an historical topic thanks to the worldwide tensions in society. However, it is unclear whether class, or even Marxism, as a form of analysis rather than a prospectus,[23] will be revived as a key conceptual device. Causality may operate both ways, as the history of society may in turn affect current and future accounts of society, while they, in turn, encourage a focus on the history of society.

TECHNOLOGY AND SCIENCE

There are also more "blue-skies" challenges worth mentioning. Genetic engineering may well lead to developments in cloning that raise fundamental questions about motivation and agency. The same may come from advances in robotics including the creation of cyborgs merging aspects of humanity and robotics, as well as advances in artificial intelligence, and in computer technology and application. Aside from the degree that such changes transform the "we" who are the stuff and source of historical work, the prospect of historical methods that make sense of initiatives by such bodies, let alone their experiences, is arresting.

Even more so is the prospect that the next millennium may see contact with other life forms in the solar system, not least if more planets are discovered. If it occurs, such contact will pose problems for a range of intellectual specialisms, notably philosophy and theology. History will not be immune, not least as it will be appropriate to devise a historiography that makes sense of human life alongside that of other life-forms. There will need to be an understanding of differing meanings of time and its impact. Geology, a historical science with a distinctive approach to the collection and evaluation of evidence,[24] already poses this challenge. Attempts in the early nineteenth century to reconcile geology and theology, attempts linked to the Christian account of the creation and the age of the world, failed. More recently, there has been scant attempt to integrate geology with history in conceptual terms. In contrast, the rise of climate change as a major issue and of environmental history as a sub-discipline, have helped to make it more important to try to reconcile human with non-human terrestrial history. At the same time, there is a danger that such an attempt leads to a geographical determinism linked to socio-biological explanations. Such an attempt, seen for example in the work of Jared Diamond,[25] has the appeal of clarity. However, it is mistaken to imagine that theories devised for the natural sciences can be readily transferred to their human counterparts.

A different direction of challenge to conventional historiography will come from a greater understanding of the human brain and of patterns of thought, motivation, and action. This understanding may provide another iteration of the impact of psychoanalysis on many historians working in the twentieth century. Scientific research on these topics will probably lead to renewed questions about how best to discuss the relationship between structure and agency, and will invite a rethinking of the nature of perception and of the character of individual and collective memory, issues which have attracted much attention over the last few decades.[26] With greater appreciation of psychological processes in the brain, the unconscious determinants of action might become better understood, notably the unconscious processes that precede conscious processes. It is unclear what affect these developments will have on notions of free will. Knowledge of brain regions has led to an appreciation of differences between episodic memory, for single events that have been experienced, and semantic memory, about the world as a whole. Research on mirror neurons has led to an appreciation of the extent to which action and perception are interwoven, with experience affecting action directly, rather than separate. There will also be better understanding of collective memories. Human beings are biologically equipped for these memories.[27]

At the same time, the understanding of the brain will not necessarily undermine a vital distinction between historical actors and historians. Historical actors were, and are, able to perceive their past and present, and to try to predict their future and to seek to influence it. In contrast, with the benefit of hindsight, historians can have a totally different knowledge of what was to come. Contrasting views on counterfactualism (what if?) arise in part from this distinction. As another instance of the interpretative role of posterity, historians will probably continue to play a major part in deciding how best to categorize periods of time. As a result, historians will encourage particular ways to understand change. Future categorization may well alter, not least as the challenge of global history leads to the reshaping of particular accounts. For example, it is possible that historians would benefit from shifting away from chronological periodization, which is currently the dominant mode, and, instead, put greater weight on considering stadial periodization, an approach with a long pedigree. Such a reorientation eases the process of considering and accounting for the persistence of particular characteristics.[28] However, stadial history risks suggesting that some societies are more advanced than others, an approach that is regarded as unacceptable.

CONCLUSIONS

Thanks to the topics mentioned in this chapter and others, historiography will be affected anew by developments in other subjects and by the pace of political, social, and cultural change. Whether discussion of the subject rises to the challenge, and recruits a public audience accordingly, is unclear. The idea that historical research and teaching is dependent on politics and events is one that will not surprise historians considering historiography. A somber instance of developments affecting the perception of the past is provided by the impact of some recent episodes, notably Rwanda in 1994, on the historiography of genocide.[29] Some academics, however, prefer to underplay, if not sometimes ignore, the dependence of historical work on politics because it challenges the ideas of professional autonomy and intellectual independence, as well as the desire for freedom of enquiry that leads to an assumption that such freedom should, and will, obviously pertain. Suggesting that this sense of entitlement may be of scant relevance for the governments of many states, and that authoritarianism may become more prominent on the world scale, raises issues of scholarly engagement. These can be seen with discussion both of the importance of Western liberal values, and of the dangers of authoritarianism. Freedom of enquiry in practice has a wider cultural value than one limited to the West. To write, therefore, of the decline of the West in terms of the "end of history," or at least of this liberal interpretation, would be overly alarmist. First, there would be states that do not develop in this direction. Secondly, authoritarian systems are less monolithic and ideologically coherent than they might seem or pretend. Thirdly, historical processes will continue, and be recorded and discussed, however much the recording and discussion are slanted and biased.

Yet, at a deep level, the decline of the West might challenge history understood as an aspiration freely to provide independent accounts of the past. That does not have the ring of the "end of history," but the prospect is alarming. Outlining such a prospect should remind us of human agency, of the role of each generation in affecting not only the present, but also in influencing the future and presenting the past. Those telling the past, both academics and others, have a particular responsibility in this sphere as they can also help shape perceptions of the present and for the future. To abdicate this responsibility by preferring to focus on points of scholarship while underrating the wider context for intellectual life is a potent neglect of a public responsibility to maintain liberal values of free inquiry and free debate. As such, a liberal interpretation of history is a good tradition that should be preserved.[30] These values are central to democratic culture and practice.

THIRTEEN

A Personal Note

IT IS NORMAL FOR ACADEMIC HISTORIANS TO SINK THEMSELVES
into their subject and to avoid personal comments, at least in print. There
are writers who prefer to offer such comments, but they are not the majority. Even in autobiographies, historians omit much and tend to repeat and represent the profession's norms and collectivity.[1] Moreover,
by maintaining an impersonal style in their scholarship, authors are assumed to demonstrate impartiality, and also to gain added credence for
their arguments. Possibly historiography requires this treatment even
more than most subjects as it represents an attempt to move beyond
the perspective of the individual in order to chart the development of a
subject and to offer judgments on others. Yet, there is also much to be
said for providing the personal account, not because it has any special
authority, or even interest, but thanks to the particular insight the individual can provide. It is also slightly strange for an historian to write
about historiography advancing general reflections, but failing to offer
an explicit engagement with the issues and closeness arising from his or
her own experience.

SCHOOL AND LIBRARIES

To divide such reflections between research and teaching is artificial
as they are closely related. Nevertheless, this division captures a functional distinction that is important to historiographical discussion. The
research I was first aware of was that of others, and that is a strand that
has to be addressed whenever an author writes of his or her engagement

with research. The conventional pattern of a high school education in history in the 1960s and early 1970s was extended by the availability of two good libraries: Edgware Public Library, in the part of London in which I grew up, and the high school library. Thus, a key element of historiography for me was the filtering provided by the acquisition policies of these bodies, an element that could be readily grasped by looking at what was on the shelves. However, access to a wider world of print was provided by inexpensive interlibrary loans through the broader public library system. These loans did not offer the scale or immediacy of the internet, but did ensure that libraries were part of broader networks of access and availability.

An element in this filtering was clearly provided by perceptions of readability, which helps explain why the titles were in English, while cost was also an issue. Yet, as part of a broader cultural policy, there was also the sense of providing a general education. This was notably the case for the public library, but was also significant for the school library, although course requirements were important for the latter. In the public library, most of the books were narratives and many were biographies, there was a heavy focus on British history, and on the twentieth century, and wars were a frequent theme. At the same time as the focus on narrative, the coverage of history was much wider in the public library than in its school counterpart. There were recent authoritative scholarly works, such as those volumes of *The New Cambridge Modern History* already published. This situation helps explain the problems in Britain created by the recent, accelerating crisis in public libraries. This is a crisis arising from changing public interests, the rise of visual and electronic material, and, in particular from 2011, grave difficulties in local governmental finances. Traditionally, the public library offered, through its selection of books, the opportunity of an informed general narrative to anyone who walked through its doors. There is no effective comparable filter of quality in what is provided for those who access material on line.

The teaching provided at high school did not offer a Plato to NATO narrative on the American pattern; but, instead, provided periods of narrative as well as history that was different in type and tone. Beginning with the Egyptians, and running on chronologically in a "Western civilization" pattern, was my fate three times from the age of seven, but narrative was abruptly dismissed at the ages of 13–16. Instead, there was somewhat of a hotchpotch, but one, nevertheless, that was extremely stimulating. I can recall the study of political thought, including having to write an essay discussing Rousseau's statement in the opening chapter of *The Social Contract* (1762) that "Man is Born Free and Everywhere is in Chains," a term re-enacting, as a game, and with different outcomes, the Congress of Vienna of 1815,[2] followed by a less successful reenactment of the Paris Peace Conference of 1919, a detailed study of the New Deal, and thorough study of twentieth-century British politics as well as of interwar Germany. The net effect was to give a clear and comprehensive narrative of the last century, but certainly not of British or world history in the longer term. In terms of identity politics, which did not seem to have been an issue at the time, this approach can rank as a failure or, possibly, as an attempt to ground identity in terms of modern British politics, with this a world of twentieth-century Conservatives and Labour; rather than eighteenth-century Tories and Whigs, let alone seventeenth-century Cavaliers and Roundheads. In so far as the developments of the twentieth century had a longer-term grounding, this approach was unsuccessful as it did not provide explanations in such terms. Most of the pupils would have stopped high school history at this point, leaving them with a far-from-complete account of national or international history.

The A-level (now in Britain AS and A level) years, the last two years at high school, involved three courses, two of them outline, and one a source-based special subject. In my case, I did an option on early modern British history, another on early modern European history, which was understood as excluding Britain, and a special subject on the reign of Henry VIII (1509–1547). Later chronological options and special subjects were also available, but nothing covering earlier periods. Again, this choice can be seen in positive terms, as providing a good account of a significant period, that of the Reformation and the growth of parliamentary government, combined with an opportunity to study a particular subject including the use of printed primary sources. Less positively, large gaps in historical coverage were readily apparent. For me, bar a valuable study day on mid-nineteenth century Britain, both the eighteenth and nineteenth centuries were unknown lands at high school.

At high school, however, there was a degree of openness to conceptual and methodological innovation. For example, I read Braudel's *The Mediterranean and the Mediterranean World in the Age of Philip II,* although, characteristically, the English translation and not the (earlier) French original was offered in the school library. Braudel's work provided an insight into research as a process of critical intelligence. It also accorded with my own interest in geography, which has remained a lasting concern, seen most obviously in my work on maps and geopolitics. As a reminder, however, that scholars, like other readers, are not guided in some determined way by the works they read, I was greatly excited by Braudel's feel for place, a feel that at times was quasi (and maybe self)-hypnotic; but rejected what I saw as the quasi-determinisms of much of his conceptualization, argument, and phrases. Despite the emphasis on the totality and unitary nature of Braudel's vision,[3] the structural, more geographical, dimension of his great work, with its stress on long-term factors, does not readily cohere with the chronological political section dealing with the late sixteenth century, the *Age of Philip II.* This problem of the relationship between structure and agency is a fundamental one for scholarship. Moreover, structural factors are not of course "little touched" by time (or events) as Braudel suggested. The difficulties inherent in Braudel's model, notably of linking the general to the particular, may help explain why those writing in his shadow have not always been successful. Yet, as a sign of a significant historiographical trend, whereas Braudel was much stronger on the Christian Mediterranean than on its Muslim rival, there has been a finer balance in scholarship since. In addition, the presentation for Egypt of a factionalism that emerged in response to deep-rooted social and demographic currents, such that political culture is regarded as running deeper than Braudel's *histoire événementielle,* offers a fruitful advance on Braudel.[4]

UNIVERSITY

At university, Cambridge (1975–1978), it was again exposure to the research of others that was important. The most significant influences were reading doctoral theses in the university library in my third year, for the three courses I covered that year; and, secondly, being taught the "Norman Conquest" Further Subject by Marjorie Chibnall, a great historian of medieval England. She let me use for that course the proofs of the volumes of Orderic Vitalis's *Historia Ecclesiastica* she was then editing. This understanding of research and writing as a protean, multi-stage, activity was particularly valuable in contributing to a view of history as an interim report on the past; a necessarily interim report, but, nevertheless, one that was of considerable value. Compared, moreover, to the excitement, as an undergraduate, of reading doctoral theses in the university library, such as the excellent ones on Spanish history produced under the supervision of J. H. Elliott, there seemed something stale about formal works on historiography. At school the prime player was E. H. Carr's *What is History?*, and at university Geoffrey Elton's *Practice of History*. I notice that these and similar modern works appear uninteresting to most current undergraduates. Written by British scholars, they engaged with European developments, but were weak on the wider global scale.

Coverage of history at Cambridge was patchy, in many respects being reminiscent of school. There were outline papers, but they did not add up to an outline in world history. I took five. In the first year, three: medieval Europe medieval British, political and constitutional, and early modern British, social and economic; in the second year, one: early modern British, political and constitutional; and one, early modern European, in the third. The other papers were Political Thought down to 1650, in the second year; and, in the third year, the Norman Conquest, and a special subject on British Foreign Policy, 1783–1793. General papers on broad questions in historical development and method, including historiography, were taken in parts one and two (in the second and third years); but the teaching for them was perfunctory in the extreme. For purposes of examination, these papers each involved one three-hour essay.

The Cambridge history course had positive points for me, with much of the teaching very good, and I benefited in particular from my exposure to medieval history, which was new to me.[5] However, the course was also somewhat bitty as, indeed, remains the case there. History after 1793 was a blank for me, as was that of the non-Western world. Both areas were on offer, but to have done either would have meant missing out large chunks of earlier history. In essence, this experience demonstrated the problem of seeking to cover such a large subject. Even the individual outline papers involved much selection, with big gaps between. Thus, the medieval British political and constitutional course meant moving at speed from constitutional crisis to constitutional crisis in England, for example the reign of John, to Simon de Montfort under Henry III, to the reign of Edward II, to that of Richard II. This approach provided opportunities for the precise analysis of documents such as Magna Carta (1215), the ordinances designed to limit the power of Edward II (1311), and the Provisions of Oxford (1258), and insights on ideas of good kingship and on the rise of Parliament. However, in its repeated focus on crisis, this course essentially omitted consideration of success. In Political Thought, I jumped from Plato, Aristotle, Cicero, and Augustine, to Marsilius of Padua and Dante, which again left a significant gap, as well, of course, of no reference to China or anywhere non-Western. Given the resources available to Cambridge, it was surprising that at least some of the lecturers were not instructed to provide a broad-brush coverage of world history, but none was available. On the other hand, given the "culture" of the subject, there should have been no surprise.

ACADEMIC ENGAGEMENT

The selection of research topic is generally critical in the trajectory of an academic's career, both in terms of deciding the field in which he or she will specialize, and in affecting the chance of being hired; chance, rather than prospect, being the key word. In my case, as in many others, an interest fired in undergraduate years led to a research focus. The special subject I took in 1977–1978, on British Foreign Policy, 1783–1793, proved particularly stimulating because I was interested in how far policy was affected by domestic politics in the form of creating what was to be called a strategic culture. I decided to work for a doctorate on the background to the collapse, in 1787 as a result of the Dutch Crisis, of the attempt to ease Anglo-French relations, only to be told in 1978 that I could not pursue the subject, as a doctoral student at London was already working on British foreign policy in those years. Ironically, he never completed. Having to find a new topic for graduate work in Oxford, I turned back to a previous period of collapse, namely from 1730, when an Anglo-French alliance was strong, to 1740 when the two powers were close to war. In practice, the introductory chapter of my thesis, on 1727–1731, took over, and those became the dates of the thesis. Chance again played a career role, as working on the pre-1750 period made it possible to apply for the early modern European post that came up at the University of Durham in 1980. In turn, that lectureship gave me the opportunity to develop both teaching and research.

There were implications for my engagement with historiography. Moving to postgraduate work had entailed, in the circumstances of doctoral study at the time, a narrowing of focus compared to undergraduate work, and a concern with sources and method, rather than general works on the nature of history. Moreover, moving to the research frontier ensured that the relevance of previous work became more conditional. The "under-theorized" nature of work on the history of eighteenth-century foreign policy was also significant.

Over a career, the broadening out of research interests to cover new fields has required an engagement with other historiographies. The value of the latter for orientation is readily apparent, not least because historiography both underlines general intellectual trends and provides insights on particular areas of study. Teaching over a range should also require an engagement with other historiographies. For individual scholars, engagement with theory varies, but there is a common need to engage with existing research work, particularly as academic history is an accretional subject, with scholarship involved in a debate both with original sources and with existing work. This is a key aspect of historiography. As a separate issue, the extent of the explicit interaction with current political concerns varies considerably.[6]

Like most scholars, alongside the development of other interests, I have remained focused on my original subject of research, in my case eighteenth-century British foreign policy. I am still going to the archives to read eighteenth-century diplomatic correspondence thirty-six years since I started to do so and, in 2010, to my surprise, discovered a new series of relevant documents that I had not hitherto worked on.

It is interesting to look back and consider what can be made of the changes in emphasis in my own published work. My first single-author

book, which was devoted to British foreign policy in the age of Sir Robert
Walpole, Britain's leading minister from 1720 to 1742, appeared in 1985.
The context then is different to that of my more recent works on the period, not because of developments in the subject of history as a whole,
but rather due to changes in the work of the other historians in the field.
Thus, in the 1980s, the dominant figure was Ragnhild Hatton, and her
approach, that of studying foreign policy in terms of diplomacy and the
international system, rather than of domestic circumstances, was also
adopted by her pupils, such as Hamish Scott. The contrasting approach,
which was one I found more pertinent, was adopted by Graham Gibbs,
following the lead of his supervisor Mark Thomson, but it had less of an
impact. I was conscious that my work on the 1980s and 1990s in this field
was written against the Hatton approach, which work in the archives
increasingly led me to conclude was inaccurate as an explanation of British policy, as well as being methodologically and conceptually flawed.
By the 2000s, however, the field was different. After the 1990s, when
there were very few working in the field, then, in the 2000s, there was
a series of major publications by younger scholars, notably Tony Clay-
don, Nicholas Harding, Brendan Simms, and Andrew Thompson. Their
work was more diverse than the Hatton school and more alive to the role
of domestic political circumstances.[7] Thus, as far as the historiography
of the subject and my own work were concerned, the key element was
the work of other scholars, rather than theoretical studies in the field
of international relations.

Yet, there is an important overlap with the general situation in historiography, as much recent work on the eighteenth century focuses on
the idea of a climate of opinion. This approach, however, poses major
problems, notably the selection and analysis of texts in accordance with
what is in effect a pre-determined thesis, and also the very notion of a
zeitgeist (spirit of the age). Historians may stress the power of particular
sets of ideas, but, to go beyond this, to suggest that one vision became
a dominant discourse, runs considerable risks. It may become self-vali-
dating; it has severe limitations in describing what is, generally in fact,
a diverse situation; and it may neglect the extent to which supposedly
hegemonic worldviews were actually divisive and polemical. Indeed,
the contested nature of the concept of national interest today makes it

easier to understand contemporary opposition criticism of the methods and objectives of British foreign policy in 1714–1757. Moreover, the role of contingency in these objectives contributed to this contested nature as well as reshaping the public debate.

More generally, in the view of this empiricist, an awareness of particular interests and specific conjunctures should take precedence over the fascination with discourse. Indeed, the reality in eighteenth-century politics was more complex and fractured than those who search for a *zeitgeist* might suggest. This of course is a fundamental challenge to the standard approach in much scholarship, with its tendency to employ discourse as a "hegemonic" concept and to argue by assertion, producing what the American historian Richard Hamilton has aptly termed "Truth by Declaration."[8] For example, to ascribe policy to a climate of opinion is not terribly helpful unless the subjective nature of the definition is accepted and the problematic character of moving from "climate" to policy is allowed for.

For all scholars, however, issues are posed by limited space, not least the difficulty of explaining the context, process, and contingencies of each choice of policy, and then of analyzing it in accordance with the chronological specificities of the debate at any particular juncture. Arguments take on meaning in that context. However, this approach poses problems of analysis, exposition, and space. As a result, factors of convenience encourage a frequently misleading tendency to emphasize the continuity of arguments.

As far as other fields are concerned, I drew on studies I wrote in the 1980s and 1990s on the causes of war, on conceptual work in international relations, notably by Jack Levy, Bill Thompson, and John Vasquez.[9] For historical cartography, in contrast, this process was more one of a reaction, as I found the theoretical accounts, in particular those of Brian Harley and Denis Cosgrove, overly instrumental, and I continue to do so.[10] In contrast, my works on the Grand Tour, the British press, eighteenth-century English culture, and the history of diplomacy[11] can all be seen as "under-theorized." However, there is a deliberate attempt in these books to focus on the "nuts and bolts" of what happened. At the same time, I have tried to advance and apply theoretical perspectives in military history.[12]

Authors of course may not be as aware of the context of their work and its impact as they think, and they certainly lack a full knowledge. Yet, the perspective of the individual acts as a valuable qualification to the tendency to emphasize general influences. Moreover, if the last are to be stressed, it is unclear why financial or institutional issues, such as the pressures to conform to particular models of academic behavior and the role of related patronage structures and disciplinary practices, should be accorded less attention than the more conceptual matters generally discussed in terms of historiography. Giving due weight to these issues is an important challenge to much historiographical literature.

In some respects, teaching takes the process of approaching new subjects further than research, as it entails trying to understand work across a wide range of sub-specialisms in order to provide students with an informed account of the interplay between established conceptual issues and cutting-edge scholarship. In teaching, as in research, I have found that the historiographical discussions that are most useful for conveying knowledge are those integral to scholarly work, rather than stand-alone texts on historiography. This point echoes the discussions, in the early years in the 1900s, of what became the International Congresses of Historical Sciences.[13] Indeed, the coverage of historiography, whether understood in terms of conceptualization, methodology, or previous work, is often better informed in specific historical works, rather than in stand-alone texts on historiography. Thus, to grasp the impact of China's Cultural Revolution on historiography, it is more useful to read an account of the Cultural Revolution, as that locates and explains the issue, whereas references to twentieth-century China in general works on historiography are not only scant but tend to lack explanatory context.

CONCLUSIONS

Reading scholarship in the round rather than any individual branch of the subject, let alone particular works, makes clear what is readily apparent from the outset: that there is no one way to present the past. Instead, there are key differences in context and approach, conceptualization and methodology. The tone and sounds vary, ranging, for example, in the coverage of North America in the nineteenth century, from the funeral laments for its indigenous cultures to the brash triumphant clarion calls of a supposed destiny for the American republic as it came to span the continent. History as the accounts (not simply account) of the past is more than the silent spectator to individual tales, for part of its value is to make overt what are often implicit choices of approach and analysis. Indeed, in making the implicit overt, it is important to turn to the writers and readers who clothe them with meaning.

The readers are the key, for it is they/you/we who decide what to take from books, the same being the case for museum displays, television programs, films, and other forms of presentation. However, by the nature of any individual book, the readers are unknown at the moment of creation. Their nationality, prior knowledge, relevant assumptions, and values are unclear, as is the impact of all these on their assessment of both subject and authorial treatment. Historiography could profitably devote more attention to these issues than it currently does. The writer possibly is less important than the reader in terms of impact, but is clearer in focus. Frequently, helpful reviewers clarify this focus by drawing attention to the assumptions that can be seen in the work. In the Anglophone tradition, authors themselves downplay such assumptions because of the intellectual, pedagogic, and cultural preference in academic life for concealing the work of the author and, in particular, for apparently letting the material dictate the treatment.

This practice is unfortunate, for conceptual and methodological issues therefore tend to be downplayed. They need to be emphasized. For example, I have written several works on global military history. These oblige both myself and my readers to confront some key conceptual and methodological points, points that can be considered in a historiographical context. Expanding the scale geographically greatly adds to analytical and comparative dimensions, but underlines the problems of balance and significance that face all historians, while enhancing the issues posed by simultaneity. Is there any significance that events in different parts of the world occurred in the same year, a question given force by books devoted to such years, for example 1000, 1492, and 1688?[14] Clearly such simultaneity is significant once we have interacting large-scale global financial and economic models, as at present, while the role of climate, notably for agricultural production and demographic trends, also makes such simultaneity significant. Yet, is the same true of military events and/or developments in different parts of the world in the early-modern period? In the jargon, are events being forced together, in a misleadingly unified whole, in the service of a meta-narrative?[15]

As this example illustrates, explanatory context is a key element in assessing historical issues, but also in explicitly discussing how this assessment reflects present assumptions, for historiography, as both subject and method, does not stand outside historical scholarship or indeed the process of time passing. Instead, while affected by both of these, historiography is a topic for historical enquiry. Far from being a branch of applied philosophy, historiography is a subject and method that takes on value through its engagement with specific issues of the past understood in terms of the shifting prism of the present. The last helps give value and values not only to the perspectives of individual writers and teachers, but also to those of individual readers and students.

Stalked by the past

PETER HAIN, former secretary of state for Northern Ireland, about
the impact of the past and the need to let go of it, 7 April 2014[1]

FOURTEEN

Conclusions

NECESSARY OR A BURDEN; GOOD, BAD, OR INDIFFERENT; THE weight of history can be seen very differently. It is, of course, in part each, and every one, of these descriptions. The awareness of historically grounded wrongs, of empowerment through grievance, of atavistic hatreds, and identities through opposition, that are all mentioned in this book, could readily be extended in terms of examples and, indeed, categories. This awareness encourages a feeling that history is a weight that should be shed, as well as a means of identity. The two, weight and means of identity, combine to emphasize difference, different views and responses. The very terms used illustrate this. Thus, the term "The American War," which is employed in Vietnam, readily deploys blame for a destructive struggle that in reality owed at least as much to the North Vietnamese determination from 1959 to overthrow any non-Communist government in South Vietnam.[2] Emphasizing this role by North Vietnam, however, is totally unacceptable to Vietnam, a state created by this very overthrow in 1975, and one still ruled by the Communist victors.

For many years, the sense of history as a weight, if not a curse, was a response that the British readily voiced in reaction to the murderous sectarian divides of Northern Ireland. The "could they not get over this" was a powerful sentiment, and one that was far from new. During the crises of the French Revolutionary and Napoleonic Wars, for example, British commentators had expressed the same view about Protestant-Catholic divides in Ireland as they had sought to use Irish resources in the war against France waged for most of 1792–1815. A similar response about accepting the past has been seen in reaction to the existential challenge posed by the demands of al-Qaeda for the withdrawal of non-Muslims from formerly Muslim lands, especially al-Andalus, southern Spain. Again, the choice of name is significant. That these lands had only ever been Muslim as a result of conquest in the eighth century was ignored by al-Qaeda. More seriously, there was no sense that distant time was anything other than an immediate issue. Whereas some episodes, such as the Holocaust or the very different Palestinian movement (forced and voluntary) from Israel in 1948–1949, were within living memory, this was certainly not true of the final extinction of al-Andalus with the conquest of the kingdom of Granada in the late fifteenth century.

Conversely, such a distinction between distant and recent episodes can be regarded as presentism. If movements such as Islam, or for that matter Christianity and Judaism, or the groups within all three, are to be regarded as long-term entities, which is how they present themselves, then it is easy to understand how an organic appreciation ensures that past events become present grievances and wrongs to be righted in the future. This was seen in Britain in 2007 with the leaders of the Church of England treating that body's attitude prior to 1807 to the slave trade as a matter for present contrition. The ideas that nobody alive was responsible, and, indeed, that another age had a very different set of values, were put to one side in the face of an assertion of corporate responsibility that could be regarded as seriously ahistorical.

The bicentenary of the abolition of the slave trade brought up also the contrast between a historicized sense of grievance, which it was easy to express, and the more complex reality of problems in the modern world. At the same time that Britain was being denounced for the historical slave trade, a denunciation in which there was scant reference to the key role of African cooperation in the trade, African regimes were doing little to criticize the dictatorial and destructive regime of Robert Mugabe in Zimbabwe who ran the country from 1980. That he was also deliberately propagating what will be a partial, if not false, history made this contrast doubly ironic. Mugabe's claim that the economic travails of Zimbabwe were due to British pressure gave no weight to the mistakes of his own government's policy, but it was a claim that was apparently accepted by many other African states. The shared history of violent opposition to white ruling systems proved more significant, notably for

South Africa. The contrasts between the extensive memorialization of the iniquities of the slave trade in Britain and the far more hesitant engagement with the devastation wrought by Mugabe were instructive. The needs in history in the public sphere for good and bad played a role in the preference for criticizing the slave trade, and in the means of doing so. Furthermore, the idea of devoting time to the complexities of issues such as the destructive impact today of First World tariffs on African producers, for example cotton farmers in Burkina Faso and Mali, was clearly not an attractive one.

Empowerment through historic grievance is a source not only of division but also of a reluctance to search for the compromises necessary if life is to continue. On the other hand, much of history does deal with conflict, and with identification through difference. To ignore this is foolish. Moreover, there is a sense that a consideration of the past can provide lessons or even what is referred to as closure. The two can be linked. A British political pamphlet of 1757 commenting on a recent passage of popular agitation, claimed: "History shows ages are necessary to obliterate national prejudices, when the populace of a nation have once been raised to acts of resentment, by their ministers, or governors, be it either for their safety, or to screen themselves; . . . by this means the people are made a party in the cause, and each individual thus imposed on, thinks himself interested, that it should not be proved, he was or could be imposed on."[3]

Whether either lessons or closure can be gained from the past is uncertain. It is also unclear what either lessons or closure means and, more particularly, means on the global scale. In practice, each idea is heavily value-laden, not least in the processes that thereby are advocated and followed. The notion of closure is particularly problematic, as the attempt to reconcile grievances can, in practice, both strengthen existing grievances and create a cause of new ones. Moreover, the idea of closure, as of lessons, assumes a fixing of the past in, and for, the present that, in reality, is an illusion: the present both encompasses a number of views and is constantly changing.

However, there is a widespread determination to search not for complex lessons, but for those that apparently offer obvious guidance. In short, the public treatment of history can take on a quasi-religious character, with episodes providing homilies about what will happen if wrong choices are made. The regeneration that is pursued rests on a presentation, of past, present, and future, in which rights and wrongs are clearly etched. The emphasis, thus, is on sin, rather than redemption; and with the latter dependent on acknowledging sin and accepting the values and methods of those who make that judgment.

Contrasting notions about learning from the past in an incremental fashion, those offered here, assume not a millenarian perfectibility of mankind nor an ending of history, but, rather, a notion of improvability. President Michael D. Higgins of Ireland, visiting Britain in 2014 on the first state visit by an Irish President, argued that "affecting a kind of amnesia is of no value" and that, instead, it was necessary to "show humility about the past" and say sorry.[4] The wrongs of the past are not forgotten, but their reiteration as admonition can only take us so far. The notion of improvability is a more helpful way of considering lessons from the past than that of perfectibility. However, like the more strident approach, improvability poses a danger, that the past may be jettisoned if it does not contribute to, or correspond with, the lesson sought. The most accurate history, one that notes the ambiguities of the past, the diversities of motives, and the complexities of causation is not one that corresponds with political and religious strategies, or with public needs for clarity, heroes, and villains. Such a history is one that tells us most about the past and about ourselves. It is one that repays examination.

Notes

Preface

1. Bob Sloan, e-mail message to Jeremy Black, April 28, 2014.

1. Academic, State, and Public Histories

1. L. Xiaoming, "China and Britain won the war together," *Daily Telegraph*, 1 Jan. 2014.

2. P. Furtado, ed., *Histories of Nations* (London, 2012).

3. N. Chen, "Putin is outflanking the West at every turn," *Observer*, 22 Dec. 2013, p. 35.

4. P. J. Corfield, *Time and the Shape of History* (New Haven, Connecticut, 2007).

5. D. J. Wilcox, *The Measure of Times Past: Pre-Newtonian Chronologies and the Rhetoric of Relative Time* (Chicago, Illinois, 1987).

6. A. Adaboe, "Babylonian Mathematics, Astrology, and Astronomy," in *The Cambridge Ancient History*, ed. J. Boardman et al, 2nd ed., vol. 3, part 2 (Cambridge, 1991), p. 281.

7. E. Robson, "Table and Tabular Formatting in Sumer, Babylonia and Assyria, 2500 BCE–50 CE," in *The History of Mathematical Tables: From Sumer to Spreadsheets*, ed. M. Croarken, R. Flood, and E. Robson (Oxford, 2003), pp. 19–48.

8. D. Feeney, *Caesar's Calendar: Ancient Time and the Beginnings of History* (Berkeley, California, 2007); A. Lianeri, *The Western Time of Ancient History* (Cambridge, 2011).

9. R. Koopmans, *Wonderful to Relate: Miracle Stories and Miracle Collecting in High Medieval England* (Philadelphia, Pennsylvania, 2011).

10. J. Hughes, *Arthurian Myths and Alchemy: The Kingship of Edward IV* (Stroud, 2002).

11. M. Kempshall, *Rhetoric and the Writing of History, 400–1500* (Manchester, 2011).

12. A. Boot, *The Ordering of Time* (Cambridge, 1993).

13. I have benefited from the advice of James Palmer on this section.

14. J. E. Lendon, *Soldiers and Ghosts: A History of Battle in Classical Antiquity* (New Haven, Connecticut, 2005).

15. J. Coffey, "'Tremble Britannia!' Fear, Providence and the Abolition of the Slave Trade, 1758–1807," *English Historical Review*, 127 (2012), pp. 844–881.

16. D. Cohn-Sherbok, *Holocaust Theology* (London, 1991) and D. Cohn-Sherbok, ed., *Holocaust Theology: A Reader* (Exeter, 2003).

17. E. Kaufmann, *Shall the Religious Inherit the Earth? Demography and Poli-*

tics in the Twenty-First Century (London, 2010).

18. R. J. Evans, *Altered Pasts: Counterfactuals in History* (London, 2014).

19. P. Burke, *The French Historical Revolution: The "Annales" School, 1929–1989* (Stanford, California, 1990).

20. M. Bentley, *Modernizing England's Past: English Historiography in the Age of Modernism 1870–1970* (Cambridge, 2006).

21. R. Perks and A. Thompson, eds., *The Oral History Reader,* 2nd ed. (London, 2006).

22. I. Mortimer, "Whose History is This?," *History Today,* 64, no. 6 (June 2014), pp. 4–5. A far more positive account of academics, and notably of their critical role, is offered by J. Tosh, "Public History, Civic Engagement and the Historical Profession in Britain," *History,* 99 (2014), pp. 191–212.

23. P. A. Cohen, *History and Popular Memory: The Power of Story in Moments of Crisis* (New York, 2014).

24. B. Stuchtey and E. Fuchs, eds., *Writing World History, 1800–2000* (Oxford, 2003).

25. S. Berger and C. Lorenz, eds., *The Contested Nation: Ethnicity, Class, Religion and Gender in National Histories* (Basingstoke, 2008); M. Spiering and M. Wintle, eds., *European Identity and the Second World War* (Basingstoke, 2011).

26. W. Cronon, *Changes in the Land: Indians, Colonists, and the Ecology of New England* (New York, 1983).

27. R. White, *The Middle Ground: Indians, Empires, and Republics in the Great Lakes Region, 1650–1815* (Cambridge, 1991).

28. Bolingbroke, *Letters on the Study and Use of History, Letter II.* The letters, the first dated 1735, were published in 1752.

29. J. B. Sykes, ed., *The Concise Oxford Dictionary of Current English,* 6th ed. (Oxford, 1977), p. 509.

30. C. Butler, *Postmodernism: A Very Short Introduction* (Oxford, 2003); G. G. Iggers, *Historiography in the Twentieth Century: From Scientific Objectivity to the Postmodern Challenge* (Hanover, New Hampshire, 1997).

31. R. Rosenzweig and D. Thelan, *Presence of the Past: Popular Uses of History in American Life* (New York, 1994).

32. P. Rau, *Our Nazis: Representations of Fascism in Contemporary Literature and Film* (Edinburgh, 2013).

33. For an effective global account, see D. R. Woolf, *A Global History of History* (Cambridge, 2011). For a more conventional, Eurocentric, account, see J. Burrow, *A History of Histories: Epics, Chronicles, Romances and Inquiries from Herodotus and Thucydides to the Twentieth Century* (London, 2007).

34. For a comparable problem, see L. Freedman, *Strategy: A History* (Oxford, 2013).

35. P. N. Stearns, *Western Civilisation in World History* (London, 2003) and "Western Civ and World History: Conflicts and Complements," *Historically Speaking,* vol. 5, no. 4 (Mar. 2004), pp. 2–4.

36. T. L. Haskell, *Objectivity Is Not Neutrality: Explanatory Schemes in History* (Baltimore, Maryland, 1998); J. Rüsen, "Morality and Cognition in Historical Thought: A Western Perspective," *Historically Speaking,* vol. 5 no. 4 (Mar. 2004), pp. 40–42.

37. J. de Groot, *Consuming History: Historians and Heritage in Contemporary Popular Culture* (Oxford, 2009).

38. D. Wengrow, *What Makes Civilisation? The Ancient Near East and the Future of the West* (Oxford, 2010).

39. For the mistake of comparing Barbary and Somali pirates, in the 1800s and today, respectively, see S. M. Carmel, "The Big Myth of Somali Pirates," *Proceedings of*

the *U.S. Naval Institute*, 136/12 (Dec. 2010), pp. 30–35.

40. D. Chuter, "Munich, or the Blood of Others," in *Haunted by History: Myths in International Relations*, ed. C. Buffet and B. Heuser (Oxford, 1998), pp. 65–79.

41. G. Martin, *Past Futures: The Impossible Necessity of History* (Toronto, 2004).

42. See the contrasting reviews in the same issue of the *Times* of J. Israel, *Revolutionary Ideas: An Intellectual History of the French Revolution from The Rights of Man to Robespierre* (Princeton, New Jersey, 2014) and J. White, *Zeppelin Nights: London in the First World War* (London, 2014), *Times, Saturday Review*, 26 Apr. 2014, pp. 14–15.

43. R. Smelser, *The Myth of the Eastern Front: The Nazi-Soviet War in American Popular Culture* (Cambridge, 2007); W. J. Astore, "Loving the German War Machine: America's Infatuation with *Blitzkrieg*, Warfighters, and Militarism," in *Arms and the Man: Military History Essays in Honor of Dennis Showalter*, ed. M. S. Neiberg (Leiden, 2011), pp. 5–30, esp. p. 20.

44. S. Wineburg et al, "Common Belief and the Cultural Curriculum: An Intergenerational Study of Historical Consciousness," *American Educational Research Journal*, 44 (2007), pp. 40–76, at p. 71.

45. V. N. Rao, D. Shulman, and S. Subrahmanyam, *Textures of Time: Writing History in South India, 1600–1800* (New York, 2003).

46. D. Turnbull, *Maps are Territories, Science is an Atlas* (Chicago, Illinois, 1993); J. B. Harley, *The New Nature of Maps* (Baltimore, Maryland, 2001).

2. A Selective Narrative to 1650

1. T. P. Wiseman, *The Death of Caligula* (Liverpool, 2013), p. 4.

2. F. Lambert, *Inventing the Great Awakening* (Princeton, New Jersey, 1999);

J. Kent, *Wesley and the Wesleyans* (Cambridge, 2002).

3. For a discussion focusing on academic history, see R. Spalding and C. Parker, *Historiography: An Introduction* (Manchester, 2007).

4. Bolingbroke, *Of the Study of History, Letter 2: Concerning the True Use and Advantages of it* in *The Works of the Rt. Hon. Henry St John, Viscount Bolingbroke* (London, 1754), II, 283.

5. Eg., *Daily Mail*, 25 October 2010.

6. Thucydides, *History of the Peloponnesian War*, 2.21.3, translated by C. F. Smith (London, 1919), p. 301.

7. J. Black, *Other Pasts, Different Presents, Alternative Futures* (Bloomington, Indiana, 2015).

8. E. Greenwood, *Thucydides and the Shaping of History* (London, 2006); D. Kagan, *Thucydides: The Reinvention of History* (London, 2009).

9. T. P. Wiseman, "Classical History: a sketch with Three Artifacts," in *Understanding the History of Ancient History: Proceedings of the British Academy*, 143, ed. H. G. M. Williamson (Oxford, 2007), pp. 71–89, at 74–76.

10. N. Luraghi, ed., *The Historian's Craft in the Age of Herodotus* (Oxford, 2007); J. Marincola, ed., *A Companion to Greek and Roman Historiography* (Oxford, 2007).

11. A. Lianeri, ed., *The Western Time of Ancient History: Historiographical Encounters with the Greek and Roman Pasts* (Cambridge, 2011).

12. Xenophon, *Cyropaedia*, translated by W. Miller (London, 1914), pp. 127–129.

13. Polybius, *The Histories*, 1.4.1, translated by W. R. Paton, revised by F. W. Walbank and C. Habicht (Cambridge, Massachusetts, 2010), p. 11.

14. Livy, *History, Book I*, translated by B. O. Foster (London, 1919), pp. 3, 7.

15. *Plutarch's Theseus*, 1.3.

16. P. Darby, *Bede and the End of Time* (Farnham, 2012).

17. M. Oja, "Fictional History and Historical Fiction: Solzhenitsyn and Kiš as exemplars," *History and Theory,* 27 (1988), p. 112; M. Baár, "Abraham Viskaski, the Patriarch of the Ruritanian Nation," *Storia Della Storiografia,* 54 (2008), pp. 3–20, esp. p. 20.

18. J. Clive, *Not By Fact Alone: Essays on the Writing and Reading of History* (New York, 1989); A. Jones, "Reporting in Prose: Reconsidering Ways of Writing History," *The European Legacy,* 12 (2007), pp. 311– 336, and "Vivid History: Existentialist Phenomenology as a New Way to Understand an Old Way of Writing History, and as a Source of Renewal for the Writing of History," *Storia della Storiografia,* 54 (2008), pp. 21–55; C. Ginzburg, *Threads and Traces: True False Fictive* (Berkeley, California, 2012)

19. K. L. Klein, "On the Emergence of Memory in Historical Discourse," *Representations,* 69 (2000), pp. 127–150; F. Bouza, *Communication, Knowledge, and Memory in Early Modern Spain* (Philadelphia, Pennsylvania, 2004); M. Elvin, *Changing Stories in the Chinese World* (Stanford, California, 1997); G. Cubitt, ed., *History and Memory* (Manchester, 2007).

20. R. Ghosh, "'It disturbs me with a presence': Hindu History and What Meaning Cannot Convey," *Storia della Storiografia,* 55 (2009), p. 98.

21. J. E. Schwartzberg, *A Historical Atlas of South Asia,* 2nd ed. (Oxford, 1992), pp. XXIX, 162–164, 182; F. E. Pargiter, *Ancient Indian Historical Tradition* (London, 1922).

22. J. Gottshcall, *The Storytelling Animal: How Stories Make Us Human* (Boston, Massachusetts, 2012); Gottschall and D. S. Wilson, eds., *The Literary Animal: Evolution and the Nature of Narrative* (Evanston, Illinois, 2005); D. Carr, *Time, Narrative,* and History (Bloomington, Indiana, 1986); R. C. Shank, *Tell Me a Story: Narrative and Intelligence* (Evanston, Illinois, 1990); M. S. Sugiyama, "Narrative Theory and Function: Why Evolution Matters," *Philosophy and Literature,* 25 (2001), pp. 233–250.

23. P. A. Cohen, *History in Three Keys: The Boxers as Event, Experience and Myth* (New York, 1997); S. A. Smith, "Talking Toads and Chinless Ghosts: The Politics of 'Superstitious' Rumours in the People's Republic of China, 1961–1965," *American Historical Review,* 111 (2006), pp. 405–427.

24. S. Baxter, "MS C of the Anglo-Saxon Chronicle and the Politics of Mid-Eleventh-Century England," *English Historical Review,* 122 (2007), pp. 1189–1227.

25. A. J. Hingst, *The Written World: Past and Place in the Work of Orderic Vitalis* (Notre Dame, Indiana, 2009).

26. P. Nabokov, *A Forest of Time: American Indian Ways of History* (Cambridge, 2002); *Atlas de la Nouvelle Calédonie et dépendances* (Paris, 1981), section 18. For a wider-ranging approach, A. D. Smith, *Chosen Peoples: Sacred Sources of National Identity* (Oxford, 2003); T. A. Davis, ed., *Place Names of the Ancestors: A Maori Oral History Atlas* (Wellington, 1990).

27. R. Landes, *Relics, Apocalypse, and the Deceits of History: Ademar of Chabannes, 989–1034* (Cambridge, Massachusetts, 1995); J. Grier, "Hoax, History, and Hagiography in Adémar de Chabannes's Texts for the Divine Office," in *Representing History, 900–1300: Art, Music, History,* ed. R. A. Maxwell (University Park, Pennsylvania, 2010).

28. J. Gillingham, "The Historian as Judge: William of Newburgh and Hubert Walter," *English Historical Review,* 119 (2004), pp. 1275–1276.

29. T. Stiefel, *The Intellectual Revolution in Twelfth-Century Europe* (London, 1985).

30. E. Freeman, *Narratives of a New Order: Cistercian Historical Writing in England, 1150–1220* (Turnhout, 2002).

31. P. Brown, *The Cult of the Saints: Its Rise and Function in Latin Christianity* (Chicago, Illinois, 1981); H. van Os, *The Way to Heaven: Relic Veneration in the Middle Ages* (Amsterdam, 2001); J. de Voragine, *The Golden Legend: Readings on the Saints,* translated by W. G. Ryan (Princeton, New Jersey, 2012); R. Bartlett, *Why Can the Dead Do Such Great Things? Saints and Worshippers from the Martyrs to the Reformation* (Princeton, New Jersey, 2014); J. Le Goff, *In Search of Sacred Time: Jacobus de Voragine and the Golden Legend* (Princeton, New Jersey, 2014).

32. B. Anderson, *Imagined Communities: Reflections on the Origin and Spread of Nationalism,* 2nd ed. (London, 1991).

33. M. E. Lewis, *China's Cosmopolitan Empire: The Tang Dynasty* (Cambridge, Massachusetts, 2010).

34. D. Twitchett, *The Writing of Official History under the T'ang* (Cambridge, 1992).

35. H. Franke and D. Twitchett, eds., *Cambridge History of China, vol. 6: Alien Regimes and Border States, 907–1368* (Cambridge, 1994), p. 93.

36. W. Gungwu, "The Chiu-Wu-tai shih and History Writing during the Five Dynasties," *Asia Major,* 6 (1958), pp. 1–22.

37. D. Twitchett and P. J. Smith, eds., *The Cambridge History of China, vol. 5, pt 1: The Sung Dynasty and Its Precursors, 907–1279* (Cambridge, 2009), pp. 41, 254.

38. Ibid., pp. 689–692.

39. H. Franke and D. Twitchett, eds., *Cambridge History of China, vol. 6: Alien Regimes and Border States, 907–1368* (Cambridge, 1994), pp. 459–460.

40. Ibid., p. 1.

41. L.-S. Yang, *Studies in Chinese Institutional History* (Cambridge, Massachusetts, 1961), pp. 1–17.

42. B. A. Elman, *From Philosophy to Philology: Intellectual and Social Aspects of Change in Late Imperial China* (Cambridge, Massachusetts, 1984).

43. Contention over his year of birth played a role in anniversary celebrations. By marking his 800th birthday in 1962, the Mongolian government asserted its view and underlined its importance in the presentation of Chinggis.

44. R. Murphey, *Exploring Ottoman Sovereignty* (London, 2008).

45. H. M. Elliot and J. Dowson, eds., *The History of India, as Told by its own Historians,* 8 vols. (London, 1867–1877); S. H. Hodivala, *Studies in Indo-Muslim History: A Critical Commentary on Elliot and Dowson's "History of India . . . ,"* 2 vols. (Bombay, 1939).

46. *Financial Times,* 14 May 2014, p. 13.

47. For European developments in a global context, see J. Rabasa, M. Sato, E. Tortarolo, and D. Woolf, eds., *The Oxford History of Historical Writing: III, 1400–1800* (Oxford, 2012).

48. F. Fernández-Armesto, *1492: The Year Our World Began* (London, 2010), p. 126, re Savonarola in Florence.

49. For the resulting neglect of episcopal spiritual jurisdiction, see S. Hamilton, "Inquiring into Adultery and Other Wicked Deeds: Episcopal Justice in Tenth and Early Eleventh-Century Italy," *Viator,* 41 (2010), p. 25.

50. S. MacCormack, *On the Wings of Time: Rome, the Incas, Spain and Peru* (Princeton, New Jersey, 2007).

51. A. Gransden, *Historical Writing in England: II. c. 1307 to the Early Sixteenth Century* (London, 1982), p. 459; J. P. Genet, "Politics: Theory and Practice," in *The New Cambridge Medieval History, vol. 7, c. 1415–c. 1500,* ed. C. Allmand (Cambridge, 1998), pp. 25–27.

52. R. Hitchcock, "The *Falsos Chronicones* and the Mozarabs," *Journal of the*

Institute of Romance Studies, 3 (1994–1995), pp. 87–96. For different readings of the Arab arrival into Spain, P. E. Grieve, *The Eve of Spain: Myths of Origins in the History of Christian, Muslim, and Jewish Conflict* (Baltimore, Maryland, 2009).

53. R. Hitchcock, "Mozarabs and Moriscos: Two Marginalised Communities in Sixteenth-Century Toledo," in *Historicist Essays on Hispano-Medieval Narrative*, ed. B. Taylor and G. West (London, 2005), pp. 175–177.

54. H. Neuhaus, ed., *Die frühe Neuzeit als Epoche* (Munich, 2009).

55. A. Wood, *The Memory of the People: Custom and Popular Senses of the Past in Early Modern England* (Cambridge, 2013).

56. K. Sharpe, *Image Wars: Promoting Kings and Commonwealths in England, 1603–1660* (New Haven, Connecticut, 2010).

57. J. P. Carley, ed., *John Leland: De Viris Illustribus/On Famous Men* (Toronto, 2010).

58. A. Frisch, *The Invention of the Eyewitness: Witnessing and Testimony in Early Modern France* (Chapel Hill, North Carolina, 2004).

59. P. Kewes, I. W. Archer, and F. Head, eds., *The Oxford Handbook of Holinshed's Chronicles* (Oxford, 2012).

60. W. H. Herendeen, *William Camden: A Life in Context* (Woodbridge, 2007), pp. 209, 217–218.

61. K. van Lière, S. Ditchfield, and H. Louthan, eds., *Sacred History: Uses of the Christian Past in the Renaissance World* (Oxford, 2012).

62. D. R. Woolf, *Reading History in Early Modern England* (Cambridge, 2000); P. Kewes, ed., *The Uses of History in Early Modern England* (San Marino, California, 2006).

63. T. A. Sowerby, "'A Memorial and a Pledge of Faith': Portraiture and Early Modern Diplomatic Culture," *English Historical Review*, 129 (2014), p. 300 fol. 162.

64. A. Walsham, *Providence in Early Modern England* (Oxford, 1999), p. 218.

65. G. Rees and M. Wakely, *Publishing, Politics, and Culture: The King's Printers in the Reign of James I and VI* (Oxford, 2009), p. 245.

66. W. Haller, *Foxe's Book of Martyrs and the Elect Nation* (London, 1963); E. Evenden and T. S. Freeman, *Religion and the Book in Early Modern England: The Making of John Foxe's "Book of Martyrs"* (Cambridge, 2011).

67. D. R. Kelley, *Foundations of Modern Historical Scholarship: Language, Law and History in the French Renaissance* (New York, 1970); G. Huppert, *The Idea of Perfect History: Historical Erudition and Historical Philosophy in Renaissance France* (Chicago, Illinois, 1970); D. Hay, *Annalists and Historians* (London, 1977); A. B. Ferguson, *Clio Unbound: Perception of the Social and Cultural Past in Renaissance England* (Durham, North Carolina, 1979).

68. J. Vansina, "Once upon a Time: Oral Traditions as History in Africa," *Daedalus*, 100 (1971), pp. 442–468; P. Thompson, *The Voice of the Past: Oral History* (Oxford, 1978); K. Thomas, *The Perception of the Past in Early Modern England* (London, 1983).

69. D. R. Woolf, "The 'Common Voice': History, Folklore and Oral Tradition in Early Modern England," *Past and Present*, 120 (Aug. 1988), p. 48.

70. D. R. Woolf, "Of Danes and Giants: Popular Beliefs about the Past in Early Modern England," *Dalhousie Review*, 71 (1991), p. 198.

3. The Long Eighteenth Century

1. P. Ihalainen, *Protestant Nations Redefined: Changing Perceptions of National*

Identity in the Rhetoric of the English, Dutch and Swedish Public Churches, 1685–1772 (Leiden, 2005).

2. U. Weiss, "'Inside was a Parchment, so beautifully painted on all sides.' The Ornate Charters of the Hanoverian Succession," in *Hand and Seal for a Kingdom: The Ornate Charters of the Hanoverian Succession in Great Britain*, ed. M. L. Babin, G. van den Heuvel, and U. Weiss (Göttingen, 2014), pp. 35, 37.

3. J. Rose, "Robert Brady's Intellectual History and Royalist Antipopery in Restoration England," *English Historical Review*, 122 (Dec. 2007), pp. 1287–1317.

4. C. Grell, *L'Histoire entre Érudition et Philosophie: étude sur la connaissance historique à l'âge des Lumières* (Paris, 1993).

5. R. MacKay, *"Lazy, Improvident People": Myth and Reality in the Writing of Spanish History* (Ithaca, New York, 2006).

6. H. R. Trevor-Roper, *History and the Enlightenment* (New Haven, Connecticut, 2010); K. O'Brien, *Narratives of Enlightenment: Cosmopolitan History from Voltaire to Gibbon* (Cambridge, 1997); M. C. Carhart and J. Robertson, "The Enlightenments of J. G. A. Pocock," *Storia della Storiografia*, 39 (2001), pp. 123–151.

7. J. Black, "The Enlightenment Historian at Work: The Researches of William Robertson," *Bulletin of Hispanic Studies*, 45 (1988), pp. 251–260.

8. P. H. Reill, *The German Enlightenment and the Rise of Historicism* (Berkeley, California, 1975).

9. D. Twitchett and P. J. Smith, eds., *The Cambridge History of China, vol. 5, pt 1: The Sung Dynasty and Its Precursors, 907–1279* (Cambridge, 2009), p. 41 fn. 5.

10. W. Franke, "Historical Writing during the Ming," in *The Cambridge History of China, vol. 7, pt 1, The Ming Dynasty, 1368–1644*, ed. F. Mote and D. Twitchett (Cambridge, 1988), pp. 781–782.

11. P. K. Crossley, *A Translucent Mirror: History and Identity in the Transformations of Qing Imperial Ideology* (Berkeley, California, 1999).

12. For an effective short introduction, see M. Pittock, "Historiography," in *The Cambridge Companion to the Scottish Enlightenment*, ed. A. Broadie (Cambridge, 2002), pp. 258–279.

13. M. Neufeld, *The Civil Wars after 1660: Public Remembering in Late Stuart England* (Woodbridge, 2013).

14. George to another brother, William, Duke of Gloucester, 9 Nov. 1771, Windsor Castle, Royal Archives, GEO/15938.

15. J. Hardman, *Louis XVI* (New Haven, Connecticut, 1992).

16. Thurlow to James Bland Burges, Under-Secretary of State for Foreign Affairs, 5 Dec. 1789, Oxford, Bodleian Library, Bland Burges papers, vol. 18 fol. 89.

17. D. Hay, *Annalists and Historians: Western Historiography from the Eighth to the Eighteenth Centuries* (London, 1977), p. 184.

18. H. Fielding, *The True Patriot*, edited by M. A. Locke (London, 1965), p. 23.

19. Anon., *Reflections on Ancient and Modern History* (Oxford, 1746), p. 25.

20. Anon., *Reflections*, p. 26.

21. Cowper, notes for parliamentary debate, 11 Jan. (os) 1722, Hertford, CRO, Panshanger papers D/EP F 182 fols. 96–104.

22. F. Nibelius, *Lord Bolingbroke (1678–1751) and History: A Comparative Study of Bolingbroke's Politico-Historical Words and a Selection of Contemporary Texts as to Themes and Vocabulary* (Stockholm, 2003).

23. R. Bentley, *Considerations upon the State of Public Affairs* (London, 1798), p. 63.

24. Montagu to Elizabeth Carter, 16 July 1762, San Marino, California, Huntington Library, Montagu papers, no. 3079.

25. G. Abbattista, *Commercio, Colonie e Impero alla vigilia della Rivoluzione Americana: John Campbell pubblicista e storico nell' Inghilterra del sec XVIII* (Florence, 1990).

26. J. Morgan, *A Complete History of Algiers*, 2 vols. (London, 1728–1729), p. ii.

27. R. Rolt, *Lives of the Principal Reformers* (London, 1759), p. 195.

28. R. Rolt, *An Impartial Representation of the Conduct of the Several Powers of Europe*, 4 vols. (1747–1750) I, p. x.

29. P. Limborch, *History of the Inquisition* (London, 1731), p. xv.

30. R. Strong, *And When Did You Last See Your Father? The Victorian Painter and British History* (London, 1978), pp. 78–85; A. Sanders, *In the Olden Times: Victorians and the British Past* (New Haven, Connecticut, 2013). This book profitably combines paintings with literary views of history.

31. M. Shaw, *Time and the French Revolution: The Republican Calendar, 1789 – Year XIV* (Woodbridge, 2011); S. Perovic, *The Calendar in Revolutionary France: Perceptions of Time in Literature, Culture, Politics* (Cambridge, 2012).

32. E. Burke, *Reflections on the Revolution in France* (Everyman ed., London, 1910), pp. 20, 29–31. The literature on Burke, the *Reflections,* and the subsequent controversy is vast. F. P. Lock, *Burke's Reflections on the Revolution in France* (London, 1985) and S. Blakemore, ed., *Burke and the French Revolution* (Athens, Georgia, 1992) are good introductions. On the controversy, see G. T. Pendleton, "Towards a Bibliography of the *Reflections* and *Rights of Man* Controversy," *Bulletin of Research in the Humanities,* 85 (1982), pp. 65–103. A crucial topic in helping to understand terms is covered in J. T. Boulton, *The Language of Politics in the Age of Wilkes and Burke* (London, 1963).

33. E. Breisach, *Historiography* (Chicago, Illinois, 1983), p. 248.

34. G. C. White, *A Versatile Professor* (London, 1903); J. M. Black, "A Georgian Fellow of Merton: The Historian Edward Nares," *Postmaster* (1987), pp. 53–59.

35. E. Nares, *A Sermon, Preached at the Parish Church of Shobdon . . .* (no place, 1798), pp. 1–18.

36. B. Melman, *The Culture of History: English Uses of the Past, 1900–1953* (Oxford, 2006).

37. H. Ben-Israel, *English Historians on the French Revolution* (Cambridge, 1968).

38. D. R. Kelley, "Grounds for Comparison," *Storia della Storiografia,* 39 (2001), p. 5.

39. J. Assmann, *Religio Duplex: How the Enlightenment Reinvented Egyptian Religion* (Cambridge, 2014).

40. M. Byrd, "Monuments to the People: The Napoleonic Scholars and Daily Life in Ancient Egypt," *Consortium on Revolutionary Europe: Selected Papers, 1997,* p. 247.

41. G. W. Bowersock, *From Gibbon to Auden: Essays on the Classical Tradition* (Oxford, 2009), p. 90.

42. George to William Pitt the Younger, the Prime Minister, 10 Feb. 1800, NA. PRO 30/8/104 fol. 263.

4. The Nineteenth Century

1. Nares papers in Merton College, Oxford, and in the Bodleian Library, Oxford; G. C. White, *A Versatile Professor: Reminiscences of the Rev. Edward Nares, D. D.* (1903); J. Black, "A Georgian Fellow of Merton. The Historian Edward Nares," *Postmaster* (1987), pp. 53–59, "A Regency Regius: The Historian Edward Nares," and "A Williamite Reprobate? Edward Nares and the Investigation of his Failure in 1832 to Deliver his Lectures," *Oxoniensia,* 52 (1987), pp. 173–178, 53 (1988), pp. 337–340.

2. Nares, *Burghley* (London, 1828), pp. xx–xxii, 3.

3. S. Sebastiani, "Conjectural History vs. the Bible: Eighteenth-Century Scottish Historians and the Idea of History in the *Encyclopaedia Britannica*," *Storia della Storiografia*, 39 (2001), pp. 51–61.

4. D. Wormell, *Sir John Seeley and the Uses of History* (Cambridge, 1980), p. 177; R. T. Shannon, "John Robert Seeley and the Idea of a National Church," in *Ideas and Institutions of Victorian Britain*, ed. R. Robson, (London, 1967), pp. 236–267; M. Bentley, "The Age of Prothero: British Historiography in the Long *Fin de Siècle*, 1870–1920," *Transactions of the Royal Historical Society*, 6th ser., 20 (2010), p. 175.

5. C. T. McIntire, *The Ongoing Task of Christian Historiography* (Toronto, 1974) and *Herbert Butterfield: The Historian as Dissenter* (New Haven, Connecticut, 2004); M. Bentley, *The Life and Thought of Herbert Butterfield: History, Science and God* (Cambridge, 2011).

6. L. Mitchell, *The Whig World, 1760–1837* (London, 2005), p. 150.

7. T. Koditschek, *Liberalism, Imperialism, and the Historical Imagination: Nineteenth-Century Visions of a Greater Britain* (Cambridge, 2011).

8. Russell to Cobden, 2 Apr. 1861, NA. PRO. 30/22/32 fol. 120.

9. B. Hingley, *The Recovery of Roman Britain, 1586–1906: A Colony So Fertile* (Oxford, 2008), p. 325.

10. [E. Nares], *Tytler's Elements* (London, 3 vols, 1801–1822), III, 417.

11. W. A. Goffart, "Breaking the Ortelian Pattern: Historical Atlases with a New Program, 1747–1830," in *Editing Early and Historical Atlases*, ed. J. Winearls (Toronto, 1995), pp. 49–81.

12. G. J. Whitrow, *Time in History* (Oxford, 1988), p. 184.

13. S. Bann et al., *Painting History: Delaroche and Lady Jane Grey* (London, 2010).

14. P. O'Keeffe, *A Genius for Failure: The Life of Benjamin Robert Haydon* (London, 2009).

15. E. G. Bouwers, *Public Pantheons in Revolutionary Europe: Comparing Cultures of Remembrance, c. 1790–1840* (Basingstoke, 2012).

16. P. Fritzsche, *Stranded in the Present: Modern Time and the Melancholy of History* (Cambridge, Massachusetts, 2004).

17. M. Baár, *Historians and Nationalism: East-Central Europe in the Nineteenth Century* (Oxford, 2010), p. 289.

18. S. Rothblatt and B. Wittrock, eds., *The European and American University since 1800: Historical and Sociological Essays* (Cambridge, 1993).

19. R. L. Geiger, *To Advance Knowledge: The Growth of American Research Universities, 1900–1940* (New York, 1986).

20. J. A. Reuben, *The Making of the Modern University: Intellectual Transformation and the Marginalization of Morality* (Chicago, Illinois, 1996).

21. D. D. Van Tassel, "From Learned Society to Professional Organization: The American Historical Association, 1884–1900," *American Historical Review*, 89 (1984), pp. 929–956; B. G. Smith, "Gender and the Practices of Scientific History: The Seminar and Archival Research in the Nineteenth Century," *American Historical Review*, 100 (1995), pp. 1150–1176.

22. R. Soffer, *Discipline and Power: The University, History, and the Making of an English Elite, 1870–1930* (Palo Alto, California, 1994).

23. D. Hay, *Polydore Vergil: Renaissance Historian and Man of Letters* (Oxford, 1952), p. 165.

24. R. Hitchcock, "The Conquest of Granada in Nineteenth-Century English and American Historiography," in *Medieval Spain*, ed. R. Collins and A. Good-

man, (Basingstoke, 2002), pp. 242–265, esp. pp. 243, 250.

25. B. Marsden and C. Smith, *Engineering Empires: A Cultural History of Technology in Nineteenth-Century Britain* (Basingstoke, 2005), pp. 89–90.

26. L. Gossman, "Imperial Icon: The Pergamon Altar in Wilhelminian Germany," *Journal of Modern History*, 78 (2006), pp. 551–587.

27. E. A. Fraser, *Delacroix, Art, and Patrimony in Post-Revolutionary France* (Cambridge, 2004).

28. O. Chadwick, *Acton and History* (Cambridge, 1998), p. 16.

29. E. Hobsbawn, *Interesting Times: A Twentieth-Century Life* (London, 2002), p. 415.

30. R. Gildea, *The Past in French History* (New Haven, Connecticut, 1994).

31. A. Forrest, *The Legacy of the French Revolutionary Wars: The Nation-in-Arms in French Republican Memory* (Cambridge, 2009).

32. S. Hazareesingh, *The Legend of Napoleon* (London, 2004).

33. M. J. Clavin, *Toussaint Louverture and the American Civil War: The Promise and Peril of a Second Haitian Revolution* (Philadelphia, Pennsylvania, 2010).

34. C. Jelavich, "Nationalism as Reflected in the Textbooks of the South Slavs in the Nineteenth Century," *Canadian Review of Studies in Nationalism*, 16 (1989), pp. 15–34.

35. L. Jensen, J. Leerssen, and M. Mathijsen, eds., *Free Access to the Past: Romanticism, Cultural Heritage and the Nation* (Leiden, 2010); M. Hall, ed., *Towards World Heritage: International Origins of the Preservation Movement, 1870–1930* (Farnham, 2011). For preservation and imperial narratives, see A. Swenson and P. Mandler, eds., *From Plunder to Preservation: Britain and the Heritage of Empire c. 1800–1940* (Oxford, 2014).

36. D. N. Myers, *Re-inventing the Jewish Past: European Jewish Intellectuals and the Zionist Return to History* (Oxford, 1995).

37. P. Brock, J. D. Stanley, and P. J. Wróbel, eds., *Nation and History: Polish Historians from the Enlightenment to the Second World War* (Toronto, 2006).

38. Z. Blažević, "Performing National Identity: The Case of Pavao Ritter Vitezović, 1652–1713," *National Identities*, 5 (2003), pp. 251–267, esp. p. 262 fn. 1.

39. G. Arnold, *Held Fast for England: G. A. Henty, Imperialist Boys' Writer* (London, 1980). The title is based on Henty's *Held Fast for England: A Tale of the Siege of Gibraltar, 1779–83*.

40. R. Torstendahl, "Fact, Truth and Text: The Quest for Historical Knowledge around 1900," *History and Theory*, 42 (2003), pp. 305–331.

41. L. Howsam, *Past into Print: The Publishing of History in Britain, 1850–1950* (London, 2009).

42. R. Mitchell, *Picturing the Past: English History in Text and Image, 1830–1870* (Oxford, 2000); M. Samuels, *The Spectacular Past: Popular History and the Novel in Nineteenth-Century France* (Ithaca, New York, 2004).

43. S. Kern, *The Culture of Time and Space, 1880–1918* (Cambridge, Massachusetts, 1986).

44. H. Gemsheim, *The History of Photography from the Camera Obscura to the Beginning of the Modern Era*, 2nd ed. (London, 1969).

45. T. Baycroft, *Inventing the Nation, France* (London, 2008); R. L. Fuller, *The Origins of the French Nationalist Movement, 1886–1914* (Jefferson, North Carolina, 2012).

46. M. Simpson, "Taming the Revolution? Legitimists and the Centenary of 1789," *English Historical Review*, 120 (2005), pp. 340–364.

47. D. Goy-Blanquet, ed., *Joan of Arc, a Saint for all Seasons: Studies in Myth and Politics* (Aldershot, 2003); F. Brown, *The Embrace of Unreason: France 1914–1940* (New York, 2014); M. Hanna, "Iconology and Ideology: Images of Joan of Arc in the Idiom of the Action française, 1908–1931," *French Historical Studies*, 12 (1985), pp. 215–239.

48. N. McWilliam, "Conflicting Manifestations," *French Historical Studies*, 27 (2004), pp. 396–401; V. Caron, "Catholic Political Mobilisation and Antisemitic Violence in Fin de Siècle France: The Case of the Union Nationale," *Journal of Modern History*, 8 (2009), pp. 315–318.

49. D. Kertzer, *The Popes against the Jews: The Vatican's Role in the Rise of Modern Anti-Semitism* (New York, 2001).

50. S. Tanaka, *New Times in Modern Japan* (Princeton, New Jersey, 2004), p. 11; T. Keirstead, "Inventing Medieval Japan. The History and Politics of National Identity," *Medieval History Journal*, 1 (1998), pp. 47–71.

51. R. S. Wortman, "'Invisible Threads': The Historical Imagery of the Romanov Tercentenary," *Russian History*, 16 (1989), pp. 389–408; A. J. Frantzen, *Bloody Good: Chivalry, Sacrifice, and the Great War* (Chicago, Illinois, 2004).

5. The Twentieth Century

1. J. Le Goff, *History and Memory* (New York, 1992), p. x.

2. E. Hobsbawm, *Interesting Times*, p. 282.

3. For the additional issues of accuracy and emphasis, J. E. Lendon, "The Ignorance Factory," *Arion*, vol. 12, no. 1 (spring/summer 2004), pp. 189–200.

4. For instructive examples of a very rich literature, W. Kidd and B. Murdoch, eds., *Memory and Memorials: The Commemorative Century* (Aldershot, 2004); S. Goebel, *The Great War and Medieval Memory: War, Remembrance and Medievalism in Britain and Germany, 1914–1940* (Cambridge, 2007); S. Heathorn, "The Civil Servant and Public Remembrance: Sir Lionel Earle and the Shaping of London's Commemorative Landscape, 1918–1933," *Twentieth-Century British History*, 19 (2008), pp. 259–287.

5. This was another instance when public history cannot be translated as popular history.

6. D. Cannadine, *G. M. Trevelyan: A Life in History* (London, 1992).

7. H. Carpenter, *The Envy of the World: Fifty Years of the BBC Third Programme and Radio 3* (London, 1996), pp. 52, 73.

8. W. E. H. Lecky, *The Political Value of History* (London, 1892), pp. 19–20.

9. M. C. Lafollette, *Science on the Air: Popularisers and Personalities on Radio and Early Television* (Chicago, Illinois, 2008).

10. A. Assman, "Europe: A Community of Memory?," and subsequent discussion, *Bulletin of the German Historical Institute, Washington*, 40 (spring 2007), p. 38.

11. D. Deletant and H. Hanak, eds., *Historians as Nation Builders: Central and South-East Europe* (Basingstoke, 1988); M. Bucur and N. M. Wingfield, eds., *Staging the Past: The Politics of Commemoration in Hapsburg Central Europe, 1848 to the Present* (Purdue, Indiana, 2001); F. Hadler and M. Mesenhöller, eds., *Lost Greatness and Past Oppression in East Central Europe: Representations of the Imperial Experience in Historiography since 1918* (Leipzig, 2007).

12. G. Bowd, *Fascist Scotland-Caledonia and the Far Right* (Edinburgh, 2014).

13. D. Hanovs and V. Tēraudkalns, *Ultimate Freedom – No Choice: The Culture of Authoritarianism in Latvia, 1934–1940* (Leiden, 2013).

14. D. E. Lorey, "The Revolutionary Festival in Mexico: November 20 Celebrations in the 1920s and 1930s," *Americas*, 54 (1997), pp. 39–82; A. Marashi, *Nationalizing Iran: Culture, Power, and the State, 1870–1940* (Seattle, Washington, 2008).

15. B. I. Schwartz, "Themes in Intellectual History: May Fourth and After," in *The Cambridge History of China, vol. 12, pt 1: Republican China, 1912–1949*, ed. J. K. Fairbank (Cambridge, 1983), p. 410.

16. P. Duara, *Rescuing History from the Nation: Questioning Narratives of Modern China* (Chicago, Illinois, 1995); L. Hosetler, "Contending Cartographic Claims? The Qing Empire in Manchu, Chinese, and European Maps," in *The Imperial Map: Cartography and the Mastery of Empire*, ed. J. R. Akerman (Chicago, Illinois, 2009), pp. 98–99.

17. S. Plokhy, *Unmaking Imperial Russia: Mykhailo Hrushevsky and the Writing of Ukrainian History* (Toronto, 2005).

18. C. A. Cline, "British Historians and the Treaty of Versailles," *Albion*, 20 (1988), pp. 43–50; W. D. McIntyre, *The Britannic Vision: Historians and the Making of the British Commonwealth of Nations, 1907–48* (Basingstoke, 2009); D. Gillard, *Appeasement in Crisis: From Munich to Prague, October 1938–March 1939* (Basingstoke, 2007).

19. E. L. Woodward, *Short Journey* (London, 1942); *Oxford Dictionary of National Biography*, 60 (2004), pp. 243–245. For a highly critical account, see A. L. Rowse, *All Souls and Appeasement: A Contribution to Contemporary History* (London, 1961). For a less critical view, see S. Aster, ed., *Appeasement and All Souls: A Portrait with Documents, 1937–9* (Cambridge, 2004). For a more favorable view, see S. J. D.

Green, "Appeasers and Anti-Appeasers: All Souls and the International Crisis of the 1930s," in *All Souls and the Wider World: Statesmen, Scholars and Adventurers, c. 1850–1950*, ed. S. J. D. Green and P. Horden (Oxford, 2011), chapter 10.

20. K. Schönwälder, "The Fascination of Power: Historical Scholarship in Nazi Germany," *History Workshop Journal*, 43 (1997), pp. 133–154; H. Schleier, "German Historiography under National Socialism: Dreams of a Powerful Nation-State and German *Volkstum* Come True," in *Writing National Histories: Western Europe since 1800*, ed. S. Berger, M. Donovan, and K. Passmore (London, 1999), pp. 176–188.

21. C. Fleck, *A Transatlantic History of the Social Sciences: Robber Barons, the Third Reich and the Invention of Empirical Social Research* (London, 2010).

22. J. Connelly and M. Grÿttner, eds., *Universities under Dictatorship* (University Park, Pennsylvania, 2005).

23. R. Harris, "Sarajevo: Where the Century of Terror Began," *Standpoint*, 64 (July/August 2014), p. 42.

24. D. B. Dennis, *Inhumanities: Nazi Interpretations of Western Culture* (Cambridge, 2012).

25. Re: Croatia, R. Yeomans, *Visions of Annihilation: The Ustasha Regime and the Cultural Politics of Fascism, 1941–1945* (Pittsburg, Pennsylvania, 2013).

26. A. G. Sepinwall, *The Abbé Grégoire and the French Revolution: The Making of Modern Universalism* (Berkeley, California, 2005).

27. I have benefited greatly from the advice of Tim May.

28. M. Goldman, "The Party and the Intellectuals: Phase Two," in *The Cambridge History of China, vol. 14, pt 1: The People's Republic: The Emergence of Revolutionary China 1949–1965*, ed. R. MacFarquhar and J. K. Fairbank (Cambridge, 1987), p. 459.

29. T. C. Fox, "The Holocaust under Communism," in *The Historiography of the Holocaust*, ed. D. Stone (Basingstoke, 2004), p. 423.

30. W. Czaplinski and T. Ladogorski, eds., *The Historical Atlas of Poland* (Wroclaw, 1981), p. 34.

31. T. Pietsch, *Empire of Scholars: Universities, Networks and the British Academic World 1850–1939* (Manchester, 2013).

32. D. Brown, "The Fate of Academic Freedom in the Age of High Liberalism: The Case of Charles Beard," *Journal of the Historical Society*, 6 (2006), pp. 1–17, esp. p. 15.

33. R. Soffer, *Discipline and Power: The University, History, and the Making of an English Elite, 1870–1930* (Stanford, California, 1994), and *History, Historians and Conservatism in Britain and America: From the Great War to Thatcher and Reagan* (Oxford, 2008).

34. E. Fitzpatrick, *History's Meaning: Writing America's Past, 1880–1980* (Cambridge, Massachusetts, 2002).

35. L. Lim, *The People's Republic of Amnesia: Tiananmen Revisited* (Oxford, 2014); *Times*, 6 May 2014, pp. 32–33.

36. S. Heathorn, "'The Long Retreat of Stone Generals': Imperial Memory, Decolonisation and the Repatriation of Monuments from Sudan, 1956–60," *Studies in Ethnicity and Nationalism*, special issue (2005), pp. 42–61.

37. M. Sandle, *Gorbachev: Man of the Twentieth Century?* (London, 2008).

38. A. Portelli, *The Order Has Been Carried Out: History, Memory, and Meaning of a Nazi Massacre in Rome* (Basingstoke, 2003).

39. A. Ichijo, *Scottish Nationalism and the Idea of Europe: Concepts of Europe and the Nation* (2004), and "The Place of Scotland's European Past," *Literaria Pragensia*,

vol. 19, no. 38 (Dec. 2009), pp. 60–74, esp. pp. 60, 65.

40. M. Pittock, "'To see Ourselves as Others See Us.' The Scot in English Eyes Since 1707," *European Journal of English Studies*, 13 (2009), pp. 293–304.

41. E. Gkotzaridis, *Trials of Irish History: Genesis and Evolution of a Reappraisal, 1938–2000* (London, 2006); J. M. Regan, "Southern Irish Nationalism as a Historical Problem," *Historical Journal*, 50 (2007), pp. 197–223; B. Girvin, "Beyond Revisionism? Some Recent Contributions to the Study of Modern Ireland," *English Historical Review*, 124 (2009), pp. 94–107.

42. C. Fraser, "New Greek Myths," *Standpoint*, 64 (July/Aug. 2014), p. 10.

43. P. Burke, *The French Historical Revolution: The Annales School, 1929–89* (Cambridge, 1990).

44. S. Conde, "Desire for History. Historiography, Scholarship, and the Vicarious (on C. Ginzburg)," *Storia della Storiografia*, 30 (1996), pp. 57–75; K. Jenkins, *At the Limits of History: Essays on Theory and Practice* (Abingdon, 2009).

45. W. O. Aydelotte, *Quantification in History* (Reading, Massachusetts, 1971), p. 15.

46. D. C. Coleman, *History and the Economic Past: An Account of the Rise and Decline of Economic History in Britain* (Oxford, 1987).

47. J. Namier, *Lewis Namier: A Biography* (London, 1971).

48. F. Braudel, *The Mediterranean and the Mediterranean World in the Age of Philip II*, 2 vols (London, 1972), I, 16, 21.

49. A. Burguière, *The Annales School: An Intellectual History* (Ithaca, New York, 2009).

50. J. Barry, M. Hester, and G. Roberts, eds., *Witchcraft in Early Modern Europe: Studies in Culture and Belief* (Cambridge, 1996).

51. J. Mali, "Real Narratives: Myth, History and Mythhistory," *Storia della Storiografia*, 30 (1996), p. 13.

52. S. Hazareesingh, *In the Shadow of the General: Modern France and the Myth of De Gaulle* (Oxford, 2012).

53. A. Megill, "Coherence and Incoherence in Historical Studies: From the *Annales* School to the New Cultural History," *New Literary History*, 35 (2004), pp. 207–231.

54. P. Burke, *What is Cultural History?* (Oxford, 2004); S. Gunn, *History and Cultural Theory* (Harlow, 2006).

55. L. Hunt, ed., *The New Cultural History* (Berkeley, California, 1989); V. E. Bonnell and Hunt, eds., *Beyond the Cultural Turn: New Directions in the Study of Society and Culture* (Berkeley, California, 1999); M. A. Cabrera, ed., *Postsocial History: An Introduction* (Lanham, Maryland, 2005).

56. For example, P. S. Carmichael, *The Last Generation: Young Virginians in Peace, War and Reunion* (Chapel Hill, North Carolina, 2005); M. A. Weitz, *More Damning than Slaughter: Desertion in the Confederate Army* (Lincoln, Nebraska, 2005).

57. A. J. Johnston, *Cultural Realism: Strategic Culture and Grand Strategy in Chinese History* (Princeton, New Jersey, 1995); H. van de Ven, ed., *Warfare in Chinese History* (Leiden, 2000).

58. H. R. Guggisberg, "American Exceptionalism as National History?," in *Bridging the Atlantic: The Question of American Exceptionalism in Perspective*, ed. E. Glaser and H. Wellenreuther (Cambridge, 2002), pp. 265–276; M. Addas, "Out of Step with Time: United States Exceptionalism in an Age of Globalization," in *Writing World History 1800–2000*, ed. B. Stuchtey and E. Fuchs (Oxford, 2003), pp. 137–154.

59. D. S. Showalter, "Europe's Way of War, 1815–64," in *European Warfare 1815–2000*, ed. J. Black (Basingstoke, 2002), p. 27; J. Black, *War and the Cultural Turn* (Cambridge, 2012).

60. P. Nora, *Realms of Memory: Conflicts and Divisions* (New York, 1996); J. Winter and E. Sivan, eds., *War Remembrance in the Twentieth Century* (Cambridge, 1999); F. Cappelletto, ed., *Memory and World War II: An Ethnographic Approach* (Oxford, 2005); A Kasabova, "Memory, Memorials, and Commemoration," *History and Theory*, 47 (2008), pp. 331–352.

61. A. H. M. Kirk-Greene, ed., *The Emergence of African History at British Universities* (Oxford, 1995).

62. A. Temu and B. Swai, *Historians and Africanists: A Critique* (1981); C. Neale, *Writing "Independent" History: African Historiography, 1960–1980* (Westport, Connecticut, 1985); B. Jewsiewicki and D. Newbury, eds., *African Historiographies: What History for Which Africa?* (Beverly Hills, California, 1986).

63. J. C. Miller, "History and Africa/Africa and History," *American Historical Review*, 104 (1999), p. 17.

64. J. Thornton, *Africa and Africans in the Making of the Atlantic World, 1400–1800*, 2nd ed. (Cambridge, 1998).

65. For example, N. Ferguson, *Empire: How Britain Made the Modern World* (London, 2003), and critical views in F. Cooper, "Empire Multiplied: A Review Essay," *Comparative Studies in Society and History*, 46 (2004), pp. 247–272 and A. Sartori, "The British Empire and Its Liberal Mission," *Journal of Modern History*, 78 (2006), pp. 641–642.

66. M. Garry and M. P. Gerrie, "When Photographs Create False Memories," *Current Directions in Psychological Science*, 14 (2005), pp. 321–325.

67. B. Chadwick, *The Reel Civil War: Mythmaking in American Film* (New York, 2001). History on film has attracted much

recent interest. Among the works, see
M. Hughes-Warrington, *History Goes
to the Movies: Studying History on Film*
(Abingdon, 2006); M. Hughes-War-
rington, ed., *The History on Film Reader*
(Abingdon, 2009); K. Machtans and M.
Ruehl, eds., *Hitler Films from Germany:
History, Cinema and Politics since 1945*
(Basingstoke, 2012); M. Stokes, *American
History through Hollywood Film: From the
Revolution to the 1960s* (London, 2013);
J. Chapman, *Film and History* (Basing-
stoke, 2013).

68. B. Bildhauer, *Filming the Middle
Ages* (London, 2011).

69. J. Chapman, *Film and History* (Basingstoke, 2013), p. 89.

6. New States and the
Possibilities of Lineage

1. L. Pawson, *In the Name of the People: Angola's Forgotten Massacre* (London,
2014).

2. P. Chatterjee, *The Black Hole of Empire: History of a Global Practice of Power*
(Princeton, New Jersey, 2012).

3. M. Mukerjee, *Churchill's Secret War:
The British Empire and the Ravaging of India
During World War II* (New York, 2010).

4. D. D. Kosambi, *An Introduction to
the Study of Indian History*, 2nd ed. (London, 1996); R. Thapar, *History and Beyond*
(New Delhi, 2000).

5. N. Ben-Yehuda, *The Masada Myth:
Collective Memory and Mythmaking in Israel* (Madison, Wisconsin, 1995).

6. Y. Shain and B. Bristman, "The
Jewish Security Dilemma," *Oribis*, 46
(2002), pp. 55–56.

7. A. Shavit, *My Promised Land: The
Triumph and Tragedy of Israel* (New York,
2013).

8. P. Bishop, *The Reckoning: Death
and Intrigue in the Promised Land* (London,
2014).

9. C. Ehret, "Africa in World History: The Long, Long View," in *The Oxford
Handbook of World History*, ed. J. H. Bentley, (Oxford, 2011), p. 472.

10. J. R. Brennan, *Taifa: Making Nation
and Race in Urban Tanzania* (Athens, Ohio,
2012).

11. For example, T. Falola, *Colonialism
and Violence in Nigeria* (Bloomington, Indiana, 2009).

12. A. Swenson and P. Mandler, eds.,
*From Plunder to Preservation: Britain and
the Heritage of Empire c. 1800–1940* (Oxford, 2014).

13. M. Monmonier, *From Squaw Tit to
Whorehouse Meadow: How Maps Name,
Claim, and Inflame* (Chicago, Illinois,
2006).

14. I. Gershoni and J. Jankowski, *Commemorating the Nation: Collective Memory,
Public Commemoration, and National Identity in Twentieth-Century Egypt* (Chicago,
Illinois, 2004).

7. THE HISTORICAL DIMENSION
OF MANIFEST DESTINY

1. J. Bodnar, *Remaking America: Public Memory, Commemoration, and Patriotism in the Twentieth Century* (Princeton,
New Jersey, 1992).

2. B. Schwartz, "The Reconstruction
of Abraham Lincoln," in *Collective Remembering*, ed. D. Middleton and D. Edwards (Newbury Park, California, 1990),
pp. 81–107.

3. Although traumatic, Pearl Harbor (1941) was an attack not an invasion,
and was not directed at the continental
landmass.

4. D. W. Blight, *American Oracle: The
Civil War in the Civil Rights Era* (Cambridge, Massachusetts, 2011).

5. R. Breitman et al, eds., *US Intelligence and the Nazis* (Cambridge,
2005).

6. F. Manchel, "A Reel Witness: Steven Spielberg's Representation of the Holocaust in *Schindler's List*," *Journal of Modern History*, 67 (1995), p. 91; M. B. Hanse, "*Schindler's List* is Not *Shoah:* The Second Commandment, Popular Modernism and Public Memory," *Critical Inquiry*, 22 (1996), p. 311.

7. A. Landsberg, *Prosthetic Memory: The Transformation of American Remembrance in the Age of Mass Culture* (New York, 2004).

8. E. Stephens, *US Policy toward Israel: The Role of Political Culture in Defining the "Special Relationship"* (Brighton, 2006).

9. L. Friedberg, "Dare to Compare: Americanizing the Holocaust," *American Indian Quarterly*, 24 (2000), pp. 353–380; W. Churchill, *A Little Matter of Genocide* (San Francisco, California, 1997).

10. P. Novick, *The Holocaust and Collective Memory: The American Experience* (London, 1999).

11. The figure of 340 chests of tea is based on the East India Company's shipping documents, whereas the more commonly used figure is 342, which came from contemporary newspaper reports.

12. P. D. G. Thomas, *The Townshend Duties Crisis: The Second Phase of the American Revolution, 1767–1773* (Oxford, 1987).

13. J. Lepore, *The Whites of Their Eyes: The Tea Party's Revolution and the Battle over American History* (Princeton, New Jersey, 2010).

14. J. J. Summerhill and J. A. Williams, *Sinking Columbus: Contested History, Cultural Politics, and Mythmaking during the Quincentenary* (Gainesville, Florida, 2000).

15. P. Nobile, ed., *Judgment at the Smithsonian* (New York, 1995); E. T. Linenthal and T. Engelhardt, eds., *History Wars: The Enola Gay and Other Battles for the American Past* (New York, 1996); K. Bird and L. Lifschulz, eds., *Hiroshima's Shadow:* *Writings on the Denial of History and the Smithsonian Controversy* (Stony Creek, Connecticut, 1997); R. P. Newman, *Enola Gay and the Court of History* (New York, 2004).

16. Editorial by Roger Kimball, *New Criterion*, 29, no. 4 (Dec. 2010), pp. 2–3. The *New Criterion* is a conservative journal that frequently criticises "politically correct" academics and universities; see, for example, "Shut up, they explained," 32, no. 10 (June 2014), pp. 1–3.

17. B. Atwood, *Telling the Truth about Aboriginal History* (London, 2005); G. Davison, *The Use and Abuse of Australian History* (Sydney, 2000); J. Hirst, *Sense and Nonsense in Australian History* (Melbourne, 2005).

18. A. E. Coombes, ed., *Rethinking Settler Colonialism: History and Memory in Australia, Canada, New Zealand and South Africa* (Manchester, 2006).

8. Post-Communism and the New History

1. P. Kenney, "After the Blank Spots Are Filled: Recent Perspectives on Modern Poland," *Journal of Modern History*, 79 (2007), p. 161.

2. R. Radosh, M. R. Habeck, and G. Sevostianov, eds., *Spain Betrayed: The Soviet Union in the Spanish Civil War* (New Haven, Connecticut, 2001).

3. T. Snyder, *The Reconstruction of Nations: Poland, Ukraine, Lithuania, Belarus, 1569–1999* (New Haven, Connecticut, 2003), p. 248.

4. H. G. Penny, "The Fate of the Nineteenth Century in German Historiography," *Journal of Modern History*, 80 (2008), p. 107.

5. A. Charlesworth, "Contesting Places of Memory: The Case of Auschwitz," *Environment and Planning D: Society and Space*, 12 (1994), pp. 579–593.

6. E. Zuroff, "Whitewashing the Holocaust: Lithuania and the Rehabilitation of History," *Tikkun*, 7, 1 (1992), pp. 43–46.

7. O. Bartov, *Erased: Vanishing Traces of Jewish Galicia in Present-Day Ukraine* (Princeton, New Jersey, 2007), and "Eastern Europe as the Site of Genocide," *Journal of Modern History*, 80 (2008), p. 593.

8. R. H. Hayden, "Schindler's Fate: Genocide, Ethnic Cleansing, and Population Transfers," *Slavic Review*, 55 (1996), pp. 727–748.

9. N. Cigar, *Genocide in Bosnia: The Policy of "Ethnic Cleansing"* (College Station, Texas, 1995).

10. J. Jacobs, "The Many Deaths of a Kazak Unaligned: Osman Batur, Chinese Decolonization, and the Nationalization of a Nomad," *American Historical Review* (2001), pp. 1290–1314.

11. R. Ostow, ed., *(Re)Visualizing National History: Museums and National Identities in Europe in the New Millennium* (Toronto, 2007).

12. T. Sindbaek, *Usable History? Representations of Yugoslavia's Difficult Past from 1945 to 2002* (Aarhus, 2012).

13. P. A. Cohen, *History and Popular Memory: The Power of Story in Moments of Crisis* (New York, 2014), pp. 1–32.

14. M. Todorova, *Imagining the Balkans* (Oxford, 1997).

15. P. Pomerantsev, "Diary," *London Review of Books*, 36/12, 19 June 2014, pp. 42–43.

16. BBC Radio Four, 8.00 AM news programme, 6 Mar. 2010.

17. H-T. H. Tai, ed., *The Country of Memory: Remaking the Past in Late Socialist Vietnam* (Berkeley, California, 2001); E. Roszko, "Commemoration and the State: Memory and Legitimacy in Vietnam," *Sojourn*, 25 (2010), pp. 1–28.

18. J. Jin-sung, *Dear Leader* (New York, 2014).

9. Western Europe

1. D. Bloxham, *Genocide on Trial: War Crimes Trials and the Formation of Holocaust History and Memory* (Oxford, 2001); L. Douglas, *The Memory of Judgment: Making Law and History in the Trials of the Holocaust* (New Haven, Connecticut, 2001).

2. N. Frei, *Adenauer's Germany and the Nazi Past: The Politics of Amnesty and Integration* (New York, 2002).

3. A. Schildt, "The Long Shadows of the Second World War: The Impact of Experiences and Memories of War on West German Society," *German Historical Institute London: Bulletin*, 29 (2007), p. 35.

4. R. Moeller, *War Stories: The Search for a Usable Past in the Federal Republic of Germany* (Berkeley, California, 2001); J. K. Olick, *In the House of the Hangman: The Agonies of German Defeat, 1943–1949* (Chicago, Illinois, 2005).

5. J. Herf, *Divided Memory: The Nazi Past in the Two Germanys* (Cambridge, Massachusetts, 1997).

6. P. O. Pendas, *The Frankfurt Auschwitz Trial, 1963–65: Genocide, History, and the Limits of the Law* (Cambridge, 2006).

7. M. Sargeant, "Memory, Distortion and the War in German Popular Culture: The Case of Konsalik," in *Memory and Memorials: The Commemorative Century*, ed. W. Kidd and B. Murdoch (Aldershot, 2004), p. 199.

8. D. Lipstadt, *Denying the Holocaust: The Growing Assault on Truth and Memory* (London, 1993).

9. E. Hellmuth, "How to Domesticate the History of a King: Reflections on the 'Friederisiko' Project," *German Historical Institute London, Bulletin*, 36, no. 1 (May 2014), pp. 49–60, esp. p. 56.

10. J. Knowlton and T. Cates, *Forever in the Shadow of Hitler? Original Documents of the Historikerstreit* (Atlantic Highlands, New Jersey, 1993).

11. G. Hartman, ed., *Bitburg in Moral and Political Perspective* (Bloomington, Indiana, 1986).

12. P. Novick, "Comments on Aleida Assmann's Lecture," *German Historical Institute, Washington*, 40 (2007), p. 31.

13. H. Heer, "The Difficulty of Ending a War: Reactions to the Exhibition War of Extermination: Crimes of the Wehrmacht, 1941 to 1944," *History Workshop Journal*, 46 (1998), pp. 187–203.

14. U. Schlie, "Today's view of the Third Reich and the Second World War in German Historiographical Discourse," *Historical Journal*, 43 (2000), p. 564.

15. K. Machtans and M. Ruehl, eds., *Hitler Films from Germany: History Cinema and Politics since 1945* (Basingstoke, 2012).

16. J. Revel and G. Levi, eds., *Political Uses of the Past: The Recent Mediterranean Experience* (London, 2002).

17. M. L. Chirico, R. Cioffi, A. Grimaldi, and G. Pignatelli, eds., *I Due Risorgimenti: La costruzione dell'identita' nazionale* (Naples, 2011).

18. D. Reid, "Resistance and Its Discontents: Affairs, Archives, Avowals and the Aubracs," *Journal of Modern History*, 77 (2005), pp. 97–137; D. Cordier, *De l'histoire à l'histoire* (Paris, 2013).

19. Eg. P. de Froment, *Un Volontaire de la Nuit dans l'Enfer des Camps Nazis* (Paris, 2005); O. Lalieu, *La Zone Grise? La Résistance française à Buchenwald* (Paris, 2005).

20. C. Callil, *Bad Faith: A Forgotten History of Family and Fatherland* (London, 2006).

21. R. J. Golsan, *Vichy's Afterlife: History and Counterhistory in Postwar France* (Lincoln, Nebraska, 2000); H. Rousso, *The Haunting Past: History, Memory and Justice in Contemporary France* (Philadelphia, Pennsylvania, 2002).

22. R. J. Golsan, ed., *Memory, The Holocaust and French Justice: The Bousquet and Touvier Affairs* (Hanover, New Hampshire, 1996).

23. N. Furman, "Viewing Memory through *Night and Fog, The Sorrow and the Pity*, and *Shoah*," *Journal of European Studies*, 35 (2005), p. 180.

24. Poll by l'Ifop for *France-Soir*, published in latter on 6 November 2010, p. 5.

25. S. Hazareesingh, *Le Mythe Gaullien* (Paris, 2010).

26. S. R. Suleiman, *Crises of Memory and the Second World War* (Cambridge, Massachusetts, 2006).

27. O. Wieviorka, *Divided Memory: French Recollections of World War II from the Liberation to the Present* (Stanford, California, 2012).

28. H. R. Southworth, *Guernica! Guernica!: A Study of Journalism, Propaganda and History* (Berkeley, California, 1977); N. Rankin, *Telegram from Guernica: The Extraordinary Life of George Steer, War Correspondent* (London, 2003).

29. For a misplaced comparison, see P. Preston, *The Spanish Holocaust: Inquisition and Extermination in Twentieth-Century Spain* (London, 2012).

30. E. Robinson, *History, Heritage and Tradition in Contemporary British Politics: Past Politics and Present Histories* (Manchester, 2012).

31. *Times*, 15 Mar. 2014, p. 21.

32. Eg., M. Houlbrook, *Queer London: Perils and Pleasures in the Sexual Metropolis, 1918–57* (Chicago, Illinois, 2005).

33. For earlier debates, see D. Cannadine, J. Keating, and N. Sheldon, *The Right Kind of History: Teaching the Past in Twentieth-Century England* (London, 2011).

34. Cameron, Speech outside No. 10 Downing Street, BBC Radio Four, 19 Sept. 2014.

35. See also, M. Hastings, "Oh, what a lovely myth," *Sunday Times*, 11 May 2014. For a longer time-scale, see S. Heathorn, *Haig and Kitchener in Twentieth-Century Britain: Remembrance, Representation and Appropriation* (Farnham, 2013).

36. H. R. Trevor-Roper, *The Invention of Scotland* (New Haven, Connecticut, 2008).

37. L. Colley, *Acts of Union and Disunion* (London, 2014).

38. J. Gibney, *The Shadow of a Year: The 1641 Rebellion in Irish History and Memory* (Madison, Wisconsin, 2013).

39. A. Jackson, "Ireland's Long Nineteenth Century of Union," *Journal of Modern History*, 86 (2014), p. 125.

40. M. Beard, *Confronting the Classics* (London, 2014), pp. 218–223, 272.

10. Contesting the Past, Claiming the Future

1. R. G. Hovannisian, *The Armenian Genocide in Perspective* (New Brunswick, New Jersey, 1986); P. G. Dwyer and L. Ryan, eds., *Theatres of Violence: Massacre, Mass Killing and Atrocity Throughout History* (New York, 2012).

2. For similar arguments leading to murderous treatment of Jews during the Russian Civil War, notably by Whites, see O. Budnitskii, *Russian Jews Between the Reds and the Whites, 1917–1920* (Philadelphia, Pennsylvania, 2012).

3. *i*, 29 Ap. 2014, p. 27.

4. N. Doumanis, *Before the Nation: Muslim-Christian Coexistence and its Destruction in Late-Ottoman Anatolia* (Oxford, 2012); E. J. Zürcher, *The Young Turk Legacy and Nation Building from the Ottoman Empire to Atatürk's Turkey* (London, 2010).

5. G. D. Brockett, "When Ottomans Became Turks: Commemorating the Conquest of Constantinople and Its Contribution to World History," *American Historical Review* (2014), pp. 399–433.

6. I have benefited from discussing this issue with Yasuo Naito.

7. W. A. Skya, *Japan's Holy War: The Ideology of Radical Shintō Ultranationalism* (Durham, North Carolina, 2009).

8. W. A. Callahan, "History, Identity, and Security: Producing and Consuming Nationalism in China," *Critical Asian Studies*, 38 (2006), pp. 179–208; Y. He, "History, Chinese Nationalism and the Emerging Sino-Japanese Conflict," *Journal of Contemporary China*, 16 (2007), pp. 1–24; T. Hasegawa and K. Togo, eds., *East Asia's Haunted Present: Historical Memories and the Resurgence of Nationalism* (Westport, Connecticut, 2008).

9. M. Macmillan, *The Uses and Abuses of History* (London, 2009), p. 167.

10. S. Schama, "His Story, Our Story," *Financial Times*, 9 June 2012.

11. D. Horspool, *The English Rebel: One Thousand Years of Troublemaking, from the Normans to the Nineties* (London, 2009); E. Vallance, *A Radical History of Britain: Visionaries, Rebels and Revolutionaries – The Men and Women Who Fought for Our Freedoms* (London, 2009).

12. See, for example, T. Snyder, *Bloodlands: Europe Between Hitler and Stalin* (New York, 2010).

13. Quoted in *Times*, 25 June 2014, p. 33.

14. See C. Tyerman, *The Debate on the Crusades, 1099–2010* (Manchester, 2011).

15. R. Ostow, *(Re) Visualizing National Identity: Museums and National Identities in Europe in the New Millennium* (Toronto, 2007).

16. J. de Groot, *Consuming History: Historians and Heritage in Contemporary Popular Culture* (Abingdon, 2008).

17. Tacitus, *Dialogus, Agricola, Germania* (London, 1914), p. 169.

11. Historiographies of the Present

1. R. Conquest, *The Dragons of Expectation: Reality and Delusion in the Course of History* (London, 2006), p. 206.

2. T. Snyder, "In Darkest Belarus," *New York Review of Books*, 10 Nov. 2010, pp. 33–35.

3. R. J. Evans, "What is history?," in *Big Questions in History*, ed. H. Swain (London, 2006), p. 6.

4. Introduction to P. Daileader and P. Whelan, eds., *French Historians 1900–3000: New Historical Writing in Twentieth-Century France* (Oxford, 2010), pp. xxiii–xxiv.

5. J. K. Fairbank, "The reunification of China," in *The Cambridge History of China, vol. 14, pt 1: The People's Republic: The Emergence of Revolutionary China 1949–1965*, ed. R. MacFarquhar and J. Fairbank, pp. 6–7.

6. For a resulting spat on radio that was more generally indicative of differences between academic and popular approaches, "In Our Time," BBC Radio Four, 23 Dec. 2010.

7. For a recent pessimistic account of the failure of this Christian tradition, S. J. D. Green, *The Passing of Protestant England: Secularisation and Social Change, c. 1920–1960* (Cambridge, 2010).

8. M. C. C. Adams, "Postwar Myth-making about World War II," in *Major Problems in the History of World War II*, ed. M. A. Stoler and M. S. Gustafson (Boston, Massachusetts, 2003), pp. 428–436.

9. M. E. Smith, "The Strategic Bombing Debate: The Second World War and Vietnam," *Journal of Contemporary History*, 12 (1997), pp. 175–191.

10. T. D. Biddle, "Shifting Dresden's Ashes," *Wilson Quarterly*, 29 (2005), pp. 60–80.

11. A. Verrier, *The Bomber Offensive* (London, 1968).

12. R. Overy, "The Post-War Debate," in *Firestorm: The Bombing of Dresden, 1945*, ed. P. Addison and J. A. Crang, (London, 2006), pp. 123–142.

13. *Observer*, 5 May 1963.

14. T. Joel, *The Dresden Firebombing: Memory and the Politics of Commemorating Dresden* (London, 2013).

15. *House of Commons Debates*, vol. 163, col. 872.

16. E. C. Corwin, "The Dresden Bombing as Portrayed by German Accounts, East and West," *UCLA Historical Journal*, 8 (1987), pp. 74–84; M. Nolan, "Germans as Victims during the Second World War. Air Wars, Memory Wars," *Central European History*, 38 (2005), pp. 7–40; A. Fuchs, *After the Dresden Bombing: Pathways of Memory, 1945 to the Present* (Basingstoke, 2012).

17. A. C. Grayling, *Among the Dead Cities: Is the Targeting of Civilians in War Ever Justified?* (London, 2006).

18. K. S. Inglis, "War Memorials: Ten Questions for Historians," *Guerres mondiales et conflits contemporains*, 167 (July 1992), pp. 5–21.

19. J. Friedrich, *Der Brand: Deutschland im bombenkrieg* (Berlin, 2002); B. von Benda-Beckmann, *A German Catastrophe? German Historians and the Allied Bombings, 1945–2010* (Amsterdam, 2010); H. Watzman, *Guilt, Suffering and Memory: Germany Remembers its Dead of World War Two* (Bloomington, Indiana, 2010).

20. B. Niven, ed., *Germans as Victims: Reading the Past in Contemporary Germany* (Basingstoke, 2006).

21. J. Black, *World War Two: A Military History* (London, 2003), pp. 34–35.

22. K.-H. Frieser, "Kursk–Turning Point of the War?," *RUSI Journal*, vol. 148, no. 5 (Oct. 2003), p. 80.

23. B. Harrison, *Finding a Role? The United Kingdom 1970–1990* (Oxford, 2010), p. 402.

24. S. Schama, "Why history still matters," *Guardian*, 9 Nov. 2010, Section two, p. 10.

25. Comparing Herbert Butterfield and Daniel Woolf, A. De Baets, "The Grandeur of Historiography," *Storia della Storiografia*, 51 (2007), pp. 141–147.

26. H. van de Ven, ed., *Warfare in Chinese History* (Leiden, 2000).

27. P. A. Elliott, *Enlightenment, Modernity and Science: Geographies of Scientific Culture and Improvement in Georgian England* (London, 2010).

28. S. Schmalzer, *The People's Peking Man: Popular Science and Human Identity in Twentieth-Century China* (Chicago, Illinois, 2008).

29. R. A. Gross, "The Transnational Turn: Rediscovering American Studies in a Wider World," *Journal of American Studies*, 34 (2000), pp. 373–393; S. F. Fishkin, "Crossroads of Cultures: The Transnational Turn in American Studies," *American Quarterly*, 57 (2005), pp. 17–57.

30. P. Ihalainen, "The Sanctification and Democratisation of 'the Nation' and 'the People' in Late Eighteenth-Century Northwestern Europe: Proposing a Comparative Conceptual History," *Contributions to the History of Concepts*, 3 (2007), pp. 125–151, esp. 128–129. For the use of comparative history to study exceptionalisms, see P. Bergmann, "American Exceptionalism and German *Sonderweg* in Tandem," *International History Review*, 23 (2001), pp. 505–534.

31. P. Duara, "Transnationalism and the Challenge to National Histories," in *Rethinking American History in a Global Age*, ed. T. Bender (Berkeley, California, 2002), pp. 25–46; B. Anderson, *Imagined Communities: Reflections on the Origin and Spread of Nationalism* (London, 1983).

32. J.-C. Schmitt and O. G. Oexle, eds., *Les tendances actuelles de l'histoire du Moyen Âge en France et en Allemagne* (Paris, 2003).

33. Stadial theories propound historical development through distinct stages.

34. R. Robertson, *The Three Waves of Globalization: A History of Developing Global Consciousness* (London, 2003); D. Northrop, ed., *A Companion to World History* (Chichester, 2012).

35. E. Breisach, *On the Future of History: The Postmodernist Challenge and Its Aftermath* (Chicago, Illinois, 2003).

36. C. B. McCullagh, *The Logic of History: Putting Postmodernism in Perspective* (London, 2004).

37. T. Dean, "How Historians Begin: Openings in Historical Discourse," *History*, 95 (2010), p. 416.

12. Historiographies of the Future

1. A. Applebaum, review in *New York Review of Books*, 24 Nov. 2010, p. 12.

2. For different editions of Lecky, see D. McCartney, *W. E. H. Lecky, Historian and Politician 1838–1903* (Dublin, 1994), p. 184.

3. W. H. Sewell, *Logics of History: Social Theory and Social Transformation* (Chicago, Illinois, 2005).

4. I. Morris, *Why the West Rules – For Now: The Patterns of History, and What They Reveal about the Future* (London, 2010).

5. W. K. Hancock, *Professing History* (Sydney, 1976), pp. 159, 167.

6. H. Nelson, "Kokoda: and Two National Histories," *Journal of Pacific History*, 42 (2007).

7. R. Bin Wong, *China Transformed: Historical Change and the Limits of European Experience* (Ithaca, New York, 1997); J. Blaut, *Eight Eurocentric Historians* (New York, 2000); J. M. Hobson, *The Eastern Origins of Western Civilisation* (Cambridge,

2004); P. Lorge, *The Asian Military Revolution: From Gunpowder to the Bomb* (Cambridge, 2008).

8. J. G. A. Pocock, *Barbarism and Religion,* first two vols. (Cambridge, 1999).

9. F. Dikötter, *Mao's Great Famine: The History of China's Most Devastating Catastrophe, 1958–62* (London, 2010).

10. "China leaders 'like Nazis' for stifling massacre memory," *Times,* 4 June 2014.

11. R. Grew, "Expanding Worlds of World History," *Journal of Modern History,* 78 (2006), p. 897.

12. J. Osterhammel, *The Transformation of the West: A Global History of the Nineteenth Century* (Princeton, New Jersey, 2014).

13. K. Naumann, "Teaching the World: Globalization, Geopolitics, and History Education at U.S. Universities," in *Beyond the Nation: United States History in Transnational Perspective,* ed. T. Adam and U. Luebken (Washington, 2008), pp. 124–126.

14. E. S. Rawski, "Reenvisioning the Qing," and H. Ping-ti, "In Defense of Sinicization," *Journal of Asian Studies,* 55 (1996), pp. 829–850 and 57 (1998), pp. 123–155.

15. C. Horner, *Rising China and Its Postmodern Fate: Memories of Empire in a New Global Context* (Athens, Georgia, 2009).

16. R. H. Fritze, *Invented Knowledge: False History, Fake Science and Pseudo-Religions* (London, 2009), pp. 96–103.

17. For a recent instance, see B. Cumings, *The Korean War: A History* (New York, 2010). See the review in *Proceedings of the U.S. Naval Institute,* 136, 12 (Dec. 2010), pp. 73–74.

18. M. Barr, *Who's Afraid of China? The Challenge of Chinese Soft Power* (London, 2011).

19. M. Clifford, C. Giangrande, and A. White, *Chinese Museums Guide* (2014).

20. M. Werner and B. Zimmermann, "Beyond Comparison: *Histoire Croisée* and the Challenge of Reflexity," *History and Theory,* 45 (2006), pp. 30–50.

21. For a volume including valuable discussion of national historiographies, W. Blockmans and J.-P. Genet, eds., *Visions sur le Développement des États Européens, Théories et Historiographies de l'État Moderne* (Rome, 1993).

22. P. Clarke and C. Methuen, eds., *The Church on its Past* (Woodbridge, 2013).

23. C. Wickham, ed., *Marxist History-Writing for the Twenty-First Century* (London, 2007); G. Eley and K. Nield, *The Future of Class in History: What's Left of the Social?* (Ann Arbor, Michigan, 2007).

24. M. J. S. Rudwick, *Bursting the Limits of Time: The Reconstruction of Geohistory in the Age of Revolution* (Chicago, Illinois, 2005).

25. Most prominently, J. Diamond, *Guns, Germs, and Steel: The Fates of Human Societies* (New York, 1997).

26. M. Halbwachs, *Collective Memory,* Lewis A. Coser (trans.) (New York, 1980); P. H. Hutton, *History as an Art of Memory* (Hanover, New Hampshire, 1993); J. V. Wertsch, *Voices of Collective Remembering* (New York, 2002).

27. M. Wilson, "Six Views of Embodied Cognition," *Psychonomic Bulletin,* 9 (2002), pp. 625–636; G. Rizzolatti and C. Sinigaglia, *Mirrors in the Brain* (Oxford, 2008); I have benefited from discussing mirror neurons with Adam Zeman.

28. G. Paquette, ed., *Enlightened Reform in Southern Europe and its Atlantic Colonies, c. 1750–1830* (Farnham, 2009).

29. D. Stone, ed., *The Historiography of Genocide* (London, 2008).

30. J. M. Headley, *The Europeanization of the World* (Princeton, New Jersey, 2008).

13. A Personal Note

1. J. D. Popkin, *History, Historians, and Autobiography* (Chicago, Illinois,

2005); P. Hollander, "Acknowledgements: An Academic Ritual," *Academic Questions*, 5 (2001–2002), pp. 63–76. For some interesting essays based on interviews, see D. Snowman, *Historians* (Basingstoke, 2007).

2. K. Dawson et al., "Congress of Vienna," in *Simulation in the Classroom*, ed. J. L. Taylor and R. Walford (Harmondsworth, 1972).

3. P. Daix, *Braudel* (Paris, 1995); C. A. Aguirre Rojas, *Fernand Braudel et les sciences humaines* (Paris, 2004).

4. G. Piterberg, T. Ruiz, and G. Smycox, eds., *Braudel Revisited: The Mediterranean World 1600–1800* (Toronto, 2010); J. Marino, ed., *Early Modern History and the Social Sciences: Testing the Limits of Braudel's Mediterranean* (Kirksville, Missouri, 2002).

5. J. Black, "Mentors: A Personal Note," *Historically Speaking*, vol. 5, no. 6 (July/Aug 2004), p. 39.

6. For reflective instances by distinguished scholars, K. Robbins, "Britain and Munich Reconsidered: A Personal Historical Journey," *Proceedings of the British Academy*, 140 (2007), pp. 231–244; and R. Hutton, *Debates in Stuart History* (Basingstoke, 2004).

7. J. Black, "Debating Britain and Europe, 1688–1815" and "Foreign Policy and the Debate over British Political Culture," *British Scholar*, 1 (2009), pp. 37–52, and 2 (2010), pp. 254–272.

8. R. F. Hamilton, *President McKinley, War and Empire: I. President McKinley and the Coming of War, 1898* (New Brunswick, New Jersey, 2006), p. 252.

9. J. Black, *Why Wars Happen* (London, 1998).

10. J. Black, *Maps and Politics* (London, 1997).

11. For example, J. Black, *The English Press, 1621–1861* (Stroud, 2001), *Italy and the Grand Tour* (New Haven, Connecticut, 2003), *A Subject for Taste: Culture in Eighteenth-Century England* (London, 2005) and *A History of Diplomacy* (London, 2010).

12. J. Black, *Rethinking Military History* (London, 2004) and *War and the Cultural Turn* (Cambridge, 2012).

13. K. D. Erdmann, *Toward a Global Community of Historians: The International Historical Congresses and the International Committee of Historical Sciences, 1898–2000*, W. J. Mommsen and J. Kocka, eds., (Oxford, 2005).

14. E.g., J. E. Wills, *1688: A Global History* (London, 2001); F. Fernández-Armesto, *1492: The Year Our World Began* (London, 2009).

15. R. E. Berkhofer, *Beyond the Great Story: History as Text and Discourse* (Cambridge, Massachusetts, 1995).

14. Conclusions

1. BBC, RADIO 4.

2. L.-H. T. Nguyen, *Hanoi's War: An International History of the War for Peace in Vietnam* (Chapel Hill, North Carolina, 2012); P. Asselin, *Hanoi's Road to the Vietnam War, 1954–1965* (Berkeley, California, 2013).

3. Anon., *Observations on the Conduct of the Late Administration* (London, 1757), p. 13.

4. Higgins, Speech to both Houses of Parliament, April 2014.

Selected Further Reading

There is an extensive literature on this subject, and this brief list restricts itself to works published since 1990. Earlier works should be approached through the bibliographies and footnotes in these books.

Anderson, B. *Imagined Communities: Reflections on the Origins and Spread of Nationalism,* Revised Ed. London: Verso 2006.

Appleby, J. L., L. Hunt, and M. Jacob. *Telling the Truth about History.* New York: Norton, 1994.

Arnold, J. *History: A Very Short Introduction.* Oxford: Oxford University Press, 2000.

Arnstein, W., ed. *Recent Historians of Great Britain: Essays on the Post-1945 Generation.* Ames: Iowa State University Press, 1990.

Ashton, P., and H. Kean, eds. *People and Their Pasts: Public History Today.* Basingstoke: Palgrave Macmillan, 2009.

Bender, T., P. M. Katz, C. Palmer, and the A H A Committee on Graduate Education. *The Education of Historians for the Twenty-First Century.* Urbana: University of Illinois Press, 2004.

Berger, S. *The Search for Normality: National Identity and Historical Consciousness in Germany since 1800.* Oxford: Berghahn, 2007.

Berger, S., M. Donovan, and K. Passmore, eds. *Writing National Histories: Western Europe since 1800.* London: Routledge, 1999.

Berkhoffer, R. F. *Fashioning History: Current Practices and Principles.* New York: Palgrave Macmillan, 2008.

Black, J. *Contesting History.* London: Bloomsbury Academic, 2014.

———. *The Curse of History.* London: Social Affairs, 2008.

Bosworth, R. J. B. *Explaining Auschwitz and Hiroshima: History Writing and the Second World War, 1945–1990.* London: Routledge, 1993.

Boyd, K., ed. *Encyclopedia of Historians and Historical Writing.* London: Routledge, 1999.

Brady, C., ed. *Interpreting Irish History: The Debate on Historical Revisionism.* Dublin: Irish Academic Press, 1994.

Breisach, E. *Historiography: Ancient, Medieval, and Modern,* 2nd ed. Chicago, Ill.: University of Chicago Press, 1994.

Brown, C. G. *Postmodernism for Historians.* London: Routledge, 2005.

Brownlee, J. *Japanese Historians and the National Myths, 1600–1945: The Age of the Gods and Emperor Jinmu.* Vancouver: University of British Columbia Press, 1997.

Brundage, W. F. *The Southern Past: A Clash of Race and Memory*. Cambridge, Mass.: Belknap Press, 2005.

Burke, P. *The French Historical Revolution: The* Annales *School, 1929–1989*. Stanford: Stanford University Press, 1990.

Cannadine, D. *Making History Now and Then*. Basingstoke: Palgrave Macmillan, 2008.

——, ed. *What is History Now?* Basingstoke: Palgrave Macmillan, 2002.

Carr, E. H. *What is History?* New York: Random House, 1961; rpt. London: Penguin, 2006.

Collini, S. *English Pasts: Essays in History and Culture*. Oxford: Oxford University Press, 1999.

Coombs, A. E. *Settler Colonialism: History and Memory in Australia, Canada, Aotearoa New Zealand and South Africa*. Manchester: Manchester University Press, 2005.

Costello, P. *World Historians and Their Goals: Twentieth-Century Answers to Modernism*. DeKalb, Ill.: Northern Illinois University Press, 1993.

De Baets, A. *Censorship of Historical Thought: A World Guide, 1945–2000*. Westport, Conn.: Greenwood, 2002.

De Groot, J. *Consuming History: Historians and Heritage in Contemporary Popular Culture*. London: Routledge, 2009.

Dummitt, C., and M. Dawson, eds. *Contesting Clio's Craft: New Directions and Debates in Canadian History*. London: Institute for the Study of the Americas, 2009.

Elton, G. R. *The Practice of History*, 2nd ed. Hoboken, N.J.: Wiley-Blackwell, 2001.

Evans, R. J. *In Defence of History*. London: Granta, 2001.

Fasolt, C. *The Limits of History*. Chicago: University of Chicago Press, 2004.

Feldner, H., et al., eds. *Writing History: Theory and Practice*. London: Bloomsbury, 2010.

Ferro, M. *Resentment in History*. Cambridge: Polity, 2010.

Frisch, M. *A Shared Authority: Essays on the Craft and Meaning of Oral and Public History*. Albany: State University of New York Press, 1990.

Fuchs, E., and B. Stuchtey, eds. *Across Cultural Borders: Historiography in Global Perspective*. Lanham, Md.: Rowman and Littlefield, 2002.

Gaddis, J. L. *The Landscape of History: How Historians Map the Past*. Oxford: Oxford University Press, 2003.

Gallego, A., ed. *Historia de la historiografía Española*. Madrid, 1999.

Gorman, J. *Historical Judgement: The Limits of Historiographical Choice*. Montreal: McGill-Queens University Press, 2008.

Grafton, A. *What Was History? The Art of History in Early Modern Europe*. Cambridge: Cambridge University Press, 2007.

Hobsbawn, E. *On History*. London: Abacus, 1998.

Hoffer, P. C. *The Historians' Paradox: The Study of History in Our Time*. New York: New York University Press, 2008.

Iggers, G. C. *Historiography in the Twentieth Century: From Scientific Objectivity to the Postmodern Challenge*. Middletown, Conn.: Wesleyan University Press, 1997.

Jager, S. M., and R. Mitter, eds. *Ruptured Histories: War, Memory, and the Post–Cold War in Asia*. Cambridge, Mass.: Harvard University Press, 2007.

Jenkins, K. *Re-Thinking History*. London: Routledge, 1991.

Jordanova, L. *History in Practice*, 2nd ed. London: Bloomsbury Academic, 2006.

Lambert, P., and P. Schofield, eds. *Making History: An Introduction to the History and Practices of a Discipline*. London: Routledge, 2004.

Lamont, W., ed. *Historical Controversies and Historians*. London: Routledge, 1998.

Lonetree, A., and A. J. Cobb, eds. *The National Museum of the American Indian: Critical Conversations*. Lincoln, Neb.: University of Nebraska Press, 2008.

McCullagh, C. B. *The Logic of History: Putting Postmodernism in Perspective*. London: Routledge, 2004.

Majumdar, R. *Writing Postcolonial History*. London: Bloomsbury Academic, 2010.

Mandler, P. *History and National Life*. London: Profile Books, 2002.

Munslow, A. *The Routledge Companion to Historical Studies*. London: Routledge, 2000.

O'Sullivan, L. *Oakeshott on History*. Exeter: Imprint Academic, 2003.

Porciani, I., and J. Tollebeek, eds. *Setting the Standards: Institutions, Networks, and Communities of National Historiography*. Basingstoke: Palgrave, 2012.

Rabasa, J., M. Sato, E. Tortarolo, and D. R. Woolf, eds. *The Oxford History of Historical Writing: III: 1400–1800*. Oxford: Oxford University Press, 2012.

Rao, V. N., D. Shulman, and S. Subrahmanyam. *Textures of Time: Writing History in South India, 1600–1800*. London: Permanent Black, 2003.

Revel, J., and G. Levi, eds., *Political Uses of the Past: The Recent Mediterranean Experience*. London: Routledge, 2002.

Rüsen, J., ed. *Western Historical Thinking: An Intercultural Debate*. Oxford: Berghahn, 2002.

Samuel, R. *Theatres of Memory*. London: Verso, 1994.

Schivelbiesch, W. *The Culture of Defeat: On National Trauma, Mourning, and Recovery*. London: Picador, 2003.

Scott, J. W. *Gender and the Politics of History*, rev. ed. New York: Columbia University Press, 1999.

Seixas, P. *Theorising Historical Consciousness*. Toronto: University of Toronto Press, 2004.

Spiegel, G. M. *The Past as Text: The Theory and Practice of Medieval Historiography*. Baltimore, Md.: The Johns Hopkins University Press, 1997.

Stuchtey, B., and E. Fuchs, eds. *Writing World History 1800–2000*. Oxford: Oxford University Press, 2003.

Stuchtey B., and P. Wende, eds. *British and German Historiography 1750–1950*. Oxford: Oxford University Press, 2000.

Thorstendahl, R., ed. *An Assessment of Twentieth-Century Historiography: Professionalism, Methodologies, Writings*. Stockholm: Almquiest & Wiksell, 2000.

Tosh, J., ed. *Historians on History: An Anthology*. Harlow: Longman, 2000.

——. *Why History Matters*. Basingstoke: Palgrave Macmillan, 2008.

Tyrrell, I. *Historians in Public: The Practice of American History, 1890–1970*. Chicago: University of Chicago Press, 2005.

Unger, J., ed. *Using the Past to Serve the Present: Historiography and Politics in Contemporary China*. Armonk, N.Y.: M. E. Sharpe, 1993.

Walls, A. *The Cross-Cultural Process in Christian History: Studies in the Transmission and Application of Faith*. London: Bloomsbury/T&T Clark, 2002.

Wang, E. Q., and F. L. Fillafer, eds. *The Many Faces of Clio: Cross-Cultural Approaches to Historiography*. Oxford: Berghahn, 2006.

Wood, G. *The Purpose of the Past: Reflections on the Uses of History*. London: Penguin, 2008.

Wickham, C., ed. *Marxist History-Writing for the Twenty-First Century*. Oxford: Oxford University Press, 2007.

Woolf, D. R., ed. *A Global Encyclopedia of Historical Writing*. London: Routledge, 1998.

——. *A Global History of History*. Cambridge: Cambridge University Press, 2011.

Index

JEREMY BLACK is professor of history at the University of Exeter. He is author of many books including *War and Technology* (IUP, 2013), *Fighting for America: The Struggle for Mastery in North America, 1519–1871* (IUP, 2011), and *War and the Cultural Turn*. Black received the Samuel Eliot Morison Prize from the Society for Military History in 2008.

CPSIA information can be obtained at www.ICGtesting.com
Printed in the USA
LVOW08s0243210815

451005LV00007B/306/P